WINNING
AT
TRIAL

Winner of the 2008 *Award of Professional Excellence*
from the Association for Continuing Legal Education.
www.aclea.org

WINNING

AT

TRIAL

D. Shane Read

NITA®

National Institute for Trial Advocacy

Reprint Permission
National Institute for Trial Advocacy
361 Centennial Parkway, Suite 220
Louisville, CO 80027
Phone: (800) 225-6482
www.nita.org

Library of Congress Cataloging-in-Publication Data
Read, D. Shane.
    Winning at trial / D. Shane Read.
       p.   cm.
    ISBN 978-1-60156-001-8
    1. Trial practice—United States.   I. National Institute for Trial Advocacy (U.S.)
II. Title.
KF8915.R43   2007
347.73'75—dc22

                                                                        2007014631

ISBN: 978–1–60156–001–8
FBA: 1001

Printed in the United States of America

For Linda
and our children,
Caroline, Will, and Christopher

CONTENTS

Preface, xi
Acknowledgments, xiii

Chapter One   Trial Strategies and Basics, 1
    Six Factors Influencing the Outcome of a Trial, 2
    Eight Qualities of Great Trial Lawyers, 3
    Bench versus Jury Trials, 21
    The Trial Process, 21
    The Trial Notebook, 23
    Study Questions for Focus Group Video Clips from *Scruggs v. Snyder,* 26

Chapter Two   Voir Dire, 31
    Strategies for Voir Dire, 32
    The Basics of Federal Court Voir Dire, 34
    Challenges for Cause and Preemptory Strikes, 36
    Prohibitions, 37
    Jury Questionnaires and Consultants, 38
    Voir Dire in a Criminal Trial, 38
    Voir Dire in a Civil Trial, 47
    Answers to Voir Dire Problems, 57
    Study Questions for Voir Dire Video Clip of *Scruggs v. Snyder*, 62

Chapter Three   Opening Statement, 65
    The Underrated Importance of the Opening Statement, 65
    The Basics, 74
    The Ten Steps of Preparing a Powerful Opening Statement, 77
    How to Deliver an Opening Statement, 93
    Seven Steps to Overcoming Courtroom Fears, 97
    The Six Don'ts of Opening Statements, 100

Examples of Themes, 106

Analysis of Prosecution's Opening Statement in *U.S. v. McVeigh*, 110

Analysis of Defendant's Opening Statement in *U.S. v. McVeigh*, 121

Study Questions for Opening Statement Video Clips from *People v. Simpson*, 129

Chapter Four   Direct Examination, 135

Strategies, 136

Techniques, 146

Organization and Style of Direct Examination, 155

How to Prepare Direct Examination, 161

Difficult Problems on Direct Examination, 164

Redirect Examination, 171

Common Mistakes on Direct Examination, 176

Expert Witness, 179

Analysis of Direct Examination (Joseph Hartzler) from *U.S. v. McVeigh*, 185

Study Questions for Direct Examination Video Clips from *People v. Simpson*, 194

Chapter Five   Cross-Examination, 201

Three Myths about Cross-Examination, 201

The Basics of CLIPS, 203

Creating an Outline, 210

How to Ask Questions, 214

Impeachment with Prior Inconsistent Statements or Omissions, 222

Logical Reasoning and Progression of Questions, 228

Control of the Hostile Witness, 232

Expert Witness, 237

Analysis of Cross-Examination from *Goldman v. Simpson,* 239

Study Questions for Cross-Examination Video Clips from *People v. Simpson*, 251

Chapter Six   Closing Argument, 257

The Overrated Importance of Closing Argument, 257

The Basics, 258

Eight Steps to a Successful Closing Argument, 266

The Three Don'ts of Closing Argument, 276

Rebuttal Argument, 279

Analysis of Closing Arguments in *People v. Simpson* and *Goldman v. Simpson*, 286

Study Questions for Closing Argument Video Clips from *People v. Simpson*, 303

Chapter Seven   Exhibits and Objections, 311

Three Types of Exhibits, 312

Majority of Exhibits Easily Admitted, 313

Laying the Foundation, 314

The Six Steps for Getting Exhibits Admitted, 314

The Right Witness, 319

Bench Memos, 320

Examples of Admitting Real and Illustrative Exhibits, 321

Persuasive Aids, 347

Examples of Persuasive Aids, 347

Objections to Exhibits and Testimony, 353

Chapter Eight   Conclusion, 359

Appendix One: Background for *People v. Simpson, 363*

Appendix Two: Background for *U.S. v. McVeigh, 369*

Appendix Three: DVD Menus, 373

Appendix Four: Sample Newspaper Ad and Focus Group Questionnaire, 377

Appendix Five: Federal Rules of Evidence, 387

Index, 415

About the Author, 425

PREFACE

The genesis of this book comes from a desire to teach trial skills in a more understandable way than has ever been presented before. To that end, the book analyzes transcripts and videos of noteworthy trials such as the O. J. Simpson criminal and civil trials and the Timothy McVeigh trial to see how trial techniques have been applied in the courtroom. Some of the techniques are so well executed—and some so badly performed—that you will never forget the techniques after analyzing them.

Moreover, although there are many textbooks available, they are either too theoretical or too elementary. Those that are too theoretical do not clearly teach trial skills and fail to recognize courtroom realities that confront lawyers. For example, answers are not provided to handle the fear of being in trial for the first time or to be successful in cross-examining a witness who won't answer your question. On the other hand, the books that are too elementary do not effectively teach in-depth trial strategies and advanced skills dealing with very difficult witnesses and situations. These topics, and more, are all addressed here against the backdrop of actual trials.

Included in this book are two DVDs that contain footage of trial techniques as they were executed in the O. J. Simpson criminal trial. There are examples from all aspects of the trial, including opening statements, direct and cross-examinations, and closing arguments. By examining these video clips in conjunction with the step-by-step guides provided in this book, the lessons in this book will become easy to learn and memorable.

In addition, many textbooks ignore how important visual aids and your knowledge of the jury are to the outcome of a trial. To that end, the DVDs show a focus group analyzing a case prior to trial, a jury selection, and some of the most modern visual exhibits at hand. For the first time, readers can see striking current resources available for the trial lawyer to use to win at trial.

This book is based on my experiences teaching law students and lawyers alike, as well as being the lead attorney on countless trials in both federal and state courts in Washington, D.C., and Texas. In many of those cases, I have been both a criminal prosecutor and a civil attorney for the U.S. Attorney's Office.[1] My goal with this book is that readers will gain new insights to the trial process that will spark their curiosity, motivate them to think creatively, and inspire them to develop a trial style uniquely their own.

For more information about this book or the author, go to www.shaneread.com.

---

1. The views expressed in this book are solely those of the author and do not necessarily reflect the views of the Department of Justice.

ACKNOWLEDGMENTS

One reason this book stands out from others is the inclusion of DVDs, which will help readers learn trial techniques in a meaningful way. I am extremely grateful to Jeff Wald at KTLA for permission to use video from the Simpson criminal trial.

I am also grateful to Chris Borowiec at Totality Productions for his magnificent skill, patience, and creativity in producing the DVDs. His professionalism is unsurpassed.

Also essential to this book are the contributions of Michael E. Cobo, Robina Royer, Paul Jepsen, Susan G. Fillichio, and many others at DecisionQuest. Their enthusiasm and expertise have improved dramatically the sections on focus groups, jury selection, and exhibits. I would also like to thank Southwestern Law School in Los Angeles, California, for use of its courtroom for the voir dire video.

In my early stages of writing, Professor Fred Moss, Southern Methodist University Dedman School of Law, provided much-needed encouragement. As the book developed, he provided invaluable suggestions that made the book far better than it would have been otherwise.

Many thanks to Don Tittle, who has been a very wise sounding board for many of the cases I have tried over the years. I have also benefited greatly from Michael Kidney's exceptional advice throughout my career. Bob Webster and John Parker generously shared their vast knowledge of trial techniques. Josh Sandler, a bright and conscientious law student at Southern Methodist University, provided thoughtful insight on the book from a student's perspective.

Bob Nichol's creativity got this book off the ground, and Bill Bailey contributed important advice regarding focus groups. There are many others to thank, and I would be remiss if I did not give special thanks to Richard Roper, Lackland Bloom, Jeanne Philotoff, Adam Slote, Steve Fahey, and Gloria Pennell.

Finally, thanks to my late father, who always wanted to write a book and whose inspiration caused me to write this one.

Chapter One

———✦———

TRIAL STRATEGIES
AND BASICS

The picture cannot be painted if the significant and the insignificant are given equal prominence. One must know how to select.

—*Benjamin N. Cardozo*

At its most basic form, a trial is nothing more than the presentation of each side's version of a dispute. However, many lawyers—trained to be masters of every detail and to make every possible argument—overwhelm jurors with a myriad of facts and possibilities. They fail to connect with them and to discover the emotions that motivate them in the decision-making process. In short, lawyers—failing to distinguish between the significant and insignificant—conduct trials that do not present a compelling story. Instead, the trials are often a study in tedium.

Winning at Trial teaches the skills to use at trial along with ideas and methods to spur your creative imagination so that you can connect with the jury and be successful. You should approach each trial not as simply a technical exercise in asking questions of witnesses and getting evidence admitted but more as an art that uses imagination to create a story grounded in fact that will persuade the jury.[1] By doing so, you will find that juries return favorable verdicts more often and more quickly because you have touched an emotional chord in them, motivating them to believe in your side.

This chapter looks first at the six factors influencing the outcome of a trial, then examines the eight qualities of great trial lawyers, and, finally, gives a brief overview of the trial process, including what is needed for your trial notebook.

1.1 SIX FACTORS INFLUENCING THE OUTCOME OF A TRIAL

The old law school saying about outcome is true: "If you have bad facts, argue the law; if you have bad law, argue the facts." For example, if you represent a plaintiff against a large company that put out a product that hurt your client, but the law is such that it would be difficult for a jury to find the company liable, argue the facts of the case: your client is badly injured, and justice must prevail. In contrast, if you represent the defendant, argue the law: there can be no finding of liability even though one naturally would feel sorry for the plaintiff.

There are other factors as well. Witnesses bring the facts to life. As a plaintiff's attorney, you may have compelling facts (e.g., the defendant admitted running the red light and hitting your client's car), but if the plaintiff is not likable, the amount the jury awards him will certainly be affected. Likewise, the biases of jurors are very important, since they see the facts of the case through the lens of their own perceptions.[2] In addition, the location of a trial is important. An argument by

---

1. *Art* is defined as "the conscious use of skill and creative imagination" in *Merriam-Webster's Collegiate Dictionary* at 69 (Merriam-Webster 11th ed. 2003).
2. Throughout this book, the fact finder at trial will be referred to as the jury. Whether or not your trial is before a jury or judge, almost all the principles discussed will be the same. The differences are addressed in the section "Bench versus Jury Trials" in this chapter.

plaintiff's counsel that a corporation should be punished severely is going to be received by jurors more readily in certain parts of the country than others depending on the jurors' prevailing attitudes.

> Six factors influence the outcome of a case: (1) the facts, (2) the law, (3) the witnesses, (4) the jury, (5) the judge, and (6) the lawyers.

The judge is another important factor. If the judge likes your case and gives you favorable rulings on evidence, that can certainly be outcome determinative. Moreover, judges sometimes fail to shield their opinion of the case from the jury. Jurors notice the tone of a judge's voice when he rules on objections, speaks to counsel, or asks questions of witnesses, and his facial expressions are noted as well.

The final factor is the attorney. The impact can be significant. The facts that a jury hears are the result of the attorney's preparation and investigation prior to trial. For example, an attorney controls what documents have been discovered and what witnesses have been interviewed prior to trial to support his case. Moreover, through effective presentation at trial, great trial attorneys get more favorable verdicts because they have been able to present a clear and compelling case. In addition, the jury is also influenced by the attitude and demeanor the attorney projects.

1.2 EIGHT QUALITIES OF GREAT TRIAL LAWYERS

To become a great trial lawyer, you need eight qualities: you must develop your own style, tell a compelling story, see your case through the jurors' eyes, be prepared, adopt an attitude of less is more (the rule of three), never compromise your integrity, passionately argue your case, and show charisma.

1. Develop Your Own Style

The goal of *Winning at Trial* is not to make every lawyer the same, even if it were possible. Instead, it is to give you the tools that have proven successful for many different types of lawyers in a wide variety of circumstances so that you can use them to develop your own style.

For example, if you are not folksy, don't try to be. If you don't remember details well, don't try to be a master of them. However, that doesn't mean you should not try to improve your skills. The first step to developing your own style is to watch other attorneys. Surprisingly, you can get through three years of law school without ever stepping foot inside a courtroom. Every law student—and even an experienced lawyer— needs to spend time at the courthouse watching different trials. You will see a variety of styles and get ideas to develop your own, based on your own strengths and weaknesses.

Once you are in trial yourself, get feedback from as many people as possible afterward: the court reporter, the judge, the bailiff, and anyone who was listening. Ask the judge if you may speak to the jury. This feedback is essential to determine how you can improve. Find out if you need to be more or less aggressive, speak softer or louder, put on more or less evidence, and so on.

The video clips on the enclosed DVDs are an excellent means for comparing different styles and deciding which you like. For example, both Barry Scheck and Johnnie Cochran were lawyers for O. J. Simpson. Yet their styles were very different. Johnnie Cochran did not try to act like Barry Scheck, and vice versa. By employing good trial skills within their own style, they were effective advocates. Whatever style you develop, it is essential to be confident and likable.

2. Tell a Compelling Story

A. Have a Powerful Beginning

There is an old proverb that states, "First impressions make lasting impressions." Our life experiences have proven the truth of this saying, whether we have learned it from meeting other people, watching a new movie, or listening to a new song. There is now a new field of psychology that studies this phenomenon. It is called the "study of the adaptive unconscious." It is the study of the unconscious part of our brain that is able to make "very quick judgments based on very little information."[3]

---

3. Malcolm Gladwell, *Blink: The Power of Thinking without Thinking* at 12 (Little, Brown 2005).

To illustrate, a psychologist once compared the snap judgments of students about a professor as compared to the judgments of students who had taken a class with the professor. The psychologist found that "a person watching a silent two-second video clip of a teacher he or she has never met will reach conclusions about how good that teacher is that are very similar to those of a student who has sat in the teacher's class for an entire semester."[4] Another study found that "within three minutes of meeting someone new, people today form an opinion about where the future of the relationship is headed."[5]

So, at trial, whether it is your opening statement or cross-examination, begin it with significance. Jurors are sizing you up and sizing up what you and your witness are saying a lot quicker than you realize.

B. Create Memorable Moments

We process information and remember it best if it is conveyed as a story.[6] Every great story has unforgettable images associated with it. Likewise, a successful trial lawyer creates situations that will capture the jurors' attention, hold it, and, in those moments, create a lasting impression that will persuade the jurors. In your opening statement, create a story so powerful that the jury will no longer be disinterested in the trial but, instead, will view the rest of the trial through your point of view

---

4. Id. at 13.
5. Jeffrey Zaslow, *First Impressions Get Faster,* Wall Street Journal at D4 (February 16, 2006), citing a 2004 study cowritten by University of Minnesota–Duluth communications professor Michael Sunnafrank. The article also cited another study that found that people register "likes and dislikes in as little as 1/20th of a second." Roger Ailes declares that "research shows that we start to make up our minds about other people within seven seconds of first meeting them"; see *You Are the Message* at 3 (Doubleday 1995).
6. Nancy Pennington and Reid Hastie, *Explaining the Evidence: Tests of the Story Model for Juror Decision Making,* 62 Journal of Personality and Social Psychology at 202 (1992). (For jurors, "ease of story construction mediates perceptions of evidence strength, judgments of confidence, and the impact of information about witness credibility. . . . These results, combined with our previous research (Pennington & Hastie, 1988) support the claim that stories are the mediating mental structures that cause decisions in the juror's judgment task.")

and quietly be cheering you on. The use of exhibits in opening statements and throughout the trial to create lasting visual images is vital.

Great communicators have always employed three tried-and-true principles: primacy, recency, and frequency. That is, people tend to remember what they see or hear first (primacy), last (recency), and often (frequency). By employing these principles, you naturally start and end your case with a memorable witness. Even better, start (primacy) and end (recency) each day with compelling testimony. A jury is paying the most attention at the start of the day and will have all evening to remember the last testimony of the day. In addition, when you are conducting an examination of a witness and you are approaching the lunch break, don't stick to your outline. Instead, ask the witness something important so that the jury will remember the important testimony over the lunch period (recency). Make the jurors look forward to entering the courtroom after each break because you have trained them to expect that you will start off (primacy) with interesting and important testimony. Finally, your direct and cross-examinations should include themes from your opening and closing arguments (frequency).

C. Develop a Great Theme

Developing a great theme is discussed in detail in chapter 3. For now, it is important that you realize that if your theme rings true with the jury, you will likely win; if it doesn't, you won't. Throughout this book, we will be looking at examples from actual trials to learn skills by either imitating good examples or by learning from the mistakes of bad examples. As you read the following, ask yourself if the prosecutor, Christopher Darden, had a good theme or not in the O. J. Simpson trial.

Example: Prosecution Closing Argument
(Christopher Darden) from *People v. Simpson*

Well, let me explain justice to you this way, and then I will sit down and I will be quiet.

The people put on their case, the defense put on their case, and I assert that the defense case is a bunch of smoke and mirrors, all about distracting you from the real evidence in this case.

So imagine the smoke and imagine a burning house. Imagine that you are standing in front of a burning house, and from inside that burning house you can hear the wail of a baby, a baby's cry, a baby in fear, a baby about to lose its life. And you can hear that baby screaming. You can hear that wail.

Now, that baby, that baby is justice. This is baby justice. Usually justice is a strong woman, but in this case justice is just a baby. And you hear that baby, and you hear that wail, and you see the smoke, you see the defense.

There is all this smoke in front of you and you feel a sense—you have a sense of justice and you have a sense of what the law requires and you have a strong commitment to justice and to the law and you want to do the right thing while justice is about to perish, justice is about to be lost, baby justice is about to be lost.

And so you start to wade through that smoke trying to get to that baby. You have got to save that baby, you have to save baby justice, and you happen to run into smoke, find your way through the smoke, and if you happen to run into a couple of defense attorneys along the way, just ask them to politely step aside and let you find your way through the smoke, because the smoke isn't over, OK? The smoke is [going] to get heavier because they are about to talk to you.

Let's use your common sense. Wade through the evidence. Get down to the bottom line.

And please do the right thing.

It has been an honor to appear before you, and we will wait for your verdict.

Court: Thank you, Mr. Darden.[7]

Does this theme present a compelling picture to you? Does it work? Darden had the entire trial to think of a theme for his closing. This theme is the last—and most important—idea he is conveying to the jury. The picture he painted for the jurors was that justice needed to be rescued from a burning house. What is he asking the jurors to do? Run into a burning house, throw aside a couple of attorneys who are blocking their way, and rescue a baby called justice. Darden is asking the jurors to do an amazing amount of work at great risk to their own lives. His story does not even make sense in connection with

---

7. *People v. Simpson* No. BA097211, 1995 WL 686428 at *28–29 (Cal. Super. Ct. Sept. 27, 1995) (closing argument of Christopher Darden).

his analogy of smoke and mirrors. In short, the metaphor does not work.

What if Darden had, instead, said the following:

> The defense in this case is nothing more than smoke and mirrors. It is using the smoke of unsupported evidence and the mirrors of illogical arguments to distract you from the truth. The smoke and mirrors it is using can't prevent you from seeing the truth. The problem with the defense is that truth lasts forever, and smoke doesn't; it fades away. Just sit back for a moment and let all of the smoke clear away. Once you do, you will see that the truth is that O. J. is guilty. An overwhelming amount of evidence points toward his guilt. Everything from O. J.'s blood, hair, and clothing fibers found at the murder scene, to the blood of the victims found in his car and at his home, to his past threats to harm Nicole Simpson—everything proves that he is guilty.

The point is to choose your theme carefully and argue forcefully. Darden's theme shows the problem with not giving enough thought to this issue. Contrast Darden's theme with that of Johnnie Cochran's. A key piece of evidence for the prosecution was a bloody glove that was found at the murder scene. During the trial, the prosecution made the mistake of having O. J. Simpson try on the leather gloves [over latex gloves Simpson was wearing to prevent evidence contamination] in front of the jury. Simpson struggled mightily to pull the glove over his hand. In his closing, Johnnie Cochran had this to say:

> *I want you to remember these words. Like the defining moment in this trial, the day Mr. Darden asked Mr. Simpson to try on those gloves and the gloves didn't fit, remember these words; if it doesn't fit, you must acquit.*[8]

Cochran knew he had a great theme that would reach the emotions of the jurors. However, he did not limit his theme to the gloves alone. Throughout the remainder of his closing, Johnnie

---

8. *People v. Simpson* No. BA097211, 1995 WL 686429 at *19 (Cal. Super. Ct. Sept. 27, 1995) (closing argument of Johnnie Cochran).

Cochran referred to the theme of "if it doesn't fit" to refer to other pieces of evidence.

> The power of clear statement is the great power at the bar.
> —Daniel Webster, 1782–1852

3. See Your Case through the Jurors' Eyes

To be successful, you must see the trial not through your perceptions but through those of the jurors'.

A. Determine a Winning Theory

You must present arguments and facts that are credible to the jury. Ironically, lawyers are generally not the best suited for determining which theory of the case will accomplish this. First, there will likely be a disconnect between the socioeconomic background of lawyers and the jurors they are trying to persuade. Second, lawyers are paid by clients to represent them, and in their zeal, lawyers often put on blinders to facts that might not be helpful to their case but will influence the outcome of the trial. This problem is exacerbated in a big case, as the lawyer spends so much time marshaling favorable facts that he unwittingly discounts the importance of facts that are detrimental to his case. Being in denial is often the Achilles' heel of a lawyer in the courtroom. Also, you need to be aware of the commonly held opinions of your jurors, which will often vary depending on the jurisdiction. For example, jurors in a large city where there has been well-publicized police corruption may view the conduct of the police less favorably than jurors from a small town where there has been no reported corruption. These opinions must be considered in determining your theory.

One way to decide your case theory is to tell your friends, family members, and associates the facts of your case, and see if they agree with your theory. Try to find people who will resemble your jury. At the very least, discuss your facts with an attorney who has represented the other side in similar cases. For example, if you are a defense attorney in a car-wreck case and your theory is that the plaintiff is faking his injuries, spend some time discussing the facts of your case with a plaintiff's attorney to get a different perspective. The insight you gain will be invaluable.

B. Employ Trial Consultants and Focus Groups

A better way to determine your theory is to hire a trial consultant. You will get the benefit of an objective analysis of your case combined with the expertise of years of experience in analyzing jurors. Too often trial attorneys go to trial with a "gut" feeling about the strength and weakness of their case based on anecdotal evidence. A trial consultant will force an attorney to see his case objectively. Trial consultants can help you develop themes and strategies of the case and determine how best to tell your story with the facts and witnesses you have.

One of the most beneficial services a trial consultant can provide is to create a focus group of potential jurors prior to trial to help you understand how jurors will perceive the most critical issues in your case. You can also elicit their evaluations of potential damages and get invaluable information that can prevent your taking a case to trial that should be settled.

On disc 1 of the enclosed DVDs, you will find an excerpt of a focus group that evaluated the facts of a hypothetical case, *Scruggs v. Snyder*.[9] The focus group was conducted by DecisionQuest.[10] A summary of the *Scruggs* case and study questions for this video can be found at the end of the chapter.

Ideally, all trial attorneys would go to trial with the benefit of a trial consultant. The small size of many cases, however, does not justify this expenditure. Unfortunately, attorneys believe that if they cannot afford a trial consultant, their only option is to bounce their ideas off friends and colleagues, as discussed above. Yet conducting your own mock trial with a focus group is relatively straightforward and inex-

---

9. The facts of the focus group were slightly modified from *Scruggs v. Snyder Case File*, by William S. Bailey and Fred Moss (NITA 2007). A NITA case file (or booklet) contains everything needed to conduct a mock trial, such as pleadings, exhibits, and witness statements.

10. DecisionQuest is a leader in the field and has consulted on more than 14,000 cases. For further information, visit their Web site, at www.decisionquest.com, for insightful articles regarding jury research and trial strategies (accessed December 1, 2006). One such article is *How Jurors Really Think: A Primer of Jury Psychology*, by Ann T. Greeley, PhD.

pensive.[11] Although such an exercise does not give an attorney the objective analysis of an outside trial consultant or the many other resources that the consultant can provide, it is a very effective tool to use. The first step is to place a classified ad offering to pay individuals fifty to sixty dollars for their participation as jurors in a four-hour mock trial (a sample advertisement can be found in appendix 4). In a city such as Seattle, 100 calls are usually generated from such an ad in the city paper. You can then choose your mock jury from the information you gather from the respondents who call. The information you ask for is: (1) contact information, (2) age, (3) occupation, (4) education history, and (5) work history.

It is important to select a diverse group of people. What is so cost-effective about this process is that the callers you don't use for your current trial can be called at a later date for future trials. The meeting place can be your office or a conference room at a centrally located hotel. Saturday morning is a convenient time to meet.

Once the mock jurors arrive, read a neutral statement of the case that summarizes both sides' positions.[12] Depending on your witnesses, you may also want to conduct a short examination of your client and show severely edited excerpts of videotaped depositions of the most important witnesses for each side. If you don't have videotape, summarize the testimony. Also, show a PowerPoint presentation of key exhibits (or just put them in a notebook for the jurors).

Your presentation should last no more than an hour. After the presentation, pass out questionnaires to the jurors before their deliberations. Forms ask questions such as (1) who should win, (2) three main

---

11. William S. Bailey contributed extensively to this section on conducting your own focus group. He is a NITA instructor and adjunct professor of Trial Advocacy at the University of Washington School of Law. He has been successfully conducting focus groups for his own cases for more than a decade. To read articles he has written, visit his law firm's Web site at www.furybailey.com (accessed December 1, 2006).

12. If you try and have two attorneys give abbreviated openings (given the time constraints of the focus group) in an adversarial context, too much of the jurors' time is spent discussing the personalities and advocacy styles of the attorneys instead of the facts of the case. Moreover, it would be impossible to duplicate opposing counsel's style.

reasons why, (3) what key issue decided who should win, (4) whether they believe everything the plaintiff is claiming, (5) whether they believe everything the defense is claiming, (6) if they would like more information to decide the case, and (7) how to assign a percentage of fault to each party involved in the case. You can then add questions about damages (see appendix 4 for this form).

The jurors take anywhere from ten to forty-five minutes to answer the questionnaire. Then, you collect the forms and ask the jurors to deliberate and reach a verdict. Turn on a camcorder (preferably with a live feed to the place where you are) as you leave the room. Tell the jurors that the video will only be used for purposes of reviewing the results of the mock trial.

Once the jurors reach a verdict, conduct an extensive debriefing of the group. A debriefing is simply asking follow-up questions based on the jurors' discussions you have watched and the individual answers they gave on the questionnaires. Obviously, you cannot rely completely on your mock jury. Your jurors at trial may consist of a completely different type of group.[13] However, your mock jury will certainly make you think in new ways about the strength and weaknesses of your case. You are guaranteed to get new insights. Most important, if you conduct the mock trial while discovery is still in progress, you will be able to fix the problems the mock jury raises. Even if you conduct it after discovery, you will be able to tailor your evidence and your themes based on what you have learned.

---

13. Surprisingly, mock jurors who respond to the ad are very diverse. While you might not expect to get many professionals, you will typically get responses from retired professionals. In short, a wide variety of people are normally interested in participating. Ideally, you should conduct two focus groups—one at the beginning of your case and a second one after discovery has been completed. In selecting people for your first focus group, pick people who will be the least likely to support your position so that you will be on notice of as many problems as possible early in your case, when you can take steps to address the problems. For the second focus group, select people who will mirror your expected jury at trial. By doing this, you can determine how to adjust your trial presentation for the most effect.

C. Research Verdicts

In addition to focus groups, you should not go to trial without knowing the verdicts other juries have returned in similar cases. Most jurisdictions have a trial-reporting service that lists a short summary of the case, the lawyers and judges involved, settlement demands and offers, and the verdict. Other sources for this information are Westlaw and LexisNexis, which allow you to search verdicts across the country.[14] For example, if you want to get an idea of jury verdicts that have been returned on gender employment discrimination cases in San Francisco, you would go to the LexisNexis database "Jury Verdicts and Settlements, Combined" and enter the following search: gender or sex! /3 discriminat! & San Francisco.

D. Jurors Don't Know the Case like You Do

Remember that jurors are trying to process the information in court for the very first time. Make it clear and memorable. Have witnesses explain complex terms. Use visual aids to help the jury understand the facts.

Don't just go through the motions. On any given day, you can watch a trial at which attorneys are standing by exhibits (which may have cost a small fortune to produce) that are too small for the jurors to see. If the lawyers even notice, their typical reaction is to keep plowing forward instead of stopping, moving the exhibits closer, or simply admitting to the jury that the exhibits are difficult to see and moving on to another area. Of course, these problems could have been prevented by visiting the

> As the witnesses testify, pretend you are hearing and seeing their testimony for the first time. Does it make sense? Can the jurors see the exhibits? Are the testimonies and exhibits understandable? By doing this, you can constantly assess how the testimony is being perceived by the jury.

---

14.   Visit Westlaw (www.westlaw.com) and LexisNexis (www.lexis.com). In addition to the Web sites, each company has very helpful reference attorneys to assist you in specialized research. The phone number for Westlaw is 800-733-2889, and the number for LexisNexis is 800-543-6862.

courtroom prior to trial to determine if the exhibits can be seen from the jury box.

Moreover, lawyers will often introduce dozens and dozens of exhibits (sometimes hundreds and hundreds) and expect the jury to figure them all out during deliberations instead of telling them in their opening and closing arguments that there are key exhibits to focus on.

4. Be Prepared

The necessity of being prepared is so obvious that it will only be discussed very briefly. Jurors expect you to be the authority in the case. You must have a command of every facet of the trial. It is better to have a memorable and short opening statement that is well prepared than a rambling and long one. Moreover, by being prepared, you will avoid surprises in the courtroom. Not only are surprises personally uncomfortable but they undercut your integrity with the jury. The corollary to being prepared is "don't underestimate opposing counsel." Instead, overestimate her potential, and you will be prepared for anything. As Muhammad Ali said, "The fight is won or lost far away from witnesses—behind the lines, in the gym and out there on the road, long before I dance under those lights."

5. Adopt an Attitude of Less Is More (the Rule of Three)

Since trial advocacy is an art, let's look at one of the greatest lessons from the arts: "Less is more." If you are guided by the philosophy of less is more, you will develop the wisdom to determine what is important and what is not, and that process will force you to present a more powerful case at trial.

The rule of three is a great tool with which to train yourself to embrace the philosophy of less is more. The rule of three is a long-standing principle of successful communicators that groups ideas and limits them by the number three. Be guided by this principle at trial. Create an opening statement that has three powerful ideas, have your witnesses testify to three important facts, and limit your cross-examinations to three important topics.

Let's see how this rule of three would apply in a simple civil case. Suppose you represent a defendant in an employment discrimination case in which the plaintiff claims he was wrongfully fired because of his age; your defense is that he was fired not because of his age but because his work product was unacceptable. In your opening, on a projection screen you could display for the jury the three best reasons why the plaintiff's work was unsatisfactory: (1) failed to work well with coworkers on team projects, (2) important deadlines were missed, and (3) work product was sloppy. Then, to support these three reasons you could display for the jury three examples to support them. For example, you could show (1) a supervisor's evaluation showing the plaintiff's lack of teamwork, (2) a chronology of an important deadline that was missed, and (3) an example of the plaintiff's sloppy work. Staying with this rule of three, when you cross-examine the plaintiff, you could show these same three examples again. Likewise, when you conduct the direct examination of the supervisor who fired the plaintiff, you could again show the jury these three examples and have the supervisor fill in details for each example.

6. Never Compromise Your Integrity

The jury rightly sees you as responsible for events in the courtroom. If you put a witness on the stand who exaggerates (or, even worse, lies), not only will your witness be disbelieved but the jury will no longer trust you or the remaining witnesses you call. Likewise, if you make promises in the opening statement that you fail to keep, or if you make disingenuous arguments, the jury will fault you for your betrayal.

A problem trial attorneys have is that they are in denial about the weaknesses of their case. They often leave common sense outside the courtroom. One reason is that lawyers are pressured by clients to assert arguments that are extreme and inconsistent because the clients are also in denial. When the lawyer compromises his integrity and makes an argument that flies in the face of common sense, this loss of integrity hurts the client because the jury will not believe the argument and will reward the other side even more because the lawyer has offended the jurors' common sense.

Being in denial about the bad facts of your case is dangerous because the scrutiny of trial almost always reveals the truth. For example, if you represent a Fortune 500 company, and your trial is in a part of the country that is distrustful of large corporations, it would be foolish to take a position that does not consider the jury's skepticism of corporate motives. You are not being honest with yourself, your client, or the jury. Moreover, if you do not address the weaknesses in your case but allow the other side to mention them first, then the jury will not only distrust you on those particular issues but will wonder what else you are hiding.

Even an attorney who is aware of weaknesses is sometimes reluctant to admit them for fear that he might reveal something the other side has not thought of. In such a situation, part of your calculation depends upon your assessment of opposing counsel. If your adversary is really bad, there is a good chance the weakness won't be discovered. Nonetheless, since the penalty of not being upfront with the jury is so great, it is almost always better to bring out a weakness, knowing that there will be the rare occasion when you will have done it unnecessarily. As is discussed in later chapters, even if you bring out a weakness, you can learn how to turn weaknesses into strengths, so there really is very little downside to preempting the other side.

Since your goal is to show the jury that you are trustworthy and, therefore, that your position represents the truth, show an abundance of fairness in the courtroom. Whatever the type of case, show the jury that you are more than fair. For example, if you are the prosecution, tell the jurors the following in the opening statement: "I strongly encourage you to keep an open mind until you have heard *all* the evidence. Remember just because a government witness says something, that doesn't mean it is true. You are the judge of his credibility. Ask yourselves, by his tone and mannerisms, is he telling the truth? If you don't believe the witness is credible, acquit the defendant." How refreshing it would be for jurors to hear this from a prosecutor. Those simple words, if sincerely spoken, would not be seen as a sign of weakness but would go a long way toward establishing trust with a jury.

Moreover, this is very effective because it is an argument almost every defense attorney makes. By making it yourself, you will gain the trust of the jury and take away a strong argument from the defense counsel.

Showing trustworthiness also applies to selecting your witnesses. For example, while you can't always choose your witnesses, you can choose how to present them. There is an old saying among prosecutors that "drug deals don't take place in front of nuns." If you don't have a nun as a witness, the worst thing you can do is pretend that you do. The jurors will see through this and hold you responsible. If your witness has faults, show them. If your witness is going to say something implausible on the stand, don't call him. And if the witness surprises you with an outrageous statement, don't accept it as being true.

Having integrity also means hiring as neutral an expert as possible. Why hire an expert for trial who is biased? It is certain that the jurors will see her prejudices. Instead, hire an expert who has a history of testifying for both sides or, better yet, the other side. Best yet, find one who is well qualified but rarely testifies. You want someone who is testifying not because she makes a living doing it but because she has an interest in getting to the truth.

Example: Prosecution Showing Fairness in Closing Argument

As with an opening statement, a prosecutor (or any lawyer) has the opportunity to show fairness in a closing argument. (Throughout the book, the author's commentary is in brackets in bold.)

> Ladies and gentlemen, I encourage you *not* [said with emphasis] to rush to judgment in this case. Take your time during deliberations. Look at all the evidence carefully, and don't convict unless there is no doubt. [Pause.] Let me show you why you will find that the only just verdict in this case is guilty.

7. Passionately Argue Your Case

Have so much confidence in your case that you bring energy and passion into the courtroom and never let them go until the trial is over. Don't play it safe, but be so confident of your preparation that there is nothing the other side can do to undermine your theory.

In a leading textbook on trial advocacy, Professor Thomas A. Mauet mistakenly advises the following: play it safe on cross-examination. He proclaims:

> The traditional approach to cross-examinations was to make all your points during the cross-examination itself. The modern approach has an entirely different emphasis and level of subtlety. You ask only enough questions on cross-examination

to establish the points you intend to make during your closing argument. This means that you will avoid asking the last question that explicitly drives home your point. Instead, your cross will merely suggest the point. During the closing argument you will rhetorically pose that last question and answer it the way you want it answered, when the witness is not around to give you a bad answer.[15]

On the contrary, modern trials are not subtle. The jury must be aware of the themes you are using with each witness. Confront the adverse witness on cross-examination with the ultimate question, not because you think he will admit to it but because you have boxed him into such a corner that the denial he makes will sound unbelievable to the jury.

Moreover, don't hide behind the burden of proof. For example, if you are a defense attorney without any burden at all, don't overemphasize that the plaintiff or prosecution has the burden of proof. Instead, when you have a case to put on, tell the jury in the opening statement that you will put on evidence (even though you are not required to) and prove your case beyond all doubt. It will show the jury how confident you are in your case. Likewise, if you are a plaintiff's attorney, don't say that all you have to do is prove your case by 51 percent; instead, declare passionately that you will prove it beyond any doubt. Are these ideas radical? Not really. Jurors make their decisions based on who is right and who is wrong, almost always regardless of who has the burden of proof or how much of a burden it is. Jurors want to resolve disputes; they take their jobs seriously. There is no quicker way to gain the confidence of the jury than to show that you are fair and that you are confident that you will prove your case (even when you don't have to) beyond any doubt.

In addition, do not make alternative arguments. An alternative argument presents the jury with a choice between two or more theories of the case of which only one may be chosen. They are a sign of weakness. They also show a lack of preparation. The jury believes that the lawyer, better than anyone else in the courtroom, knows the truth

---

15. See Thomas A. Mauet, *Trial Techniques* at 253 (Aspen 6th ed. 2002).

about the case. When you make an alternative argument, it signals to the jury that you do not believe strongly in either alternative argument.

Example: Alternative Argument

Look at the problems caused by making an alternative argument for the defense in a murder case. The defendant, Doug, was accused of shooting and killing Dwayne late one night outside a crowded bar. In the closing argument, Doug's attorney made the following alternative arguments to the jury:

> On the night of the shooting, Doug was with his friend Todd at Todd's house watching TV when the shooting took place. There is no reason to doubt Todd's testimony.[16] That is what happened. However, if during your deliberations, you do not believe Todd's testimony regarding Doug's alibi and you conclude that Doug was at the scene of the murder, then you can still conclude that Doug acted in self-defense. Witnesses said the person who looked like Doug was first attacked by Dwayne and acted in self-defense.

The inconsistent arguments defeat any hope of credibility.

8. Show Charisma

Charisma is defined as the "capacity to inspire followers with devotion and enthusiasm."[17] Trial lawyers must have charisma; otherwise, it is more difficult to persuade the jury to see their clients' point of view. Some lawyers are lucky enough to be born with charisma, but for the rest of us, it takes a lot of hard work to develop. Roger Ailes, a media consultant to Presidents George Bush and Ronald Reagan, created a quotient to determine how much charisma a person has. Take the following test he devised, scoring yourself from a minimum of one ("Not true of me at all") to a maximum of five ("Describes me exactly"):

---

16. Doug did not testify.
17. *The Concise Oxford Dictionary* at 167 (Oxford 6th ed. 1976).

- Self-confident (in myself, as opposed to confidence related to my job or material possessions)
- Content with myself
- Can make others comfortable
- In control of my life
- Having definite goals and a sense of purpose
- Viewed by others as a leader
- Natural and unpretentious, no matter what the circumstances are.[18]

Ailes explains that after rating yourself, add up your score and divide by seven. If your average score is one or two, you are low on charisma. Discuss the categories with friends and work on your weak areas. If your score is three or four, you have a good charisma quotient but could still improve. If you got a five, you are very charismatic.[19]

EIGHT QUALITIES OF GREAT TRIAL ATTORNEYS

1. Develop your own style.
2. Tell a compelling story.
3. See your case through the jurors' eyes.
4. Be prepared.
5. Adopt an attitude of less is more (the rule of three).
6. Never compromise your integrity.
7. Passionately argue your case.
8. Show charisma.

---

18. Roger Ailes, *You Are the Message* at 111 (Doubleday 1995).
19. Ailes further explains: "To determine whether you have the ingredients to be charismatic, answer the following questions: What are your real feelings about who you are? What do you believe in? Do you have goals or a mission in life? Do you project optimism? Do others turn to you for leadership? Noncharismatic people spend their lives auditioning for others and hoping they'll be accepted. Charismatic people don't doubt their ability to add value to a situation, so they move forward with their mission"; *You Are the Message* at 106.

When you walk into a courtroom, you need to act like you own it. Don't be brash, but have confidence in your case and your abilities. When surprises at trial happen, don't lose control; take charge instead. The jury is looking for a leader it can trust. Let there be no doubt you are that person.

1.3 BENCH VERSUS JURY TRIALS

Bench trials and jury trials are very similar. The main difference is that, compared to a jury, a judge is usually better educated. He also has intimate knowledge of the law and has taken part in hundreds of trials. So, your presentation of argument and evidence needs to be tailored to this more sophisticated audience. Obviously, there is no need to explain in great detail the law in the closing argument.

One mistake lawyers make, however, is that they assume that all a judge wants to hear are the facts presented in a short and dry recitation. Judges are no different from jurors in that you need to find the emotion that will motivate them to decide in your favor. Likewise, in a bench trial, visual aids and persuasive themes are just as important as if you were before a jury.

1.4 THE TRIAL PROCESS

Before any trial starts, there is a pretrial conference. Depending on the jurisdiction, this conference can be very detailed and can occur a month before the trial, or it can be a perfunctory meeting on the day of trial. Whatever the situation, the judge will want to know from the lawyers (1) if efforts have been made to resolve the case, (2) the number of witnesses each side expects to call and the length of time the trial is expected to last, (3) any scheduling problems, (4) outstanding evidentiary issues, and (5) unresolved motions.

At the pretrial conference, it is important to raise objections you may have to the other side's evidence.[20] Only raise important objections. You need to pick your battles carefully because a judge will soon

---

20. This process and the terms used in this paragraph will be explained in greater detail in chapter 7.

grow tired of lawyers who fight over everything. You will find that the more you agree with the other side on items of evidence she wants to admit, the more reciprocal agreements you will get. In general, most items of evidence can be authenticated and admitted with the proper witness. Judges want you to agree on the admission of exhibits that can be introduced.

On the day of trial, the judge will confirm that both sides are ready and then notify the jury room that a panel of jurors is needed for voir dire.[21] Voir dire is that process in which the court and attorneys question potential jurors (the voir dire panel) to determine their views on the issues in the case. After the jury is selected, the court will give the jurors preliminary instructions explaining how the trial will proceed and their duties as jurors. Each side then gives opening statements (the defense can—but should not—waive his opening until it is time to put on his case) that explain the case to the jury. The plaintiff then puts on her case in chief, in which she asks a witness questions (called direct examination). The defense then cross-examines the witness, followed by—in most courts—redirect examination (sometimes there is even recross).

After the plaintiff puts on her case in chief, the plaintiff rests. The defense then moves the court to dismiss the plaintiff's case (a directed verdict in civil cases or a motion for judgment of acquittal in a criminal case). If the motion is denied, the defendant puts on its case in chief if he wants. At the conclusion, the defendant rests, and the plaintiff may ask the court to put on rebuttal evidence. Plaintiff then closes, followed by the defendant.

The parties then deliver closing arguments, followed by the court's instructions to the jury regarding the law that governs the case.[22] Once the jury retires to deliberations, the attorneys meet with the courtroom staff and agree upon which exhibits have been admitted into evidence

---

21. The plaintiff or prosecution sits at the table closest to the jury box. It is widely believed this tradition comes from the idea that since the plaintiff/prosecution has the burden of proof, it should be given the advantage (although there isn't any) of being closest to the jury.

22. During a break near the end of the trial, the court will conduct a charge conference. This is a meeting where the court will go over the proposed jury instructions and objections submitted by both sides and determine which instructions will be given.

so that the staff can take the exhibits back to the jury room for deliberations. After the jury has reached a verdict, its decision is returned on a verdict form and delivered to the court. The verdict is then read in court with the parties and jurors present.

1.5 THE TRIAL NOTEBOOK

The trial notebook is the staple of any successful trial attorney. It is nothing more than a three-ring binder with dividers that you take to court that has the most important documents you will need for trial. For example, while your case files will have all the discovery documents, your trial notebook will only have the most important ones. When you first get a case, set up a binder to be filled in as the case progresses. This is not a task for an assistant. You need to decide what is important and how you want it organized.

The goal is to have one (maybe two if it is a big case) binder that you will be able to have in court at counsel table that you can quickly refer to during trial in response to a judge's questions, opposing counsel's arguments, or the presentation of your case. Below is a sample table of contents of a typical trial notebook for a medical malpractice case. Develop your own table of contents that fits your particular style and case.

**Example: Table of Contents for
Defendant's Medical Malpractice Trial Notebook**

Defendant's Table of Contents

Contact Info and Tasks
1. To-Do List
   At the beginning of your notebook, have a list of the most important tasks you must complete.

2. Contact List
   It is essential that you have the contact information (addresses, phone numbers, and e-mails) of all the important witnesses, attorneys, court reporters, etc., in your case.

3. Division of Labor
   If you are trying the case with another attorney, list each person's tasks.

Important Pleadings and Court Orders

4. Plaintiff's First Amended Complaint
   This section is for the most recent complaint since it will govern the allegations during discovery and trial.

5. Defendant's First Amended Answer

6. Court's Scheduling Order and Stipulations
   As trial approaches, the parties will reach stipulations (or agreements) regarding particular pieces of evidence. Include the stipulations here. Obviously, the court's scheduling order of important deadlines is critical. This section might also include important correspondence in the case.

7. Miscellaneous Court Orders
   Have all of the court orders here, even the unimportant ones. You never know what the court might think is important in the heat of a trial.

Chronology

8. Chronology of Events
   Generally, even the simplest cases need a timeline of important events.

Discovery Materials

9. Plaintiff and Defendant's Initial and Supplemental Disclosures
   In federal court, the parties are required to provide the names and other identifying information of witnesses and documents that may be used to support their claims and defenses.[23] There is also a duty to supplement this information throughout discovery.

10. Important Discovery Pleadings
    Here, include only the most important discovery pleadings or excerpts from them.

Pretrial Materials

11. Joint Pretrial Order
    In federal court, the parties submit a joint pretrial order just prior to trial that sets forth estimates about the length of trial, contested and uncontested facts at trial, names and other identifying information of

---

23. See Fed. R. Civ. P. 26(a)(1).

witnesses, testimony that will be provided by deposition, and other important information.[24]

12.   Plaintiff's and Defendant's Trial Exhibit Lists

13.   Plaintiff's and Defendant's Trial Witness Lists

14.   Plaintiff's and Defendant's Proposed Jury Instructions

15.   Motions in Limine and Other Motions
      Any significant motions for trial should be included here.

Trial Materials

16.   Order of Call
      List your witnesses and the expected order in which you intend to call them at trial.

17.   Outline of Opening Statement
      Begin working on this as soon as you get your case. Add to it, change it, and make it a working document throughout discovery until trial.

18.   Outline of Closing Argument

19.   Cross of Plaintiff *(Outline Form)*
      This section and the other sections for witnesses should contain the following: (1) outline of cross-examination, (2) prior statements made by each witness, (3) highlighted copies of prior inconsistent statements with which you intend to cross-examine each witness, (4) summary of each witness' deposition,[25] and (5) highlighted copies of exhibits you intend to use on cross.

20.   Cross of Plaintiff's Spouse *(Outline Form)*

21.   Cross of Plaintiff's Expert Witness *(Outline Form)*

22.   Cross of Other Plaintiff's Witnesses *(Outline Form)*
      If there are a number of witnesses who have a small amount of testimony, their outlines can be put in this section.

23.   Direct of Defendant's Expert Witness *(Outline Form)*
      This section and the other sections for witnesses should contain your outline of direct examination and highlighted copies of exhibits you expect to use with each witness. It should also have a copy of the witness' prior statements (including a summary of his deposition) for you to access if necessary on redirect examination.

24.   Direct of Treating Doctors[26] *(Outline Form)*

---

24.   See Fed. R. Civ. P. 26(a)(3).
25.   The witnesses' depositions will be too bulky to put in the notebook.
26.   As opposed to a hired expert who reviews medical records, a treating doctor or nurse is the person who actually took care of the patient.

25. Direct of Treating Nurses *(Outline Form)*

26. Direct of Other Defendant's Witnesses *(Outline Form)*

Important Exhibits and Research

27. Most Important Defense Exhibits

     Concentrate on your most important exhibits, and put them here.
     You should have copies of the most important medical records.
     Include copies of your medical expert's written report. In large cases,
     you will need to create a chart that summarizes the most important
     documents in your case. By starting the summary when you first
     begin working on your case, you will discipline yourself to look for
     and focus on only the most critical documents.

28. Most Important Plaintiff Exhibits

29. Research on Important Legal Issues

1.6 STUDY QUESTIONS FOR FOCUS GROUP VIDEO CLIPS FROM *SCRUGGS V. SNYDER* (DISC 1) (37 MIN.)[27]

Prior to the excerpt shown on disc 1, the focus group was read a statement of the case (as set forth below) and told that the plaintiffs were seeking $200,000 in past medical expenses, $300,000 in future medical expenses, and $5 million for loss of enjoyment of life.

The focus group consisted of the following people from the West Coast: (1) Amy, a human resource specialist; (2) Sidney, an information technology specialist (who had a degree in psychology); (3) Bill, a beginning law student who was formerly a sixth-grade teacher; (4) Naomi, who worked in accounting; (5) Jim, a law-enforcement officer with twenty-eight years' experience; (6) Amanda, an office receptionist (who had a degree in psychology); (7) Joe, a retiree; (8) Doreen, a prin-

---

27. You can go to different parts of this clip by using the "seek" button. The first chapter is at Part One: Liability and Past Medical Expenses (11 min. duration). Part Two is Future Medical Expenses (6 min. duration). Part Three is Loss of Enjoyment of Life Damages (4 min. duration). Part Four is Conclusions (7 min. duration). Part Five is Discussion with Moderator after Verdict (9 min. duration).

Figure 1.1. View of Pedestrian Tunnel.

cipal of an elementary school; and (9) Lynn, a former auditor who is now a stay-at-home mom.[28]

The focus group was asked to answer two questions: (1) whether the defendant is liable and (2) if so, how much damages the plaintiffs are entitled to for past medical damages, future medical damages, and loss of enjoyment of life for the child and his parents. The focus group was also shown three photographs (see figures 1.1–1.3).

Statement Read to Focus Group

This is a personal injury case involving a six-year-old child, Sam Scruggs, who ran across a busy two-lane highway while his family was camping at a state park over the Fourth of July weekend.[29] The highway runs through the middle of the park. People in the park can cross the highway by way

---

28. Their profiles are also shown on a chart under Juror Profiles on disc 1.
29. The facts were modified slightly from *Scruggs v. Snyder Case File,* by William S. Bailey and Fred Moss (NITA 2007).

Figure 1.2. Aerial Photo of Highway and Child's Path Across It.

of a pedestrian tunnel that connects both sides of the park. On the evening of the accident, Sam was being watched by his fourteen-year-old sister, Robin (who was momentarily distracted), when he tried to cross the highway from a softball field on one side of the highway back to his family's campsite on the other side.

A number of motorists, including the defendant, Lynn Snyder, who hit the child, noticed Sam on the southbound shoulder before he attempted to dash across it. A southbound pickup truck pulling a boat on a trailer in the lane closest to the boy was able to slow down enough to avoid hitting him as he crossed the highway. The defendant, who was coming in the other direction, hit the boy with the right front of her rental car as the boy almost made it across both lanes.

The child survived with two broken legs and a head injury. He was initially unconscious and then was crying at the scene. Sam has completely recovered from the two broken legs. However, his parents claim that he suffered some residual mental impairment (such as mild learning and memory issues) as a result of the collision. The parents seek damages from the defendant, both for their son and their own sake, alleging that

Pedestrian is adjacent to the estimated location of impact.

Photo is taken from the point where braking would <u>need</u> to begin to avoid contact.

Figure 1.3. Street Level View from Defendant's Car.

the defendant failed to keep a proper lookout and was going too fast for the conditions.

Defendant denies any negligence on her part and claims that the child suffered no lasting injury or impairment from the accident. The state highway patrol officer who investigated the accident determined that the defendant could not have done anything to avoid the accident. However, the plaintiffs' accident reconstructionist[30] and an eyewitness state that there was enough time for the defendant to have avoided hitting the child.

The plaintiffs' accident reconstructionist further maintains that Snyder should have anticipated a potential emergency when she saw the child on the opposite shoulder before he darted across the highway. Even if Snyder

---

30. An accident reconstructionist is a hired expert who analyzes information about an accident—including eyewitness testimony—and testifies regarding how the accident occurred.

had not seen the child at this point, when the southbound truck slammed on his brakes and skidded, Snyder should have seen and heard this, and if she had, she would have been able to stop in time. Further evidence that Snyder was at fault is the fact that the heavier southbound truck with the boat trailer took twice as long to stop after braking as compared to the defendant's lighter Kia. Given that the truck was able to slow enough to avoid hitting the boy, the defendant should have done so even more easily.

There is also another witness for the plaintiffs who will testify that she was driving southbound behind the truck and saw that the defendant was using a cell phone at the time of the collision (the defendant denies this and claims that the "on" cell phone found in the front of the car was being used by her passenger).

The defendant alleges that the accident was the result of the negligence of the child in attempting to cross a busy highway when there was a pedestrian walkway under the highway nearby. The defendant also alleges that the child was being improperly supervised by his parents, who put the child under the supervision of his fourteen-year-old sister while they remained at their campsite some distance away.

Study Questions

Before viewing the clip, answer the following questions.

1. How would you decide liability and damages?
2. How do you think the focus group will decide liability and damages?
3. What do you think are the three issues the group will determine are important?
4. How significant will the issue of the defendant's use of the cell phone be?
5. What are the two most important facts the group will want to know that are not in the statement above?

As you watch the clip, notice which people are the leaders and the followers. Notice how important that is in the outcome of the discussion. After you watch the clip, decide how you would build your case based on the discussion if you represented the plaintiffs.

Chapter Two

———— ❧ ————

VOIR DIRE

The only place where a man ought to get a square deal is in a courtroom, be he any color of the rainbow, but people have a way of carrying their resentments right into a jury box.

—*Harper Lee,* To Kill a Mockingbird

oir dire is the selection process where potential jurors are asked questions to determine whether they can be fair in a particular trial. Depending on the court, it can be conducted entirely by the attorneys, entirely by the judge, or by a combination of both.

When courts permit attorneys to ask questions, the scope of what the attorneys can say varies widely. For example, some courts allow attorneys to explain their case in great detail without the necessity of posing a lot of questions to the jurors.[1] Such a scenario offers a unique chance for an attorney to build an emotional bond with the jurors and

---

1. The potential jurors participating in voir dire are sometimes called venire members, members of the jury panel, jurors, and other names. For ease, they will be referred to as jurors throughout this chapter.

can be one of the most important parts of a trial. If this is the case, many of the principles stated in chapter 3, "Opening Statement," apply. That is, in addition to identifying unfavorable jurors (see discussion below), voir dire should be seen as a virtual opening statement with some questions interspersed throughout.

In most courts, however—even where lawyers are allowed a chance to participate—the court will not permit the attorneys to do anything other than ask questions (the amount of particular facts an attorney can discuss with the jury varies among courts). In addition, there is often a court-imposed time limit that restricts questioning. Moreover, when judges conduct the entire voir dire, the process can be even more perfunctory.

The custom in federal courts is that judges conduct the majority of the questioning with some involvement from the attorneys. The judges are strict in prohibiting statements or arguments from counsel and requiring that only questions be asked. There are also time limits set by individual judges. Given the variance among local jurisdictions, the federal court process is discussed below.

2.1 STRATEGIES FOR VOIR DIRE

The hardest part of voir dire is getting the jurors to talk. It is very difficult because the setting is formal, and you are necessarily asking jurors questions about their own biases. Not many people are willing to talk openly about their prejudices and shortcomings in front of a group of strangers. Plus, everyone likes to think of himself as fair. So, getting jurors to talk about their failings and then to admit that they cannot judge the case fairly because of their biases is a rare event.

In addition, the limited amount of time allowed prevents a thorough voir dire. There is simply not enough time to get adequate information from each juror to make very intelligent decisions. If a lawyer has only twenty minutes to question thirty to forty jurors, that leaves about thirty to forty-five seconds per juror—hardly enough time to get a juror comfortable with revealing long-held biases.

Some lawyers think they can watch jurors' body language during voir dire to gain insight into what type of juror they will be. However, trying to evaluate jurors by dress, mannerisms, and body language is often pure speculation. It is naive to think that a lawyer can consistently predict how complete strangers will decide a complex matter by evaluating their body language and mannerisms.

Given the difficulties in getting information from jurors, you must have realistic goals. There are four things you can accomplish in most voir dires: (1) identify the obviously biased jurors who speak out against your position, (2) get the jurors to like you, (3) make the jurors interested in your position, and (4) educate the jury by discussing the critical legal issues that will apply to your case.[2]

First, voir dire is your chance to weed out the obviously biased jurors who can't wait to tell you their opinions about your case. For example, some people believe that if a defendant is innocent, he ought to testify at trial even if the Constitution gives him the right not to. If you are a defense attorney and you plan to instruct your client not to testify and discover such a juror, you have achieved success.

Second, voir dire is a wonderful opportunity to let the jury get to know you. First impressions are everything. You may be taking written notes on the jurors, but they are making mental notes about you. Are you likable? Do you know the case?

Third, try to create an emotional bond between the jurors and the facts of your case. Make the jurors feel the trial is important for your client so they will want to be on the jury to return a verdict in your favor.

Fourth, since you cannot discuss the details of the law in your opening statement, voir dire affords an excellent opportunity to do so. For example, criminal defense attorneys will often spend significant time emphasizing how high the burden of proof is in a criminal case. Defense attorneys can also explain elements of the crime in a

To get jurors talking, a good trick is to pick a juror who has been vocal and ask him an important question. After the juror has stated his view, then ask other jurors who you are curious about if they agree or disagree with the first juror. After significant questions, ask if there are other jurors who haven't spoken who agree or disagree with the point you are trying to make.

---

2. Some courts restrict the discussion of the law by attorneys.

way that shows how difficult it should be for the prosecution to get a conviction.

Finally, ask individual jurors short, open-ended questions to encourage them to talk. Ask what they like about their jobs, why they chose to live in this particular city, what kind of previous jury service they have, and so forth. At first, it may feel like you are trying to pull teeth, but soon they will warm up to your questions.

2.2 THE BASICS OF FEDERAL COURT VOIR DIRE

After the parties have announced they are ready for trial, the judge notifies the jury room that a panel of jurors is needed. Spectators in the courtroom are asked to give up their seats for the panel when it arrives. The number in the panel varies from court to court but is usually between twenty and fifty.

Prior to the panel's arrival, the court provides the lawyers with a list of people on the panel. The list has identifying information such as address, occupation, age, prior jury service, and spouse's occupation.

One of the first things you should do upon arriving at court is to ask the bailiff how the panel will be seated. Will it be in rows of six starting with juror number one on the left of the courtroom or something different? The reason is that you need to create a chart so that you can quickly put a name and occupation with a face as the jurors take their seats. There will inevitably be some time to do this after you get your list and before the jury arrives.

To create a chart, turn a legal pad of paper sideways and draw a box that represents each seat in the courtroom.[3] In the upper left-hand corner of the box, put the juror's number, and then fill the top part of the box with the juror's last name and occupation. By the time the panel arrives in the courtroom, you will have a chart that has the jurors' identifying information. As the jurors answer questions, fill in the boxes with only the most important responses.

---

3. Draw two horizontal parallel lines across the pad for each row of seats in the courtroom (or however your courtroom is configured). Then draw vertical lines connecting the horizontal lines so that you will have a box for each seat.

The court begins voir dire by explaining the selection process to the jurors and summarizing each side's contentions. The panel is administered an oath to tell the truth, and the judge asks some basic questions, followed by the attorneys' questions.

First, the court will usually question the jurors about (1) whether they can be fair based on the short summary of the case they have just heard, (2) if there are scheduling problems, and (3) whether they know any of the parties, lawyers, or potential witnesses. The court will then ask more specific questions relevant to the particular case.

The attorneys are then sometimes given twenty to thirty minutes to ask questions. The plaintiff (or prosecution) goes first and then the defendant. The questioning takes place from the podium (which has been turned around to face the jurors).[4]

After the attorneys question the jurors, the lawyers approach the bench, and the judge calls certain jurors up to the bench—one at a time—who have been requested by the attorneys. The attorneys then ask follow-up questions that would not be appropriate in front of a group. Such questions might include the nature of an illness that would prevent jury service or other reasons that a juror felt he would be unfit. After this, the attorneys make their challenges for cause and preemptory strikes (discussed in more detail below), and the remaining number of jurors that are needed are seated in the jury box.

The size of the ultimate jury depends on the jurisdiction. In federal court, civil juries must consist of a minimum of six people and no more than twelve, criminal juries must consist of twelve people, and unanimity is required for both types of verdicts.[5] Often, one or more alternate jurors will be seated depending on the length of the trial. For nonfederal cases, the jury can be anywhere from six to twelve people for civil and criminal trials depending on the particular state. The verdicts do not necessarily have to be unanimous—even for criminal trials. For example, in civil cases, generally a simple majority is needed. In criminal cases, most jurisdictions require unanimous verdicts, but pluralities of ten out of twelve have been allowed. When juries number only six,

---

4. In most state courts, the questioning usually takes place from the counsel table (where the chairs have been repositioned on the other side of the table so that the table is between attorneys and the jurors).
5. Fed. R. Civ. P. 48 and Fed. R. Crim. P. 23(b)(1) and 31(a).

however, verdicts must be unanimous in both civil and criminal cases.[6]

2.3 CHALLENGES FOR CAUSE AND PREEMPTORY STRIKES

Jurors may be struck for cause if their answers show that they cannot be fair and impartial. Jurors may also be excused if they

> When asking voir dire questions, do not pay much attention to jurors in the back of the courtroom (i.e., those at the bottom of the list) since they probably won't be on the jury. Courts call for panels that have far more jurors than are needed. In the limited amount of time you have, concentrate on the jurors in front, who matter.

cannot serve on a jury because of health or serious scheduling problems. After the attorneys question the panel, the judge speaks with the attorneys (outside of the panel's presence). She asks the attorneys to name jurors they want to question further to determine if they should be struck for cause. Then, one by one, the judge asks these jurors to approach the bench for a private discussion with the attorneys. Each side has an opportunity to ask the juror questions. Once the questioning of the juror is complete, the juror returns to his seat. Then, before calling the next juror up to the bench, the judge asks the attorneys if there is a motion to strike for cause and hears a brief argument from counsel before ruling. After the judge rules, the next juror is called up to the bench, and the process is repeated until all the relevant jurors have been questioned. There is no limit to the number of jurors that can be struck for cause.

After the court rules on the strikes for cause, the stricken jurors are excused, and the attorneys then make their preemptory strikes. Unlike a strike for cause, a preemptory strike allows an attorney to strike a juror for any reason, as long as it is not based on race or gender. The

---

6. See, e.g., *Apodaca v. Oregon,* 406 U.S. 404, 411 (1972) (Oregon's requirement that all that was needed in conviction in noncapital criminal cases was a plurality of ten out of twelve jurors was constitutional) and *Burch v. Louisiana,* 441 U.S. 130 (1979), six-person juries must be unanimous; Fed. R. Crim. P. 31(a) requires unanimous verdicts in federal criminal cases.

number of preemptory strikes varies from jurisdiction to jurisdiction. In a federal civil case, each side gets three.[7] In a federal criminal trial, there are six for the prosecution and ten for the defendant.[8] The attorneys submit their strikes to the court personnel on a piece of paper that the court provides. Then, depending on the number of jurors and alternates needed (see discussion in previous section), the court reads in numerical order the names of the jurors who will be on the jury. The jury sits in the jury box and is sworn in.

> Don't start the trial on the wrong foot by getting the court upset with you for making unreasonable strikes for cause. Here is a great opportunity to show the court your fairness by readily agreeing to opposing counsel's legitimate strikes and only asserting clearly meritorious ones yourself.

2.4 PROHIBITIONS

Under *Batson* and its progeny, you may not use preemptory strikes on jurors based on race or gender (whether in a civil or criminal trial).[9] Consequently, after you submit your preemptory strikes and the jury is seated, the judge will ask if there are any challenges to the jury. Opposing counsel may make a *Batson* challenge. If your opponent makes out a prima facie case of prohibited discrimination, you must provide a reason for your strike that is not prohibited by *Batson*. The reason does not need to rise to the level of proof, as in a challenge for cause (e.g., that the juror cannot be fair), but does need to be on its face legitimate and nondiscriminatory. Your opponent can respond, and then the judge rules. If you lose the *Batson* challenge, the juror you struck is replaced in his original order on the panel and seated on the jury if his position would have dictated this action. If he is seated, the effect is that the last juror seated before the challenge is removed from the jury.

Another prohibition is the arguing of your case to the panel instead of asking questions. However, if the court allows attorneys to

---

7. 28 U.S.C. section 1870 (2006).
8. Fed. R. Crim. P. 24(b).
9. *Batson v. Kentucky,* 476 U.S. 79 (1986) and, e.g., *Hernandez v. New York,* 500 U.S. 352 (1991).

conduct the entire voir dire, as is done in some state courts, the attorney is usually allowed great latitude to argue a point—or several points—to a jury as long as there is a question at the end of the topic. In short, not every statement must be a question, but in general, after a few statements, you need to ask the panel a question. Be aware of your particular court's practice and the freedom given to lawyers by the court.

Finally, an attorney cannot discuss evidence that won't be admissible at trial or misstate the law. Consequently, most questions are permissible as long as they go to a juror's particular qualifications or are relevant to the facts that will come out at trial.

2.5 JURY QUESTIONNAIRES AND CONSULTANTS

To get more information from jurors, some courts will allow you to mail (through the court) a jury questionnaire to the jurors on your panel that is returned prior to trial.[10] The jury questionnaire can give you a lot of very helpful information and allow you to save time by getting jurors to answer questions in advance. These questions can be anything that would be appropriate to ask during voir dire.

In larger cases where resources are justifiable, jury consultants are extremely helpful. They can help you (1) prepare a jury questionnaire, (2) draft voir dire questions, (3) pick the jury, and (4) hire a mock jury to provide feedback while the trial is in progress.

2.6 VOIR DIRE IN A CRIMINAL TRIAL

As you read the summary of facts for the criminal and civil trials below, try to spot the relevant issues. Decide how you would handle the voir dire, and compare your results with the examples.

---

10. Some courts allow questionnaires to be passed out on the day of trial to the jurors while they are waiting to be called into the courtroom for the first time. In any case, the questionnaires are typically one or two pages long.

1. Summary of Facts

The following voir dire is based on the facts in a National Institute for Trial Advocacy (NITA) case file about an aggravated assault that occurs in an alley.[11] The victim is Henry Fordyce. The defendant is Edward Felson. (For this example, assume that codefendant Gerry Harris will be tried separately.)

Henry is expected to testify that on the night of March 2, he and his friend, Eva, went to Gus' Bar & Grill at 10:30 p.m. They both ordered a couple of drinks (Henry had already drunk two scotches earlier at another bar). Henry noticed two tough-looking guys—who he now knows as Gerry and Edward—sitting a couple of tables away. Gerry kept staring at Eva. Henry told him to "knock it off." Gerry laughed and shouted to Eva, "Honey, drop the stiff and come over here. I'll show you a real good time." Edward then said to Eva, "I remember you from down on the corner. What's the matter—business bad—too many cops around?"

Eva started to cry. Henry went over to the table, grabbed Edward by his shirt, and pushed him off his chair. Edward got up, broke a beer bottle, and came after Henry. In defense, Henry used a chair to protect himself. Then, Gerry punched Henry in the stomach. By this time, the police arrived and broke up the fight. Officer Logan took down everyone's identifying information but made no arrests.

Henry and Eva left the bar at 11:30 p.m. Henry will testify that they walked about fifty feet when Gerry jumped out of a very dark alley. He shoved Eva away and pulled Henry into the alley and clobbered him on the head with a broom handle. While Henry was on the ground, Gerry struck him again. Then, as Henry was losing consciousness, he saw Edward approach him, stomping on his stomach twice before he passed out. At the hospital, Henry told the police that the two men at the bar (Edward and Gerry) had attacked him, but he was groggy from medication when he made this statement.

---

11. The case file is *Fordyce v. Harris and Felson*, by Abraham P. Ordover (NITA 1992). The facts used in the voir dire have been modified to adapt the case from a civil assault to a criminal assault and are reprinted here with NITA's permission. The names of the jurors and attorneys used in the examples are fictitious.

Eva will testify similarly to her friend, Henry, except that she will say that both Gerry and Edward jumped out of the alley and "clobbered us" (while Henry says it was just Gerry.) She will also say that although she saw Edward near Gerry in the alley, it was Gerry who kicked Henry in the stomach (not Edward as Henry claims).

Edward may not testify because of his felony convictions. If he does, however, he will testify that he has a felony conviction for auto theft—and was arrested and convicted for armed robbery after the incident at Gus' Bar & Grill while on release in this case. Edward claims that he was talking with his friend, Gerry, when Henry came over to their table—smelling of alcohol—and knocked him off of his chair, spilling a beer on Gerry. Edward started "mixin'" it up with Henry but never used a broken beer bottle as Henry claims. After the police broke up the fight, Edward took a cab home. While waiting for the cab, he noticed Gerry walking toward the alley where the assault occurred.[12]

The officer who responded to Eva's cries for help will testify that he was on his beat when Eva ran to him and yelled, "They are killing my friend!" When the officer arrived in the alley, no one was there except Henry, who was lying on the ground, bleeding from the head. Eva told the officer that the assailants were the same two people who had fought with Henry in the bar.[13]

2. Prosecution's Voir Dire

> Q: *Good morning, ladies and gentlemen. I have the honor of representing the people of NITA. First, don't worry*

---

12. Because of his pending trial, Gerry will not testify. At his own trial, he will assert an alibi defense. He will testify that he and Edward were at the bar and had a few beers. Edward started staring at Eva when all of a sudden Henry—who was very drunk—came flying across the room and knocked Edward to the floor and spilled some beer on Gerry. He then went after Henry, and they were wrestling on the floor when the police arrived. After the fight was broken up, Gerry walked to the apartment of his girlfriend, Glenda Barkan, around 11:30 p.m.

13. A couple of days later, after Gerry and Edward were arrested, a lineup was conducted. Eva immediately picked Gerry and Edward out, but the officer's conversations with her later revealed that although she was positive of the Gerry identification, she was much less sure of her identification of Edward.

*about being nervous. That is natural. It is not fun an-
swering questions that are very personal. So, if at any
time you feel uncomfortable, feel free to let me know,
and we can discuss your answer in private at the bench
with the judge.*

At the outset, try to create a bond with the jurors. If you accomplish nothing else during voir dire, get them to like you.

Q: *One point I anticipate that the defense will discuss at
length is the burden of proof. Does everyone understand
that the government does not have to prove its case beyond all doubt?*
A: *[No response from panel]*
Q: *Ms. Kim, does that make sense to you?*
A: *Yes, I guess. Could you explain it some more?*

If jurors don't respond, one way to get the conversation started is
to select a particular juror, as above.

Q: *"Beyond all doubt" leaves no room for any error at all.
Beyond all doubt is sometimes referred to as a scientific
or mathematical certainty. On the other hand, "beyond a
reasonable doubt" means that you* can *have a doubt and
still convict, as long as the doubt is not a reasonable one.
Ms. Kim, does that explanation clear up any confusion
you might have?*
A: *Yes.*
Q: *Have any of you watched the TV show C.S.I.? I see there
are a lot of hands. Mr. Norman, are you aware that many
of the crime-solving technologies and resources available
to the police on that show simply don't exist?*
A: *Well, now that you say it, I guess so.*
Q: *The reason I ask that question is that, as we all know,
C.S.I. is not a documentary. It is fiction. So, as you might
expect in the real world, there is often not scientific evidence like that shown in C.S.I. that links a defendant to a
crime. In the case before you, there will be no such scientific evidence. What there will be are eyewitnesses. Having said that, is there anyone here who could not convict
the defendant if the government proved its case beyond a
reasonable doubt through eyewitness testimony—but did
not have any scientific proof?*

A: *[No response from panel]*

Q: *Mr. Fahey, could you convict if the government proved its case beyond a reasonable doubt with eyewitness testimony but did not have any scientific proof?*

A: *Yes.*

Q: *Mr. Parker, do you disagree with Mr. Fahey?*

A: *No.*

Q: *All right, by a show of hands, does anyone disagree with Mr. Fahey and Mr. Parker and instead believe the government can't rely on eyewitness testimony alone, no matter how strong it is, but must put on scientific evidence to link the defendant to the crime?*

A: *[No hands are raised.]*

The above question is not intended to elicit any juror responses since it is unlikely someone would volunteer this information because doing so invites some ridicule from the other jurors. The point of the question is to begin to persuade the jurors how strong your eyewitness testimony is.

Q: *Do any of you have moral or religious beliefs that would prohibit you from judging the guilt or innocence of another person?*

A: *[No response from panel]*

Q: *Ms. Holmes, do you?*

A: *I kind of have a problem with . . .*

Q: *Has anyone ever had any experience with law enforcement that you were dissatisfied with?*

A: *[Mr. King] I was once falsely arrested for drinking while driving. The charges were later dropped.*
[For this witness, the attorney should follow up with these questions: How do you feel about the police? How do you feel about the criminal justice system? After those questions, you could ask the following question:]

Q: *Could you keep an open mind in this case, or does your experience make you—as you sit here today—favor the defendant before the trial begins?*

A: *Well, the prosecutor dropped the case. So, I could be fair.*

King's answers would probably prevent him from being struck for cause by the prosecution. Even though King claims he could be fair, however, the prosecutor would be wise to use a preemptory strike.

Q: *Anyone else had a bad experience with law enforcement?*

A: *[Ms. Bell] I have a brother serving time for a crime he didn't commit. He was framed by the police.*

[Additional questions for this witness include the following: What was the nature of the crime? Was there a trial? Were you a witness? Why do you say he was "framed" by the police?]

Q: *Given what you believe happened to your brother, could you be a fair juror in this case, or right now do you lean toward the defense?*

A: *I couldn't be fair.*

Bell can be struck for cause.

3. Defendant Edward Felson's Voir Dire

A. Introduction

Q: *Ladies and gentleman, as the court mentioned, I have the privilege of representing Edward Felson. I will be brief, but I need to ask you a few questions about the case.*

First, Edward graduated from Hillcrest High School, served in the Persian Gulf War, was honorably discharged, and volunteers at the First Baptist Church here in town, where he has been a member since childhood. Does anyone know Edward?

A: *[No response from panel]*

Q: *Everyone's goal here is to find fair jurors for this case. Let me give you an example of what I mean. You might be the fairest person in the world, but there are certain trials where you just might not be a good juror. For example, I am a father of three little children. If a defendant were accused of child abuse, it would be very hard for me to keep an open mind in such a trial. We are all more open-minded about some issues than others.*

So, let me ask you some questions about this case. First, this case involves an allegation of aggravated assault. Everyone feels sorry for what happened to Mr. Fordyce in the alley. No one deserves to be beaten over the head with a stick. Is there anyone who is thinking to himself, "I'm a fair person, but given what happened, I don't think this is a trial where I could keep an open mind"?

A: *[No response from panel]*

Q: *Ms. Leedy, how do you feel about what happened to Mr. Fordyce?*

A: *Of course, I think it is tragic, but I could be fair.*

Q: *Let me turn to a few of the instructions you will hear from the judge during the trial. One instruction concerns the credibility of witnesses. You will be instructed by the court that you—not the attorneys and not the judge—determine the credibility of a witness. You may believe everything a witness says, part of it, or none of it.*

What is important about that fact is that every witness enters this courtroom on equal footing. Is there anyone who is more likely to believe a witness just because that person is called by the prosecution to testify?

[No response from panel]

Q: *In other words, the fact that the prosecution or defense calls a witness is not a factor you can consider in determining whether you believe a witness. Does everyone understand that?*[14]

A: *[No response from panel]*

The previous two questions are not intended to identify unfavorable jurors but rather to educate them on important legal issues.

Q: *Another instruction you will hear concerns a defendant's absolute right not to testify. Now, some believe that if you are an innocent person, you should testify. Who feels like that?*[15]

---

14. If you are going to challenge a police officer's credibility, the following question is appropriate. Q. Nowhere does it say in the instructions that just because a witness is a police officer, he can't make mistakes or has to be believed. Is there anyone here who believes that before an officer testifies, you are going to believe what he says just because he is a police officer?

15. The following are questions to ask if you think it is very likely Edward Felson will testify.

Q. *You may hear my client was convicted of a felony a few months ago; would that cause anyone automatically to disbelieve my client?*

Q. *You will be instructed by the court that you may consider my client's prior conviction only as it may affect his believability as a witness, not as evidence of guilt of the crime for which he is on trial. Does anyone believe that because my client was recently convicted of another crime that he is guilty of the crime charged today?*

A: [Mr. Brickman] I believe that if a defendant doesn't testify, he is hiding something.

Q: Does anyone else agree with Mr. Brickman?

A: [No response from panel]

Q: All right, Mr. Brickman; can you think of some other factors at work other than the defendant trying to hide something?

A: No. I just think if you've got nothing to hide, you ought to defend your name at trial and testify. It's that simple.

Q: All right. Mr. Black, let me ask you a question about this. If you hired a lawyer, wouldn't you take the advice of your lawyer if he told you that you did not need to testify if the government had failed to meet the burden of proof?

A: Yes.

Brickman can be struck for cause. Since no one else agreed with him, the attorney asks a series of questions to educate the jury. Note that the above question is only successful if you are certain that your client is not going to testify. It can backfire if he does testify since jurors may remember this question and assume you believe the government has met its burden of proof.

Q: Another factor is that prosecutors are in trial all the time. They are highly educated, very skilled, and experts at making witnesses look bad. On the other hand, this is my client's first time to be in a courtroom. So, can you see another reason why I may not let Edward testify is that I don't want to put him in such an unfair battle?

A: [Mr. Black nods.]

Q: Another factor is that innocent people are nervous. I am nervous. Anyone here nervous?

A: [A few hands are raised.]

Q: Remember how awkward and nervous you felt when the judge first started asking questions? Well, imagine being on the witness stand being charged with a felony you did not commit. How nervous would you be? Mr. Black, do you see now that there are at least three reasons why an innocent defendant wouldn't testify?

A: Yes.

Q: This is a related question: who thinks my client, as he sits here today, is just as innocent of the alleged crime as the person sitting next to you? Ms. Roberts?

- A: *I think he must have done something, or he would not have been arrested.*
- Q: *Ms. Roberts, thank you for your candid response. That is such a natural reaction. Tell me, why do you feel that way?*
- A: *My brother was a criminal defense attorney, and he told me about the cases he handled. He told me that almost every client he represented was guilty of something.*
- Q: *By a show of hands, who else agrees with Ms. Roberts that because Edward is sitting here in this courtroom that he must have done something wrong?*
- A: *[No hands are raised.]*
- Q: *Let me explain the law. There is a complete presumption of innocence for my client. Just because he has been arrested, or charged with a crime, doesn't mean he has done anything wrong. And there is a reason for that. Our country was founded on the principle that before someone's liberty could be taken away, the government had to prove its case at a trial. It is safe to say that there is a presumption of innocence because our Founding Fathers wanted to force the government to get it right. The only way to ensure this was that an accused citizen is presumed innocent until the government proves its case beyond a reasonable doubt.*
- Q: *Mr. Briggs, does that make sense to you?*
- A: *Yes.*

By asking Ms. Roberts how she feels, the juror reveals the reasons for her conclusion. The reasons will allow the defense attorney to strike her for cause unless the prosecution can rehabilitate her. The attorney then educates the other jurors and lays the groundwork for his opening and closing arguments.

- Q: *I know the prosecution has asked you some questions about the burden of proof, but let me ask you about different types of proof. Has anyone heard of a reasonable suspicion?*
- A: *[Several jurors raise hands.]*
- Q: *For example, reasonable suspicion is what is required for a police officer to search a defendant if he suspects that he has unlawful drugs in his possession. Another type of proof is "probable cause," and that is what is necessary for a grand jury to return an indictment. Another type of proof is "more likely than not," or 51 percent, that is all*

that is required in a civil case. There are two other types of burdens of proof. One is "clear and convincing evidence." "Clear and convincing evidence" means that you have a firm belief or conviction. Does everyone understand that the standard in Edward's case is even greater than all of the ones I just mentioned? [**Pause and speak with emphasis.**] *It is beyond a reasonable doubt. It is the highest standard any court has in this country. Ms. Henderson, let me ask you, do you understand that beyond a reasonable doubt is a burden heavier than "a reasonable suspicion"?*

A: *Yes.*

Q: *Heavier than "probable cause"?*

A: *Yes.*

Q: *Heavier than "51 percent"?*

A: *Yes.*

Q: *Heavier than "clear and convincing evidence"?*

A: *Yes.*

Q: *Another instruction you will hear from the judge relates to evidence. Mrs. Monnick, do you understand that my client has no burden to put on any evidence?*

A: *Yes.*

Q: *Well, even though the burden of proof is on the government, we will prove my client's innocence. Let me turn to another topic.*

The key is to develop your own style. Use the above questions merely as a guide.

2.7 VOIR DIRE IN A CIVIL TRIAL

To give readers the most current insights into the science of jury selection, the author has collaborated with DecisionQuest,[16] a preeminent

---

16. Paul Jepsen, a director with DecisionQuest, collaborated with the author on this section. He has been involved in the development of trial strategies from a social-science perspective for two decades. He has written many articles, including "Revealing the Hearts and Minds of the Jury—Six Best Practices for Improving Voir Dire Results," which he coauthored with Peter A. Moir. Visit DecisionQuest's Web site, at www.decisionquest.com, to read this article and others on jury selection and trial strategies (accessed December 1, 2006).

trial research consultant firm, to create the following civil voir dire and its analysis for *Scruggs v. Snyder*. The facts of that case can be found in chapter 1. DecisionQuest has also produced the mock plaintiffs' voir dire of *Scruggs v. Snyder* contained on disc 1.

1. Plaintiffs' Voir Dire

Q: *I am nervous because this is a very important day in the life of Sam and his family. I want to summarize briefly the facts in this case so you can decide whether or not you are the best person to sit as a juror on this particular type of case. [The lawyer briefly summarizes the case.]*

Q: *From what you have heard so far, is there anyone who has the slightest concerns about sitting on this type of case?*

A: *[No response from panel]*

Q: *Mr. Jones, I see from the jury questionnaire that you have been in a car accident before. What were the details of that accident?*

A: *[Mr. Jones relates the details.]*

Q: *Mr. Jones, given the fact that you were a defendant in a lawsuit because of the accident, do you think that you might come into this trial leaning in favor of the defendant?*

A: *Yes, I think I would not start out with a clean slate and probably favor the defendant.*

Q: *Ms. Smith, you stated on the questionnaire that you were also in an accident. Do you have the same feelings as Mr. Jones?*

A: *No, I think I could be fair.*

Do not use voir dire to identify good jurors for your side. If you do, the other side will surely use its preemptory strikes on them. Instead, identify the bad jurors for your case so that you can strike them. Do not be afraid if a juror gives a strong opinion against your side. For example, if you represent a defendant and the juror says, "I am sick of defense attorneys because all they do is get guilty people off." Many attorneys believe that such a comment will "poison the well." On the contrary, jurors are not going to change their beliefs based on a stranger's comments. However, it is vital that such a juror be identified.

Q: Tell me the details of your accident.

A: While crossing the street, I was hit by a teenager who ran a red light. . . .

Q: So, Ms. Smith, what you're saying is that you can listen with an open mind and won't hold the defendant liable unless we prove our case?

A: Yes, that's right.

Analysis: This last question is an effort by plaintiffs' counsel to inoculate Ms. Smith from a strike for cause by the defendant because she was a victim in a car accident somewhat similar to the plaintiff in this case.

A. Burden of Proof

Q: Unlike a criminal case, in a civil case, the burden of proof is a preponderance of the evidence. That is a fancy way of simply saying "more likely than not." All we have to prove is that the evidence is just slightly in our favor— just 51 percent. We will prove it by more than that, but that is all the law requires us to do. Is there anyone who would have the slightest hesitation in finding a verdict against the defendant if the evidence in the case was just slightly in our favor?

A: [No response from panel]

Q: Ms. Miller, how do you feel about the plaintiff only having to prove his case by 51 percent?

A: [Ms. Miller] Well, I think . . .

B. Damages

Q: Now, like I said, we will bring you overwhelming evidence, but the law only requires us to prove it more likely than not. Let's turn to the real issue in this case: damages. At the outset, let me assure you that I am not going to ask you to award any amount of damages that I have not proven. You will hear from an expert that Sam's actual damages are $200,000. Is there anyone, for whatever reason, who thinks that he or she could not consider that amount of damages even if there were proof?

A: [Mr. King] I believe . . .

Notice how the attorney signals to the jury that "the real issue in this case" is damages. She is also telling the jury that it will be easy to decide that the defendant was at fault.

> Q: *Now, there is also another type of damages: pain and suf-fering. These are intangible damages. There will not be an expert witness to testify regarding the amount of those damages. The evidence for these damages will come from Sam and his parents. Is there anyone who feels that, although they could award actual damages if an expert testified about them, they could not award damages for something like pain and suffering?*
>
> A: *[No response from panel]*
>
> Q: *Mr. Wade, do you feel that you would need an expert's testimony before you could award damages for pain and suffering?*
>
> A: *I haven't given it much thought, but I guess . . .*
>
> Q: *As I mentioned earlier, we are not going to ask for any-thing that the evidence does not support. In addition to past medical bills, we are going to prove to you that the plaintiffs are entitled to millions of dollars for pain and suffering and loss of enjoyment of life. Is there anyone, for whatever reason, who thinks he could not consider a multimillion-dollar verdict even if there were proof?*
>
> A: *[Mr. Staniar] I believe that . . .*

The attorney is laying the groundwork for her closing argument, where she will ask the jury to return a large verdict. Also, now is the time to find out who the reluctant jurors are.

The following are additional questions that should be asked. The answers have been omitted. These questions are intended to reveal potential jurors who have opinions and beliefs most harmful to the plaintiffs' case. Some attorneys are reluctant to ask questions like these because they fear the jurors' responses will influence, or "poison," the beliefs and opinions of their fellow jurors. However, it is better to hear jurors discuss these issues in voir dire than to hear about them later in deliberations.[17] Where indicated, some of the questions are discussed in more detail in the problem section below and at the end of the chapter.

> Q: *Who here feels that lawsuits these days have gotten out of hand—that too often people file frivolous lawsuits and*

---

17. Many judges will permit follow-up questions on sensitive areas at the bench. What a judge considers "sensitive" varies. Nonetheless, what-ever happens, the questions need to be asked.

collect damages they do not deserve? [See problem 1 below.]

Q: *Who thinks that the amount of money awarded in some lawsuits is way too large, such as people getting millions of dollars for spilled coffee or paint scratches on their car?*

Q: *Who here has been sued? Or accused of wrongdoing by a fellow employee or some other acquaintance? How did you feel about that experience?*

Q: *What do you think about those ads on TV with personal-injury lawyers who tell you to call an 800 number and recover loads of money?* [See problem 2 below.]

Q: *As you started to hear about this case, whose first reaction was something like "Well, if a six-year-old child gets to the edge of the highway all by himself, his parents must have been really careless or negligent"?* [See problem 3 below.]

Q: *Who has difficulty with the idea of awarding money for things like "pain and suffering" and "loss of enjoyment in life"?* [See problem 4 below.]

Often, the most important question attorneys can ask is the "second," or follow-up, question. Sometimes, because attorneys are too focused on simply getting through a list of prepared questions, or are reluctant to hear more of jurors' adverse opinions, they fail to hear what jurors have said and ask an effective second question. Too often, this results in an exchange such as the following:

Q: *Have you or your spouse suffered any recent health problems?*

A: *I just had to go in for a biopsy, and I am waiting for the results.*

Q: *OK. And how is your husband's health?*

By not listening to the answer, the attorney has unintentionally shown a lack of compassion for the juror. If the attorney had listened to the answer, she should have responded: "If you don't mind, I would like to ask you a follow-up question later at the bench. May I ask you how your husband's health is?"

Below, for each question and resulting juror reply, select the best potential follow-up question. The answers can be found at the end of this chapter.

Problem 1

Q: Who here feels that lawsuits these days have gotten out of hand—that too often people file frivolous lawsuits and collect damages they do not deserve?

A: I agree with that. I think some lawsuits are just driving up the cost of insurance for the rest of us.

    Q1. But you understand, don't you, that many studies have shown that lawsuit damages have not caused insurance rates to rise?

    Q2. Tell me more about why you feel some lawsuits are driving up the cost of insurance.

    Q3. But you would agree with me, wouldn't you, that everyone deserves his or her day in court and that it is important for you to put this bias about lawsuits aside and fairly and impartially reach a just verdict for this case?

    Q4. Thank you. Let's change subjects and talk about damages for pain and suffering.

Problem 2

Q: What do you think about those ads on TV with personal-injury lawyers who tell you to call an 800 number and recover loads of money?

A: I have seen that—that old Hollywood guy is on every night saying to call this 800 number and "get money damages fast."

    Q1. In what ways do those kinds of ads influence how you might listen to and judge a case like this?

    Q2. You realize, don't you, that those are not my ads?

    Q3. Have you seen any ads against "lawsuit abuse" or for limiting the amount of damages from lawsuits?

    Q4. How do you feel about those ads?

Problem 3

Q: As you started to hear about this case, whose first reaction was something like "Well, if a six-year-old child gets to the edge of the highway all by himself, his parents must have been really careless or negligent"?

A: Yes, when I go to someplace like the grocery store, I am amazed by how many parents let their children run around.

Q1. Do you understand that, in this case, the Scruggses' fourteen-year-old daughter was supervising Sam?

Q2. Do you really think it is possible to keep an eye on a busy six-year-old every second of the day?

Q3. And what did you think about Ms. Snyder and her level of watchfulness while driving?

Q4. As you started to picture this scene in your mind, what did you picture that the parents were doing when Sam was hit by that car?

Problem 4

Q: Who has difficulty with the idea of awarding money for things like "pain and suffering" and "loss of enjoyment in life"?

A: I can see paying for the medical bills. I have no problem with that. These days those medical costs are plenty high. But I have trouble with something like pain and suffering.

Q1. The judge will instruct you that plaintiffs are entitled, by law, to ask for pain and suffering damages. Can you be a fair and impartial juror and follow the judge's instructions?

Q2. What experiences have you had with pain and suffering and medical bills?

Q3. OK. Does anyone know, or has anyone heard anything about, Dr. Wilson, our expert economist witness?

Q4. But you would be willing to pay something to avoid pain and suffering, wouldn't you? In that sense, you could see how it has economic values, right?

2. Defendant's Voir Dire

Q: *Good morning. Ladies and gentlemen, I have the honor of representing Lynn Snyder in this case. This is a very important day for her as well. She has waited a long time to be able to show that the plaintiffs' claims have no merit. Does everyone understand that—unlike a criminal case, where a grand jury investigates facts before charges are brought—in a civil case, anyone can pay a filing fee to the clerk and file a lawsuit?*

A: *[No response from panel]*

Q: *Have you or a family member ever been in a car wreck?*

A: *[Ms. Reeves raises her hand.]*

Q: Ms. Reeves, tell me the details about it.
A: Well, last year, I was driving down the highway and a car in the other lane cut in front of me, and I hit it. My car was damaged, but I wasn't hurt.

Do not ask any more questions of this juror because the juror is likely to be helpful since—like the defendant—she was unable to stop quickly enough. Let the plaintiffs' attorney try and get her removed for cause or by using a preemptory strike.

Q: Anyone else?
A: [No response from panel]
Q: Is anyone familiar with the crossing in the state park where this occurred?
A: [No response from panel]
Q: Has anyone taken or taught a course in defensive driving?
A: [No response from panel]
Q: Has anyone or a family member ever had his or her leg broken?
A: [Ms. Madison] I broke my leg skiing.
Q: Did you experience any lasting injuries?
A: No.
Q: Has anyone or a family member had a head injury of any kind?
A: [Mr. Lee] My child fell off a swing and had a concussion.
Q: Mr. Lee, did your child suffer any lasting effects from the concussion?
A: No.
Q: Now, you will hear that there was a truck trailering a boat that was able to stop and avoid hitting Sam. Does anyone believe that since the truck was able to stop, then the defendant should have been able to?
A: [Mr. Solomon] Well, I'm really not sure. I kind of think that since the truck was on the same side of the road and was able to stop, then your client should have been able to stop.
Q: Mr. Solomon, what if you learned that there were cars on both sides of the road that made it harder for my client to see the child; would that change your view?
A: Well, maybe.
Q: Mr. Solomon, in your opinion, how close to perfect would a driver need to be to not be at fault for hitting a pedestrian?

A: *In my mind, the driver has to do pretty much everything right. If they are going too fast, or they're distracted, then they could be at fault, but you'd have to look at all the evidence.*

Q: *Who agrees with Mr. Solomon?*

A: *[Ms. Newman] I do. I have been driving for a long time and . . .*

Solomon appears likely to have an unfavorable bias. His qualified "Well, maybe" response is a warning of underlying trouble. Asking him to elaborate provides the opportunity to further gauge the extent of the bias and evaluate whether a peremptory strike should be used later to remove him from the panel. His continued qualifying of his answers makes it unlikely he can be successfully struck for cause. Rather than argue with Solomon with follow-up questions, it often works best to ask the other jurors if they agree with Solomon. This will provide the opportunity to identify other unfavorable jurors.

Q: *Now this is a very important question. Would any of you have the slightest bit of trouble in returning a verdict for the defendant if the plaintiffs failed to prove their case?*

A: *[No response from panel]*

In this situation, it is likely that juror silence to the above question arises because the jurors feel they are being asked to provide an obviously wrong answer. The question sounds too much like "Is there anyone here so stupid he or she would still find for the plaintiffs even though the defense won the trial?" Since the question was asked, you should follow it up with the following:

Q: *The reason that I ask is that it is natural to feel sympathy for a child. Who here—knowing their heart—would find it very hard to reach a verdict that would give nothing to the child who suffered this accident?*

The following additional defense-oriented questions should be asked. The answers have been omitted. In a manner similar to the plaintiffs' questions listed above, these questions are also intended to reveal potential jurors with harmful opinions and beliefs—this time with biases adverse to the defense. Again, the goal for the defense is to have these most dangerous jurors do most of the talking during voir dire. Where indicated, some of the questions are discussed in more detail in the problem section below and at the end of the chapter.

> Q: *Who here feels that cell-phone use by drivers has become a real safety menace?* [See problem 1 below.]
>
> Q: *Who thinks that too many people just drive too fast these days?*
>
> Q: *Who would agree that if you hurt somebody, you are automatically responsible to pay for his damages? For example, if the mail carrier falls on your steps, then you are liable?*
>
> Q: *Have you ever sued someone? How did that turn out?*
>
> Q: *Have you ever felt you could have sued someone but chose not to?* [See problem 2 below.]
>
> Q: *Who here feels they would struggle with listening to the testimony in this case, because it will be too close to home, that you know someone who has suffered like Sam Scruggs and his family?* [See problem 3 below.]
>
> Q: *Who feels, in the grand scheme of things, that knowing who is responsible for Sam's injuries is not as important as making sure this little boy and his family are taken care of financially?*

Below, for each question and resulting juror reply, select the best potential follow-up question. The answers can be found at the end of this chapter.

Problem 1

Q: Who here feels that cell-phone use by drivers has become a real safety menace?

A: I think cell-phone use can be a problem.

    Q1. But you understand, don't you, that Ms. Snyder will testify that she was not talking on the phone at the time of the accident?

    Q2. Do you think that if someone is using a cell phone while driving and gets into an accident, he or she is automatically negligent?

    Q3. But you would agree with me, wouldn't you, that because the plaintiffs have the burden of proof, they have to prove to you that Ms. Snyder was distracted by using a cell phone?

    Q4. Who has concerns about a radio being a distraction for drivers?

Problem 2

Q: Have you ever felt you could have sued someone but chose not to?

A: My wife had a horrible boss at her old job, lots of abuse and discrimination. She thought about suing him and the company.

    Q1. Tell me more about that. Why did she choose not to sue?

    Q2. OK. Are there any other times you might have sued but chose not to?

    Q3. Do you think too many people do choose to file lawsuits?

    Q4. Can you promise me to put that experience aside and decide this case fairly and impartially and base your verdict only on the evidence and the law?

Problem 3

Q: Who here feels they would struggle with listening to the testimony in this case, because it will be too close to home, that you know someone who has suffered like Sam Scruggs and his family?

A: I don't know if this is what you mean, but my sister's son drowned in a pool two years ago.

    Q1. I am very sorry to hear that, but since this case does not involve water or any drowning, you can put that experience aside, can't you?

    Q2. OK. Has anyone else suffered a recent tragedy?

    Q3. I am very sorry to hear that. But the judge will instruct you that you must not allow sympathy to influence your verdict. Are you willing to follow that instruction as a juror in this case?

    Q4. I am very sorry to hear that. What a horrible tragedy. Can I ask you, in your mind, how did such a terrible tragedy occur?

2.8 ANSWERS TO VOIR DIRE PROBLEMS

1. Plaintiffs' Voir Dire

Problem 1

Q: Who here feels that lawsuits these days have gotten out of hand—that too often people file frivolous lawsuits and collect damages they do not deserve?

A: I agree with that. I think some lawsuits are just driving up the cost of insurance for the rest of us.

    Q1. But you understand, don't you, that many studies have shown that lawsuit damages have not caused insurance rates to rise?

Q2. Tell me more about why you feel some lawsuits are driving up the cost of insurance.[18]

A: I think a lot of these lawsuits are just driven by greedy lawyers. Instead of having people sit down and try and work things out, they just push people to sue, sue, sue. I think it just has to stop.

Q3. But you would agree with me, wouldn't you, that everyone deserves his or her day in court and that it is important for you to put this bias about lawsuits aside and fairly and impartially reach a just verdict for this case?

Q4. Thank you. Let's change subjects and talk about damages for pain and suffering.

Analysis: Often, the best "question" (Q2) is simply to request more information. When doing so, it is important to repeat, exactly, a portion of the juror's prior answer. The goal is to move past what the juror believes to why the juror has the belief. Avoid arguing with (Q1) and preaching to (Q3) potential jurors. Ignoring a juror's response (Q4) will not make it go away.

Problem 2

Q: What do you think about those ads on TV with personal-injury lawyers who tell you to call an 800 number and recover loads of money?

A: I have seen that—that old Hollywood guy is on every night saying to call this 800 number and "get money damages fast."

Q1. In what ways do those kinds of ads influence how you might listen to and judge a case like this?

A: Well, I guess I would have to say that those ads have left a bad taste in my mouth, and it would bias me against a lawsuit where someone is claiming all sorts of injuries.

Q2. You realize, don't you, that those are not my ads?

Q3. Have you seen any ads against "lawsuit abuse" or for limiting the amount of damages from lawsuits?

---

18. In some jurisdictions, such as Minnesota and Texas, it is grounds for a mistrial to mention insurance in the courtroom. In other states, such as Wisconsin, insurance companies are explicitly mentioned in the complaint. In jurisdictions that do not allow mention of insurance coverage, the question can be rephrased as, "Tell me more about why you feel lawsuits are driving up the cost of products/medical care/daily life."

Q4. How do you feel about those ads?

Analysis: This follow-up question (Q1) is phrased to lead a juror to identify and state potential bias. The question is neutral and does not pass judgment on the juror's opinions. Rather, the emphasis remains on the ads. The question is open-ended and calls for more than just a yes or no answer. Note that (Q2) argues with the juror, (Q3) preaches to the juror, and (Q4) is too vague in comparison to (Q1).

Problem 3

Q: As you started to hear about this case, whose first reaction was something like "Well, if a six-year-old child gets to the edge of the highway all by himself, his parents must have been really careless or negligent"?

A: Yes, when I go to someplace like the grocery store, I am amazed by how many parents let their children run around.

Q1. Do you understand that, in this case, the Scruggses' fourteen-year-old daughter was supervising Sam?

Q2. Do you really think it is possible to keep an eye on a busy six-year-old every second of the day?

Q3. And what did you think about Ms. Snyder and her level of watchfulness while driving?

Q4. As you started to picture this scene in your mind, what did you picture that the parents were doing when Sam was hit by that car?

A: It was the Fourth. They were at a campground, staying there for a few days. You know, I've been to that campground before—it is quite a party spot. I've got to figure they were just sitting around drinking; they should have been watching their child.

Analysis: Jurors often use extra-evidentiary information to help resolve cases, and they usually supply that information from their own lives and experiences. Ask jurors to describe how they visualize or perceive a situation. Note that Q4 is not phrased as a yes or no question; if jurors are alive and breathing, they are forming perceptions and visualizing situations. Again, avoid arguing (Q1), preaching (Q2), and changing the subject (Q3).

Problem 4

Q: Who has difficulty with the idea of awarding money for things like "pain and suffering" and "loss of enjoyment in life"?

A: I can see paying for the medical bills. I have no problem with that. These days those medical costs are plenty high. But I have trouble with something like pain and suffering.

Q1. The judge will instruct you that plaintiffs are entitled, by law, to ask for pain and suffering damages. Can you be a fair and impartial juror and follow the judge's instructions?

Q2. What experiences have you had with pain and suffering and medical bills?

A: I was in a car accident five years and two months ago. I was hospitalized for a week, and I still feel the pain. But no one gave me a bunch of money for my pain. Sometimes you just have to suck it up and get on with your life. You can't expect everyone to always take care of your problems. God helps those who help themselves.

Q3. OK. Does anyone know, or has anyone heard anything about, Dr. Wilson, our expert economist witness?

Q4. But you would be willing to pay something to avoid pain and suffering, wouldn't you? In that sense, you could see how it has economic values, right?

Analysis: This follow-up question (Q2) probes for experiences that may underlie a belief. An opinion based on hard-won experience is likely to be much stronger than an opinion based just on "things I've heard and read." Use "what" questions often in voir dire. Like the "Tell me more" phrasing, they encourage thoughtful replies.

2. Defendant's Voir Dire

Problem 1

Q: Who here feels that cell-phone use by drivers has become a real safety menace?

A: I think cell-phone use can be a problem.

Q1. But you understand, don't you, that Ms. Snyder will testify that she was not talking on the phone at the time of the accident?

Q2. Do you think that if someone is using a cell phone while driving and gets into an accident, he or she is automatically negligent?

A: Yes, that's all I need to hear. If drivers get in an accident because they are talking on a phone while they are driving, they are guilty. You would have to prove to me otherwise to get me to side with the driver in this lawsuit.

Q3. But you would agree with me, wouldn't you, that because the plaintiffs have the burden of proof, they have to prove to you that Ms. Snyder was distracted by using a cell phone?

Q4. Who has concerns about a radio being a distraction for drivers?

Analysis: This follow-up question (Q2) is a stronger example of attempting to lead a juror into admitting a bias. Going further than the earlier example ("Plaintiffs' Voir Dire, Problem 2"), this question narrows the juror's reply options and adds a reference to a legal standard. This type of follow-up question works best in response to a juror with a clear, strongly expressed opinion. (For example, most people are more likely to have a strong preexisting opinion about cell-phone abuse than about lawsuit abuse.)

Problem 2

Q: Have you ever felt you could have sued someone but chose not to?

A: My wife had a horrible boss at her old job, lots of abuse and discrimination. She thought about suing him and the company.

> Q1. Tell me more about that. Why did she choose not to sue?
>
> > A: Nowadays, everything is stacked up against the little guy. If she had complained, they probably would have fired her and brought in some fancy big-city lawyers like you guys to file some counter-suit against her. It's not worth sticking your neck out and making waves.
>
> Q2. OK. Are there any other times you might have sued but chose not to?
>
> Q3. Do you think too many people do choose to file lawsuits?
>
> Q4. Can you promise me to put that experience aside and decide this case fairly and impartially and base your verdict only on the evidence and the law?

Analysis: As with "Plaintiffs' Voir Dire, Problem 1," this follow-up question (Q1) is phrased with a statement. This time, the statement is accompanied with a question that narrows the focus of the reply. Otherwise, there is too much chance the follow-up question will produce an unfocused rant from the juror. Again, it is important to seek the "why" behind the "what."

Problem 3

Q: Who here feels they would struggle with listening to the testimony in this case, because it will be too close to home, that you know someone who has suffered like Sam Scruggs and his family?

A: I don't know if this is what you mean, but my sister's son drowned in a pool two years ago.

Q1. I am very sorry to hear that, but since this case does not involve water or any drowning, you can put that experience aside, can't you?

Q2. OK. Has anyone else suffered a recent tragedy?

Q3. I am very sorry to hear that. But the judge will instruct you that you must not allow sympathy to influence your verdict. Are you willing to follow that instruction as a juror in this case?

Q4. I am very sorry to hear that. What a horrible tragedy. Can I ask you, in your mind, how did such a terrible tragedy occur?

A: I blame the pool company. The way the cover was designed, it was too easy for a child to be trapped underneath the cover. They should have done more to change the cover and warn people about the danger.

Analysis: Preliminary voir dire often provides plenty of information about jurors (e.g., where they live, what they do, and major life traumas). Use voir dire to learn the "why." Ask jurors why they have chosen to live in their neighborhood and why they choose to do the work they do. Most important, ask jurors to explain why they feel bad things that have happened to them have occurred. When jurors describe adversity, express sympathy and empathy, and ask them about why they feel it happened. By asking "why," you can learn a juror's feelings, which may reveal a bias against your case.

2.9 STUDY QUESTIONS FOR VOIR DIRE VIDEO CLIP OF *SCRUGGS V. SNYDER* (DISC 1)

A mock voir dire can be found on disc 1 under the heading "Voir Dire." The voir dire is a sample of questions that a plaintiff's attorney might ask based on *Scruggs v. Snyder*.[19]

1. Are appropriate follow-up questions asked? Identify which ones are good and which ones are bad.
2. Which jurors, if any, are bad for the plaintiffs?

---

19. Note that in an actual trial there would be many more jurors. In some courts, all the jurors are sitting in the audience section of the courtroom for voir dire, while in other courts some jurors are seated in the jury box and the audience section.

3. Which jurors, if any, are bad for the defendant?
4. Is the attorney effective in eliciting answers from the jurors?
5. Is it easy for the attorney to get the jurors to reveal their feelings?

Chapter Three

OPENING STATEMENT

It usually takes more than three weeks to prepare a good impromptu speech.

—*Mark Twain*

3.1 THE UNDERRATED IMPORTANCE OF THE OPENING STATEMENT

Unless you are before a court that gives attorneys wide latitude to explain and argue their case to the jurors during voir dire, the opening statement is the most important part of a trial. Research shows that at least 80 percent of jurors reach a decision about a case based on the persuasion of opening statements.[1] While this does not mean that jurors fail to listen to the rest of the trial, it does mean that the opening statement steers jurors to think a certain way about a case and frames

---

1. James F. McKenzie, *Eloquence in Opening Statement,* Trial Dipl.J. at 32 (Spring 1987); Donald E. Vinson, *Jury Psychology and Antitrust Trial Strategy,* 55 Antitrust L.J. at 591 (1986) (based on 14,000 actual or surrogate jurors, "80 to 90 percent of all jurors come to a decision during or immediately after the opening statements").

the way they will filter the testimony that follows.[2] Unfortunately, in courtrooms across the country, the majority of opening statements do not achieve their most basic goal: to convey clearly to the jury what the lawyer believes the evidence at trial will be. Few rise to a higher level, where a story is told that effectively moves a jury to produce maximum results. The reason for this is twofold. First, lawyers do not realize the importance of an opening statement and, thus, spend too much time on less-important aspects of the trial. Second, lawyers have not learned the art of giving a persuasive opening statement.

An opening statement is much like a speech: it must be well organized, easy to understand, and easy to remember. Juries appreciate presentations that are thoughtfully crafted, leading them step-by-step to a clearly defined conclusion. Attorneys who carefully organize their opening statements are perceived as more knowledgeable and believable than those who give rambling and disjointed statements.

The opening statement takes serious effort. Not only do you have to win over the jury but you set the tone for the rest of the trial. Make no mistake: the opening dictates the tenor and logic of things to come.

First of all, know your jurors (see the discussion on focus groups in chapter 1). Knowing them will yield useful information that will ingratiate you with them and make your message more effective. If you lose them at the outset, you're going to have a hard time reeling them back in. You want the jurors to find you credible, to like you, and to accept the logic of your information and your version of things. It all begins at the beginning.

The most basic job is to persuade. Have the ring of truth. Supply the conviction that will make your case. In the crowded field of statistics, numbers, and sheer rhetoric, your opening needs to start with a bang. It is the first chance the jury has to assess your case. The dynamics of most trials cause many jurors to lose interest in the proceedings. There is too much of everything: too many witnesses, too many exhibits, too many objections, and too many delays. Even if you put on a perfect case, you won't be able to control the length of the other attorney's presentation,

---

2. Kurt A. Carlson and J. Edward Russo, *Biased Interpretation of Evidence by Mock Jurors*, 7 Journal of Experimental Psychology: Applied at 100 (2001) ("jurors predecisionally distort case evidence as it is presented").

and the jury may very well be exhausted by the time of closing argument. Your opening, then, is your best chance to persuade the jurors while they are fresh, receptive, and interested in the trial.

Present information in ways that appeal to the jurors so that they will want to hear what follows. The words you use should be descriptive but easy on the ear. Phrase your opening statement from the jury's viewpoint. Don't be self-important, or you will seem pompous. Your opening statement should contain your best arguments.

1. Make It Important and Interesting

Although the subject matter of a typical trial may at first seem mundane, there is a way to make your case significant even if it involves a simple case of breach of contract or shoplifting. Find it. Believe in what you have to say, and the jury will pay attention to you and be willing to consider your viewpoint.

To make an important and interesting opening statement, it is helpful to read great speeches. All great speeches (and opening statements) have an attention getter, a theme, and a strong idea that is powerful and easy to remember. If, in addition, they tell a story that is potent enough to move the audience emotionally, so much the better.

Because juries have a limited capacity to follow an intricately presented opening statement or to absorb vast quantities of information, making your case by pulling the strings of emotion is a smart thing to do. In fact, some speeches are remembered more for the emotion produced by a single statement than for the speech itself.

Sparking the American Revolution, Patrick Henry proclaimed, "I know not what course others may take; but as for me, give me liberty, or give me death."

In Shakespeare's *Julius Caesar*, Antony uttered the lines that have stood the test of time: "Friends, Romans, countrymen, lend me your ears. . . . This [Brutus' killing of Caesar] was the most unkindest cut of all."

Every grade-school child identifies our first president the way Henry Lee described him, as "first in war—first in peace—and first in the hearts of his countrymen."

Excommunicated, Martin Luther was defiant: "Here I stand, I cannot do otherwise."

Steadying his countrymen for the long war against Nazi aggression, British prime minister Winston Churchill gave his "blood, toil, tears, and sweat" (altered now to "blood, sweat, and tears") speech.

Franklin Delano Roosevelt will always be associated with the admonition, "The only thing we have to fear is fear itself." Who knows that the line came from his first inaugural address, intended to give confidence to a nation laid low by the Depression?

2. Reach the Jurors' Emotions

Sometimes emotion is all you need. Senator George Graham Vest, a member of the Confederate Congress during the Civil War, is remembered to this day for a winning argument made as a young lawyer. He was representing a plaintiff who sued a neighbor for the killing of his dog.[3]

> Gentlemen of the jury:
> The best friend a man has in the world may turn against him and become his enemy. His son or daughter that he has reared with loving care may prove ungrateful. Those who are nearest and dearest to us, those whom we trust with our happiness and our good name may become traitors to their faith. The money that a man has, he may lose. It flies away from him, perhaps when he needs it most. A man's reputation may be sacrificed in a moment of ill-considered action. The people who are prone to fall on their knees to do us honor when success is with us may be the first to throw the stone of malice when failure settles its cloud upon our heads.
> The one absolutely unselfish friend that man can have in this selfish world, the one that never deserts him, the one that never proves ungrateful or treacherous is his dog. A man's dog stands by him in prosperity and in poverty, in health and in sickness. He will sleep on the cold ground, where the wintry winds blow and the snow drives fiercely, if only he may be near his master's side. He will kiss the hand that has no food to offer; he will lick the wounds and sores that come in encounter with the roughness of the world. He guards the sleep of his pauper master as if he were a prince. When all other friends desert, he

---

3. Even though this is a closing argument, its use of powerful themes is instructive for opening statements.

remains. When riches take wings, and reputation falls to pieces, he is as constant in his love as the sun in its journey through the heavens.

If fortune drives the master forth an outcast in the world, friendless and homeless, the faithful dog asks no higher privilege than that of accompanying him, to guard him against danger, to fight against his enemies. And when the last scene of all comes, and death takes his master in its embrace and his body is laid away in the cold ground, no matter if all other friends pursue their way, there by the graveside will the noble dog be found, his head between his paws, his eyes sad, but open in alert watchfulness, faithful and true even in death.

The key is to make the facts of your case more important than they might appear to you at first glance. The reason is that the case is very significant to your client, and you need to convey that to the jury. You do not need an important event in order to give a memorable opening. Keep in mind the argument regarding the dog's simple faithfulness and how memorable it was.

3. Examples from Famous Speeches

Emotion and theme are so bonded that it may be said that the single most important ingredient of a good opening statement is the theme for your story. The three short speeches that follow illustrate how you may capture the jury's attention in your next opening statement. Obviously, these speeches have the benefit of discussing very important events. Don't let that discourage you. A memorable event does not automatically produce a good speech. There are a lot of historical events that have resulted in forgettable speeches.

But one event that resulted in arguably the most memorable speech of all time is the battle at Gettysburg. In the Gettysburg Address, Lincoln focused on the theme of the nation's rededication to the principle of freedom. The dominant word, *dedicate,* is used six times. Count them. Developing the theme, there are four final "that" clauses, ending with the stirring "that government of the people, by the people, for the people, shall not perish from the earth."

Four score and seven years ago our fathers brought forth on this continent, a new nation, conceived in liberty, and *dedicated* to the proposition that all men are created equal.

Now we are engaged in a great civil war, testing whether that nation, or any nation so conceived and so *dedicated,* can long endure. We are met on a great battlefield of that war. We have come to *dedicate* a portion of that field, as a final resting place for those who gave their lives that the nation might live. It is altogether fitting and proper that we should do this.

But, in a larger sense, we cannot *dedicate*—we cannot consecrate—we cannot hallow—this ground. The brave men, living and dead, who struggled here, have consecrated it, far above our poor power to add or detract. The world will little note, nor long remember, what we say here, but it can never forget what they did here. It is for us the living, rather, to be *dedicated* here to the unfinished work which they who fought here have thus far so nobly advanced. It is rather for us to be here *dedicated* to the great task remaining before us—*that* from these honored dead we take increased devotion to that cause for which they gave the last full measure of devotion—*that* we here highly resolve that these dead shall not have died in vain—*that* this nation, under God, shall have a new birth of freedom—and *that* government of the people, by the people, for the people, shall not perish from the earth. *(emphasis added)*

To grab the attention of his listeners, President Franklin D. Roosevelt certainly started with a bang delivering his "date of infamy" speech.

Mr. Vice-President, Mr. Speaker, members of the Senate and the House of Representatives:

Yesterday, December 7, 1941—a date which will live in infamy—the United States of America was suddenly and deliberately attacked by naval and air forces of the empire of Japan.

In this speech asking Congress to declare war on Japan, he gives historical background:

The United States was at peace with that nation and, at the solicitation of Japan, was still in conversation with its government and its emperor looking toward the maintenance of peace in the Pacific.

Indeed, one hour after Japanese air squadrons had commenced bombing in the American island of Oahu the Japanese ambassador to the United States and his colleague delivered to our secretary of state a formal reply to a recent American message. And, while this reply stated that it seemed useless to continue the existing diplomatic negotiations, it contained no threat or hint of war or of armed attack.

It will be recorded that the distance of Hawaii from Japan makes it obvious that the attack was deliberately planned many days or even weeks ago. During the intervening time the Japanese government has deliberately sought to deceive the United States by false statements and expressions of hope for continued peace.

And then he vividly describes the current situation:

The attack yesterday on the Hawaiian Islands has caused severe damage to American naval and military forces. I regret to tell you that very many American lives have been lost. In addition, American ships have been reported torpedoed on the high seas between San Francisco and Honolulu.

Yesterday the Japanese government also launched an attack against Malaya.

Last night Japanese forces attacked Guam.

Last night Japanese forces attacked the Philippine Islands.

Last night the Japanese attacked Wake Island.

And this morning the Japanese attacked Midway Island.

Japan has therefore undertaken a surprise offensive extending throughout the Pacific area. The facts of yesterday and today speak for themselves. The people of the United States have already formed their opinions and well understand the implications to the very life and safety of our nation.

He follows up with steps taken:

As commander in chief of the army and navy I have directed that all measures be taken for our defense, that always will our whole nation remember the character of the onslaught against us.

He concludes with the rousing declaration of war after the unprovoked attack by Japan:

No matter how long it may take us to overcome this premeditated invasion, the American people, in their righteous might, will win through to absolute victory.

I believe that I interpret the will of the Congress and the People when I assert that we will not only defend ourselves to the uttermost but will make it very certain that this form of treachery shall never again endanger us. Hostilities exist. There is no blinking at the fact that our people, our territory, and our interests are in grave danger.

With confidence in our armed forces, with the unbounding determination of our people, we will gain the inevitable triumph. So help us God.

I ask that the Congress declare that since the unprovoked and dastardly attack by Japan on Sunday, December 7, 1941, a state of war has existed between the United States and the Japanese Empire.

Roosevelt's outline can be used for any opening statement: (1) start with a bang, (2) provide important background, (3) describe the current situation, (4) detail steps that need to be taken for justice, and (5) deliver a rousing conclusion.

Less known, certainly, but highly effective is Gerald Ford's short speech with the theme "our long national nightmare is over." Ford had been appointed by Richard Nixon to replace Vice President Spiro Agnew after Agnew stepped down to avoid prosecution. When Nixon resigned his presidency, Ford then became the nation's first appointed president.

After the trauma of Watergate, Ford kept his first address as president humble and simple—but deeply moving.

The oath that I have taken is the same oath that was taken by George Washington and by every president under the Constitution. But I assume the presidency under extraordinary circumstances never before experienced by Americans. This is an hour of history that troubles our minds and hurts our hearts.

Therefore, I feel it is my first duty to make an unprecedented compact with my countrymen. Not an inaugural address, not a fireside chat, not a campaign speech—just a little straight talk among friends. And I intend it to be the first of many. I am acutely aware that you have not elected me as your president by your ballots, and so I ask you to confirm me as your president with your prayers. And I hope that such prayers will also be the first of many.

If you have not chosen me by secret ballot, neither have I gained office by any secret promises. I have not campaigned either for the presidency or the vice-presidency. I have not subscribed to any partisan platform. I am indebted to no man, and only to one woman—my dear wife—as I begin this very difficult job.

I have not sought this enormous responsibility, but I will not shirk it. . . .

I believe that truth is the glue that holds government together, not only our government but civilization itself. That bond, though strained, is unbroken at home and abroad.

In all my public and private acts as your president, I expect to follow my instincts of openness and candor with full confidence that honesty is always the best policy in the end.

My fellow Americans, our long national nightmare is over.

Our Constitution works; our great Republic is a government of laws and not of men. Here the people rule. But there is a higher power, by whatever name we honor him, who ordains not only righteousness but love, not only justice but mercy.

As we bind up the internal wounds of Watergate, more painful and more poisonous than those of foreign wars, let us restore the golden rule to our political process, and let brotherly love purge our hearts of suspicion and of hate. . . .

With all the strength and all the good sense I have gained from life, with all the confidence my family, my friends, and my dedicated staff impart to me, and with the good will of countless Americans I have encountered in recent visits to forty states, I now solemnly reaffirm my promise I made to you last December 6: to uphold the Constitution, to do what is right as God gives me to see the right, and to do the very best I can for America.

God helping me, I will not let you down.

Thank you.

Of course, a good opening statement depends for its effectiveness not only on content but also on delivery. If poorly delivered, the best-written opening statement can fall flat.

The Pulitzer Prize–winning historian Taylor Branch made the following observation about Dr. Martin Luther King Jr.'s "I have a dream" speech:

> Critics would point out that the dream was ethereal, and people who yearned for simple justice would object that the content was too simple. Still, precious few among millions detected lightness or naïveté in the speech. On the contrary, the

> There are secrets to a good opening statement, and you can learn them. To make an opening statement interesting and important, you must give it a theme. Organize it. Give it with persuasion.

emotional command of his oratory gave King authority to reinterpret the core institution of democratic justice. More than his words, the timbre of his voice projected him across the racial divide and planted him as a new founding father.[4]

While few have the command of oratory that gave King's and Churchill's speeches the wallop they had, one can certainly speak with sincerity and conviction.

3.2 THE BASICS

1. When, Where, and How Long

After the jury has been selected, the judge will give it preliminary instructions. Those instructions include a brief explanation of the claims and defenses of each party, instructions on the jurors' duties (e.g., not to discuss the case during breaks), and a general overview of the trial process. After these instructions, the judge will ask the plaintiff (or prosecutor) if he wishes to give an opening statement, and then the opening statement is delivered.

> In an opening statement, captivate the jurors. *Don't* make them feel like a captive audience. A good rule of thumb is to give an opening that is no more than twenty minutes in length for each week you expect to be in trial. A ten-minute opening for a two- or three-day trial is certainly sufficient. Remember, less is more.

In federal court, the attorney must stand in the center of the courtroom at a podium turned to face the jurors. The attorney is not allowed to leave the podium (e.g., to walk toward the jury) unless it is to get an exhibit. In most state courts, attorneys may walk freely in front of the jury box and are not limited by a podium.

---

4. Taylor Branch, *Parting the Waters: America in the King Years, 1954–1963* at 887 (Simon and Schuster 1988).

2. Prohibitions

A. Rule against Argument

How forceful can you be in your opening statement? Although it is prohibited to argue inferences from the evidence (the domain of the closing argument), the rule is becoming antiquated.[5] The reality is that great trial lawyers and experienced judges expect opening statements to be powerful stories that go well beyond openings of the past that used the recitation "the evidence will show" throughout. As Judge Herbert Stern declared, "the object of the opening is to argue your case to the jury."[6]

Another reason the rule against argument is fading away is that lawyers rarely object during opening statements because they are arguing in their own opening statement. And when they do, judges have difficulty in ruling on the objection because of the vagueness of the rule.[7] So, in the unusual situation where there is an objection, the judge will most often overrule it and remind the jury that an opening statement is not evidence.

So you won't be surprised, find out from other lawyers or from the court during the pretrial conference what the court's view of the opening statement is regarding permissible argument. If for some reason you can't find out the court's view of opening statements and you find yourself before a judge who believes that openings should be restricted to a simple recitation of what the exhibits are and what the witnesses will testify to, then you can always scale back the opening you have

---

5. However, even though arguing in an opening statement is common, the use of rhetorical questions, famous quotations, and comparisons of the facts at trial to famous stories (e.g., Aesop's Fables) is still usually the province of closing arguments. Nonetheless, their successful use in openings is on the increase.

6. Herbert Stern, *Trying Cases to Win* at 138 (John Wiley & Sons, 1991).

7. "Unfortunately, determining the precise parameters of 'argument' is extraordinarily difficult, often leaving lawyers, commentators, and even judges confused or uncertain." Timothy Perrin, *From O. J. to McVeigh: The Use of Argument in the Opening Statement* 48 Emory L.J. at 107, 112 (Winter 1999).

prepared and make it less argumentative. It is much easier to scale back a creative opening than to make a bland opening more interesting.

A perfect example of a powerful opening is the prosecution's opening statement in *U.S. v. McVeigh*, discussed at length at the end of this chapter. Opposing counsel did not make one objection.

The following is an example of a statement that some attorneys would object to as "argumentative" or "stating an opinion."

Example: Prosecution Opening Statement
(Christopher Darden) from *People v. Simpson*

Darden: The man you'll see [defendant O. J. Simpson] will be the face of a batterer, a wife beater, an abuser, a controller.[8]

In the above example, let's assume there was an objection—even though there was not one at the trial. If there had been the objection "argument," simply rephrase as follows: *"**We will prove that** the man you'll see [defendant O. J. Simpson] will be the face of a batterer, a wife beater, an abuser, a controller."*

B. Other Prohibitions

There are, however, four other prohibitions that should be followed strictly. First, attorneys should not discuss the details of jury instructions until the closing argument after the court has told the lawyers the precise instructions on the law it will give to the jury. Second, lawyers are limited to discussing only the evidence that they have a good-faith belief is admissible. Third, prosecutors cannot comment on the defense's case or suggest in any way that the defense has a burden of proof.[9]

Fourth, lawyers are also not supposed to state their opinions. This is a difficult concept to understand, since in any good opening state-

---

8. *People v. Simpson* No. BA097211, 1995 WL 25440 at *19 (Cal. Super. Ct. Jan. 24, 1995) (opening statement of Christopher Darden).
9. For example, it would be improper as a prosecutor to state, "The defendant can offer no innocent explanation as to why his fingerprints were found on the murder weapon." However, a prosecutor could say, "The defendant's fingerprints were found on the murder weapon. The only explanation for this is that he is the one who killed John."

ment the jury should be fully aware of your opinion of the case. Consequently, in enforcing this rule, judges listen for key phrases such as "I think," "I believe," and "you must." When attorneys use these phrases, the objection will be sustained. To avoid the objection, do not use the pronoun *I,* and when asking the jury to do something, avoid the pronoun

> There is a way to inoculate yourself from objections in opening statements. Simply say "I will prove" before statements that you think might be too strong in an opening. If you have evidence to prove them, you can say them in your opening.

you. Instead, keep the command in the third person. For example, instead of saying, "I think [or believe] the only true verdict you can return in this case is one for the plaintiff," declare, "The only true verdict in this case is one for the plaintiff."

3. The Typical Juror's Perspective

To realize the importance of the opening statement, put yourself in the shoes of a typical juror. For this discussion, assume the juror is a working mother. She has been dreading this moment for a while. She has had to interrupt life's routines and make arrangements for work and family to come to the courthouse, not to mention the fact that she has had to fight rush-hour traffic to go to an unfamiliar building early in the morning. Once at the courthouse, she has been told to wait in a large room until needed and then, finally, herded up to the courtroom for voir dire. During voir dire, she has had to sit for an hour or more while the judge and attorneys, from what she perceives, ask boring, repetitive, and very personal questions.

Once selected for the jury, she is anxious to find out if all of the inconvenience is going to be rewarded. The successful trial attorney will give that reward.

3.3 THE TEN STEPS OF PREPARING A POWERFUL OPENING STATEMENT

The following ten steps will help you prepare a persuasive opening statement that will truly make a difference: (1) make a list of the good and bad facts in your case; (2) determine your theory of the case; (3)

create a theme for your case; (4) tell a story that begins powerfully, addresses weaknesses, and ends memorably; (5) write an outline of your first draft; (6) write a first draft of your entire opening; (7) practice memorizing ideas, not words; (8) use visual aids; (9) know your ending cold; and (10) create a final one-page topic outline.

1. Make a List of the Good and Bad Facts in Your Case

What should you cover in your opening? The easiest way to start is to create a document on your computer that has two headings: "Good Facts" and "Bad Facts." Under the heading "Good Facts," list all the facts and exhibits that support your case; under the heading "Bad Facts," list all those that do not. Be inclusive in making your lists. Highlight the most important ones from each list. The highlighted items on the entire document are the foundation of your opening.

2. Determine Your Theory of the Case

You must have a theory of your case. Lawyers do not spend nearly enough time determining this. *Webster's* dictionary defines *theory* as "the analysis of a set of facts in their relation to one another."[10]

To arrive at a theory, you must successfully answer this question: "At the end of the trial, what conclusion must the jury be compelled to reach after hearing *all* the important good and bad facts of the case?"

Developing a theory of the case should start as soon as you begin working on the case and continue to evolve throughout the litigation. Once discovery is complete and the trial is approaching, finalize your theory.

An adequate opening will candidly account for some of the bad facts you have highlighted. An extraordinary opening will not only admit that there are bad facts but will weave them naturally into the strong points, making a coherent story that the jurors will believe after hearing all the evidence.

---

10. *Merriam-Webster's Collegiate Dictionary* at 1296 (Merriam-Webster 11th ed. 2003).

A. Transforming Bad Facts to Good Facts in Nichols v. Frank

If you develop a successful theory, it will transform the bad facts into good facts for your side. Even if you haven't mastered this skill, the mere fact that you have acknowledged the existence of weak points will garner you several points with the jury because it raises your credibility with them.

In *Nichols v. Frank,* the plaintiff was a deaf-mute woman who brought a sexual harassment lawsuit.[11] She claimed that her supervisor forced her to have sex in a room at the office late at night. The following "bad" facts existed for the plaintiff: there were no corroborating witnesses, the plaintiff did not tell anyone at work about the harassment, the plaintiff did not tell her husband, and the assault happened more than once (suggesting consensual sex).

If you were the plaintiff's attorney, your opening would need not only to mention the bad facts but to turn them into good facts. Here's how:

> Ladies and gentlemen, you will hear that Terri Nichols' supervisor, Ron Francisco, had all the power. He forced Terri to have sex. He did not make her do this when there was a chance of being caught; instead, he assaulted her late at night when no one was around. Because there were no witnesses, and they were all alone, he knew that he could assault her over and over again.
>
> Terri was simply scared to death. She was afraid of losing her job, and if she lost her job, she knew that she would be unable to make her mortgage payments and would then lose her house. Mr. Francisco injured and scared her so much that she did not tell any coworkers. Who could blame her? She was so traumatized and embarrassed that she did not even tell her husband. It was an absolute nightmare, made even more difficult because she had to face this harassment alone.[12]

---

11. *Nichols v. Frank,* 42 F.3d 503 (9th Cir. 1993).
12. In order to personalize their clients, some attorneys address them by their first name in openings and closings. There is no set rule how you should address your client or the opposing party other than you should not refer to the opposing party by his first name. The key is to be consistent at trial and to use the style you are comfortable with for the particular case. In the above example, the plaintiff's attorney effectively personalizes his client by using her first name and referring

B. Transforming Bad Facts into Good Facts in People v. Simpson

Another example comes from the defense in the O. J. Simpson trial. The defense was faced with the following bad facts, to name a few: One of Simpson's gloves was found at the murder scene; the other was found in his side yard. Blood that matched the blood of the victims (Nicole Brown and Ron Goldman) was found in Simpson's Ford Bronco. A bloody shoe print at the murder scene was the same size as O. J.'s foot. DNA evidence (hair) consistent with Simpson's was found at the murder scene. Blood consistent with Simpson's was found at the murder scene. With so much evidence against him, Simpson's defense was that the evidence had been planted. If the jurors believed the police were corrupt and the evidence was planted, it did not matter how much evidence (bad facts) there was linking O. J. to the murders. In short, bad facts became good facts (police corruption).

For the bad facts that you cannot transform into good ones, you will succeed by dealing with them. The defense in the Simpson trial had to respond to the prosecution's evidence that O. J. stalked Nicole Brown after she left him, and his motivation for killing her was that if he could not have her, no one could. One way the defense dealt with this fact was to argue that the "stalking" had occurred long before the murder and that there were studies showing it was rare for a stalker to murder the person with whom he was obsessed.[13]

3. Create a Theme for Your Case

After you have determined the most important facts and made a theory for your case, think of an image—a theme—that will persuade the jury that your position at trial is the truth and the only reasonable resolu-

---

to the opposing party as "Mister" to show the power he had. However, notice in the examples at the end of the chapter from *U.S. v. McVeigh* that the prosecutor refers to the defendant by his last name only (no "Mister"), and the defense counsel refers to his client as "Mr. McVeigh."

13. The defense also made the argument that near the time of the murders it was Nicole who was obsessed with O. J., and it was she who kept coming back to him, so there could not have been any stalking on O. J.'s part.

tion of the disputed facts. The success of your case depends on this step. If your theme is not credible, you will most likely lose.

Why is a theme so important? It ties everything in a trial together. It gives the jury a simple idea that it can hang its hat on. When you are first starting as a trial lawyer, an easy tool to force yourself to develop a theme is to say, "This case is about _____." For example, this case is about "greed," "carelessness," "doing the wrong thing at the wrong time," "denial," "broken promises," or "the abuse of power." Like a Broadway musical, where the melody of the theme song recurs throughout the musical, the theme of your case should set the tone of the trial that characterizes all the evidence that is presented later. In essence, the theme frames your argument.

Developing a theme is the heart of your opening and will dictate the manner in which you present evidence and cross-examine witnesses. You need to spend plenty of time on this step. Your theme can't be corny, trite, or off the mark, but it must be just right. For example, in a sexual-harassment case where a woman complained that male coworkers constantly told off-color jokes and made fun of her physique, it would certainly not be wise—let alone, decent—for the defense attorney to assert, as a theme, "This is a case about a woman who can't take a joke." A theme that is off the mark is worse than no theme at all.

Once you have mastered the technique of "This case is about _____," leave off the crutch "This case is about" and weave the key words of your theme throughout the opening. You can also try expanding your theme to include three powerful ideas using the rule of three discussed in chapter 1. For example, if you are the prosecutor in a drunk-driving case, instead of just having a theme of "driving dangerously," you could say: "This case is about driving *d*angerously, being *d*runk, and an officer's *d*uty." It is not required, but it is sometimes a helpful device for the three ideas to begin with the same letter. See how this works in the example below.

Example: Prosecution Opening in a Drunk-Driving Trial

This case is about three very important things: being dangerous, being drunk, and an officer's duty. First, we will prove that Mr. Stewart, on the night of August 3, was driving dangerously. He could not stay in his lane and was traveling at an unsafe speed. Second, we will prove that Mr. Stewart's alcohol level in his blood was twice that of the legal limit. In short, he was drunk. Finally, we will prove that Officer Slote removed a dangerous driver from the road and was very professional in carrying out his duties when he administered the field sobriety tests to Mr. Stewart. Now, I would like to discuss each of these facts in detail. Let's first look at how Mr. Stewart was driving dangerously on the night of August 3.

4. Tell a Story That Begins Powerfully, Addresses Weaknesses, and Ends Memorably

The art of delivering a successful opening statement is simply the art of telling a good story. Remember that not all stories are told chronologically. Be creative.

The only introductory statement you should make—if you choose—before beginning powerfully is, "May it please the court, [name of opposing counsel], ladies and gentlemen of the jury." Why? This phrase is part of trial culture and lends solemnity to what you are about to say.[14] Whether you make this statement is a matter of personal preference.

After this introductory phrase, start your opening with your theme or a powerful image, repeat it and build on it throughout, and end memorably.

Why? As mentioned in chapter 1, there are three well-known principles of memory: primacy, recency, and frequency. That is, people remember most what they see or hear first (primacy), last (recency), and often (frequency). So, apply these principles in your opening.

Your mind-set has to be one of confidence but not arrogance. You can't be timid. Nonetheless, Mauet instructs that "if you do err, do so

---

14. It is also a chance to show your sportsmanship. Most attorneys refer to opposing counsel as, "Counsel," barely showing acknowledgment. Instead, show respect to all involved by stating the names of the attorneys on the other side. Your attention to detail in saying opposing counsel's name will be noticed by the jury, and if you say the phrase with sincerity, it will show your professionalism and raise your credibility.

on the side of caution. When in doubt, understatement is the better part of wisdom. The jury will be pleasantly surprised to learn that your case is even better than it had expected."[15] If you embody this attitude, it will not only lead you to being overly cautious in your opening statement but throughout the trial. It is true that if you mislead the jury, your credibility will be damaged irreparably. However, the solution is not to understate your case but to be certain and confident. Don't wait until closing argument to surprise the jury with how strong your case is.

Example: Plaintiff's Opening Statement with Weak Beginning (Car Wreck)

Plaintiff's counsel: May it please the court, Ms. Smith [defense counsel], ladies and gentlemen of the jury. I first want to thank you for your patience in being here today. I expect that it will be a long trial, but hopefully you can rely on your patience and sense of duty to get through. I would first like to introduce you to my client, Ms. Ken [have client stand]. Next, I would like to tell you how the trial will proceed. The opening statement is my chance to give you a preview of what I expect the evidence to show. A trial is like a giant puzzle. I will bring you witnesses who will fill in pieces of the puzzle. You may wonder what the purpose of a particular exhibit is or why a certain witness is testifying, but trust me that all the pieces will fit by the end of the trial. If you have any questions at the end of the trial, I hopefully can answer them in my closing.

Example: Plaintiff's Opening Statement with Powerful Beginning (Car Wreck)

Plaintiff's counsel: May it please the court, Ms. Smith [defense counsel], ladies and gentlemen of the jury. July 5th was the start of a nightmare for my client, Sally Ken. Her life was changed forever, when—through no fault of her own—her car was rear-ended by the defendant. Sally has never been the same since the accident. She has had constant pain in her

---

15.   Thomas A. Mauet, *Trial Techniques* at 69 (Aspen 6th ed. 2002).

back, has been unable to lift her toddler, has lost her job, and isn't able to sleep comfortably. The defendant has caused a nightmare for Sally, which continues today.

The first example begins well enough by thanking the jury for their service, but those words are wasted. Show your thanks by getting to the point (after all, they have been waiting most of the day to hear from you) and making the moment significant. Although many experienced trial lawyers begin their openings by introducing their client and themselves to the jury and then explaining to them how the trial will proceed, it defies common sense to do so because the client has already been introduced in voir dire, and the judge has already told the jury how the trial will proceed.

One reason lawyers make this mistake is that they have not spent the time to put a coherent opening statement together. It is easy, then—but not effective—to fill the time by talking to the jury about the trial process.

Example: Addressing Weaknesses—Prosecution Opening Statement (Christopher Darden) from *People v. Simpson*

Darden: Why would he do it? ... [This is] not the O. J. Simpson ... we've seen over the years. But that is another question, and that question is, do you know O. J. Simpson?

We've seen him leap turnstiles and chairs and run to airplanes in the Hertz commercials, and we watched him with a 15-inch afro in Naked Gun 33½, *and we've seen him time and time again, and we came to think that we know him.*

What we've been seeing, ladies and gentlemen, is the public face, the public persona, the face of the athlete, the face of the actor.

It is not the actor who is on trial here today, ladies and gentlemen. It is not that public face. It is his other face, like many men in public. Like many public men, they have a public image, a public persona, a public side, a public life, and they also have a private side, a private life, a private face. And that is the face we will expose to you in this trial, the other side of O. J. Simpson, the side you never met before.[16]

---

16. *People v. Simpson* No. BA097211, 1995 WL 25440 at *19 (Cal. Super. Ct. Jan. 24, 1995) (opening statement of Christopher Darden).

The major weakness in the prosecution's case was that the defendant was a huge celebrity: a Hall of Fame football player, television star, and movie star. Darden admits that it might be hard to be convinced that the O. J. Simpson persona the public has seen on TV could be a murderer. He then points out that many public people have a public image that is different from reality, from the way they act in private. Darden assures the jury that the prosecution will put on evidence revealing the true O. J. Simpson, a man who murdered.

It is also vitally important to address, but not dwell on, the significant weaknesses in your case. Your integrity with the jury depends on it. The worst thing that can happen is to sit down after giving your opening and hear opposing counsel exclaim to the jury: "I would first like to talk to you about what my opposing counsel *did not mention and did not want to talk about in his opening.*"

Example: Ending Memorably—Prosecution Opening Statement (Christopher Darden) from *People v. Simpson*

Darden: This is not character assassination. This is not some tabloid prosecution. The evidence you hear in this case will be evidence of this defendant's life, of his conduct, the things he did.

You will hear evidence of his relationship with one of the victims. And as you hear it, you will—as you hear the evidence and as you listen to Ms. Clark—you'll see how it is that Ron Goldman happened to be at the wrong place at the wrong time.

As you listen to the evidence, you will see that his decision to kill finally was merely a final link in a progressive chain of abusive and controlling conduct, and it was a chain that consisted of fear and intimidation and battery and emotional and mental abuse and economic abuse and control and stalking.

And you'll see that there was a common scheme and common plan in all of this, and that was to control, to control her. It was all designed just to control her. And in controlling her, it was the private man, private O. J. Simpson, it was the defendant who committed that final ultimate act of control.

She left him. She was no longer in his control. He was obsessed with her. He could not stand to lose her, and so he murdered her.

And as you hear the evidence in this case, it will become
clear that in his mind, she belonged to him; and if he couldn't
have her, then nobody could.
Thank you.[17]

Darden leaves the jury with a powerful image of the private persona of O. J. Simpson seeking to control Nicole Brown. The image
leaves little doubt for the motive: "He could not stand to lose her, and
so he murdered her." There were many problems with other parts of
the prosecution's opening and its obvious failure to present evidence in
a compelling manner to back up this powerful image, but standing by
itself, Darden's ending is an excellent example of how to end an opening statement.

5. Write an Outline of Your First Draft

After starting out powerfully, how do you explain your version of
events? Should you tell your story chronologically, categorically, or
summarize each witness' testimony? The answer is to make it memorable and believable. The following outline and steps have proven to be
very effective for a wide variety of cases.[18]

1. *Begin powerfully with a memorable theme.* Tell the jury your
theme of the case and briefly summarize the facts that support your
theme.

2. *Discuss the important details of the story.* Give the jury all—but
only—the *important* details about the case. Paint a compelling picture

---

17. *People v. Simpson* No. BA097211, 1995 WL 25440 at *30–31 (Cal.
    Super. Ct. Jan. 24, 1995) (opening statement of Christopher Darden).
    See also DVD disc 1, "Darden Opening Statement," clip 4.
18. Compare this outline with Mauet's, which is far too complicated and does
    not force an attorney to tell a powerful and concise story. Mauet suggests
    the following outline: (1) introduction, (2) parties, (3) scene, (4) instru-
    mentality, (5) date, time, weather, and lighting, (6) issue, (7) what hap-
    pened, (8) basis of liability/nonliability or guilt/nonguilt, (9) anticipating
    and refuting the other side, (10) damages (civil cases only), and (11) con-
    clusion. See Thomas A. Mauet, *Trial Techniques* at 74 (6th ed. Aspen
    2002). Notice how the most important part of the outline, "what hap-
    pened," is buried at number 7 on his list.

for the jury. Tell a coherent story built around your theme. Although telling a story chronologically is typical, don't be bound by this form. Instead, tell it in whatever way makes the most lasting impression. An effective style is to give first an overview of strong facts and then set forth significant evidence that supports those facts. It also is important to use visual aids to explain your case.

3. *Address candidly—but don't dwell on—weaknesses in the case and turn them into strengths.* Every case has its weaknesses. There is a strong urge to avoid talking about bad facts in the naive hope that the other side won't recognize them. You must be upfront with the jury. Handled well, an admission of weak facts increases your trustworthiness with the jury and takes the sting out of facts that must be dealt with at some point in the trial.

4. *Briefly discuss the elements of the claim/defense and the burden of proof.* Although it is improper to discuss jury instructions in detail in an opening statement, it is permissible and necessary to explain very briefly to the jury the legal issues involved in the case. For example, it is important to summarize the elements of your claim if you are the plaintiff or explain your legal defense (e.g., self-defense) if you are on the other side. Also, no matter which side you are on, don't shy away from discussing the burden of proof. It is a great chance to show the jury the confidence you have in your case.

Example: Prosecution Discussion of Burden of Proof (Joseph Hartzler) from *U.S. v. McVeigh*

Hartzler: As you already know and as His Honor instructed you again this morning, our burden in this case is to prove the guilt of Timothy McVeigh beyond a reasonable doubt. We welcome that burden. We will meet it.[19]

5. *End memorably.* Before you conclude, summarize the most significant facts that you have discussed in your opening. This can be done in just a few sentences. Most important, return to your theme and convince the jurors they must find for your side.

---

19. *United States v. McVeigh,* No. 96-CR-68, 1997 WL 198070 at *25 (D. Colo. Apr. 24, 1997) (opening statement of Joseph Hartzler).

> ## Opening Statement Outline Form
>
> I.   Begin Powerfully with a Memorable Theme.
> II.   Discuss the Important Details of the Story.
>   A. Give an Overview of Strong Facts.
>   B. Present Significant Evidence That Supports Strong Facts.
>   C. Use Visual Aids.
> III.   Address Candidly—but Don't Dwell on—Weaknesses in the Case and Turn Them into Strengths.
> IV.   Briefly Discuss the Elements of the Claim/Defense and Burden of Proof.
> V.   End Memorably.

6. Write a First Draft of Your Entire Opening

Write every single word of your opening for your first draft by following the outline above. This is beneficial because the hardest step is getting started. Just fill the pages on your notepad or computer. It does not matter if what you write is good or bad; there will be plenty of time to improve your initial ideas later. If you are having writer's block, that means you are trying too hard to choose the perfect word or ideas. Lower your expectations and write something!

> The acronym KISS (keep it simple, stupid) applies to opening statements. If it is not important or memorable or easy to understand, don't say it.

Most likely, the opening you give will be quite different from this first draft. By forcing yourself to write every word, however, you will get the creative juices flowing and discipline yourself to think about the structure of your opening and how you would like to deliver it.

7. Practice Memorizing Ideas, Not Words

After you have written the first draft, move on and never look back. From then on, develop your opening by thinking about it or speaking it. There is nothing worse than an opening statement that is memorized. By disciplining yourself not to write multiple drafts of your opening, you will avoid the pitfalls of trying to write and memorize the exact words you want to use at trial. You also will maintain your creativity and communicate broad ideas in a story form to the jury.

By avoiding the trap of trying to memorize your opening word for word, you will be more conversational, sincere, and relaxed, as if you are trying to tell a story as opposed to reciting from memory. In addition, you need to have flexibility, especially if you represent the defendant. Something surprising always comes up in the plaintiff's opening. The defendant's opening needs to be able to address a surprise issue if it's important. A memorized speech does not allow this flexibility.

Practice your opening by speaking it out loud and silently to yourself many times until you consistently have the same ideas (not words) in the same order each time. Fight the urge to rewrite your first draft. Make all the changes and improvements you want, but make them silently as you are thinking about the opening or as you speak it in practice.

If you are in law school preparing your first opening at a mock trial, you can probably think of many seemingly good reasons to write more than one draft. First, the professor will never know, so what's the harm? Second, you probably have never given a speech for a grade in front of colleagues before, so you feel the need for the crutch of a second draft. *Don't do it!* As Samuel Johnson said, "The chains of habit are generally too small to be felt until they are too strong to be broken." Once you start relying on written speeches for your presentation, it is an extremely difficult habit to break later on. Anyhow, it won't help you. You will always do better speaking naturally without a script.

What if you forget a great idea that you had the day before because you have not written a second draft? Now you are mad at yourself for not following your nagging urge to write a second, third, and fourth draft. The answer is that if you forgot the great idea you had the day before, it must not have been a very good idea. This does not mean you should not write several drafts of an outline, as long as you keep the outline topic oriented and not structured with complete sentences.

As you get closer to your final version of the opening, practice once or twice in a more formal setting. Find out the best way for you to practice. Some attorneys will find an empty courtroom to practice in; others will practice in front of colleagues at their firm. Tape-recording or

> **Although practice is important, don't overpractice. If you do, you will lose the spontaneity and the conversational tone so important in an opening.**

videotaping your opening is invaluable. Only through these objective media can you see whether or not the tone and pacing of your voice is effective or whether your physical gestures are helpful or distracting. The old adage of practicing in front of a mirror is bad advice, since it makes you self-conscious, and it is difficult to practice and analyze yourself at the same time.

8. Use Visual Aids

Since the goal of an opening is to paint a convincing picture of your case that the jury won't forget, what better way than to use a visual aid or an actual piece of evidence? Studies show that people learn best from a combination of seeing and hearing. For example, use a timeline of events, a chart of the main characters, a diagram of the scene, or anything to vary your presentation. Challenge yourself to be creative. If your opening is built around five important facts you are going to prove, list them on a poster board in large lettering. Why not show the jury evidence you are actually going to use at trial?

> **By using exhibits in your opening, not only do you get the benefit of making a strong impact on the jury first (primacy) but you will also benefit from the rule of frequency because the jury will get to see the important exhibit again when it is introduced into evidence at trial.**

Most attorneys are afraid to refer to exhibits in the opening for fear that the exhibits might not get admitted into evidence. This fear is unfounded. If you can talk about what the evidence will be, you can certainly show the jury as well.[20] If there is a 911 tape of the victim of a burglary calling the police as the crime is happening, play it for the jury. Is there a letter that proves the defendant sexually harassed the plaintiff? Show it to the jury. Why wait? Remember, at least 80 percent of the jurors are making up their minds as you give your opening. Don't hold back.

---

20. Prior to the opening statement, inform the court and opposing counsel of your intentions to see if there are any objections.

9. Know Your Ending Cold

Although the cardinal sin is to memorize the words of your opening, you must memorize your concluding words. Why? No matter how well prepared you are, there will be the occasion when, for some unknown reason, you forget part of your opening. If you have memorized your concluding thought, you will always have a way to end the opening memorably. Moreover, by memorizing the words of your conclusion, you will gain confidence for the rest of the opening. It will give you a target to aim at, and if you forget part of your opening, at least you will have the ability to end your opening strongly and confidently. As music teachers are fond of saying, "During a performance, you must at least know the last note so that the audience will know the piece is over and can applaud."

10. Create a Final One-Page Topic Outline

When you deliver your opening, it is best to have no notes or, at most, a one-page outline. Having no notes forces you to maintain constant eye contact with jurors and keep a conversational tone. It also forces you to have confidence in the ideas you have developed, since you do not have the crutch of notes or an outline to fall back on. If you have written out the words of your opening, it is guaranteed that you will at some point, probably multiple times, look down at your notes. Why? Because if you have written down every word, you must fear you will forget to say some word. That fear will become a self-fulfilling prophecy that will force you to look at your notes.

Another way to understand the rationale of this step is to put yourself in the shoes of the jurors. They dread seeing a lawyer walk toward them from the counsel table with a notebook full of paper. Their immediate thought: the slow torture of being on a jury is beginning, and this attorney is causing the pain! Instead, you will be pleasantly surprised at the welcoming smiles you get from the judge and jurors as you stand up to begin your opening without any notes in your hands.

Nonetheless, most beginning lawyers will need the comfort of a one-page outline. Here is a way to make it successful. Do not write complete sentences. The reason is that when you become nervous, the act of reading, especially small print, is very difficult. If you have to

Here is a way to have it all. Very few young attorneys achieve the advanced level of advocacy to deliver an opening statement with complete confidence without notes. Here is a tip that is rarely used but extremely effective. While at the counsel table, take your one-page outline and turn it upside down and put it at the edge of the table away from you. Put a cup of water next to it.

Now, when the judge asks if you are ready, stand up confidently and walk before the jury without any notes. Why are you so confident? Your outline is just a few steps away at the corner of the table. During your presentation, if you feel that you are about to forget your next idea, simply walk over to your table, get a drink of water, and read your outline. Then return to the jurors. They will never know what happened.

refer to your outline during your opening, it is because you have forgotten an idea, so it is a guarantee that you will be nervous.

Limit your topic outline to five or six important ideas and write them in LARGE LETTERS with LARGE SPACES between the lines. Your outline will then be much easier to read when you are nervous and need your memory refreshed.

Instead of writing an outline, you could create a one-page diagram with pictures that describe the topics in your opening. This technique is not for everyone but has proven helpful. It is a wonderful way to avoid the pitfalls of trying to remember the exact words of an opening. For example, if you are defending a driver in a typical car-wreck case, your diagram could have five pictures on it connected by arrows that remind you of the topics you want to cover. One picture could be the scales of justice to signify your discussion of the burden of proof; another picture could be two streets intersecting to remind you to discuss the scene; a cell phone could remind you

of the most important fact in your case (that the plaintiff was distracted because he was talking on his cell phone just prior to the accident). An X drawn over a drawing of a Band-Aid could represent a lack of significant injuries for the plaintiff.

The important point is that when you take the time to think of the pictures, to draw them, and create a diagram, the opening becomes more of a conversation of ideas and not a memorized speech. In addition, when you refer to them during a nervous moment in your presentation, the pictures are easier for your brain to process than words.

3.4 HOW TO DELIVER AN OPENING STATEMENT

Step 1: Make Good Eye Contact

The concept of making good eye contact is obvious, yet it is rarely achieved effectively. It is paramount to engage jurors so that they will be convinced of the importance of your opening statement. You must start by looking them in the eye. This creates a personal connection to the words you are speaking. It also provides you with a tremendous amount of feedback. Among other things, eye contact enables you to see if jurors are able to hear you or whether they seem bored. Do you get a questioning look when you say something? Correct it right there. If your head is buried in your notes, the opportunity will be missed.

When you give your first opening, you may find it too intimidating to look jurors straight in the eye. A wonderful trick is to look at their foreheads instead. From the jurors' perspective, they will think you are looking them in the eye. For you, it will significantly ease the pressure of having to make direct eye contact with a stranger. So, just talk to their foreheads. You will be surprised how relaxed you will be.

One common mistake is that attorneys make eye contact with only a couple of jurors—usually those directly in front of them—when they are speaking. Be sure you make eye contact with *all* the jurors. There is nothing worse than having some of the jurors feel left out.

Step 2: Limit Physical and Vocal Distractions

Gestures are an important tool in communicating effectively and should be used liberally. Particular thought should be given to coordinating them with the words spoken (see step 5 for more discussion). However, certain mannerisms can be distracting.

Do not lean on the podium if the court requires you to speak from one. The podium is your worst enemy. Don't slouch on it, don't put your hands on it, and don't bend over it or rock your body against it.

What do you do with your hands? Put your elbows at your side and bend your forearms at a ninety degree angle so that your hands are in front of you. From this position, you can gesture naturally in accordance with what you are saying. Concentrate on what you are saying, and your hands will move naturally. With practice, your gestures will become second nature, and you will develop your own style. It goes without saying that you should not wave your arms wildly. Also, do not cross them below your waist or hold them straight at your sides (like a toy soldier) or clasped behind your back. Obviously, do not put them in your pockets.

If you are in a court that allows you to move freely, be careful about walking around too much at first. Most young attorneys wind up pacing—three steps to the right, three steps to the left, three steps to the right, three steps to the left; this first engenders sympathy from the jurors and then resentment because they have to follow you around as they listen. Instead, be natural and find out what works for you.

As for vocal distractions, avoid using uhs and ums. These words and others are spoken to give your brain time to think of the next thought to say. Instead, realize that silence is your friend. Replace the distracting words with a silent pause.

Step 3: Vary Your Voice

Keep your delivery interesting by varying the pace, tone, and volume of your voice. Be creative; do anything to avoid a monotone delivery. This is true whether it is your opening, direct examination, or any other part of the trial.

Be aware of what your voice is doing. Do you have a tendency to speak fast? Then remind yourself to speak slowly. Write in large, bold letters on your outline: "SLOW DOWN." If you naturally speak quietly, write "LOUDER." The best way to know how you are speaking is to get feedback. Tape-record yourself or ask a friend for some honest criticism.

As you conclude your opening, you might want to lower the volume of your voice, speak slower, and pause just before your concluding remark. Your mission is to highlight the idea you are conveying by a change in pace, tone, or volume consistent with your message, signaling the jury to pay attention.

Step 4: Speak with Conviction

No opening is going to be effective if it is not delivered with conviction. If you do not believe wholeheartedly the words you are saying, don't say them. You have to believe that what you say is the absolute truth in the case. Remember, the jury believes that you know all the facts in the case and a lot of facts that won't come out at trial.

Step 5: Develop Gestures for the Most Important Points

Make sure you give a lot of thought to developing gestures that coordinate with your most important points. Throughout the trial, your goal should be to create several memorable moments that the jury will remember during deliberations. In an opening, you might create these moments at the very beginning and end. To create such a moment, think how your voice and body are going to gesture.

There is no hard-and-fast rule about how you should do this because it will depend on what is being said. What is significant, however, is that you recognize the occasions and gesture accordingly.

Although the following is an example from a closing argument, its lesson is no less instructive for an opening statement. The lawyer for Ron Goldman, Daniel Petrocelli, in the wrongful death civil case against Simpson, described an important gesture he made with his feet to emphasize a significant point in his closing. What follows is an excerpt from that closing with Petrocelli's comments in boldface. In the excerpt, Petrocelli is describing the murder scene, where the dead bodies of Nicole Brown and Ron Goldman lay on the ground covered in blood and surrounded by bloody footprints.

Example: Effective Gestures (Daniel Petrocelli) from *Goldman v. Simpson*

> And by [Ron Goldman's and Nicole Simpson's] blood, they forced him [Simpson] to *step, step, step,*—**I [Petrocelli] just began stepping! I hadn't planned to, but I picked up my feet gingerly; you could almost hear the wet blood sticking to my soles**—as he walked to the back, leaving shoe prints that are just like fingerprints in this case, that tell us who did this, who did this unspeakable tragedy.[21]

Step 6: Get Feedback

Getting feedback is a simple but important task. Either review your own videotape or audiotape or ask a friend, but get some feedback on whether your delivery is compelling.

Step 7: Dress Appropriately

As Mark Twain remarked, "Clothes make the man. Naked people have little or no influence on society."

Checklist for Delivery of Opening

1. Make good eye contact.
2. Limit physical and vocal distractions.
3. Vary your voice.
4. Speak with conviction.
5. Develop gestures for the most important points.
6. Get feedback.
7. Dress appropriately.

---

21. See Daniel Petrocelli and Peter Knobler, *Triumph of Justice: The Final Judgment on the Simpson Saga* at 602 (Crown Publishers 1998) (emphasis added).

3.5 SEVEN STEPS TO OVERCOMING COURTROOM FEARS

Stage fright is no stranger to the courtroom. Consequently, you need to employ the same seven tools that performers—whether they are actors, athletes, or musicians—use in combating nervousness.

1. Be Prepared

The first key to success is preparation. No one can perform well in court or onstage without the necessary preparation. The downfall of most people, however, is listening to the subconscious voice that says, "You need more time to prepare." Recognize that if you listen to that voice of doubt, you will never be ready because there has yet to be a trial where every possible surprise has been anticipated. Relax by knowing that one mistake to make is to overprepare. All good conversations, or openings, have spontaneity and enthusiasm. Overpreparation takes those two vital elements out of your delivery.

2. Permit Yourself to Make Mistakes

It's not surprising that, after hundreds of years of jurisprudence, the perfect opening statement has not yet been given. It is unlikely that you are going to be the first to do it. Relax! Going into your opening, know that when you are finished, you will have forgotten to say something. It is bound to happen.

For example, everyone has given a toast at a rehearsal dinner for a wedding or some other event. Isn't it true that after you sit down, no matter how good the toast was, you remember something you wish you had said or you think of a better way to say the toast? Didn't you have the urge to stand back up and correct the "mistake"? In truth, you did not make a mistake, you just weren't perfect. Performers of all types will say that there is no perfect "live" performance.

Realize that so-called mistakes are an inherent aspect of any live performance. What distinguishes great lawyers, or performers, is how they deal with the mistakes that are bound to happen. The only way to

There may come a time in your delivery when you have stumbled badly, and you suddenly have an overwhelming urge to start over. Don't do it! The urge to start over is based on the false assumption that if you start over, you will perform better the second time around. Almost every time you won't. The best strategy is to keep pushing forward and to keep your mind focused on the moment—not your past mistakes or the parts of the opening you have not reached yet.

deal successfully with problems is to ignore that they have happened and move on.

3. Realize the Jury Wants You to Succeed

Every audience wants the speaker to succeed. Have you ever been to a lecture where the speaker forgot his place in the speech or had trouble with the microphone working? Didn't you have sympathy for him and want him to succeed? Jurors are no different. Although your jurors probably did not want to be selected for the jury, now that they are on it, they want the trial to be interesting, and they want you to succeed. They know they need the attorneys to explain the case to them. They want to understand the case, and they believe that you are the expert who will explain it to them.

You have every reason, then, to be confident. The jury wants you to do well. They will be forgiving if you make a mistake.

4. Visualize

One of the best ways to enhance performance is to visualize your success. Athletes and musicians have been using this technique for years. A day or two before the trial, set aside fifteen minutes to visualize the delivery of your opening. Picture the judge on the bench, the jury in the box, and so on. See yourself confidently getting up from the counsel table to deliver your opening. Picture the good eye contact you want to make. Visualize the faces of the jury, receptive to your ideas. Hear yourself vary the tone, speed, and volume of your opening. Really hear it! See yourself as being calm and confident.

Why is this important? You have spent time worrying about your opening so that your brain has some negative images that will affect your performance. This process of visualization will correct that problem and produce fantastic results.

5. Visit the Courtroom

Ask the courtroom staff when you can go to the courtroom when it is empty. Walk around the courtroom. Sit in the jury box. Become familiar with it. Speak some phrases from the counsel table, the podium, or the middle of the courtroom to see if you are speaking loud enough. Practice some of your hand gestures for your opening. Are they effective now that you are in a formal courtroom?

The idea is to become comfortable with your surroundings. By doing so, you will naturally be more relaxed. You might even find it helpful to practice your opening in the courtroom. If you can't get access to your courtroom, practice it in another one that is available.

6. Breathe Deeply and Slowly

Have you ever heard someone jokingly tell a nervous performer, "Don't forget to breathe!" The same is true when making opening statements. Research has proven that deep, slow breaths relax the body and mind. Before you give your opening, the judge will read some preliminary instructions to the jury that explain the trial process to them. While you are waiting, it is natural for you to become tense. You can't walk around; you just have to sit there. Don't forget to breathe, but also breathe deeply and slowly. Do this ten or fifteen times, and you will definitely feel a difference.

7. Recognize Your Nervous Energy

What happens when you get nervous? Do you get dry mouth? Then bring a water bottle to the courtroom. Does your breathing become restricted? Breathe deeply. Do your hands move

> One of the best ways to ease your nerves before a trial is to watch other attorneys give an opening. In most courtrooms, juries are selected and opening statements begun on Mondays—usually just before or after the lunch break. Take the time before your first trial to spend a Monday at the courthouse watching as many openings as you can.

around when you talk? Then hold your hands behind your back when you deliver your opening.

The important point to remember is that everyone gets nervous. Find a tool that helps you. To relax, some attorneys think about their favorite vacation spot in the few minutes right before giving an opening. Others find a quiet place in the hallway to give themselves a pep talk during a break before opening statements.

Checklist for Overcoming Courtroom Fears

1. Be prepared.
2. Permit yourself to make mistakes.
3. Realize the jury wants you to succeed.
4. Visualize.
5. Visit the courtroom.
6. Breathe deeply and slowly.
7. Recognize your nervous energy.

3.6 THE SIX DON'TS OF OPENING STATEMENTS

Having looked at what you need to do to deliver a memorable opening statement, let's look at the most important things not to do.

1. Don't Make the Jurors' Job More Difficult

Although you have the burden of proof as a plaintiff or prosecutor, you want to make the jury feel that a verdict in your favor is very natural and an easy decision to reach. Jurors do not want to hear how difficult their job is or how complicated the case will be.

Look at how such a mistake was made by prosecutor Christopher Darden in the Simpson criminal trial. Imagine all the resources Darden had at his disposal. What would your first words be to a jury that has just been chosen and sequestered for the most famous trial of the twentieth century?

Example: Prosecution Opening Statement
(Christopher Darden) from *People v. Simpson*

Darden: I think it's fair to say that I have the toughest job in town today except for the job that you have. Your job may just be a little bit tougher. It's your job—like my job, we both have a central focus, a single objective, and that objective is justice obviously.[22]

Why would he choose those words as his first ones? It is the last thing the jury wanted to hear. How incredible that Darden would volunteer that his job was tough and then declare that the jurors had an even tougher job.

What if, instead, Darden had said the following:

Ladies and gentlemen, this is a straightforward case. All the evidence points toward O. J. Simpson's guilt. There is the defendant's glove and DNA evidence found at the murder scene. There is blood from the victims found in Mr. Simpson's car. There is blood from Nicole found on Mr. Simpson's socks. Your job will be easy.

Contrast what Darden said with what the prosecution said in the *McVeigh* opening:

Example: Prosecution Opening Statement
(Joseph Hartzler) from *U.S. v. McVeigh*

Hartzler: As you see—as you'll see, there was a lot of evidence against McVeigh. We'll present a lot of evidence against McVeigh. We'll try to make your decision ultimately easy. That's our goal.

There are a number of us, but we won't stumble over each other. You'll see that each of us has a different role, presenting different segments and different types of evidence. We intend to do so fairly.[23]

---

22. *People v. Simpson* No. BA097211, 1995 WL 25440 at *18 (Cal. Super. Ct. Jan. 24, 1995) (opening statement of Christopher Darden). See also DVD disc 1, "Darden Opening Statement," clip 1.
23. *United States v. McVeigh* No. 96-CR-68, 1997 WL 198070 at *10–11 (D. Colo. Apr. 24, 1997) (opening statement of Joseph Hartzler).

2. Don't Explain to the Jurors What an Opening Statement Is—They Already Know

In the court's preliminary instructions to the jurors—after they have been sworn in but before the lawyers give opening statements—the judge will instruct the jurors that the opening statements they are about to hear are not evidence. Nonetheless, a majority of lawyers still feel a need to repeat this instruction to the jury. It is redundant. It also takes away from the effectiveness of the opening. Why would an attorney remind jurors that what they are hearing is not important because it is not evidence? You want to convey the exact opposite unspoken thought: "Jurors, listen up, because after I sit down, you will be so convinced that my client is right that you won't need to hear any evidence." Let's look at the O. J. Simpson case again.

Example: Prosecution Opening Statement
(Christopher Darden) from *People v. Simpson*

Darden: As the judge instructed you already, opening statements are not evidence. Opening statements are given by lawyers. And in an opening statement, we inform the jury of what we think the evidence will show in this case, what we believe the evidence will show.[24]

Darden clearly knew the judge had already instructed them, but he inexplicably felt the need to do it again. So, now he reminded them that his opening was not important, but he took it one step further in his next few sentences.

Darden: But we're lawyers, we're not witnesses. We're not under oath. Nothing we say is evidence. The things we say to you today are not the things that you should carry into the jury room and into deliberations.[25]

---

24. *People v. Simpson* No. BA097211, 1995 WL 25440 at *19 (Cal. Super. Ct. Jan. 24, 1995) (opening statement of Christopher Darden). See also DVD disc 1, "Darden Opening Statement," clip 1.
25. *People v. Simpson* No. BA097211, 1995 WL 25440 at *19 (Cal. Super. Ct. Jan. 24, 1995) (opening statement of Christopher Darden). See also DVD disc 1, "Darden Opening Statement," clip 1.

This is a wonderful example of how to sabotage your opening. "We're not under oath." Although technically you are not under oath, the jury expects you to tell the truth as if you were. Why say such a thing? Perhaps Darden said these words out of a fear that Cochran's opening statement would not be based on the evidence, but even if this were his intent, it backfired by undercutting the credibility of what he was saying at the moment.

3. Don't Forget to Listen

It is very important to listen to opposing counsel's opening statement. Johnnie Cochran made the mistake of not doing so.

Example: Defense Opening Statement
(Johnnie Cochran) from *People v. Simpson*

Johnnie Cochran, having heard Darden's opening, told the jury the exact same thing that Darden did.

> Cochran: As the court has so appropriately indicated, what I
> say is not evidence; it is just to aid you and guide you.[26]

If he had listened to Darden's opening carefully, he would have realized that Darden had already mentioned this point. It makes no sense to repeat it to the jury for a *third* time.

However, there is an even more important reason to listen to opposing counsel's opening. What the opposing attorney says can be a powerful weapon for you to use in your opening, if you represent the defendant, or in your closing. When opposing counsel gives her opening, jot down the main ideas she states. She is giving the jury a preview of the trial and also giving it to you!

If there are any statements that you know the evidence will show to be untrue, write the phrase in quotation marks. At the end of trial, you can refer to opposing counsel's exact misstatement in the opening to undermine her credibility.

---

26. *People v. Simpson* No. BA097211, 1995 WL 25440 at *12 (Cal. Super. Ct. Jan. 24, 1995) (opening statement of Johnnie Cochran).

What an opposing attorney says, then, or fails to say in an opening can be a powerful tool to use in your opening. Why wait until closing to highlight for the jury the lack of integrity in the opposing side's position?

4. Don't Use Legal or Difficult to Understand Words

Remember that the jurors are hearing the facts of this case for the first time. Make them simple to understand. Attorneys have unfortunately acquired a lot of legal jargon; never use it with the jury. The same goes for difficult to understand words. You job is not to impress them with your knowledge. Many attorneys use complicated words without even realizing it. Be aware that you are talking to people who want to understand what you have to say, and the quickest way to turn them off is to use language they can't understand. An analogous situation occurs when you go to the doctor's office seeking an answer to a medical problem. The last thing you want to hear from the doctor is an explanation using medical terms you don't understand.

5. Don't Talk Down to Jurors

Patronizing or lecturing jurors is another problem. Usually, jurors are less educated than the lawyers in the courtroom. They are also amateurs concerning court proceedings and legal procedure, and they know nothing about the case. Until you lose their trust, jurors perceive you as an officer of the court, highly educated and an expert in the case. Unfortunately, attorneys—often without realizing it—talk down to jurors. It is an easy mistake to make, but it invades the province of the jurors as the final decision makers.

Example: Defense Closing Argument
(Johnnie Cochran) from *People v. Simpson*

Although this example is from the closing, its lesson is applicable to an opening statement. Johnnie Cochran violated the principle of not talking down to the jurors in his closing:

> Cochran: You will do the right thing. . . . By your decision you control his very life in your hands. Treat it carefully. Treat it fairly. Be fair. . . . [A]nd beyond the dim unknown standeth the same God for all people keeping watch above

his own. He watches all of us and he will watch you in your decision.[27]

No one wants to be talked down to. Why would jurors want to be told that God is watching over them to ensure that they render a verdict that the lawyer wants?

6. Don't Use Uhs, Ohs, or Ums or Repeat Curse Words

As stated previously, when you are nervous, or trying to remember a word, the natural reaction is to say "Uh," "Oh," or "Um" until you can think of the word you are trying to say. Once or twice is OK, but more than that becomes a distraction to the jury. These sounds are made because you are afraid of silence. Don't be. Silence can be very dramatic.

Another issue that comes up is whether an attorney should repeat a curse word that is a key piece of testimony. A few attorneys can repeat the curse word in a natural way that is not offensive, but the better course is to delete the reference. The following is an excellent example of how to handle the situation that was used by the prosecutor in *McVeigh* when he referred to a statement found on the defendant's computer. (See p. 106)

Checklist of the Six Don'ts of Opening Statements

1. Don't make the jurors' job more difficult
2. Don't explain to the jurors what an opening statement is—they already know.
3. Don't forget to listen.
4. Don't use legal or difficult to understand words.
5. Don't talk down to jurors.
6. Don't use uhs, ohs, or ums or repeat curse words.

---

27. *People v. Simpson* No. BA097211, 1995 WL 27396 at *49–50 (Cal. Super. Ct. Sept. 28, 1995) (closing argument of Johnnie Cochran).

> *Hartzler: You'll see the chilling words in that computer file.
> I'm going to delete the expletive. It said, "All you tyrannical
> M.F.ers will swing in the wind one day for your treasonous
> actions against the Constitution and the United States."*[28]

3.7 EXAMPLES OF THEMES

There is an art to developing a theme for your case. The theme must be succinct and accurate, and it must convey a memorable image to the jury. The examples of themes below can be used in a variety of cases.

1. Car Wreck

Let's look at the facts from a car-wreck case. Assume the following: The plaintiff had to slow down for a stopped car on the highway. The defendant driver was unable to slow down quickly enough and rear-ended the plaintiff's car. The plaintiff went to the emergency room that night and more than a year later had lower-back surgery. The plaintiff claims at trial that the crash required him to have surgery, although he complained to emergency room doctors on the night of the accident only of pain in his neck. Photos of the rear bumper of the plaintiff's car showed no dents and only a few scratches at the point of impact.

Example: A Defendant's Opening

Defense counsel: May it please the court, Ms. Smith [plaintiff's counsel], ladies and gentlemen of the jury. This is a case where a picture tells a thousand words. [Note the theme.] In a few moments, you will see a picture that settles this dispute.

Mr. Jones [the plaintiff] has two claims that could not be further from the truth. First, he claims that my client's driving caused such pain that he had to go to the emergency room for treatment. Second, Mr. Jones wants you to believe that the accident caused him to have lower-back surgery more than a year later.

---

28. *United States v. McVeigh* No. 96-CR-68, 1997 WL 198070 at *19 (D. Colo. Apr. 24, 1997) (opening statement of Joseph Hartzler).

The plaintiff will admit on the stand that he had no abrasions, bruising, or bleeding of any kind.[29] In fact, he will testify that he did not have one single scratch on his body. He will even admit that on the night of the accident when asked by doctors and nurses where he was feeling pain, he said it was in his neck, not his lower back, which he now claims was injured in the accident.

But there is more. As I mentioned, this is a case where a picture tells a thousand words. [Show the picture of minor damage to the rear bumper to the jury.] This [point to rear bumper in picture] is what this case is all about. This picture tells the story of what happened that night, and no matter what the plaintiff says, there is nothing he can do about this photo.

2. Employment Discrimination

Now, let's look at an employment discrimination case with the following facts. A male employee (the plaintiff John Smith) was a good friend of his male supervisor (the defendant Bob Wallace), and they often played practical jokes on each other. One day, the plaintiff asked the supervisor for a letter of recommendation for a promotion to another office with the same company. When the plaintiff arrived at work the next day, the supervisor had circulated a mock letter of recommendation among several of the plaintiff's coworkers. The letter, written on official letterhead, said that the supervisor was not aware that the plaintiff still worked at the office because he called in sick so much, that he often had sex with women in the office, that he would go on drinking binges and have sex with sheep, and that the plaintiff often could be found with his hand up the skirts of subordinates.

There were witnesses who said that the plaintiff was laughing when he saw the letter and that he even made copies of the letter and showed it to other employees. The letter was never sent to the location where the plaintiff was seeking a job, and no one from that location ever learned about the letter. The plaintiff sued for sexual harassment.

Example: A Defendant's Opening

Defense counsel: May it please the court, Ms. Andrews [plaintiff's counsel], ladies and gentlemen of the jury. Mr. Smith has

---

29. The reason the attorney can be so confident is because the plaintiff has made these admissions in his deposition and to the emergency room doctors.

> Don't feel trapped by thinking that your theme *has* to use the wording, "This case is about _____." While that phrasing is helpful when you are starting out because it forces you to find a succinct theme, it is not necessary or always advisable. Be creative.

taken this joke too far. [Note the theme.] We will prove to you four important facts in this case: (1) Mr. Smith was seen laughing and making copies of the letter for coworkers, (2) not one coworker will testify that the letter was taken seriously, (3) as soon as management found out about the letter, Mr. Smith's supervisor, Bob Wallace, was demoted and moved to a separate area of the office from Mr. Smith, and (4) Mr. Smith was not damaged by this letter in any way. Mr. Smith never missed a day of work, never saw a mental health counselor of any kind, and he never formally applied for the promotion he claims he was denied because of the letter.

In this example, a theme is used (plaintiff has taken the joke too far), but it would also be effective to tell the jury that you will prove three or four facts that, if they believe them, will win the case for you. This is particularly powerful since the defendant has no burden of proof.

3. Medical Malpractice

Assume the following facts in a medical malpractice case. The plaintiff, Bill Harada, who was very ill with end-stage liver disease and respiratory problems, went to the hospital because he had an obstruction in his small intestine. Before taking an X-ray, the radiologist gave him some oral barium to drink to determine the nature and location of the blockage. This procedure was used because the barium (a pink liquid) travels through the stomach and intestines and stops where the obstruction is, and this location will show up on the X-ray. Forty-five minutes after drinking the barium, the plaintiff died in the hospital.

The medical testimony revealed that oral barium had never caused a person's death except when there was an allergic reaction. This reaction in patients was rare, less than 1 in 1,000,000, and the reactions were associated with typical symptoms of allergic reactions, such as hives and shortness of breath. The plaintiff did not suffer any of these symptoms but rather became unconscious and could not be resuscitated.

Example of a Plaintiff's Opening

Plaintiff's counsel: [no introductory phrase such as "May it please the court" is said in this example] Bill Harada was a loving father and caring husband. He served in the Vietnam War, was honorably discharged, worked for the local post office, and ceaselessly served his community by volunteering with Habitat for Humanity. But most important, he cared about his wife and looked forward each weekend to seeing his five young grandchildren. Bill cannot be replaced. This is a case about the carelessness and arrogance of the doctors to whom Bill entrusted his life. [**Note the theme.**] Their actions caused his untimely death and robbed his family of years of companionship and emotional and financial support.

Example of a Defendant's Opening

Defense counsel: May it please the court, Mr. Bell [plaintiff's counsel], ladies and gentlemen of the jury. First, I would like to express my sympathies to Mr. Harada's [the deceased] family. There is nothing worse than losing the life of a loved one, and I know that this trial is not an easy process to go through. But neither is the process easy for the doctors accused of killing Mr. Harada. The doctors tried everything they could to save a very sick man.

Whatever evidence Mr. Bell brings to court, he cannot get around the fact that the odds of dying from an allergic reaction to oral barium are less than 1 in 1,000,000. In short, Mr. Bell is long on odds and short on proof. [**Note the theme.**] There is not one witness who will testify that Mr. Harada—who was near death when he came to the hospital—suffered any symptoms of an allergic reaction, such as breaking out in hives or shortness of breath. . . .

> Although the general rule is that your opening should begin powerfully with your theme, this is a case where an exception on the defense is prudent to follow. By showing sympathy for the deceased's family, you will gain credibility with the jury by revealing yourself as a kind and caring person. Offering sympathy does not mean that you are conceding liability, and the jury will understand the difference.

[Ending] Mr. Harada did not die from drinking oral barium but, rather, from the end stages of liver disease and respiratory failure. This is not that one-in-a-million case.

3.8 ANALYSIS OF PROSECUTION'S OPENING STATEMENT IN *U.S. V. MCVEIGH*

Having looked at the steps necessary to prepare and deliver an opening, let's look at the openings in one of the most famous trials of the twentieth century, *U.S. v. McVeigh*.[30] Timothy McVeigh was on trial for driving a Ryder truck filled with homemade explosives to the Murrah Building in Oklahoma City on April 19, 1995. He detonated the bomb, which shattered the building and others nearby. It was the greatest act of domestic terrorism on U.S. soil. The explosion killed 168 people, including 19 children. By chance, McVeigh was stopped for driving without a license plate seventy-five minutes after the bombing and was arrested for possession of a concealed weapon. The prosecution's theory was that McVeigh bombed the federal building to seek revenge against the United States for its "attack" against citizens at the Branch Davidian Compound in Waco, Texas.

The opening for the prosecution was one of the best openings ever given. The lessons it teaches are applicable to both civil and criminal trials. The opening for the defense—while not as good—was creative, and there is much to learn from it. Let's look at excerpts of the opening for the prosecution first and then excerpts from the defense. The headings below are taken from the outline discussed earlier in this chapter. Notice how well the outline is used in the two openings that follow.

1. Begin Powerfully with a Memorable Theme

Before analyzing the opening statement, ask yourself what is the best fact or image you could begin your opening statement with if you were delivering it. Would it be the image of McVeigh building the bomb, or would it be the reaction of a paramedic arriving at the scene of massive

---

30. A more detailed summary of facts is contained in appendix 2.

destruction? Would you structure your opening chronologically (e.g., beginning when McVeigh first hatched this idea) or witness by witness (e.g., "You will hear from Mrs. Smith that . . .")? See how your answer compares with what was actually delivered.

Hartzler: May it please the court. . . .

The court: Counsel.

Hartzler: Ladies and gentlemen of the jury, April 19th, 1995, was a beautiful day in Oklahoma City—at least it started out as a beautiful day. The sun was shining. Flowers were blooming. It was springtime in Oklahoma City. Sometime after six o'clock that morning, Tevin Garrett's mother woke him up to get him ready for the day. He was only sixteen months old. He was a toddler; and as some of you know that have experience with toddlers, he had a keen eye for mischief. He would often pull on the cord of her curling iron in the morning, pull it off the countertop until it fell down, often till it fell down on him.

That morning, she picked him up and wrestled with him on her bed before she got him dressed. She remembers this morning because that was the last morning of his life.

That morning, Mrs. Garrett got Tevin and her daughter ready for school, and they left the house at about 7:15 to go downtown to Oklahoma City. . . . She did not work in the Murrah Building. She wasn't even a federal employee. She worked across the street in the General Records Building.

She pulled into the lot, the parking lot of the federal building, in order to make it into work on time; and she went upstairs to the second floor with Tevin, because Tevin attended the day-care center on the second floor of the federal building. When she went in, she saw that Chase and Colton Smith were already there, two years old and three years old. Dominique London was there already. He was just shy of his third birthday. So was Zack Chavez. He had already turned three.

When she turned to leave to go to her work, Tevin, as so often, often happens with small children, cried and clung to her; and then, as you see with children so frequently, they try to help each other. One of the little Coverdale boys—there were two of them, Elijah and Aaron. The youngest one was two and a half. Elijah came up to Tevin and patted him on the back and comforted him as his mother left.

> *As Helena Garrett left the Murrah Federal Building to go to work across the street, she could look back up at the building; and there was a wall of plate glass windows on the second floor. You can look through those windows and see into the day-care center; and the children would run up to those windows and press their hands and faces to those windows to say good-bye to their parents. And standing on the sidewalk, it was almost as though you can reach up and touch the children there on the second floor. But none of the parents of any of the children that I just mentioned ever touched those children again while they were still alive.*[31]

Before looking at what Hartzler did, let's look at what he did not do. He did not introduce his colleagues or himself to the jury. Nor did he explain to the jurors what an opening statement is.

The prosecution began powerfully with an unforgettable image of an innocent child. As mentioned above, the prosecution could have started its opening with a variety of compelling facts. However, Hartzler picked the most powerful and persuasive image to begin his opening: the innocent children who were victims. But he accomplished even more through his attention to detail. Hartzler knew the ages of the children as well as their first and last names: "One of the little Coverdale boys—there were two of them, Elijah and Aaron. The youngest one was two and a half. Elijah came up to Tevin and patted him on the back and comforted him as his mother left."

How did he make this image even more powerful? Which child should he pick to focus his opening on? He picked a child whose mother did not even work in the federal building to show the defendant's utter ruthlessness. Remember, McVeigh's hate was for the federal government. By showing that children who were not even associated with employees of the federal government were indiscriminately killed, Hartzler heightens one's anger about the crime. However, he did not confine his opening to just one theme of innocent children. He added two more, which will be shown below. Look for the themes the prosecution used.

---

31. *United States v. McVeigh* No. 96-CR-68, 1997 WL 198070 at *7 (D. Colo. Apr. 24, 1997) (opening statement of Joseph Hartzler).

Hartzler: At nine o'clock that morning, two things happened almost simultaneously. In the Water Resources Building—that's another building to the west of the Murrah Building across the street—an ordinary legal proceeding began in one of the hearing rooms; and at the same time, in front of the Murrah Building, a large Ryder truck pulled up into a vacant parking space in front of the building and parked right beneath those plate glass windows from the day-care center.

What these two separate but almost simultaneous events have in common is that they—they both involved grievances of some sort. The legal proceeding had to do with water rights. It wasn't a legal proceeding as we are having here, because there was no court reporter. It was a tape-recorded proceeding, and you will hear the tape recording of that proceeding. It was an ordinary, everyday-across-America, typical legal proceeding in which one party has a grievance and brings it into court or into a hearing to resolve it, to resolve it not by violence and terror but to resolve it in the same way we are resolving matters here, by constitutional due process.

And across the street, the Ryder truck was there also to resolve a grievance; but the truck wasn't there to resolve the grievance by means of due process or by any other democratic means. The truck was there to impose the will of Timothy McVeigh on the rest of America and to do so by premeditated violence and terror, by murdering innocent men, women, and children, in hopes of seeing blood flow in the streets of America.

At 9:02 that morning, two minutes after the water rights proceeding began, a catastrophic explosion ripped the air in downtown Oklahoma City. It instantaneously demolished the entire front of the Murrah Building, brought down tons and tons of concrete and metal, dismembered people inside, and it destroyed, forever, scores and scores and scores of lives, lives of innocent Americans: clerks, secretaries, law enforcement officers, credit union employees, citizens applying for Social Security, and little kids.

All the children I mentioned earlier, all of them died, and more; dozens and dozens of other men, women, children, cousins, loved ones, grandparents, grandchildren, ordinary Americans going about their business. And the only reason they died, the only reason that they are no longer with us, no longer with their loved ones, is that they were in a building owned by a government that Timothy McVeigh so hated that with premeditated intent and a well-designed

A very persuasive weapon a lawyer has is the power to choose how a fact is proven during a trial. Here, Hartzler could have chosen any number of ways to introduce the jurors to the devastation of the blast: witnesses on the street, emergency personnel responding to the scene, and so forth. Instead, he reveals the devastation from the viewpoint of the innocent people participating in a legal proceeding.

plan that he had developed over months and months before the bombing, he chose to take their innocent lives to serve his twisted purpose.

In plain, simple language, it was an act of terror, violence, in-tend—intended to serve selfish political purpose.

The man who committed this act is sitting in this courtroom be-hind me, and he's the one that committed those murders.

After he did so, he fled the scene; and he avoided even dam-aging his eardrums, because he had earplugs with him.[32]

Two other themes are introduced: resolving grievances by violence and the cowardice of McVeigh. Hartzler contrasted the orderly, established, and respected American process of resolving grievances, like those taking place in the Water Resources Building, with the way McVeigh decided to resolve his grievances. The contrasting image is persuasive. But Hartzler does more. He shows that McVeigh is a coward. For all the death and destruction he is going to cause, McVeigh wants to flee the scene and protect his eardrums from the loud explosion.

2. Discuss the Important Details of the Story

After discussing how McVeigh was stopped for a traffic violation seventy-five minutes after the explosion and the evidence in his car linking him to the crime, the prosecution then set forth the details of the case.

> *Hartzler: As it's turned out, the bombing in Oklahoma City was the first event in a series of events that would lead each of you to be in this courtroom today as jurors; but you'll*

---

32. *United States v. McVeigh* No. 96-CR-68, 1997 WL 198070 at *8–9 (D. Colo. Apr. 24, 1997) (opening statement of Joseph Hartzler).

learn as jurors that the bombing was a premeditated act. It was part of a plan that McVeigh set in action long, long before April 19, 1995. And that's why the evidence will take so much time, because we will go back, not from the beginning of time but from a certain stage in McVeigh's life and walk through the various details of what he was doing and how it all fit into his plan to kill people in the Murrah Building.

Timothy McVeigh grew up in upstate New York; and after high school, he joined the army. He first went to Fort Benning in Georgia, and that's where he met Terry Nichols. They served in Fort Benning in the same platoon.

After he and Nichols completed their basic training at Fort Benning, they were both sent to Fort Riley, in Kansas. They became friends, in part because they both shared a distaste for the federal government.

McVeigh's dislike for the federal government was revealed while he was still in the army. Even at that early time in his life, he expressed an enthusiasm for this book, The Turner Diaries. *And you will hear more about that book during this trial. It's a work of fiction, like I said. It follows the exploits of a group of well-armed men and women who call themselves "patriots," and they seek to overthrow the federal government by use of force and violence.*

In the book they make a fertilizer bomb in the back of a truck and they detonate it in front of a federal building in downtown Washington, D.C., during business hours and they kill hundreds of people.

Friends, acquaintances, and family members of McVeigh will testify that he carried the book with him, gave copies to them, urged them to read this book.

We will show you passages from the book, and you'll see how the bombing in the book served as a blueprint for McVeigh and for his planning and execution of the bombing in Oklahoma City.[33]

After establishing themes to provide a framework for his opening, Hartzler then lays out the important—and *only* the important—facts of his case. He wants to show that McVeigh's rage against the government had been simmering for a long time.

---

33. *United States v. McVeigh* No. 96-CR-68, 1997 WL 198070 at *11 (D. Colo. Apr. 24, 1997) (opening statement of Joseph Hartzler).

3. Address Candidly—but Don't Dwell on— Weaknesses in the Case and Turn Them into Strengths

As with any complicated case—and even many simple cases—there will be inconsistencies. Sometimes you will have witnesses who you believe are telling the truth but have made so many inconsistent statements that their credibility will be attacked. Don't shy away from this problem in your opening. Watch how Hartzler handles these "obstacles."

> *Hartzler: As you can probably tell from what I've said, there is no single witness who is going to come in here and tell the whole sad story. Our case consists of dozens of pieces of evidence put together. His Honor referred to that earlier this morning, when he was speaking with you. And those pieces will come in like bricks building a brick wall.*
>
> *Now, some of the bricks won't fit tightly together, because memories will be slightly different; and as I think we spoke to some of you in jury selection, there will undoubtedly be some unanswered questions. There always are in a case of this complexity.*
>
> *But in the end, we will build a solid wall of evidence against McVeigh, making your job of determining his guilt easy, I believe. You'll get a clear picture of what happened, and it won't depend on any one witness. There will be overlapping proof, and you'll be convinced beyond a reasonable doubt that he's responsible for the bombing in Oklahoma City.*[34]

Hartzler, through his integrity, is admitting to the jury that there will be some unanswered questions, but he makes the problem go away by assuring them that such a problem is perfectly natural. He also admits that there will be inconsistencies, but he tells the jurors not to worry since there will be overlapping proof, and in the end they will have a "clear picture of what happened."

Such an argument is effective because if the defense were to argue that the prosecution's case is full of inconsistencies, the prosecution has

---

34.   *United States v. McVeigh* No. 96-CR-68, 1997 WL 198070 at *31 (D. Colo. Apr. 24, 1997) (opening statement of Joseph Hartzler).

already inoculated itself from such an attack. Let's look at another example of addressing weaknesses.

> *Hartzler: But there is one witness who is very close to McVeigh and who knows a lot. I haven't mentioned him yet. Our case does not depend on him. We could prove the case without him, but he was very close to McVeigh. I'm referring, of course, to Michael Fortier, his other army buddy. We will call him as a witness because he provides insight into McVeigh's thinking, his intent, and his premeditation; and he knows a few details that other witnesses do not know. . . .*
>
> *Although he did not join the conspiracy and he didn't participate in the bombing—in fact, he rejected McVeigh's proposal—he did have knowledge of McVeigh's plans. He knew about McVeigh's criminal activity. He didn't report it. He didn't report it to anyone who could have stopped it. He made no effort to stop it.*
>
> *In addition, he actually participated with McVeigh in transporting stolen guns. These were guns that were stolen from Bob, the gun dealer in Arkansas. I told you about the trip the two of them made up to Kansas. Well, the purpose of the trip was to go up and get some of the stolen guns. Fortier participated in transporting them back to Arizona; so he transported stolen guns, which is a federal violation.*
>
> *So while he will not plead guilty to the bombing, he won't plead guilty to the conspiracy that he was not involved in, he will plead guilty to some of the crimes. He'll plead guilty to transporting the guns and to conspiring with McVeigh to transport the guns; and there are two other violations he'll plead guilty to—he's already pled guilty to.*
>
> *You'll hear that he and his wife were also involved in drug use. They used marijuana and speed. And immediately following the bombing, when Fortier could have been remorseful and could have reported what he knew, he lied. He lied to the FBI, he lied to news reporters, he lied to his friends, he lied to his parents, he lied to his family; and Lori Fortier, his wife, lied, too. They lied because they were scared. They were afraid of what could happen to them. They had known about McVeigh's plans. They had done nothing to stop it. Scores of people had died, and they were afraid that they could be prosecuted. They were afraid they could be subjected to the death penalty, and they lied.*
>
> *And the lies were bad. You'll hear from Fortier—he will admit that he lied, told reporters, told others that he thought*

> McVeigh was innocent and that he had no reason to believe McVeigh was involved.
>
> Law enforcement agents obtained a wiretap on McVeigh's house—on Fortier's house, on his telephone. The effort proved totally unfruitful in part because Fortier and his wife, as they will say, suspected that their house was being tapped.
>
> The agents then obtained subpoenas to bring the Fortiers before the grand jury in Oklahoma City; and before they appeared before the grand jury, they had lawyers appointed for them. And when they got their attorneys, they admitted they had been lying and they told us what they know; and they will tell you what they know.
>
> Michael Fortier is now in prison awaiting sentence. He pled guilty to lying to the FBI, to concealing his knowledge of this bombing, to transporting guns; and he will testify pursuant to a plea agreement with the government. He faces a maximum of twenty-three years in prison, but he's hoping to get a much, much shorter sentence than that.
>
> At the conclusion of the case, the judge will instruct you must consider Michael Fortier's testimony with care and caution; and we encourage you to do that and to consider his testimony in the context of all the other evidence we will present. And much of what he tells you will be corroborated independently.
>
> As I've said, our evidence is not dependent on any one witness. It's certainly not dependent on Michael Fortier, but he will provide you some understanding of McVeigh's thinking, especially during the last few months and up until the time the bombing actually occurred.[35]

Hartzler leaves nothing for the defense to seize upon regarding Michael Fortier. He confronts all the important weaknesses in Michael Fortier's credibility: he's a liar, drug user, convicted felon, a coward for not stopping the bombing, and is going to get a break from the government for testifying against McVeigh. However, Hartzler gains credibility by candidly admitting the weaknesses even by encouraging the jury to treat Fortier's testimony with caution. Moreover, he gives a very rea-

---

35. *United States v. McVeigh* No. 96-CR-68, 1997 WL 198070 at *31, 34–35 (D. Colo. Apr. 24, 1997) (opening statement of Joseph Hartzler).

sonable explanation why Fortier would lie about his involvement and McVeigh's: he was scared.

4. Briefly Discuss the Elements of the Claim/ Defense and the Burden of Proof

> *Hartzler: I'm not going to again detail the charges. The judge has already explained them to you; but in presenting all of this evidence to you, we obviously are going to be able to prove the eleven counts against McVeigh.*
>
> *The judge has explained to you [that] one of the counts is a conspiracy. That's an agreement between two people to commit a crime, two others involved blowing up the building. And then there are eight counts involved of murder, involving eight different law enforcement agents. And I want you to understand that those eight counts are not there because we value the lives of law enforcement agents any more than lives of any of the other people who were lost in that building. There is a specific federal statute that subjects the defendant to the death penalty for murdering a law enforcement agent in the line of duty, and that's why those eight counts are charged.*
>
> *Each of the crimes has various elements. The judge at the end of the case will instruct you on those elements. It's our burden to prove each of the elements for each of the counts.*
>
> *We will meet that burden. We will make your job easy. We will present ample evidence to convince you beyond any reasonable doubt that Timothy McVeigh is responsible for this terrible crime.*[36]

It is improper in opening statements to discuss in detail the elements of the offense or other jury instructions. It is also unnecessary since the trial judge will have briefly discussed them with the jury in his preliminary instructions prior to opening statements. Hartzler spends just enough time to explain briefly what a conspiracy is and why there is not a separate count for each person who was murdered that day. He also eagerly embraces the burden of proof the government has, and, by

---

36. *United States v. McVeigh* No. 96-CR-68, 1997 WL 198070 at *35 (D. Colo. Apr. 24, 1997) (opening statement of Joseph Hartzler).

doing so, he actually eases that burden by making it sound like it will be easily met.

5. End Memorably

Remember the themes Hartzler started his case with? They were the innocence of children, resolving grievances by violence, and cowardice. Let's see how Hartzler ties this all together in his conclusion. For the purposes of context, it is helpful to know that when McVeigh's car was pulled over by police after the bomb had exploded, he had with him written quotes from the American Revolutionary War. One was from a Founding Father who—in complaining about British rule—said, "When the government fears the people, there is liberty." Earlier in his opening, Hartzler had related some of these quotes to the jury.

> Hartzler: You will hear evidence in this case that McVeigh liked to consider himself a patriot, someone who could start the second American Revolution. The literature that was in his car when he was arrested included some that quoted statements from the Founding Fathers and other people who played a part in the American Revolution, people like Patrick Henry and Samuel Adams. McVeigh isolated and took these statements out of context, and he did that to justify his antigovernment violence.
>
> Well, ladies and gentlemen, the statements of our forefathers can never be interpreted to justify warfare against innocent children. Our forefathers didn't fight British women and children. They fought other soldiers. They fought them face-to-face, hand to hand. They didn't plant bombs and run away wearing earplugs.
>
> The court: Thank you.
>
> Hartzler: Thank you, Your Honor.[37]

Hartzler concludes the opening with a powerful image tying in the themes mentioned at the beginning of the opening: innocent children killed, revenge against the government, and cowardice. The beginning of his opening concerned the last few hours of Tevin Garrett's life, and

---

37. *United States v. McVeigh* No. 96-CR-68, 1997 WL 198070 at *35–36 (D. Colo. Apr. 24, 1997) (opening statement of Joseph Hartzler).

the conclusion of the opening set forth McVeigh fleeing the scene of devastation wearing earplugs because he did not want to hurt himself.

3.9 ANALYSIS OF DEFENDANT'S OPENING STATEMENT IN *U.S. V. MCVEIGH*

Having analyzed the prosecution's opening, let's look at how the defense responded. See if Stephen Jones, counsel for Timothy McVeigh, presented a compelling argument.

1. Begin Powerfully with a Memorable Theme

> *Jones: May it please the court. . . .*
> *The court: Mr. Jones.*
> *Jones: Special attorney to the United States Attorney General, Mr. Hartzler, and to Mr. Ryan, the United States Attorney for the Western Judicial District of Oklahoma, and to Mr. Timothy McVeigh, my client, I have waited two years for this moment to outline the evidence to you that the government will produce, that I will produce, both by direct and cross-examination, by exhibits, photographs, transcripts of telephone conversations, transcripts of conversations inside houses, videotapes, that will establish not a reasonable doubt but that my client is innocent of the crime that Mr. Hartzler has outlined to you.*[38]

Jones tells the jury that he "has waited two years" to prove that his client is innocent. How much stronger can a defense attorney start than by taking on a burden—which he does not have—to prove his client innocent? Most defense attorneys make the mistake of hiding behind the prosecution or plaintiff's burden of proof. However, that mind-set can often lead to a very defensive posture at trial, which jurors see as a weakness.

Here, Jones has told the jury he will prove his client's innocence: his first theme. Although his statement may seem rather bold, it is very much in keeping with the reality of the way jurors view a trial. Jurors

---

38. *United States v. McVeigh* No. 96-CR-68, 1997 WL 198070 at *36 (D. Colo. Apr. 24, 1997) (opening statement of Stephen Jones).

expect defense attorneys—at least through cross-examination—to prove their client's innocence in a criminal case or lack of liability in a civil case. Given the jurors' expectation, Jones is simply saying in a very bold way what any good defense attorney would do during trial but is often afraid to say in an opening statement.

> *Jones: And like Mr. Hartzler, I begin where he began. As he said, it was a spring day in Oklahoma City. And inside the office of the Social Security Administration located in the Alfred P. Murrah Building . . . [Dana Bradley] wandered out into the lobby of the Alfred P. Murrah Building. And as she was looking out the plate glass window, a Ryder truck slowly pulled into a parking place and stopped. She didn't give it any particular attention until the door opened on the passenger side, and she saw a man get out.*
>
> *Approximately three weeks later, she described the man to the Federal Bureau of Investigation agents, as indeed she did to us and to others, as short, stocky, olive-complected, wearing a puffy jacket, with black hair, a description that does not match my client. She did not see anyone else. . . .*
>
> *In addition to the members of [Dana Bradley's] family who died that morning, the bomb claimed Charles E. Hurlburt; John Karl Vaness III; Anna Jean Hurlburt; Donald Lee Fritzler; Eula Leigh Mitchell; Donald Earl Burns Sr.; Norma Jean Johnson; Calvin C. Battle; Laura Jane Garrison; Burl Bloomer; Luther Treanor; Rheta Long; Juretta Colleen Guiles; Robert Glen Westberry; Carolyn Ann Kreymborg; Leora Lee Sells; Mary Anne Fritzler; Virginia Mae Thompson. . . . [Jones names the remaining victims.]*
>
> *For those of us from Oklahoma, the bombing of the Alfred P. Murrah Building is the event by which we measure time. It is to my generation in Oklahoma what Pearl Harbor was to my mother and father's generation.*[39]

Jones follows his promise of proving his client innocent by relating an eyewitness' account that claims a person very different looking from the defendant got out of the Ryder truck that contained the bomb. Notice what Jones does next. He is aware of what an emotional impact

---

39. *United States v. McVeigh* No. 96-CR-68, 1997 WL 198070 at *36–37 (D. Colo. Apr. 24, 1997) (opening statement of Stephen Jones).

the bombing had on Oklahoma. He realizes it is necessary to show the jury that he is compassionate about what happened, and he creates a wonderful image to relate his empathy: "For those of us from Oklahoma [the trial was held in Colorado], the bombing of the Alfred P. Murrah Building is the event by which we measure time."

However, Jones goes too far in reading the names of all the people killed in the bombing. He does this to show the jury his empathy and to show that his client has nothing to fear from the list of victims because he did not commit the crime. The same effect could have been achieved by reading a few of the names, perhaps just the names of the children, without running the risk of offending jurors who might think that it crossed the line and became disrespectful to the victims.

At the outset, Jones used the theme of innocence. Notice how he expands on this below.

> Jones: In reviewing the evidence in this case and in the proof that will come, you know, and certainly it will be in evidence, that this was the largest domestic terrorism act in the history of this country. The president of the United States and the attorney general of the United States went on nationwide television within hours after the bombing. The president came to Oklahoma City for the memorial funeral service at which 12,000 people attended. The federal government offered a $2 million reward for information leading to the arrest and conviction of those involved.
>
> And I think it fair to say that this was the largest criminal investigation in the history of this country.
>
> The question is, did they get the right man. . . .
>
> I believe that when you see the evidence in this case, you will conclude that the investigation of the Alfred P. Murrah Building lasted about two weeks. The investigation to build the case against Timothy McVeigh lasted about two years. But within seventy-two hours after suspicion first centered on Mr. McVeigh, we will prove to you that even then, the government knew, the FBI agents in the case, that the pieces of the puzzle were not coming together; that there was something terribly wrong, something missing. And as Paul Harvey says, our evidence will be the rest of the story.[40]

---

40. *United States v. McVeigh* No. 96-CR-68, 1997 WL 198070 at *38 (D. Colo. Apr. 24, 1997) (opening statement of Stephen Jones).

Jones declares, much like the defense in the O. J. Simpson case, that this case was a rush to judgment: "The investigation to build the case against Timothy McVeigh lasted about two years," while the investigation of the crime only lasted "two weeks." It is a powerful image that is designed to give the jurors pause about the claims made in the prosecution's opening.

2. Discuss the Important Details of the Story

Jones: So let me begin first with Timothy McVeigh . . . he was born on April 23, 1968, in Lockport, New York, son of William and Mildred McVeigh; and as Mr. Hartzler has indicated to you, he has a sister, Jennifer, younger by six years, and an older sister, Patricia, older by two years. Tim's dad, Bill McVeigh, had been an auto worker since 1963, and his mother, Micki, worked at various jobs, including most frequently as a travel agent. . . .

He continued through all of his schooling at Lockport. He made good grades except perhaps in his senior year—in fact, well-above-average grades. He got a[n] honor pass award, which is reserved for students who exhibited above-average academic performance and initiative, in his senior year; and when he graduated from the Star Point High School in Lockport in June of 1986, he had a small regents' scholarship to a state university in New York; but he didn't go to college. . . .

Then he went to work at the Burns International Security Service, March of 1992. He had a supervisory position there, and he left it in January of 1993. He came to Arizona, where his friends Mike and Lori Fortier lived; and Tim worked at the TruValue Hardware store in Kingman beginning in 1993 and again as a security guard at State Security during the same period of time. And then he went to work, so to speak, on his own, buying and selling and trading weapons at the numerous gun shows held throughout the country, of which there are probably anywhere from 2,000 to 3,000 a year.

But in May of 1988, he entered the armed services and stayed there until December of 1991, in the United States Army. After Fort Benning, his permanent station duty was Fort Riley, Kansas. And there he became a gunner for a Bradley fighting vehicle and repeatedly throughout his army service, as his friends will testify here, he achieved a top-gun ranking. In fact, first among ninety-three other Bradley gunners.

He achieved extraordinary advancement in the enlisted ranks from a private E1 to a sergeant E5 in less than three years. And then when the Operation Desert Shield, which became Operation Desert Storm, started, he served in the front-line assault, in the Kuwait-Iraq operations. He was literally on the front line and made one of the first invasions into the enemy area.

During this service in the military, he earned one of our highest awards, the Bronze Star. He also earned the Army Commendation Medal with an upgrade for valor. He received the Army Commendation Medal, two Army Achievement Medals, and several others. In fact, his unit was chosen to be the inner perimeter guard at the site where General Schwarzkopf and his opposite number in the Iraqi army arranged the terms of the armistice that ended the war.

After the war, he returned to the United States.[41]

The details are important to Jones because they allow him to paint a different picture of his client from the inhuman terrorist the prosecution has portrayed. As any good defense attorney should do—whether civil or criminal—Jones is humanizing his client for the jury: he is not the violent rebel and murderer that the prosecution has claimed but, rather, an ordinary American who had a typical upbringing with some extraordinary achievements in the army. Jones knows that if he can get the jury to like his client, it is more likely that the jury will acquit.

3. Address Candidly—but Don't Dwell on— Weaknesses in the Case and Turn Them into Strengths

The defense needed to address its weaknesses, which were many. Here is one example of how Jones accomplished this task.

> *Jones: Mr. McVeigh's motives as described by the government in Mr. Hartzler's opening address are that he is antigovernment,*

---

41. *United States v. McVeigh* No. 96-CR-68, 1997 WL 198070 at *39–40 (D. Colo. Apr. 24, 1997) (opening statement of Stephen Jones).

that he has a hatred for the United States, and that he conspired with others to build a terrible explosive device, which he initiated because he was angry at the government of the United States.

Mr. Hartzler has told you that the government's evidence will consist of, among other things, a shirt that Mr. McVeigh was wearing when he was arrested and that in his car he had all this patriot literature—it was, after all, incidentally, Patriots' Day, as Mr. Hartzler said—quotations from John Locke, Patrick Henry; but on this shirt, he had "sic semper tyrannis," the words spoken by John Wilkes Booth when he assassinated Abraham Lincoln in Ford's Theatre. And the government suggests to you that as an expression of his motive.

Well, "sic semper tyrannis" is also the official slogan of the state of Virginia and had been for almost 100 years before John Wilkes Booth appropriated it. And it was chosen by three men: George Mason, a member of the Virginia House of Delegates, a member of the Constitutional Convention at Philadelphia. He authored several amendments to the Constitution that were later adopted.

Another person who designed that slogan and adopted it was the famous general Richard Henry Lee of the American Revolutionary Army, who signed the Declaration of Independence. . . .

The third person who participated in the selection was George Wythe, who signed the Declaration of Independence and was a delegate to the Continental Congress.

So "sic semper tyrannis" is not the exclusive property of John Wilkes Booth. It has a meaning in the historical conservative community of people who follow the revolutionary rule and its antecedents, has really nothing to do only with John Wilkes Booth; likewise with the statement that Mr. McVeigh made to his sister that something big is going to happen. Well, we will give you proof that in the last of March and the first part of April of 1995, the something big that was going to happen didn't have anything to do with the bombing in Oklahoma City. Those words and expressions and communications and conversations were all over the Internet, in which thousands of people exchanged communication back and forth because they believed that the federal government was about to initiate another Waco raid, except this time on a different group.

Now, we're not concerned with whether the federal government was going to do that. The point is that Mr. McVeigh *was just one of tens of thousands of people of his political persuasion who believed that something big was going to happen in April of 1995. . . .*

Much of the rhetoric and writing that the government will introduce and call to your attention was virulent and caustic. It was extreme in some cases.

But there are many examples of materials—and some of them, we will introduce—possessed and studied by Tim McVeigh that were not. Among the items found in Mr. McVeigh's car at the time of his arrest was a statement in reference to gun control. And along with the items that Mr. Hartzler said was found and read from, this was found: "Well, that's part of my contribution to defense of freedom, this call to arms. In the past, I put to use the above points. I intend to become more active in the future. I would rather fight with pencil lead than bullet lead. We can win this war in [the] voting booth. If we have to fight in the streets, I would not be so sure. . . . Start your defense today. Stamps are cheaper than bullets and can be more effective." This was also in Tim McVeigh's car.

And among the others was one by Abraham Lincoln: "To sin by silence when they should protest makes cowards of men."

We will prove to you that the evidence that the government brings to you, which they call the motive for blowing up the building, proves nothing; that millions of innocent people fear and distrust the federal government and were outraged and that being outraged is no more an excuse for blowing up a federal building than being against the government means that you did it.[42]

The defense confronts head-on some of the most damaging evidence in the case: McVeigh's very hostile views and the documents found in his car after the explosion. Jones turns these weaknesses into strengths. He admits that some of McVeigh's views are extreme but points out that he has softened his views, as evidenced by some of the documents found in his car. Furthermore, he declares that the government is overreaching by trying to establish McVeigh's motive through

---

42. *United States v. McVeigh* No. 96-CR-68, 1997 WL 198070 at *39–43 (D. Colo. Apr. 24, 1997) (opening statement of Stephen Jones).

beliefs that are shared by some who signed the Declaration of Independence and millions of Americans today. Finally, observe how Jones again takes on a burden of proof—which he does not need to do—by saying, "We will prove to you that the evidence . . ."

4. Briefly Discuss the Elements of the Claim/Defense and the Burden of Proof

The defense did not discuss the elements of the offense or any special legal defense (e.g., self-defense or insanity) since the issues were straightforward. It did effectively take on a burden of proof at the beginning of its opening, as shown in the first example.

5. End Memorably

> *Jones: Tim McVeigh had earplugs. He was a hunter and a shooter, and he carried a gun with him, just like many hunters and shooters do.*
>
> *He had nitrates on him because that's found on guns and ammunition. And whether he had PETN or EGDN[43] depends upon the evidence of contamination and the qualifications of the people that reached that conclusion. It also depends on whether PETN and EGDN were found at the scene. If it wasn't, it has no significance.*
>
> *If Tim McVeigh built the bomb and put it in the truck, our proof will be that his fingernails, his nostrils, his hair, his clothing, his car, his shoes, his socks would have it all over them. They don't.*
>
> *Out of 7,000 pounds of debris, there is less than half a dozen pieces of evidence of a forensic nature; and we will go over each one of them with you. And our evidence will be that they do not prove Mr. McVeigh guilty or a participant in this bombing.*
>
> *I apologize for the time—I don't apologize. I take it back. I don't apologize for the time. This is an important case. You know it. It's the only opportunity I will have probably for several weeks, if not several months, before we put on our case. I*

---

43.   PETN is a fine powder, which is an explosive residue. It was found at the bombing scene and on McVeigh's shirt and pants' pockets. EGDN is also a high explosive residue that was found on McVeigh's clothing.

> *thank you for your attention, and I believe that you now*
> *know what I meant when I said every pancake has two sides.*
> *Thank you.*[44]

Confronted with the prosecution's powerful image of McVeigh driving away with earplugs as the bomb exploded and killed innocent children, Jones offers a credible explanation for the earplugs: McVeigh was a hunter. This explanation also shows the importance of having a flexible outline so that you can respond to the plaintiff's or prosecution's opening statement. He then highlights the lack of forensic evidence at the scene and asks rhetorically why there isn't any DNA evidence of McVeigh at the crime scene.

However, the persuasiveness of the prosecution's opening is obvious from Jones' admission. Jones, apparently noticing that the jury is tired—at the very peak of his argument—apologizes. An attorney should never have to apologize for an opening statement. Perhaps Jones lost the interest of some of the jurors when he read the very long list of the names at the beginning. In any event, if you have to apologize, your opening has been too long. You have lost before you have begun.

3.10 STUDY QUESTIONS FOR OPENING STATEMENT VIDEO CLIPS FROM *PEOPLE V. SIMPSON* (DISC 1)

Having analyzed the transcripts of the *McVeigh* trial, let's examine video excerpts of the opening statements of *People v. Simpson*. These excerpts are contained on the enclosed DVD (disc 1).

1. Darden Opening

Clip 1: Darden's Opening Remarks (12 min.)[45]

Background: Christopher Darden's first words to the jury are that he has the toughest job in the city today and that the jury's job is even

---

44. *United States v. McVeigh* No. 96-CR-68, 1997 WL 198147 at *27 (D. Colo. Apr. 24, 1997) (opening statement of Stephen Jones).

45. Running time has been rounded off to the nearest minute. The transcript can be found at *People v. O. J. Simpson* No. BA097211, 1995

tougher. Next, Darden explains to the jury what evidence is and what it is not. Darden then discusses the weakness in his case: the defendant is a celebrity. The clip concludes with Darden establishing a theme for his case.

Study Questions

1. Do you agree with the subject of Darden's opening remarks?
2. Are his gestures effective or distracting?
3. Is Darden effective when he discusses the promises jurors made in voir dire?
4. How good is Darden's eye contact?
5. Does he anticipate issues in the defense opening?
6. What theme does Darden establish at the end of the clip?

Clip 2: Darden Discusses Beating on New Year's Day, 1989 (6 min.)[46]

Background: Darden relates the 911 call from Nicole Brown on New Year's Day, 1989, at 4:00 a.m. Darden tells the jury they will hear the sound of Simpson beating Brown in the background of the 911 recording. Darden relates that when police respond to the scene, they see a disheveled Nicole, partially clad, running from the darkness of the bushes toward the security gate of the home. She repeats, "He's going to kill me." An officer sees that there is the imprint of a hand around Brown's neck and that her face is bruised and battered.

Study Questions

1. How well does Darden relate the story of the police arriving in response to Nicole's 911 call?
2. Compare this clip to the preceding one. Is Darden's technique better or worse in this one?
3. What good and bad mannerisms does Darden use?

WL 25440 at *17–20 (Cal. Super. Ct. Jan. 24, 1995) (opening statement of Christopher Darden).

46. *People v. Simpson* No. BA097211, 1995 WL 25440 at *23–24 (Cal. Super. Ct. Jan. 24, 1995) (opening statement of Christopher Darden).

Clip 3: Darden Concludes Opening Statement (3 min.)[47]

Background: Darden concludes his opening statement. He states that this is not a case of character assassination but a case of a controlling personality. The clip ends with Darden saying, "And if he couldn't have her, then nobody could."

Study Questions

1. How is Darden's eye contact?
2. How is Darden's tone of voice?
3. What is Darden's theme?
4. How would you improve his concluding remarks?

2. Clark Opening

Clip 1: Clark's Opening Remarks (4 min.)[48]

Background: Marcia Clark begins by introducing her cocounsel to the jury and starts to describe for the jury the people and places involved in the murder.

Study Questions

1. Does Clark persuasively confront a weakness in her case?
2. Is Clark's opening powerful?
3. Compare her theme to Darden's. Which is better?
4. Compare her physical and verbal expressions to Darden's. Whose style is better?

Clip 2: Clark Explains the Scientific Evidence Linking O. J. to the Crime (6 min.)[49]

Background: This clip is near the conclusion of Clark's opening. She summarizes the DNA and blood evidence and anticipates the defense's

---

47. *People v. Simpson* No. BA097211, 1995 WL 25440 at *30–31 (Cal. Super. Ct. Jan. 24, 1995) (opening statement of Christopher Darden).
48. *People v. Simpson* No. BA097211, 1995 WL 25440 at *31–32 (Cal. Super. Ct. Jan. 24, 1995) (opening statement of Marcia Clark).
49. *People v. Simpson* No. BA097211, 1995 WL 25440 at *19 and 20–21 (Cal. Super. Ct. Jan. 24, 1995) (opening statement of Marcia Clark).

argument of reasonable doubt. To better understand the clip, it is necessary to know that Clark had explained earlier in her opening that there were two kinds of DNA testing: restriction fragment length polymorphism (RFLP) and polymerase chain reaction (PCR). Both tests were used in the crime-scene investigation, and both are tests of exclusion rather than inclusion. That is, you compare the sample from the crime scene to a sample of the defendant to see if you can exclude the defendant as a suspect. Note that hair and fiber analysis are not DNA testing but comparisons under a microscope.

Study Questions

1. How could Clark have phrased her words differently to avoid Cochran's "argumentative" objection, which was sustained?
2. Is Clark's summary of the physical evidence convincing?
3. Should Clark have reminded the jurors about their promises made in voir dire?

3. Cochran Opening

Clip 1: Cochran's Opening Remarks (8 min.)[50]

Background: Johnnie Cochran begins his opening by thanking the jury. Cochran quotes Dr. Martin Luther King Jr. and Abraham Lincoln in the first three minutes of his opening. He then reminds the jury that it is the conscience of the community. Cochran then introduces the themes of his case.

Study Questions

1. Is it helpful for Cochran to remind the jury that opening statements are not evidence?
2. Is it effective when Cochran reminds the jurors of their promises in voir dire?

---

50. *People v. Simpson* No. BA097211, 1995 WL 27396 at *11–14 (Cal. Super. Ct. Jan. 25, 1995) (opening statement of Johnnie Cochran).

3. What can be learned from the prosecution's objection during this clip?
4. Does Cochran respond well to the prosecution's argument?
5. What are Cochran's themes?
6. Compare Cochran's eye contact with that of Darden's and Clark's. Which is more effective, and why?

Clip 2: Cochran Responds to Darden's Claim That Wife Beating Leads to Murder (3 min.)[51]

Background: Cochran discusses Simpson's remorse for battering and his pleading no contest to a criminal charge for it.

Study Questions

1. Is Cochran's response to Darden's argument convincing?
2. Are Cochran's tone of voice and gestures effective?

Clip 3: Cochran Attacks Forensic Evidence (4 min.)[52]

Background: In this short excerpt, Cochran attacks the forensic evidence Clark discussed in her opening.

Study Questions

1. Does Cochran present compelling arguments of reasonable doubt?
2. If you were on the jury, how would you decide the case after having heard the openings?

---

51. *People v. Simpson* No. BA097211, 1995 WL 27396 at *21–22 (Cal. Super. Ct. Jan. 25, 1995) (opening statement of Johnnie Cochran).
52. *People v. Simpson* No. BA097211, 1995 WL 27397 at *10 (Cal. Super. Ct. Jan. 25, 1995) (opening statement of Johnnie Cochran).

Chapter Four

———————⸱⊰∘⊱⸱———————

DIRECT
EXAMINATION

The drunkard smells of whiskey—but so does the bartender.
—Jewish proverb

The above proverb reveals the importance of a good direct examination. If your direct examination does not convince the jury that your witness is a bartender, opposing counsel will certainly prove on cross-examination that he is a drunkard. As with opening statements, approach the preparation and delivery of your direct examination by keeping the perceptions of the jurors at the forefront of your thoughts. You need to tell a compelling story. Unless you are a misdemeanor prosecutor, it is likely that you have spent weeks, months, or even years learning your case. In contrast, the jury is trying to process information about it for the very first time. So, make the testimony of your witnesses easy to understand and unforgettable. In addition, build your trust with the jury by making your witnesses unimpeachable on cross-examination.

> Remember the three *U*'s of direct examination. Make the testimony of your witnesses understandable, unforgettable, and unimpeachable.

For the most part, questions asked on direct examination cannot suggest the answer to the witness. The reason for this is one of fairness. If the attorney suggests the answer, then the witness is no longer testifying from his personal knowledge. The problem with the rule is that it makes it very difficult to get information from the witness. Imagine how difficult it would be to carry on a conversation with someone in a social setting if you could only ask questions that began with *who, what, when, where, how,* and *why* (nonleading questions), and the person you were talking to could not ask you questions.

The section on techniques in this chapter explains how to meet this challenge. But first, let's examine strategies to determine the order of witnesses and their preparation.

4.1 STRATEGIES

1. Order of Witnesses

A. Begin Powerfully
One of the most important—and often most neglected—trial strategies is the determination of the order of your witnesses. After giving a compelling opening statement, it is now time to tell that story through witnesses. Too often, attorneys will give a good opening statement and follow it with several witnesses who give boring testimony. Your goal—if you are the plaintiff—should be to build on the momentum of your opening statement with the compelling testimony of your first witness. Remember, a vast majority of the jurors come to a decision about your case during or immediately after opening statements.[1] Don't give them the chance to change their minds. If your evidence does not back up

---

1. James F. McKenzie, *Eloquence in Opening Statement,* Trial Dipl.J. at 32 (Spring 1987); Donald E. Vinson, *Jury Psychology and Antitrust Trial Strategy,* 55 Antitrust L.J. at 591 (1986) (based on 14,000 actual or surrogate jurors, "80 to 90 percent of all jurors come to a decision during or immediately after the opening statements").

your promises in opening, the jury won't trust you by the time you deliver your closing argument, and the outcome will be disastrous. Don't make the jurors wait for the key evidence. A lot of thought needs to be put into deciding how you are going to order your witnesses so that your case is presented in the clearest, most compelling, and most concise manner.

Every case at trial will have at least two good witnesses, or you should not be going to trial. At a minimum, then, your case should start and end with those two witnesses so that you will begin and end on a high note. After deciding which two witnesses you will start and end with, fill in the remaining order of witnesses in any way that explains your case in an understandable and unforgettable way.

A secondary consideration is the fact that your witnesses are the vehicles for introducing evidence. Consequently, some thought needs to be given to the order of witnesses so that the appropriate foundations for evidence are laid with each particular witness. For example, in a car-wreck case, it would be a mistake to have an accident reconstructionist[2] explain photos of the scene of the accident if those photos had not already been introduced into evidence (because they were only admissible through a witness who had not yet testified).[3]

Example: Start with Strong Witness
(Joseph Hartzler) from *U.S. v. McVeigh*

The prosecution had any number of memorable witnesses it could have started with. It might have started chronologically with a witness such as Lori Fortier, who could have told of McVeigh's early discussions with her about the plot to bomb a federal building. Or the prosecution could have started with Tevin Garrett's mother, who was mentioned prominently in the opening statement because she had dropped her toddler off at the day-care center in the federal building just moments before the bomb exploded. The only mistake would have been to start

---

2. An accident reconstructionist is a hired expert who analyzes information about an accident—including eyewitness testimony—and testifies regarding how the accident occurred.

3. Sometimes this problem can be solved by conditionally admitting an exhibit. See chapter 7.

with a witness who would undercut the momentum created by the opening statement.

The prosecution chose an excellent first witness, Cynthia Lou Klaver. She worked for the Oklahoma Water Resources Board. Klaver was a powerful witness because when the bomb exploded, she was participating in an administrative proceeding in the Water Resources Building, next to the federal building. In the prosecution's opening statement, the government introduced the theme that McVeigh was settling his grievance against the government through the killing of innocent children, in contrast to the American tradition of handling disputes with proceedings that involve due process. Klaver was presiding over such a due process proceeding at the very moment McVeigh was bombing the federal building.

Klaver testified that she was conducting a civil proceeding at 9:00 a.m. when the bomb hit and severely damaged her building, killing a coworker. Also, through Klaver, since she was an eyewitness to the destruction, the prosecution showed the jury photographs of the Murrah Building before and after the explosion. Moreover, the prosecution also used Klaver to introduce into evidence a tape recording of the proceeding, which had recorded the sound of the explosion and the screams of people afterward.[4]

The second witness was a U.S. Marine Corps recruiter working in the federal building who had seen the Ryder truck parked in front of the federal building on the morning of the explosion. He further vividly testified about the destruction the explosion caused in his building, about coworkers who were killed, and how the bombing caused him to lose his eyesight.[5]

From these two witnesses, the jurors heard the explosion through the use of an audiotape; they saw the explosion through photographs; they heard firsthand accounts of the destruction of two buildings, of deaths and injuries to people; and they were given an identification of

---

4. See *United States v. McVeigh* No. 96-CR-68, 1997 WL 200045 at *2–10 (D. Colo. Apr. 25, 1997) (direct examination of Cynthia Lou Klaver).
5. See *United States v. McVeigh* No. 96-CR-68, 1997 WL 200045 at *10–17 (D. Colo. Apr. 25, 1997) (direct examination of Michael Norfleet).

the Ryder truck that contained the bomb. The prosecution had indeed followed its persuasive opening statement with its two best witnesses.

B. End Memorably

Not only must you start powerfully but you must end memorably. Jurors remember most what they hear first and last. Don't let witnesses' schedules dictate your order of witnesses. You need to maintain control.

Example: End with Memorable Witness (Vicki Behenna)[6] from *U.S. v. McVeigh*

The prosecution's last witness was the chief medical examiner of Oklahoma. His testimony included a description of the location of the bodies of the 163 victims and a determination of how they were identified (some by fingerprints and some by dental records only). He was a logical and compelling witness to conclude with. The witness conveyed the magnitude of the human loss and the sheer force of the explosion since many of the dead were unrecognizable without the aid of scientific examination.[7]

Since the plaintiff, or prosecution, gets to put its witnesses on first, it may be several days before the jury hears any of the defendant's witnesses. That fact, coupled with the jury's temptation to reach conclusions early in a case, makes it vital for the defendant to have a compelling opening statement. If the defendant does not open strongly and waits until it is his turn to put on evidence to tell the jury about his best facts, it may very well be too late to convince the jury.

C. Less Is More

As was discussed in chapter 1, "less is more" is a characteristic of great trial lawyers and should not be forgotten on direct examination. Before you call a witness, he should meet the two following criteria: (1) the witness is the best person to support a theme from the opening statement, and (2) if he corroborates other testimony, the corroboration must be important and not unnecessarily cumulative of that of

---

6. Vicki Behenna assisted Joseph Hartzler in the prosecution of the case.
7. See *United States v. McVeigh* No. 96-CR-68, 1997 WL 266800 at *27–38 (D. Colo. May 21, 1997) (direct examination of Dr. Frederick Jordan).

If your case has many witnesses, take a digital photograph of each witness when she is in the witness room before she testifies. Having the photograph will help you immensely in closing argument. When you summarize an important part of a witness' testimony, you can project the photograph on your screen in the courtroom. This will aid the jury in recalling exactly which witness you are referring to and help you refresh the jurors' memory regarding her testimony.

any other witnesses. There is only one other type of witness you should call: the witness who is needed solely so that you can get evidence admitted. One example is a custodian of records. The custodian needs to be called if an agreement (i.e., stipulation) regarding his testimony cannot be obtained. For instance, if you need to get bank records admitted at a trial, one way to do this is to call an employee at the bank who can testify to their authenticity—a custodian of records.

Obviously, do not call a "bad" witness. If the witness' testimony does more damage than good, you should not call him in your case in chief but rather handle his testimony on cross-examination in your adversary's case. Since you have addressed the weaknesses of your case in your opening statement, the jury won't be surprised when the "bad" testimony comes out, and you will be better able to deal with the damaging testimony through cross-examination.

Example: Order of Plaintiff's Witnesses (Car-Wreck Trial)
1. Objective eyewitness to the accident
2. Officer who responded to the accident
3. Custodian of the plaintiff's medical records[8]
4. Plaintiff
5. Plaintiff's medical expert
6. Plaintiff's spouse (to corroborate plaintiff's pain and suffering).

---

8. Often the custodian of medical records does not need to be called because these records are admissible under Fed. R. Evid. 902(11) and (12) or similar state rules that allow for certification of medical records prior to trial.

Here, the plaintiff starts with his most powerful witness, an objective eyewitness who has no interest in the outcome of the case. The last witness, the plaintiff's spouse, is a memorable witness because the jury will be very sympathetic toward her description of the plaintiff's pain and suffering. She will also be difficult to cross-examine.

The order of the other witnesses simply shows a logical way to present the evidence. The defendant's order of witnesses might be as follows: (1) passenger in defendant's car (assuming no objective eyewitnesses available), (2) defendant's medical expert, and (3) the defendant.

2. Witness Preparation

A. Make the Witness Comfortable

Preparing your witness for the courtroom is the key to a successful direct examination. Most witnesses—except for experts, law-enforcement officers, and a few others—are not used to testifying in court. It is your task to make them feel comfortable so that you can elicit the facts you need for your case. Even in a civil case where many of the trial witnesses have given their depositions (a very formal and stressful situation), the courtroom setting is very different and far more intimidating to them.

Let's look at a trial from a witness' perspective. First, the witness never expected a trial. He has rightly assumed that almost all cases settle or end in a plea bargain. Now, his overriding emotion is fear. He sees the courtroom as a very formal setting. He is intimidated and feels that no matter what he says, he cannot please the attorneys on both sides and the judge.

One of the best ways to relieve a witness' anxiety is simply to ask him at the beginning of an interview prior to trial, "Before I start, what questions do you have for me? What can I do to

In a misguided attempt to ease the anxiety of a witness and gain his cooperation, an attorney often tells him that there is no need to worry about a trial because the case will get resolved. Although the odds greatly favor such a statement, there is nothing worse than to find the day of reckoning has come for trial, and the witness has lost all trust in you because of your prior assurances. Instead, inform the witness that you will do everything you can to resolve the case but do not guarantee that there won't be a trial.

make you more comfortable?" This may sound trivial, but it is amazing what a reaction these thoughtful questions will cause. The witness will be shocked that the busy lawyer, frantically getting ready for trial, starts the interview not with his own concerns but with those of the witness.

A good example occurred in the prosecution of a particularly cruel murderer. One of the key witnesses was a codefendant who had pled guilty to taking part in the murder, was already serving a thirty-year prison sentence, and had agreed to testify for the government against his partner in crime. A few weeks before trial, the witness had been brought over from the jail at 5:30 a.m. to the prosecutor's building and had been waiting several hours for space to open up in the interview room. Trying to build rapport with a vicious murderer is no easy task. The prosecution team asked the cooperating witness those very questions mentioned in the preceding paragraph.

It was the first time in months anyone with authority had talked to him like a human being. Although the prosecutors—due to regulations—could not make the witness more comfortable by loosening his handcuffs or getting him a cigarette, as he requested, the fact that the prosecutors cared went a long way toward building trust with the witness.

The same questions work for a civilian witness. Put him at ease, and show him you care. Next, tell the witness, "The only thing you need to do at trial is tell the truth." This instruction is important for two reasons. First, it relaxes the witness (unless the witness has something to hide). Many witnesses feel that they will be pressured to remember something they can't, use certain words the lawyer wants, and so forth. This instruction immediately calms them. Second, it protects your witness on cross-examination. If the cross-examiner suggests the witness has been told what to say, the witness simply answers, "I was told to tell the truth!"

In addition, the witness needs to be told why he is being called to testify. A good way of explaining this is to tell the witness that he is a small but necessary piece of a puzzle. This relieves the sense of burden the witness has that the case will fall apart if he forgets something. Also, it relieves a sense of responsibility if the witness feels reluctant to testify against the other side.

Finally, tell the witness that the direct examination will begin with a general question about what he saw or heard, followed by background questions. Tell the witness that you are going to start out with the background questions because they take little thought on his part and allow him to get used to the surroundings before moving to the specifics of his testimony.

B. Discuss Testimony in Context of Themes

In your preparation, discuss the witness' testimony in the context of themes. There is no need to tell the witness word for word what the theme is, but certainly convey the big ideas to the witness so she will have a good idea why she is being called and what information you need from her. For example, in a sexual harassment case, you might tell a witness who is a coworker of the plaintiff the following:

Example: Plaintiff's Attorney Preparing Witness (Sexual Harassment Trial)

Q: I know you cannot remember the exact words of all the inappropriate jokes you heard or the time and place in which they occurred. That is perfectly all right. All I want you to do is tell the jury—as best you can—what you remember about Mr. Smith's harassment of Karen [the plaintiff].[9]

Witnesses have an urge to try to memorize their answers and become frustrated if they can't remember the exact details of events you are asking them about. This urge can result in disaster if, when faced with the pressure of testifying in court, the witness tries to recall the exact words of a rehearsed answer. Give your witness the freedom to answer fully by incorporating the following phrases in your trial questions: (1) Tell the jury—*as best as you can,* (2) I know you may not remember word for word your conversation with Mr. Jones, but tell us *the essence* of your conversation, and (3) I realize the collision took place three years ago, but tell us *your best memory* of what happened.

At the end of the interview, tell the witness the categories of questions (themes) you will ask. This is an excellent way of reminding the witness what is needed at trial. In the above example, you would tell the witness that you are going to begin by asking a general question

---

9. Here, the defendant is referred to as "Mr." to show that he had the power (as indicated by the more formal reference) over the plaintiff who is humanized by using her first name.

Many great trial lawyers realize the importance of saving the witness' emotions for trial. For example, in an armed-robbery case, the highlight of the trial would probably be the victim's testimony about the moment when the defendant pointed a gun a few inches from her face and demanded her purse. In your witness interviews, it would be a mistake to ask the victim several times over the course of many meetings, "How did you feel when you were staring down the barrel of a gun?" If she recounts the horrific event multiple times prior to trial, she may very well get in the courtroom and matter-of-factly talk about the traumatic event.

about what she heard and some background questions; then, questions about inappropriate jokes in the workplace; and finally, finish with the plaintiff's reaction to them.

Finally, be aware that it is important not to get the witness too comfortable by going over the testimony too much, despite the great urge to do so. Some lawyers believe that for key witnesses, every question should be rehearsed in such detail and with such repetition that the result in court is testimony that appears flawless. Some attorneys even practice with the witnesses in a mock courtroom. However, multiple rehearsals can have unintended consequences.

With too many rehearsals, the witness often will appear nervous as she tries to remember *everything*. Also, a nonclient witness—depending on the jurisdiction—may be vulnerable on cross-examination to the subject matter of the rehearsals and to questions about the amount of time spent with attorneys in preparation for trial. Juries don't want to see witnesses who are more like actors speaking rehearsed answers in court.

So, how do you prepare the witness and preserve emotion? Ask the witness *once* about the trauma of having a gun pointed in her face, so you will know the answer (i.e., the description given can be used in the opening statement). In all subsequent interviews, talk about other parts of her testimony as much as you want, but don't revisit the details of the gun. By waiting until trial, you will have preserved the emotion of the moment for the jury.

C. Make Your Witness Unimpeachable on Cross-Examination

Your integrity is crucial from the beginning of the opening statement until the end of the closing argument. If you don't elicit damaging testimony on direct that is later brought out on cross-examination, your integrity and your case will suffer potentially devastating harm. Be aware of the adage that those who lie in small things will lie in big things. Jurors are perceptive and will quickly lose their trust in you if you are not seen as forthcoming and trustworthy.

During the witness interview, it is paramount that you prepare the witness for cross-examination. First, explain the dynamics of the trial to her. If opposing counsel is abrasive, let the witness know. Tell her if you expect the judge to interrupt and ask questions. Some witnesses are totally shocked by the judge's asking questions because they simply were not prepared.

Second, go over with the witness the expected topics of cross-examination. Then, explain that there is no need to worry, since you will discuss these areas on direct examination.

It is essential that you build a relationship of trust with the witness so that you can find out all her weaknesses. Explain to the witness that the courtroom is not the time for surprises for anyone. Ask the witness if she has given any statements to the other side that you don't know about, and ask if there are going to be witnesses who will testify to negative things that you as the attorney might not know. Stress to the witness that now is the time to come clean. Let the witness know that any issues she might be concerned about can be handled before trial, but once in trial, if an embarrassing or damaging issue comes up, it may be impossible to fix.

Finally, the two greatest downfalls for a witness on cross-examination are guessing at an answer and becoming argumentative with opposing counsel. The reasons for these downfalls are understandable. A witness believes that when she is on the witness stand, the jury expects her to know the answer. Certainly, the opposing lawyer is encouraging her through his questioning to guess at answers. The opposing lawyer is motivated to get your witness to guess since he knows he can use that guess later in cross-examination to destroy your witness' credibility by using questions grounded in common sense (this is discussed in a section of chapter 5: Logical Reasoning and Progression of Questions). To avoid guessing, teach your witness to say, "I don't know" and "I don't remember."

It is also human nature for a witness to become argumentative when opposing counsel suggests through his questioning that the witness is

Tell your witness the following: "You know what you know, and you don't know what you don't know. In other words, don't guess on cross-examination, but also don't let opposing counsel shake you from the truth." The witness will always smile when given this command. "What a relief!" the witness thinks. "All I have to do is tell what I remember, don't guess, and don't let the other attorney talk me out of the truth!" This is the heart of witness prepara-tion to trial. This guidance avoids the trap at many trials where a witness is asked on cross-examination in an accusatory tone, "Did you discuss your testimony with [opposing counsel] prior to trial?" The witness, fearing she has done something very wrong, lies and answers no or tries to minimize the substance of the interview.

lying or is very biased. A witness also feels it is unfair that she must answer yes to leading questions without having the opportunity to explain her answers. Opposing counsel is aware of this. His goal is to get the witness to become emotional. By making a witness emotional, the lawyer can show that the witness is biased for the other side or can cause the witness to make a mistake. Remind your witness to stay calm. Any confusion that opposing counsel creates can be cured on redirect examination.

Finally, explain to the witness that there is nothing improper about discussing her testimony with you prior

4.2. TECHNIQUES

Having examined the strategies behind choosing the order of witnesses and preparing the witness for trial, let's analyze the techniques of direct examination. Several skills need to be mastered to become an effective direct examiner.

1. How to Ask Nonleading Questions

A leading question is one that suggests the answer. In general, questions asked on direct examination cannot be leading (although leading is permitted and preferable under certain circumstances discussed below).[10]

---

10. Fed. R. Evid. 611(c). The rule provides, in part, "Leading questions should not be used on the direct examination of a witness except as may be necessary to develop the witness' testimony."

Example: Leading and Nonleading Questions
Leading
Q. It was sunny on Monday, wasn't it?

A. Yes.

The question suggests the answer yes, and, thus, it is objectionable under Federal Rule of Evidence 611(c).

Nonleading
Q. What was the weather like on Monday?

A. Sunny.

Q. On Monday, was it sunny, rainy, snowy, or cloudy? (better question)

A. Sunny.

The last question will survive a "leading" objection since the witness is provided several choices. By providing the witness choices, the attorney is able to direct the witness to the answer he wants without leading him. On the other hand, by simply asking a very open-ended question, such as "What was the weather?" the witness may answer that it was windy and hot when you needed the witness to say that it was sunny.

As a general rule, as long as the questions are not leading, their form can be as creative as the lawyer desires.

2. Ask a Variety of Short, Specific, Open-Ended Questions

A direct examination should contain a variety of short, specific, open-ended questions that seek relevant information. Such questions usually begin with one of the following words: *who, what, when, where, how,* or *why*. Questions that begin with these words do not suggest the answer to the witness and are the substance of direct examination. The questions should ask the witness to relate one fact in his answer.

Example 1: Witness of a Car Wreck
Q: **When** were you at the intersection of 9th and K Street?

A: It was on the afternoon of July 1.

Q: **Where** were you going after you arrived at that intersection?

A: I was walking to the supermarket across K Street.

Q: **What** color was the traffic light facing you?

A: Red.

Q: **How** do you know it was red?

A: I saw it change from yellow to red.

Q: **Why** were you looking at the traffic light?

Q: I was trying to cross the street and could not because the light changed to red before I could cross.

Example 2: Witness of a Robbery

Sometimes open-ended questions can be too vague. This example shows the difference between vague questions that begin with *who, what, when, where, how,* and *why* and better ones that are more specific because they include more facts. In the example, the witness saw the defendant rob her friend as they were walking on the sidewalk.

Vague: Where was the defendant?

Specific: Where was the defendant when you **first** saw him?

Vague: What did he do?

Specific: After he approached your friend, what did he **say** to her?

Vague: What happened next?

Specific: 1. When he approached your friend, what, if anything, was he **carrying** in his hands? [Answer: a gun in his left hand]
2. What did you see him do **with the gun** he was holding in his left hand?

3. Transitions

Every direct examination should have transitions—a word or phrase that moves the questioning along, often in a new direction. Transitions are essential because they direct the witness—and the jury—to the next topic you want to discuss. Some attorneys call this skill "sign posting" or "headlining." The transitions in the example below are in italics.

Example: Transitions

1. Now that we have discussed the color of the traffic light, *let me now direct your attention* to what you saw that was unusual as you tried to cross the street. What did you see?

2. I'd like to stop you right there for a moment and *return to your testimony* earlier today regarding the traffic light at the intersection. I forgot to ask you about . . .

3. *Let's fast-forward* to the time when the ambulance arrived at the intersection. Tell the jury what you saw the paramedics do.
4. *Let's return to your discussion* of the collision. Can you give us some details regarding the cars that collided?

Not only are transitions permissible, they are essential to create a coherent and free-flowing examination.

4. Commands

Many attorneys feel helpless on direct examination because they are under the mistaken belief that they cannot control the witness and are at the mercy of the witness' answers. Nothing could be further from the truth. It is the attorney's task to control the witness and develop the important information needed for the case. One such device is a command. The following should be used unhesitatingly when needed.

Example: Commands

1. Please speak up so all of us can hear you.
    If the witness still doesn't speak loud enough, walk up to the witness stand (ask the court for permission to approach the witness) and adjust the microphone so everyone can hear.
2. Ms. Smith, you need to slow down so that we can all understand you.
3. Ms. Smith, let me stop you right there. Before you discuss the robbery, let me ask you who you were walking with that night.
4. Ms. Smith, as you were pointing on the diagram, you had your back to the jury, and we could not see what you were pointing to. Please take a couple of steps back and do it again.

5. Looping

Another device is "looping." A looping question takes the answer the witness has just given and loops or incorporates it into the following question. By incorporating part of the witness' answer into the next question, an attorney is able to create a thread for the examination and repeat an idea several times so that the jury will remember it better. Although this is an effective technique, if overused, it will become a distraction and lose its effectiveness. There are two types of looping, simple and advanced. Simple looping will be discussed first. Below, the ideas that are looped are in boldface.

Example: Simple Looping (Joseph Hartzler) from *U.S. v. McVeigh*

Q. *When he [McVeigh] first arrived, where did he stay?*

A. *[Lori Fortier]: He stayed with us [Lori and Michael Fortier] approximately for a few weeks, and then he got his **own house**.*

Q. *When you [Lori Fortier] say he got his **own house**, what do you mean?*

A. *He **rented a house**.*

Q. *Where did he **rent a house**?*

A. *It was a **block house** out in Golden Valley, about 10 miles outside of Klingman. . . .*

Q. *And you referred to a **block house**. What's a block house?*

A. *Like a concrete-**block house**.*

Q. *During the time that McVeigh had **rented** this **block house** in 1994, did you ever visit him there?*

A. *Yes, we did.*[11]

Throughout the direct examination, one of the prosecutor's goals was to show that Lori Fortier knew the details about McVeigh's actions prior to the bombing. With simple looping, the prosecutor creates a thread so the jury and witness can follow the topic of the testimony.

While simple looping repeats a fact given in the preceding answer, advanced looping involves using the question to summarize an important answer (or answers) given prior to the preceding answer. This allows you to reintroduce important information at the critical time you need it to refocus the jury. Both simple *and* advanced looping should be in direct examination. Below, the looped answers are in boldface.

---

11. *United States v. McVeigh* No. 96-CR-68, 1997 WL 206800 at *15 (D. Colo. Apr. 29, 1997) (direct examination of Lori Fortier) (emphasis added).

Example: Advanced Looping (Joseph Hartzler)
from *U.S. v. McVeigh*

Q. *Did you have any further contact with either of them after that?*

A. Yes; in about three days, Tim **called** before Michael had got home.

Q. *Just tell us what the conversation was that you had with McVeigh.*

A. He **called to say that he had been in a wreck, that a car rear-ended him, and he was upset because the blasting caps were in the back of the car,** so he fled the scene. And he was calling to ask if Michael was home yet.

Q. *And did he tell you where he was calling from?*

A. No, not that I recall.

Q. *I may have gotten ahead of myself a little bit, or you did. You said that when you arrived at that motel room, McVeigh had some items other than the blasting caps; and I also think you said you guys brought something to the motel room.*

A. Yes, we did. We brought a stock from a Mini-14.

Q. *What is that?*

A. It's a rifle. It's a stock off of a rifle that we gave to Tim. And in turn, Tim gave us an AR-15 rifle; and he gave us some gold coins, also, or some copper coins.

Q. *Anything further?*

A. No.

Q. *Was there any discussion about that exchange?*

A. Yes. He said it was like good faith; that there was more like that where the guns were; that Mike could have more money by selling the guns.

Q. *After the call that you received from McVeigh in which he said he had been in a wreck with the blasting caps in the back of his car, did you have any further contact with McVeigh or with your husband?* [The prosecutor uses looping, not from the previous answer but from six and seven answers earlier to focus the witness and jury on the blasting caps McVeigh possessed.]

A. Yes. Michael showed up a few hours after that.

Q. *Just describe for us what happened.*[12]

---

12. *United States v. McVeigh* No. 96-CR-68, 1997 WL 206800 at *30–31 (D. Colo. Apr. 25, 1997) (direct examination of Lori Fortier) (emphasis added).

6. Leading Questions

Although leading questions are generally prohibited, they are necessary and preferable in certain situations. For a typical witness, they are acceptable to use in discussing a witness' background and other areas of testimony where there is no dispute. Don't be shy about leading questions when the subject matter of the testimony is not in dispute. If you do not use any leading questions, the pace of direct examination will get bogged down. Leading questions are also permissible when the witness or testimony presents special circumstances, for example, with (1) a hostile witness,[13] (2) a young child, (3) an elderly or sick witness, and (4) a witness who is testifying about sensitive areas.[14]

7. The Importance of Exhibits and Demonstrations

The importance of visual aids is twofold. First, visual aids allow your witness to explain in more detail what he has already testified to. Second, they allow the jury to both see and hear the information and, therefore, remember it better.

One of the easiest ways to incorporate visual aids is for a witness to testify from a diagram or a photograph. In a criminal case, this is very simple since a crime had to occur somewhere. For example, have the witness point on a diagram where he was when he saw the assault, where in his house the burglary occurred, where he was when he was robbed on the street corner, and so forth.

In civil cases, use discovery as an opportunity to take photos or make diagrams of anything relevant so that your witness can use them during his trial testimony.

---

13. A hostile witness is a witness who is identified with the opposing side. See Fed. R. Evid. 611(c).
14. Fed. R. Evid. 611(a) provides that a court "shall exercise reasonable control over the mode and order of interrogating witnesses . . . so as to make the interrogation and presentation effective for the ascertainment of the truth."

Example: Use of Illustrative Exhibit
(Patrick Ryan)[15] from *U.S. v. McVeigh*

The prosecution's first witness, Cynthia Lou Klaver, has just told the jury about the bomb's explosion. Now, the prosecutor allows her to explain visually the destruction she saw by using a pointer on a photograph (exhibit 944).

> Q. *All right. Now, may I ask you to look at exhibit 944. Now, can you see exhibit 944 on the screen?*
> A. *Yes.*
> Q. *And where are you?*
> A. *I'm—let me just—I'm right here, this—that's me walking down the sidewalk right there.*
> Q. *And what are you doing right there?*
> A. *I'm walking westward, away from the Water Board and the Murrah Building. I was going down this direction to see if I could find any Water Board employees. We weren't yet sure what had happened and who was where, so I was trying to find my coworkers.*
> Q. *What are you—you see the streets there beside you on the left?*
> A. *Yes.*
> Q. *What are we looking at on the ground there?*
> A. *There was twisted—twisted metal everywhere, glass all over, debris. It looked like a war zone to me when I stepped out. The ground was littered, covered.*[16]

The witness gets to tell what happened with the benefit of a powerful visual image. Her words, "It looked like a war zone to me when I stepped out," make her testimony unforgettable.

The use of visual aids in civil cases may at first blush appear more challenging, but it isn't. If it is breach of contract, have the witness talk about the contract and then explain it with the use of the contract itself, or, if the witness was the brunt of workplace harassment on the factory floor, have the witness explain on a diagram of the factory where the harassment occurred.

---

15. Patrick Ryan assisted Joseph Hartzler in the prosecution of the case.
16. *United States v. McVeigh* No. 96-CR-68, 1997 WL 200045 at *7–8 (D. Colo. Apr. 25, 1997) (direct examination of Cynthia Lou Klaver).

Whenever a witness talks about distances or sizes of areas, try and relate them to something in the courtroom. Here is an example.

Q. You testified that you saw the black car hit the white car. Can you tell us about how far away you were?

A. I'm not really sure, about 20 feet or so.

Q. Can you point to something in this courtroom that shows the jury about how far away you were when you saw the collision.

A. If I were at the witness stand, the collision would have occurred over there. [The witness points to the counsel table.]

Q. So, it is fair to say that the distance is the same as from where you are right now to plaintiff's counsel table.

A. Yes.[17]

Demonstrations are also very helpful. Actively look for these opportunities throughout an examination, and you will see them where you never saw them before.

Example: Demonstrations

Illegal Gun Possession Trial
Q. Officer, you testified earlier that when you approached the defendant in his car, you saw the defendant bend over and try and hide something with his hand.
   Your Honor, may the witness step down from the witness stand for a demonstration?
The court: Yes.
Q. Thank you. Now, to aid the jury, I want you to take this chair and assume it is the driver's seat of the car you stopped. Now, sit where the defendant was and reenact for the jury what you saw the defendant do when you walked up to his car.

Sexual Harassment Trial[18]
Q. Ms. Weeks, you testified that your supervisor put M&M's in the breast pocket of your shirt as

---

17. Check with the courtroom staff before trial to see if the judge has measured distances in the courtroom. If so, your next question would be: "Your Honor, for the record [i.e., record of trial for appeal], does the court have a measurement of the distance from the witness stand to the plaintiff's counsel table?" Likewise, if opposing counsel's witness conducts an in-court demonstration that is unintentionally helpful to you, interrupt the direct examination after the demonstration is complete and state, "May the record reflect the witness has just . . ." This not only makes the record for appeal more understandable but highlights the witness' error for the jury.

18. Facts modified from *Weeks v. Baker & McKenzie*, 74 Cal. Rptr. 2d 510 (Cal. Ct. App. 1998).

you were walking with him in the parking lot of the Sizzler restaurant. Your Honor, may the witness step down from the witness stand for a demonstration?

The court: Yes.

Q. Now, Ms. Weeks, for this demonstration, I want you to assume the role of your supervisor, and I will pretend to be you. Show the ladies and gentlemen of the jury what happened.

> As you begin to draft your direct examination outline, it is essential to create as many visual opportunities as possible for your witness to relate to the jury what happened.

Divorce Trial

Q. You testified that your husband chased you into the bathroom, you locked the door, and he tried to get in. Can you demonstrate for the jury how loud he was knocking on the door?

A. Yes. It was like this. [Witness repeatedly bangs her closed fist on the witness stand.]

Since only witnesses can testify, it is important that if the attorney is involved in the demonstration, all the important actions are done only by the witness.

The purpose of a visual aid or demonstration is not to repeat verbatim what has previously been said by the witness. Instead, it is an opportunity to show the jury what happened and provide greater details that you have not elicited from the witness.

4.3. ORGANIZATION AND STYLE OF DIRECT EXAMINATION

The order of your questions, like the order of your witnesses, is critically important.

1. Goal

The goal of direct examination is to incorporate the themes from your opening in your questions to the witness in a way that will have a lasting impact on the jury. One of the most common mistakes a lawyer makes is to assume a passive role on direct examination and simply let the witness talk. It is very tempting to do because it is easy and has been encouraged in law school. Thomas A. Mauet, in *Trial Techniques,* declares that "[e]ffective direct examinations are best achieved by using open-ended questions that elicit descriptive responses. . . . [Open-ended questions] minimize the presence of the lawyer. Remember during direct examinations the witness should be the center of attention."[19] The problem with this advice is that it puts a tremendous burden on the witness to convey the necessary information to the jury. In reality, if you use Mauet's technique, the witness often just rambles.

While it is true that at the critical part of his testimony the witness should be the center of attention, for the remainder of the direct examination, the attorney needs to be of equal importance with the witness. Ask specific, short, open-ended questions. By varying your tone of voice, pace of questions, and words used, and by mixing in looping and leading questions, the jury will know where the critical part is, pay better attention to the witness, and process the information more easily.

Mauet's theory would work if the witness knew the themes of your case and what was important for the jury to understand. But witnesses don't have the big picture like you do. Expert witnesses are the worst because they think they know what is important and will try to resist your guidance. By following Mauet's advice, you would give control of the delivery of information to a witness unaccustomed to conveying it in a clear manner or to an expert who has made the wrong assumptions. In the example at the end of this chapter, notice how attorney Joseph Hartzler shares the spotlight with the witness. He asks short and long questions, leading and nonleading questions, uses transitions, loops answers into the next question, interrupts the witness, and summarizes testimony—all in a successful effort to artic-

---

19. Thomas A. Mauet, *Trial Techniques* at 110 (6th Aspen ed. 2002). Mauet further states to use "short, open-ended and non-leading [questions], so that the witness does the talking and becomes the center of attention." He gives the example of asking, "What happened?" and "What did you see?" Although he instructs to "periodically mix the short, open-ended questions with more focused questions," the reverse is true as discussed more fully in the following paragraphs above.

ulate his themes to the jury through his witness. Obviously, it would be wrong to dominate a witness on direct examination. Hartzler does not make that mistake.

See yourself as the facilitator of information in the courtroom. It is your job to ask questions in such a manner as to keep the testimony interesting. By doing so, you will naturally share the stage with the witness.

2. Primacy, Recency, and Frequency

Lawyers often fail to employ the techniques of primacy, recency, and frequency. When beginning to draft questions, ask yourself what is the most important information this witness can provide related to a theme from the opening. The question seeking that information should be your last. This will achieve recency for the jury.

The way to achieve frequency is to have your witness first tell his relevant testimony in his own words and then again through the use of exhibits such as diagrams, photos, or documents. That way, the jury hears the important information at least twice.

As for primacy, almost every lawyer fails to take advantage of it sufficiently. The reason is that lawyers begin their direct examinations by asking the witness about his background information. There are two disadvantages to this. First, it ignores the rule of primacy, since the first thing you are asking about a witness is unimportant to the case. Second, remember that jurors don't know how a particular witness fits into the trial. By starting with the background, the jury is left in the dark about the significance of the witness' testimony until the background information is completed.

Example: Primacy *Not* Achieved (Patrick Ryan)
from *U.S. v. McVeigh*

The direct examination of this witness begins like that of almost every witness who testifies in court: there are background questions, but no context is given for the jury to determine what the witness will testify about.

> Courtroom deputy: *Thank you. Would you have a seat, please. Would you state your full name for the record and spell your last name, please.*

The witness: My name is Cynthia Lou Klaver, K-L-A-V-E-R.
Courtroom deputy: Thank you.
The court: Mr. Ryan?
Ryan: Thank you, Your Honor.
Q. *Good morning.*
A. *Good morning.*
Q. *Would you tell the members of the jury where you live.*
A. *Well, I live in Oklahoma City, 2219 Dawn Marie; middle of Oklahoma City.*
Q. *And do you have a family?*
A. *I do. I have a son who's almost one year old and a sister who lives with me in Oklahoma City.*
Q. *How long have you lived in Oklahoma?*
A. *Eleven years.*
Q. *Would you tell the jury what you do for a living in Oklahoma.*
A. *Well, in—I am an attorney—I have been an attorney . . .*
Q. *Where were you born and raised?*
A. *I was born and raised in Hutchinson, Kansas.*
Q. *And where did you go to high school?*
A. *Hutchinson High School.*
Q. *Graduating in?*
A. *1974.*
Q. *Where did you—what did you do after high school?*
A. *Went to college at Kansas State University and graduated in 1979 from Kansas State, Manhattan, Kansas.*
Q. *With a degree in?*
A. *English, BA in English.*
Q. *Now, did you go to law school after that?*
A. *I worked for a while, and then I went back to law school; and I went to Washburn University School of Law in Topeka, Kansas, and graduated from law school in 1985.*[20]

Although this will eventually be a strong direct examination, there is no primacy, and the jury is left to guess the relevance of this witness to the case. There is also too much discussion about the witness' background. See if the following would have been better.

---

20. *United States v. McVeigh* No. 96-CR-68, 1997 WL 200045 at *2 (D. Colo. Apr. 25, 1997) (direct examination of Cynthia Lou Klaver).

Q. Good morning.

A. Good morning.

Q. Did you witness anything unusual on the morning of April 19, 1995?

A. Yes, I was working next door to the Murrah Building when a bomb exploded.

Q. Before I get to what you saw and heard, let me back up and ask you briefly to describe your background. Where do you live?

A. Well, I live in Oklahoma City, 2219 Dawn Marie; middle of Oklahoma City. . . .

Q. Where did you go to high school?

A. I went to high school in . . .

In this second example, primacy is achieved, and the jury knows where the climax of the testimony will be and will be looking forward to it. In the first example, the jury has to wait several minutes before determining how the witness fits into the trial.

3. Delivery

Like with an opening statement, an attorney should vary his voice and the pace of delivery. Keep it interesting. When discussing a witness' background, be quick and efficient. When you get to the most important part of the testimony, however, make sure the pace of your questioning reflects the mood of the answers you are soliciting. Whether you pick up the pace or slow it down will depend on the nature of the testimony. For example, if you are eliciting answers from a robbery victim, the pace of questions might have a sense of urgency regarding the anxious moments right before the robbery when the witness fears he might get robbed. Then, when you discuss the robbery itself, you could slow down the questioning to reflect the drama of the moment. Tone of voice is also very important.

Where should you stand? In federal court, you must ask your questions from a podium in the center of the courtroom. State courts vary their requirements. Some require attorneys to remain seated at the counsel table. Other courts have fewer restrictions. If you are not bound by court rules to question from either standing at the podium or sitting at the counsel table, it is best to stand behind the counsel table out to the side (toward the jury box—if you won't be too close). The reason for this—as opposed to walking around the courtroom or standing close to the witness—is that it forces the witness to speak loud enough so that you and, more important, the jury can hear him.

4. Eye Contact

Eye contact with the witness is very important. Many attorneys make the mistake of being wedded to their notes when asking questions. For example, an attorney will ask a question, and while the witness answers, the attorney will check off the question he just asked and read ahead to see what the next question is. The problem is that when an attorney's head is down, he misses crucial facial expressions from the witness. Another problem of looking at notes is that it distracts the attorney from listening carefully to the answer that is being given. Also, he loses the connection with the witness, which is important when the critical part of the testimony is told to the jury. By maintaining eye contact with the witness, the attorney can show interest and convey confidence, which the witness almost always needs. The attorney can also make facial expressions and motion with his hand for the witness to slow down or stop. If the attorney loses eye contact with the witness, the witness will turn his attention elsewhere and might not see the gestures you make.

In addition, if the attorney looks down at his notes, he is also discounting the importance of the testimony. The jury will notice and take its cue: if the attorney is not paying attention to the answer, the jury will love the excuse that it does not have to pay attention either.

A similar problem is that some attorneys believe it is best for the witness to look at the jury when answering questions. While, in theory, this might make sense because it might create a bond between the witness and the jury, in the end, it is not wise. By looking at the attorney, the witness can tell when the attorney is ready to ask the next question. Otherwise, the witness will tend to give long rambling answers, and you will lose the flow of your direct examination. More important, many jurors feel that the testimony is staged when the witness directly looks at them. Likewise, although the trial experience of expert witnesses makes them feel comfortable looking directly at the jury, it is better for them to look at the attorney for the same reasons mentioned above.

It should go without saying that attorneys should not look at the jury during examination of witnesses. Some attorneys feel that they can emphasize a point to the jurors by looking at them briefly when an important question is asked or an important answer is given. Such a tactic backfires because the jurors see the attorney as trying to get an unfair advantage over his adversary by trying to communicate directly with them.

4.4 HOW TO PREPARE DIRECT EXAMINATION

1. Select Themes for the Witness

The themes from the opening statement provide the guide for your direct examination. What theme from your opening will your witness testify about? Once you have decided, develop a few major points for your direct examination, but use no more than three unless there are special circumstances.

2. Use an Outline

Many attorneys mistakenly think it is helpful to write out each question they intend to ask. While this may be beneficial prior to trial, in the courtroom it can be detrimental. Why? Detailed questions force you to lose eye contact with the witness and take your attention away from listening to the witness' answer. Have an outline instead.

In your trial notebook, you should have a section for direct examinations with a divider for each witness (for more on creating the trial notebook, see chapter 1). In the divider, have an outline that lists the ideas you will discuss with the witness. Ideas usually translate into answers, and that is a good way to structure your outline. For example, instead of having an outline of the questions you are going to ask, create an outline that has the answers you intend to elicit from the witness.

Also, have a list of exhibits that you need to discuss with the witness and/or admit into evidence. Put a line next to each exhibit, and check it at some point before you "pass the witness" for cross-examination.[21]

---

21. When an attorney concludes an examination—whether it be direct or cross—the attorney should say to the court, "Pass the witness" or "No further questions."

Example: Direct Examination Outline

The following is a good outline for a simple car-wreck case that will work for almost every witness in any trial. The answers are in parentheses.

I.   **Reason for testifying** (e.g., saw a car accident at the intersection of 9th and K Street)
II.   **Background**
      A.   **Education** (e.g., Ryder High School and BA from Kansas University)
      B.   **General personal info** (e.g., married with three children; elementary school teacher, etc.)
III. **Details of observations** (e.g., walking on sidewalk, saw black car run red light and hit white car in middle of intersection)
IV.   **Address important weaknesses** (e.g., witness was talking on cell phone but knew that light was red because the witness was trying to cross the street and had looked at signal)
V.   **Visual aids/exhibits** (e.g., witness explains in further detail what he saw by referring to diagram of intersection)
      A.   Diagram of intersection (exhibit 1)
      B.   Photos of damaged cars (exhibit 2)
VI.   **End memorably** (e.g., the crash was very loud, "glass everywhere," the driver screaming in pain was taken away on stretcher in ambulance)

Let's briefly look at each topic of the outline. As discussed earlier, it is important that your witness immediately explain in summary fashion why he is testifying. Otherwise, while you are trying to develop background information, the jury will be wondering how this witness is relevant. Be aware that your question to the witness will need to be fairly specific so the witness will know what information you are trying to elicit.

The second category, background, is basic but important. Courts allow you to develop briefly a witness' educational, professional, and family background. The reason is that the jury's judgment of the credibility of the witness is central to determining which side to believe.

Third, develop the details of the witness' observations. This is why the witness is testifying, so make it memorable. Keep in mind that, although you and the witness know the testimony inside and out, the jury is hearing it for the first time. Emphasize the important points.

Fourth, as with opening statements, acknowledge the weakness in your witness' testimony. After you finish your direct examination, you should feel that there is no important question that can be asked on cross-examination that has not been dealt with on direct. This topic is discussed in greater detail later in this chapter in section 4.5, "Difficult Problems on Direct Examination."

Fifth, after the witness has related the events, have him discuss the events in the context of exhibits or visual aids. This achieves the effect of frequency by allowing the jury to hear the important testimony again. It is also easier for the jurors to process the information, since now they can both see and hear the important information.

Sixth, you need to end memorably. Return to the details of the observation and ask a question that you have not asked before. Leave the jury with an unforgettable image.

> Don't distract from an important answer at the end of direct examination by going to the counsel table to check your notes or to ask cocounsel if you have forgotten to ask anything.
>
> The trick is not to wait until after your last question to confer with cocounsel. When you are approaching the end, but before you reach the climatic question, go—if you must—to the counsel table, ask if there is anything else that needs to be asked, and if you have left something out, ask it *and then* conclude by eliciting an important answer from the witness.

3. Use of Deposition or Videotaped Testimony

Under certain circumstances, if the witness is unavailable for a civil trial, you may use the written transcript or videotape of the witness' deposition. What constitutes "unavailable" varies from jurisdiction to jurisdiction.[22] If a witness is declared unavailable, however, great care

---

22. See, e.g., Fed. R. Civ. P. 32(a). One of many reasons a witness may be "unavailable" is that he is more than 100 miles from the place of trial and refuses to attend voluntarily.

needs to be taken in selecting the deposition excerpts. The strategies discussed in this chapter apply equally to the testimony of live witnesses and those testifying by deposition, so put your excerpts in the outline form discussed in this chapter. Don't forget to address weaknesses and end memorably.

Preferably, you will have a videotaped deposition. Create a seamless videotape or video feed on your computer that has the selected video clips. This takes a tremendous amount of time, but there is no quicker way to lose a jury's interest than to play an unedited videotape of a deposition that has unnecessary questions, pauses, and irrelevant testimony.

As a last resort, you can use the deposition transcript at trial. Nothing could be less persuasive. If you must, select from your office a person who resembles—or at least projects—the unavailable witness' demeanor. Then, read the questions from the transcript and have the witness read the selected answers from the witness stand. Avoid a stale recitation of the questions and answers. Likewise, don't have the stand-in be so animated that the testimony seems unduly staged.

4.5 DIFFICULT PROBLEMS ON DIRECT EXAMINATION

1. Getting More Details from the Witness

Often a witness will give you an answer, thinking it is complete, when the reality is that you need more details. Many attorneys freeze with the incomplete answer, not realizing how easy it is to get more information from the witness. At your disposal, you need to have the correct phrases that draw out needed details from the witness. These phrases are highlighted below in bold.

Example: Commanding Witness to Give More Details (Joseph Hartzler) from *U.S. v. McVeigh*

The following are two examples from *U.S. v. McVeigh*. The prosecutor needs more information than was given by the witness, Lori Fortier. Observe the techniques he uses.

> Q. *And do you know what his job—what McVeigh's job was?*
> A. *He worked out back.*

Q. *Meaning what?*
A. *He worked in the lumberyard part of the store. . . .*
Q. *And did you ever observe him make phone calls during this period of time?*
A. *He used the phone pretty regularly.*
Q. *Did you see whether or not he simply dialed direct, charging the calls to your phone, or did he have some other means to make phone calls?*
A. *He said he had a calling card, and he had memorized the number.*
Q. *Did you ever see the card actually?*
A. *No, I did not.*
Q. *Do you know what name that card was in?*
A. *No, I do not.*
Q. *Did he in any way **further describe** the card to you?*
A. *At one time he called on the card to see if it had any minutes left on it, so I thought it was like a prepaid calling card. That would be it.*[23]

Since leading questions are generally prohibited, there is a tendency to believe that the witness controls the flow of information and not the attorney. The opposite is true. If the witness is not forthcoming with details, keep asking the question in as many different ways as possible (which helps avoid the "asked and answered" objection) to get the information you need. If you have prepared the witness for trial, the witness will usually quickly understand what additional information you are seeking. The following are useful phrases to remember

1. Please explain.
2. Give the jury an example of what you mean.
3. Tell us some other details you remember.
4. Give us some specifics of what you mean.

---

23. *United States v. McVeigh* No. 96-CR-68, 1997 WL 206800 at *16 (D. Colo. Apr. 25, 1997) (direct examination of Lori Fortier) (emphasis added).

2. Refreshing Recollection

It is a nightmare for a young attorney when she asks her witness an important question, and the witness answers, "I don't remember." Fortunately, there is a simple way to solve this lapse of memory. Under Federal Rule of Evidence 612, a witness' memory can be refreshed by a writing. This can be the witness' prior statement, the witness' notes, or anything tangible. Simply follow the six steps in the following example.

Example: Refreshing Recollection

Attorney: Officer, tell the jury what part of the minivan was damaged when you arrived at the scene of the collision?

Officer: I don't remember.

Step 1: Determine if memory can be refreshed without directly asking witness

Attorney: Did you prepare an accident report on the day of the accident?

Officer: Yes.

Attorney: Did you list in that report the damage to the cars?

Officer: Probably.

Step 2: Confirm by asking witness

Attorney: Would that document refresh your recollection?

Officer: Yes.

[The attorney shows opposing counsel the accident report (if he has not seen it already) and approaches the witness stand after asking the court's permission.]

Step 3: Let witness read document

Attorney: Officer, I am showing you your accident report, which has been marked for identification only as exhibit 10. Take a moment and read your accident report to yourself. . . . Have you had a chance to read it?

Officer: Yes.

Step 4: Take document away from witness

[The attorney takes the document away from the witness and returns to the podium.]

Step 5: Ask witness if document refreshes memory

Attorney: Does your accident report refresh your recollection as to what part of the minivan was damaged?

Officer: Yes.

Step 6: Ask witness the original question that he could not answer

Attorney: What part of the minivan was damaged?
Officer: The rear bumper.

Refreshing a witness' memory on matters that a witness might naturally forget does not hurt the credibility of a witness. However, to the extent that the jury feels that his lack of memory is the result of failing to prepare for his testimony, then his credibility suffers.

3. Confronting Prior Convictions

In criminal trials, it is not unusual for witnesses for both the prosecution and defense to have prior convictions. The Federal Rule of Evidence that governs the use of prior convictions is somewhat complicated, but, in short, a witness may be impeached[24] with any felony conviction or any type of conviction (whether a felony or not) that involves proof or admission of an act of dishonesty or a false statement. In general, the conviction cannot be used for impeachment if more than ten years have elapsed from the date of the witness' release from confinement or the date of conviction if the witness did not go to jail.[25]

In attempting to refresh a witness' recollection, be careful not to rush and ask the question, "Is there anything that would refresh your recollection?" If the witness answers no, you are in a trap from which it is very difficult to escape. Most courts will not allow you to refresh a witness' recollection from a document he does not even remember writing (e.g., an accident report). Instead, as the above example illustrates, ask the witness if he has prepared or has seen a specific document, photo, or tangible object. This will remind the witness that there may be information in the item that will refresh his memory. The best way to avoid this problem is by having the witness review all of his documents before testifying.

How much a witness can be asked about the conviction varies among jurisdictions. For example, some jurisdictions allow an attorney

---

24. Impeachment is discussed at length in chapter 5. In short, it means to challenge the credibility of a witness.
25. Fed. R. Evid. 609 also provides that the convictions cannot be used if the court determines the prejudicial effect of the conviction outweighs its probative value.

simply to inquire if there is a prior conviction, while others allow an attorney to ask not only about the type of conviction (felony or misdemeanor) but what kind it was (e.g., drug distribution) and even how long a sentence the witness received. The wise practice is to ask the court at the pretrial conference for a ruling regarding the extent your witness can be cross-examined about the conviction.

At what point should you ask your witness about his prior conviction? Whether you are the prosecution or defense, it is best to weave the conviction into your examination and put it about two-thirds through your examination, where it is less noticeable.[26] Consistent with the theory mentioned in chapter 1 that jurors are making quick judgments about witnesses and evidence, it would be a mistake to mention the conviction at the beginning of the direct examination and have the jury filter the remainder of the testimony through the lens of a prior conviction. Allow yourself time to bring out the conviction; then, end on a strong note by getting back to the strengths of your witness' testimony. Likewise, when you are mentioning the conviction, maintain your credibility with the jury by addressing the problem with the proper sincerity (i.e., don't be flippant).

There is one caveat to the above rule. Many attorneys are scared they will forget to ask a witness about a conviction if they wait and question the witness about it two-thirds through the examination. The fear is well founded since it is hard to remember to weave the conviction into your other questions when your direct examination is well under way. The impact of the failure to take the sting out of a conviction by failing to bring it out on direct examination cannot be overstated. Having opposing counsel destroy the witness' credibility and yours by declaring on cross-examination that the jury has been misled (e.g., "The prosecutor never asked you about your felony conviction for rape, did he?") is a horrible moment at trial everyone wants to avoid. Consequently, attorneys often ask about a conviction at the be-

---

26. If you have a cooperating witness who is testifying pursuant to a plea agreement, such a fact is not a weakness like a prior conviction. In this case, it is a strength because the witness is taking responsibility for the crime in contrast to the defendant, who is forcing a trial. Thus, prosecutors often discuss plea agreements at the beginning of direct examination.

ginning of direct examination. If you choose to do this, ask about it matter-of-factly in your background questions.

4. Addressing Important Weaknesses

Almost all witnesses have a weakness. Their testimony may be inconsistent with something they have said—or failed to say and should have—prior to trial. Or they may be biased because they have a personal relationship with the side for which they are testifying. Perhaps they have prior criminal convictions or have been promised leniency by the prosecution for their testimony. In any of these situations, your goal is to build your questions on direct examination in such a way that the jury has no doubt they are telling the truth.

For example, if you are the prosecution and your star witness was high on crack cocaine at the time he saw the murder, one way surely to lose your case is to not address the issue of drug use on direct examination and have defense counsel hammer the witness with the information on cross-examination. When a witness' observations or memory is shaky, corroborate as many details as possible about what he saw. If a large part of his testimony can be corroborated by other testimony or evidence, you will have gone a long way toward making the witness' testimony unimpeachable.

Example: Addressing Important Weaknesses (Joseph Hartzler) from *U.S. v. McVeigh*

The following example shows how the prosecution dealt with Lori Fortier's previous lies about her knowledge of McVeigh's criminal activities.

> Q. *Who else did you lie to?*
> A. *My parents; Michael's parents; our friends, Matt and Michelle; Norma. Pretty much everybody we had contact with.*
> Q. *What lies did you tell these people?*
> A. *That we didn't think Tim [McVeigh] was involved.*[27]

---

27. *United States v. McVeigh* No. 96-CR-68, 1997 WL 206800 at *42 (D. Colo. Apr. 25, 1997) (direct examination of Lori Fortier).

A few moments later, the prosecutor asks Fortier about the moment she started to tell the truth, which was just prior to her testifying before the grand jury.

> A. We got a motel room in Oklahoma City, and we called like two FBI agents and had them come out to the motel.
> Q. Tell us what happened.
> A. They got there, and we told them that we wanted to correct our statements.
> Q. What caused you to want to change your statement?
> A. Because I had to testify the next day [before the grand jury], and I didn't want to have to lie on the stand. I wanted to like come forward and say what I knew. . . . [28]
> Q. Did you find it fairly easy to lie to the FBI agents in your meetings with them [these were previous meetings] in Kingman?
> A. No, not really, because all the whole time I wanted to tell the truth.
> Q. Why didn't you tell the truth?
> A. Because I was scared for my family.
> Q. And for yourself?
> A. Yes.
> Q. What were you afraid might happen to you?
> A. That like we might be prosecuted because we knew something about it. [29]

Observe how Hartzler has turned the weakness of lying into a strength. The witness has provided very believable explanations why she would have lied to everyone, including close family members; she was scared to death of being prosecuted for her involvement. Hartzler also asks her about the moment she started telling the truth, and she declares it was just before she would have to "take the stand" before the grand jury and take an oath. By asking this question, Hartzler gives the jury another reason to believe her trial testimony: it is given under oath, while the witness' prior lies were not under the solemnity of an oath and were told for self-preservation.

---

28. *United States v. McVeigh* No. 96-CR-68, 1997 WL 206800 at *43 (D. Colo. Apr. 25, 1997) (direct examination of Lori Fortier).
29. *United States v. McVeigh* No. 96-CR-68, 1997 WL 206800 at *46 (D. Colo. Apr. 25, 1997) (direct examination of Lori Fortier).

4.6 REDIRECT EXAMINATION

In most courtrooms, the sequence of examination goes as follows: direct examination, cross-examination, and then redirect examination. However, some judges allow for recross after redirect.[30]

The purpose of redirect examination is to clear up any confusion created on cross-examination. Consequently, it is limited to topics raised on cross-examination. It is not a time to be defensive, however. Instead, redirect is a special opportunity for an attorney to highlight important themes from a witness' testimony and to end on an unforgettable note for the jury.

The most common mistake attorneys make is to conduct redirect examination on too many topics in an effort to clear up *all* the confusion from cross-examination. Limit yourself to only the most important points that have been raised. By doing so, you will further minimize the minor points you don't discuss, and you will have the last word on the important ones.

Having said that, there are occasions when nothing is left to clear up, and the wiser practice is not to conduct a redirect examination. This advice almost always applies if the judge allows recross, since if you engage in redirect, opposing counsel will be allowed to cross-examine your witness again and have the last word.

Where redirect is the last round of questioning, however, it should be embraced as a useful tactic. There is always something discussed on cross-examination that will give you the chance to hammer home an important point again on redirect examination. In both examples below, the attorney on redirect clears up the confusion left after cross-examination and also shows the jury that opposing counsel was unfair to the witness.

Example 1: Plaintiff's Attorney Allowing Plaintiff to Explain on Redirect (Car-Wreck Trial)

Attorney: Do you recall on cross-examination that [opposing counsel] asked you a series of questions about what happened in the hospital after the collision?

---

30. Fed. R. Evid. 611(a) provides that the court may exercise reasonable control over the mode and order of interrogating witnesses.

Witness: Yes.

Attorney: You were asked about your last day there. Do you remember that question?

Witness: Yes.

Attorney: You answered that you also wanted to explain how you have suffered in addition to your stay in the hospital but you were cut off. I would like to give you that opportunity. Explain to the jury what you wanted to say about your additional suffering.

Witness: My life has been changed forever. I can no longer play with my children . . .

Example 2: Correcting Confusion Created by Opposing Counsel's Cross-Examination

Attorney: On cross-examination, do you recall being shown a statement in your deposition?

Witness: Yes.

Attorney: And [opposing counsel] read a portion of that deposition that implied that you had previously testified that the light was green instead of red as you have testified today?

Witness: Yes.

Attorney: I am now showing you the entirety of page 19 from your deposition. Read along silently as I read lines one to three. Isn't it a fact that you said, "the light was green and then **turned** red?

Example 3: Letting Witness Explain (Joseph Hartzler) from *U.S. v. McVeigh*

Examples 3 and 4 are excerpts from the redirect examination of Lori Fortier. Observe how the prosecutor is able to clear up confusion left by cross-examination and also assert his themes of the case to the jury through his questioning.

> Q. *Miss Fortier, Mr. Jones asked you about the interview you had with two FBI agents in the motel room in Oklahoma City on May 17.*
>
> A. *Yes.*
>
> Q. *And you were going to explain why that was, to use your phrase, "cut short." Could you do that?*

A. Yes. Because I talked, I referred—I talked with my attorney, and then we decided to meet with them later.[31]

The prosecutor begins his redirect examination by allowing his witness to explain an answer that she was unable to do on cross-examination. That is, she cut her interview with the FBI short because she wanted to talk to her attorney. Then, after talking with her attorney, she met with the FBI again.

If the issue is important, redirect is the perfect opportunity to allow your witness to explain an answer that opposing counsel has prevented through the use of leading questions. In addition, it is a chance to make opposing counsel seem unfair for not allowing the witness to answer fully during cross-examination.

Example 4: Defusing Opposing Counsel's Suggestions (Joseph Hartzler) from *U.S. v. McVeigh*

Here, Hartzler skillfully defuses opposing counsel's suggestion on cross-examination that the witness was basing her knowledge about McVeigh's actions on reports in the media instead of on her personal knowledge.

Q. Mr. Jones asked you about knowledge and information you acquired from newspaper articles and information you heard from friends. You recall that series of questions?

A. Yes.

Q. Do you have any difficulty, as you testified here today, and yesterday, distinguishing between what you heard and read and what you know from your own firsthand information?

A. No.

Q. What you testified to was based on what you know from your own information, or what McVeigh or your husband told you?

A. Yes.

Q. Prior to your disclosure of the soup-can incident to federal agents and prosecutors, had you read anything

---

31.   *United States v. McVeigh* No. 96-CR-68, 1997 WL 209726 at *17 (D. Colo. Apr. 30, 1997) (redirect examination of Lori Fortier).

about that or heard anything about that from friends or in the news?

A. *No.*

Q. *Prior to your disclosure that McVeigh described the bomb as a shape charge, had you heard that phrase from any friends or read anything about that phrase in the newspaper?*

A. *No.*

Q. *Prior to your disclosure to federal prosecutors and federal agents about the letter that you and your husband received saying McVeigh was prepared to take action, had you heard anything or read anything in the news about a "take action" letter?*

A. *No.*

Q. *Prior to your disclosure to federal agents and prosecutors that McVeigh had said he would use sausage explosives inside the barrels, had you heard anything or read anything in the news about sausage explosives?*

A. *No.*

Q. *Prior to your disclosure to federal agents about the pipe bomb incident in the summer of 1994, had you read anything or heard any news about a pipe bomb incident involving McVeigh?*

A. *No.*

Q. *Prior to your disclosure to federal officials about the use of anhydrous hydrazine, had you read anything in the newspaper or heard any news about McVeigh's use of anhydrous hydrazine?*

A. *No.*

Q. *Prior to your disclosure to federal officials about McVeigh's being in your living room and diagramming a bomb that he would use in Oklahoma City, had you read anything or heard any news about McVeigh diagramming a bomb?*

A. *No.*[32]

Recognize Hartzler's brilliant series of questions that summarize the most important points of Fortier's direct testimony again on redirect. He uses redirect not just to gain further information but, more

---

32. *United States v. McVeigh* No. 96-CR-68, 1997 WL 209726 at *18–19 (D. Colo. Apr. 30, 1997) (redirect examination of Lori Fortier).

important, to persuasively convince the jury of McVeigh's guilt through his questioning. By using a persuasive tone of voice in his "questioning," Hartzler delivers a short closing argument in the middle of the trial. Realize that on redirect, judges are more lenient about leading questions, since the witness needs to be guided to the areas of cross-examination that will be covered on redirect. The preceding example and the one below show how Hartzler takes advantage of this leeway.

> Q. *Mr. Jones asked you about a number of meetings we've had; and indeed, we've met a number of times—*
> A. *Yes.*
> Q. *—is that not true? Spent many hours together going through questions?*
> A. *Yes.*
> Q. *Is there one thing that I have told you to do, one directive I've given you at every meeting we've had?*
> A. *Yes.*
> Q. *Tell the jury.*
> A. *Always tell the truth.*
> Q. *Nothing further.*[33]

Hartzler ends his redirect on a high note. He deflates opposing counsel's suggestion on cross-examination that Fortier is telling the jury what the prosecutor has told her to say. Observe how precise Hartzler's questions have been throughout redirect. This is not the time to explore new issues and muddy the waters. Instead, after hours and hours of cross-examination, Hartzler asks only twenty-nine questions on redirect.[34] He accomplishes three important tasks: (1) lets the witness explain an important answer that was cut short, (2) uses opposing counsel's suggestion that Fortier was not testifying from personal

---

33. *United States v. McVeigh* No. 96-CR-68, 1997 WL 209726 at *19 (D. Colo. Apr. 30, 1997) (redirect examination of Lori Fortier).
34. Included in the twenty-nine questions was also a series of questions to clear up confusion about whether Fortier had told federal agents or prosecutors certain things she saw McVeigh do, such as having in his possession blasting caps contained in Christmas wrapping paper. See *United States v. McVeigh* No. 96-CR-68, 1997 WL 209726 at *18 (D. Colo. Apr. 30, 1997) (redirect examination of Lori Fortier).

knowledge to summarize the most important things she heard or saw McVeigh do, and (3) rehabilitates Fortier from the suggestion that she is not telling the truth but instead telling the jury what prosecutors want her to say.

4.7 COMMON MISTAKES ON DIRECT EXAMINATION

The most common mistakes made on direct examination are discussed below.

1. Not Simplifying Testimony for the Jury

Throughout the trial, you need to put yourself in the shoes of the jurors. As an attorney, you have been living and breathing the case for a long time. At trial, however, you must remember that jurors are processing all this information for the first time. Ideas need to be repeated, difficult terms need to be defined, and visual aids need to be used to help jurors process the information easily.

For example, attorneys should not allow witnesses to use language so complex that it is not understood by the jury or else makes no sense.

Example: Complex Language

A police officer will often testify using police jargon. *Officer: We initiated a stop and ordered the subject to exit his vehicle.* Instead, remind the officer before she takes the stand to use everyday words. *Officer: We pulled the suspicious car over and ordered the driver to get out of his car.*

If the officer uses police jargon on the stand, simply have her explain what she is saying to the jury. *Officer: We initiated a stop and ordered the subject to exit his vehicle. Prosecutor: Officer, explain to the ladies and gentlemen of the jury what you mean when you say "we initiated a stop."*

Expert witnesses are notorious for using complicated words. Remind the experts before they take the stand and during their testimony to explain what they mean so the jury can understand, and you will win friends with the jurors by making the testimony more understandable and unforgettable for them.

2. Not Addressing Important Weaknesses Completely

As mentioned earlier, when you finish your direct examination, you should feel that there is nothing opposing counsel can ask on cross-examination to hurt your case that you have not already addressed. The mistake of not addressing weaknesses completely is made because an attorney has a naive hope that opposing counsel may not ask about the weakness during cross-examination. Occasionally, opposing counsel will be so bad that this strategy will work. However, experience shows that the more reasonable approach is to bring out the important weaknesses on direct examination because if you do not and the other side does, your integrity in the courtroom will suffer, and you may not be able to repair it. Obviously, this strategy will sometimes cause you to discuss weaknesses on direct that opposing counsel has not discovered. However, almost every weakness can be turned into a positive, and by dealing with the issue on direct examination, you will build trust with the jury and be far ahead of opposing counsel in the jury's eyes.

3. Not Controlling the Witness

Often, attorneys feel that since they cannot "lead a witness," all questions must be open-ended. However, "what happened next?" is the enemy of a successful direct examination. The problem is that often the witness doesn't know how to answer such a broad question. Moreover, the broad question suggests a broad and rambling answer. Beginning attorneys ask this question because it relieves them of the burden of having to ask a specific question. However, such questions give control to the witness since the witness is free to answer any way he chooses. When an attorney cedes control to the witness, he is no longer conveying his themes of the case through the witness.

The other problem is that once the beginning attorney realizes that the "what happened next?" question has failed, he resorts to asking leading questions to elicit the information he needs.[35]

---

35. Generally, the beginning attorney will ask leading questions that begin with a form of the verb "to be" (e.g., "Was the traffic light red?").

Consequently, ask specific nonleading questions, use transitions, mix in some leading questions, and use commands so that the witness will provide the jury the specific information you need for your theme in your opening statement.

4. Not Listening to Answers

Routinely, attorneys will silently read their next question while the witness is answering the previous question. The witness occasionally may not answer the question as intended. If the attorney is not listening to the answer, he is unable to have the witness give more details or correct the mistake.

Example 1: The Importance of Listening to Witness' Answer (Joseph Hartzler) from *U.S. v. McVeigh:*

In this example, the prosecutor asks the witness to describe a time when she saw McVeigh explode a pipe bomb in the mountains. Instead of silently reading the next question, however, the prosecutor notices that the witness is not being clear in her answer regarding exactly who is involved.

> Q. *Describe that experience for us.*
> A. *We drove to an area between Golden Valley and Laughlin, Nevada. It's a mountain range called Union Pass, and we walked up about a mile, maybe two miles into the mountains.*
> Q. *You've been saying "we." Can you tell us who you're talking about?*
> A. *Me, Michael, and Tim [McVeigh]. We walked into the mountains, and Tim put it [pipe bomb] under a boulder and set it off.*[36]

Example 2: The Importance of Listening to Witness' Answer (Joseph Hartzler) from *U.S. v. McVeigh:*

Below, the prosecutor—by listening—is able to correct a mistake made by the witness.

---

36. *United States v. McVeigh* No. 96-CR-68, 1997 WL 206800 at *17 (D. Colo. Apr. 29, 1997) (direct examination of Lori Fortier).

Q. *Just a moment ago, you said that the next time you saw him was in November. And now you said that you purchased your Jeep on Halloween.*

A. *I'm sorry. It was October.*[37]

5. Not Creating Themes for the Witness

Resist the urge simply to have the witnesses tell their story. Given this kind of freedom, witnesses can easily get sidetracked from the themes of the case. Before their testimony, explain the themes or topics you want them to discuss and have the witnesses stick to them during trial.

4.8 EXPERT WITNESS

For the most part, expert witnesses are just like any other witness. The essential difference is that experts can give specialized opinions and can comment on the testimony or expected testimony of an opposing expert. Moreover, since an expert witness is one who has certain knowledge that will assist the jury, extra care is needed in asking the appropriate background questions to qualify the witness as an expert under the Federal Rules of Evidence and to ensure that the witness is understood by the jury.[38]

---

37. *United States v. McVeigh* No. 96-CR-68, 1997 WL 206800 at *27 (D. Colo. Apr. 25, 1997) (direct examination of Lori Fortier).

38. Fed. R. of Evid. 702 provides the following: "If scientific, technical, or other specialized knowledge will assist the trier of fact to understand the evidence or to determine a fact in issue, a witness qualified as an expert by knowledge, skill, experience, training, or education, may testify thereto in the form of an opinion or otherwise. . . . Rule 104(a) provides that the court shall determine whether a witness is qualified to testify.

Be careful of long narrative answers (testimony given without the customary question-and-answer format) given by your expert. This often happens because experts feel a need to lecture the jury. Although narrative answers are often allowed for experts, you need to maintain control through your questions so you can elicit the facts that you need, not what the expert thinks is necessary.

In federal court and most state courts, an expert, to testify, must meet certain qualifications as established by the Supreme Court in *Daubert v. Merrell Dow Pharmaceuticals, Inc.,* 509 U.S. 579 (1993). Under *Daubert,* a trial judge must make a preliminary assessment whether the reasoning or methodology underlying the testimony is scientifically valid and whether that reasoning or methodology can be properly applied to the facts in issue.[39] This determination is made prior to the witness' testimony.

Even if the court has determined prior to the witness' testimony that she is qualified, your background questions need to be detailed so that the jury will see the witness as someone with specialized knowledge. During the background questions, elicit the most important parts of the witness' education, special training, board certifications, published works, and experiences handling the type of issue in question. Many attorneys get bogged down in the details of an expert's background. Your questions need to be specific. Saying "Tell the jury about your qualifications" is a sure way to put everyone to sleep.

When asking the expert her opinion, the form of your question can help strengthen the importance of the answer. For example, in the *Simpson* criminal trial, a significant issue was whether the gloves found at the crime scene (Bundy) and O. J.'s home (Rockingham) could have become smaller because of their exposure to the elements. This was an important issue since they did not appear to fit O. J. when he tried

---

39. Pertinent considerations in making this determination are whether a theory or technique can be (and has been) tested, whether it has been subjected to peer review and publication, the known or potential rate of error, and whether the theory or technique is generally accepted. Unless a *Daubert* challenge is raised by opposing counsel, there is no need to go into all the details to satisfy *Daubert.* Generally, if a *Daubert* challenge is made, a hearing will be held outside of the jury to determine if the witness is qualified.

them on in court. See how the prosecutor handled this issue well in questioning the glove expert.

Example: Asking the Expert His Opinion
(Christopher Darden) from *People v. Simpson*

Darden: Mr. Rubin, given your expertise in manufacturing and designing gloves, your own personal experience with wet gloves, your own personal experience in trying to manipulate gloves back into their original position after they have been wet, do you have an opinion as to how close we can come to reshaping the Bundy and Rockingham gloves back to their original condition?

Cochran: Your Honor, I object. That question was asked before, Your Honor. . . .

The court: Overruled.

The witness: I don't think that those gloves in that condition could get back closer to 90, 90 percent of their original size at this point in time.[40]

If your witness is a doctor, courts generally require that the opinion be based on a "reasonable degree of medical probability" (or "certainty"). So, either have that language in your ultimate question or, better yet, declare to the doctor in a preliminary question that the jury will assume her opinions are based on a "reasonable degree of medical probability" unless she tells them differently.

Now, let's look at a more detailed excerpt of a direct examination of an expert.

Example: Direct Examination (Patrick Ryan)
of Forensic Pathologist from *U.S. v. McVeigh*

The following are excerpts of the prosecution's examination of Dr. Frederick Jordan, a forensic pathologist. The first excerpt shows the detail of the background questions that are needed for an expert to ultimately give his opinion. Notice that whenever the witness uses a word or phrase the attorney believes the jury does not understand, the witness is asked to explain it.

---

40. *People v. O. J. Simpson* No. BA097211, 1995 WL 366155 at *24 (Cal. Super. Ct. June 16, 1995) (direct examination of Richard Rubin).

Qualifying Witness as an Expert

Q. All right. Now, after you graduated from medical school in 1966, did you attend a residency or internship of some type?

A. Yes. . . . And I did a three-year residency in anatomic and clinical pathology, which is learning to do—interpret surgical biopsies, do autopsies, and run a clinical laboratory. . . . [A]nd following that residency in Maine, I . . . did a two-year fellowship in forensic pathology and legal medicine.

Q. Now, for those of us who aren't doctors, could you explain for us in laymen's terms what you mean or what the term means "forensic pathologist"? [**Attorney asks for explanation.**]

A. Pathology is the study of disease, basic study of disease, how disease presents itself, how it manifests itself, how you make the diagnosis. And forensic pathology is . . .

Q. What are you trying to determine when a—when you, as a forensic pathologist or state medical examiner, examine a body following a criminal act or an act involving unusual circumstances? What is your objective?

A. Basically our objective is to determine the identification, to recover any evidence that may be present on or around that body . . . to try to determine the cause of that death. . . .

Q. In terms of cause of death, what does that mean? [**Attorney makes sure the jury understands the term.**]

A. Cause of death is what caused—what happened to the person, why did they die. . . .

Q. All right. Now, are you licensed to practice medicine in Oklahoma?

A. Yes, sir.

Q. Are you licensed in any other states?

A. Yes, sir.

Q. What states are those?

A. I'm licensed in my old home state of Maine, in Oklahoma, in Arizona, and in Virginia.

Q. Are you a member of any hospitals, on the hospital staff?

A. Yes. I'm on the courtesy staff at our teaching hospitals, at our university, and emeritus staff at Columbia Presbyterian Hospital in Oklahoma City.

Q. Do you teach as well as . . . ?

A. Yes, I'm clinical professor of pathology at the University of Oklahoma Health Sciences Center and assistant clinical professor of pathology. . . .

Q. Now, are you board certified in any fields?

A. Yes, sir.

Q. And what fields are you board certified in?

A. Anatomic pathology and forensic pathology.

Q. Explain to the jury briefly what is meant by the term "board certification." **[Attorney asks for explanation.]**

A. In order to become board certified . . .

Q. All right. Now, Dr. Jordan, have you been recognized and honored throughout your career?

A. Occasionally, yes.

Jones: If Your Honor please, I know Dr. Jordan is modest. I'm well familiar with him, stipulate to all his qualifications. He's an eminently qualified pathologist.

The court: All right.

Ryan: I'll accept that stipulation, Your Honor.[41]

Through your questions, show the jury that your expert can be trusted. While these excerpts do not reveal all the questions asked of the expert about his background, we can see that the prosecutor brings out the relevant education of the witness, including teaching responsibilities and board certifications. In addition, whenever a difficult term is used, such as *board certification,* the witness is asked to explain it.

Although in this case, after a lengthy background examination, the defense attorney interrupted to offer a stipulation, many attorneys will interrupt earlier in the examination to try and prevent the jury from hearing about the witness' extensive qualifications. If this happens to you, don't agree to the stipulation until you have elicited all that you need from the witness. Simply respond, "Your Honor, I will be brief, but I believe it is important for the jury to hear a little more about the witness' qualifications."

Asking Expert His Opinion

Q. How many bodies were removed from the Alfred P. Murrah Building?

---

41. *United States v. McVeigh* No. 96-CR-68, 1997 WL 266800 at *27–29 (D. Colo. May 21, 1997) (direct examination of Dr. Frederick Jordan) (emphasis added).

A. 163.

Q. *And how many of these bodies did you conduct an autopsy on?*

A. *We only autopsied, I think, 13.*

Q. *And why did you autopsy 13, as opposed to the 163?*

A. *We autopsied ones in which we were not clear as to what the manner of death was from the initial examination.*

Q. *Now, what is an autopsy in a very general sense?* [**The attorney asks the witness to explain a scientific term.**]

A. *Autopsy is just simply a systemic examination of an individual where you open that individual and examine all the organs of the head, neck, chest, abdomen, and pelvis.*

Q. *And with respect to the other 150, it was not necessary to do that?*

A. *That's correct.*

Q. *Cause of death was obvious [homicide]?* [**The attorney asks expert for opinion.**]

A. *We believe that's correct, yes.*[42]

This excerpt shows the prosecutor asking the expert his opinion, whether the deaths were caused by homicide or were accidental. The question is leading and certainly does not have the buildup that Christopher Darden used in the example with the glove expert. Here, however, the prosecutor knows that this is not a contested issue and simply elicits the information through a short leading question. The prosecutor later will introduce through this witness the death certificates for the victims, listing the expert's conclusions of homicide.

Use of Exhibit with Expert

Q. *Dr. Jordan, in connection with your duties as the chief medical examiner, did you also, you and your investigators who were in the building, attempt to determine the location where each of these persons was at the time of the blast?*

A. *Yes, sir.*

Q. *And did you do that?*

A. *Yes, we did.*

---

42. *United States v. McVeigh* No. 96-CR-68, 1997 WL 266800 at *32 (D. Colo. May 21, 1997) (direct examination of Dr. Frederick Jordan).

Q: Now, if I could ask the marshal there to please place on the board the next chart, which is already in evidence. It's exhibit 952. This is a chart of the 1st floor.

Using visual aids with all witnesses is important, but with experts it is paramount so that jurors can easily process information. Here, the prosecutor provides the witness a chart so he can explain where each body was recovered.

Although it was not necessary with this witness because there was no forensic pathologist for the defense, if there is an expert for the other side, you would also ask your expert if he disagreed with the conclusions of that expert and why.

4.9 ANALYSIS OF DIRECT EXAMINATION (JOSEPH HARTZLER) FROM *U.S. V. MCVEIGH*

The skills and strategies discussed above apply equally to civil and criminal trials. The only significant difference between the two types of trials is that in criminal trials, witnesses are more likely to have prior criminal convictions that will need to be addressed. However, this is simply a weakness like any other that needs to be taken up during direct examination. The following are excerpts from the direct examination of Lori Fortier, one of the key witnesses for the prosecution. The examination incorporates many of the skills and strategies discussed in this chapter.

1. Establishing Background

Direct Examination by Mr. Hartzler
Q. *Could you tell us where you presently live.*
A. *I live in Kingman, Arizona. . . .*
Q. *Were you born and raised in that area?*
A. *Yes, I was.*
Q. *And did you graduate from high school in Kingman?*
A. *Yes, sir, I did.*
Q. *How many high schools are there in the Kingman area?*
A. *When I was going to high school, there was one. There are two now.*
Q. *What year did you graduate?*

A. *January of 1990.*
Q. *Are you married?*
A. *Yes, I am.*
Q. *What is your husband's name?*
A. *Michael Fortier.*[43]

These are typical background questions. The direct would have been more understandable for the jury if the prosecutor had started off by asking, "What is one of the important things you remember about your interactions with Timothy McVeigh?" The witness would have answered, "He told me about his plot to bomb a federal building in Oklahoma City." After the jury understood the reason for calling the witness, it then would have made sense to ask the above background questions.

2. Letting Witness Approximate

Q. *How long **approximately** had he had that job?*
A. *Probably not even a month.*
Q. *Do you recall when McVeigh left, **approximately**?*
A. *A couple weeks after he showed up.*[44]

The prosecutor gives the witness plenty of comfort room on the stand by not asking for exact time periods but using the word "approximately."

3. Looping

Q. *How long approximately did he stay in the Kingman area?*
A. ***Until late summer of '93.***
Q. *So it was for **a number of months**?*
A. *Yes.*

---

43. *United States v. McVeigh* No. 96-CR-68, 1997 WL 206800 at *9–10 (D. Colo. Apr. 29, 1997) (direct examination of Lori Fortier).
44. *United States v. McVeigh* No. 96-CR-68, 1997 WL 206800 at *13 (D. Colo. Apr. 25, 1997) (direct examination of Lori Fortier) (emphasis added).

> Q. During those **number of months**—*that would have been sometime from spring **until late summer of 1993**—did you on occasion see McVeigh?*
>
> A. *Yes.*
>
> Q. *Approximately how often did you see McVeigh? And I'm just going to use the shorthand to say it's through the **summer of '93** that he was there. Approximately how often did you see him through the **summer of '93?***
>
> A. *Approximately monthly.*
>
> Q. *For what purposes?*
>
> A. *Weekly, I'm sorry.*
>
> Q. *For what purposes did you see him?*
>
> A. *Just socializing.*[45]

McVeigh made several trips to Kingman to visit Lori and Michael Fortier. The prosecutor uses questions that loop previous answers into his questions to distinguish McVeigh's visit in the summer of 1993 from the other visits so the jury won't be confused. He also uses "looping" to highlight for the jury that McVeigh stayed for several months during this visit.

4. Corroborating Details

> Q. *Do you recall your next contact with McVeigh after that telephone call?*
>
> A. *Yes.*
>
> Q. *When was it, approximately?*
>
> A. *Approximately the first part of February.*
>
> Q. *What year?*
>
> A. *'94.*
>
> Q. *How is it that you recall that approximate date?*
>
> A. *Because I remember that Tim [McVeigh] was not there for the Super Bowl of 1994.*
>
> Q. *How do you remember that?*
>
> A. *Because the Bills were playing in the Super Bowl, and that was his favorite team.*
>
> Q. *Buffalo Bills?*

---

45. *United States v. McVeigh* No. 96-CR-68, 1997 WL 206800 at *14 (D. Colo. Apr. 25, 1997) (direct examination of Lori Fortier) (emphasis added).

A. Yes.

Q. Do you recall who they played?

A. They played the Cowboys.

Q. And you recall watching the game?

A. Yes, I do.

Q. He was not there in that area?

A. No, he was not.

Q. All right. How do you recall when he arrived?

A. Because he was there for our daughter's first birthday party, which would have been Valentine's Day of 1994.[46]

The prosecutor knew that Fortier's credibility was going to be attacked on cross-examination for a number of reasons, including prior drug use. It was therefore critical to corroborate as much of her testimony as possible. By linking the chronology of McVeigh's actions to important events in Fortier's life, the prosecutor increases the certainty of the witness' recollection of events and gives the jury confidence that the witness is not guessing at dates but has reason for remembering them.

5. Developing Important Details

Q. And did you have a conversation with McVeigh during this visit about the bombing plans that he had previously disclosed to you?

A. Yes.

Q. Do you recall that discussion?

A. Yes.

Q. Who else was present?

A. Me and Michael [Fortier] and Tim [McVeigh].

Q. And where did the discussion take place?

A. In our living room.

Q. What time of day, if you recall? [The prosecutor seeks as much detail as he can to make witnesses' recollection as credible as possible.]

A. It was the evening.

Q. As best you recall now, tell us what you remember McVeigh saying and what you remember you or Michael

---

46. *United States v. McVeigh* No. 96-CR-68, 1997 WL 206800 at *15 (D. Colo. Apr. 25, 1997) (direct examination of Lori Fortier).

saying to him. [Saying "as best you recall" frees the witness from the impossibility of trying to remember the exact words of the conversation.]

A. *Tim specified that the building he was planning on bombing was the Oklahoma City building. And he went into detail. He diagrammed what he was planning on doing.*

Q. *What do you mean he diagrammed it?* [By looping the word *diagrammed* from the previous answer, the prosecutor highlights this fact for the jury and seeks more details.]

A. *He diagrammed like circles inside of what he was—he said he was going to rent a truck; and he diagrammed circles inside of a box that was supposed to re—like resemble the box of a truck.*

Q. *What were the circles to represent?*

A. *Barrels.*

Q. *Of what?* [The prosecutor seeks more details.]

A. *He was thinking about using racing fuel and ammonium nitrate.*

Q. *Anything else?* [The prosecutor draws out even more details because the witness answered incompletely.]

A. *Yes, he was going to put—what do you—fuse, like inside the barrels.*

Q. *Did he describe any other explosives that you would use in this device?* [The prosecutor seeks more details.]

A. *Yes, he did. He described the sausage things that they had stolen from the quarry.*

Q. *What do you mean "they had stolen from the quarry"?* [The prosecutor uses looping: "they had stolen from the quarry."]

A. *He told us how Tim and—he and Terry [Nichols] had robbed a quarry outside of Kansas.*

Q. *When did he tell you that?*

A. *That night.*

Q. *What did he say about the robbery of a quarry?* [The prosecutor uses looping: "robbery of a quarry" from the second previous answer.]

A. *He said that him and Terry broke into a mining quarry one night while it was raining, and they drilled a lock on a building, and they stole the explosives.*

Q. *Did he tell you where the quarry was that they broke into?*

A. *Somewhere in Kansas.*

Q. *And did they tell you how they drilled the lock at the quarry?*

A. *With a drill. That's all that I know.*

Q. *OK. You said that he also actually drew a diagram of a truck?* [The prosecutor uses looping from several answers earlier.]

A. *Yes.*

Q. *The box—what part of the truck was drawn? I'm sorry.*

A. *There was just a box, and then he filled the box in with circles that were representing barrels.*

Q. *And I think I broke you off where you were talking about some kind of sausage explosive that had been stolen from the quarry.*

A. *Yes. That was one of the things that was stolen; and he was going to like fuse into the sausage that he would put inside the barrels that contained racing fuel and ammonium nitrate.*

Q. *I think you said he told you he was going to bomb a building in Oklahoma City; is that right?* [The prosecutor uses "looping," not from the previous answer but from fourteen answers earlier to focus the jury on the precise building McVeigh planned to bomb.]

A. *Yes.*

Q. *Did he describe the building any further?*

A. *Yes, he did. He said it was a U-shaped building that had a glass front.*

Q. *And did he describe what type of building it was?*

A. *Yes. A federal building.*

Q. *Did he specify a particular building or use a particular name?*

A. *No. He just said "the federal building."*

Q. *But he definitely named the city?*

A. *Yes.*

Q. *Did he explain to you why he had selected a federal building in Oklahoma City?* [The prosecutor uses looping: "federal building."]

A. *He said it was an easy target and that it was a building that housed some of the people that were in the Waco raid.*

Q. *Did he give you any further description of the nature or the type of explosive device he was planning to use?*

A. *Yes, he did.*

Q. *What did he say?*

A. *He used the term "anhydrous hydrazine" once.*

Q. *How is it that you can remember that term?* [**The prosecutor corroborates her memory.**]

A. *Just because it was a strange term.*

Q. *Any other reason?* [**The prosecutor seeks further details because witness did not answer fully.**]

A. *Yes. Because he had looked the term up in our dictionary.*

Q. *Was that that evening?*

A. *No. I think that was the next day, when I was alone with Tim and Michael was at work.*

Q. *And did he describe how he was going to detonate this device in the truck?* [**Notice how throughout the remainder of this questioning the prosecutor deftly continues to seek from the witness more details than her initial answer.**]

A. *Yes. He did.*

Q. *What did he—*

A. *He wasn't sure whether he was going to drill holes into the cab of the truck, or if the truck had windows, he was going to like just put them through the windows.*

Q. *Put what through the windows?*

A. *The fuse. There would be two separate fuses.*

Q. *Did he explain to you in any way how the explosion would work?*

A. *Yes. He used the term "shape charge."*

Q. *Were you familiar with that term?*

A. *No, I was not.*

Q. *Did he describe what "shape charge" meant?* [**The prosecutor seeks more details.**]

A. *Yes, he did. By drawing the barrels in the truck, he formed them in a triangle shape so the biggest part of the triangle would be facing the building to get the most—*

Q. *What do you mean "the biggest"? The flat of the triangle?*

A. *Yes.*

Q. *Which direction would the point of the triangle be pointed toward?*

A. *Away from the building.*

Q. *OK. So the flat or the bottom part of the triangle would be facing?*

A. *The building.*

Q. *And what did he describe the purpose of that to be?*

A. *That it would get the most impact that way.*

Q. *And did he tell you how he was going to manufacture this device?*

A. *Yes, he did. He said that he and Terry would do it to-*
   gether; that Terry would mix the bomb.[47]

The prosecutor has painted a vivid picture of McVeigh's conversation. No detail of this important part of the testimony has been left out. Where the witness did not answer fully, the prosecutor follows up with more questions. If there was a term the jury would not understand, such as *shape charge*, the witness was asked to explain it.

6. Addressing Important Weaknesses

Q. *When you testified before the grand jury, was there any*
   kind of condition under which you testified?
A. *Yes. I testified under immunity.*
Q. *Can you describe what your understanding of immu-*
   nity is?
A. *Anything I say like can't be used against me, unless I*
   don't tell the truth.
Q. *And what happens if you don't tell the truth?*
A. *I'd be prosecuted for perjury.*
Q. *And are you testifying here today also under an order of*
   immunity?
A. *Yes, I am.*
Q. *How did that come about?*
A. *I went this morning and got a grant of immunity.*
Q. *When you say you went, sounds like you went to a store.*
A. *I went in front of a judge this morning and got a grant of*
   immunity.
Q. *You went before Judge Matsch?*
A. *No.*
Q. *Tell us about the experience.*
A. *I went up there and my lawyer talked for me, and I got*
   immunity.[48]

---

47. *United States v. McVeigh* No. 96-CR-68, 1997 WL 206800 at *23–25 (D. Colo. Apr. 25, 1997) (direct examination of Lori Fortier) (emphasis added).
48. *United States v. McVeigh* No. 96-CR-68, 1997 WL 206800 at *45 (D. Colo. Apr. 25, 1997) (direct examination of Lori Fortier).

The witness was testifying under a grant of immunity. It was essential that the prosecutor take the sting out of this information by letting the jury hear it on direct examination instead of being surprised by the revelation on cross-examination. Notice how the prosecutor then takes the weakness and makes it a strength by informing the jury—through his questions—that even though the witness has immunity, she can be prosecuted for perjury if she does not tell the truth.

7. End Memorably

Q. *Did you ever say anything to him [McVeigh] to indicate that you did not approve of this plan?*

A. *No, I didn't.*

Q. *Did you ever say anything to indicate you disapproved of his plan?*

A. *No.*

Q. *Did you ever say anything to indicate that you approved of his plan?*

A. *No, I did not.*

Q. *Did you approve of his plan?*

A. *No.*

Q. *Why didn't you say anything?*

A. *Because I guess on some level, I—Tim was my friend and I thought that he wasn't capable of it at that time. I don't know.*

Q. *He told you that he had the materials. Is that right?*

A. *Yes.*

Q. *He diagrammed the bomb. Is that right?*

A. *Yes.*

Q. *He told you what his target was. Is that correct?*

A. *Yes.*

Q. *He indicated he was capable, didn't he?*

A. *Yes, he did.*

Q. *Why did you think he wasn't?*

A. *Because I guess on some level I was in denial that he really was capable of this.*

Q. *You recognize today that you could have stopped this from happening, do you not?*

A. *Yes, I do.*

Q. *Do you feel responsible?*

A. *Yes, I do.*

Q. *Why do you think you didn't stop it?*

A. I don't know. I mean, I wish I could have stopped it now.
    If I could do it all over again, I would have.
Hartzler: May I have a moment, Your Honor?
The court: Yes.
Hartzler: Pardon me, Your Honor. Nothing further. Thank you.[49]

As mentioned above, one of this witness' many weaknesses was the defense contention that she was implicating McVeigh so that she would not have to go to jail because of her involvement. Indeed, she was testifying with a grant of immunity. However, the prosecutor takes this weakness and turns it into a strength and ends the direct examination memorably. In short, the witness says she had all of this intimate knowledge about the plot and gives a very plausible explanation why she did not try to stop it: "I guess on some level I was in denial that he really was capable of this." Not only does the witness give this explanation but she shows sincere remorse by saying she would do things differently if given the chance again.

But notice how the prosecutor makes the mistake of distracting from this emotional ending by asking the court for a moment (presumably to check with cocounsel about further questions to ask or to look at his notes) instead of simply ending the testimony with Fortier's words of sincere regret.

4.10 STUDY QUESTIONS FOR DIRECT EXAMINATION VIDEO CLIPS FROM *PEOPLE V. SIMPSON* (DISC 2)

Clip 1 (Clark): Fuhrman Begins Direct— Nervous and Denies Racism (4.5 min.)[50]

Background: Detective Mark Fuhrman was one of the first detectives to arrive at Bundy (Nicole's home). He also accompanied three other detectives to Rockingham (O. J.'s house) to notify him of Nicole's

---

49. *United States v. McVeigh* No. 96-CR-68, 1997 WL 206800 at *52 (D. Colo. Apr. 25, 1997) (direct examination of Lori Fortier).

50. *People v. Simpson* No. BA097211, 1995 WL 97332 at *35–36 (Cal. Super. Ct. Mar. 9, 1995) (direct examination of Mark Fuhrman) and *People v. Simpson* No. BA097211, 1995 WL 97333 at *2 (Cal. Super. Ct. Mar. 9, 1995) (direct examination of Mark Fuhrman).

death. While there, he found a bloody glove that matched the other glove found at Bundy.

Kathleen Bell was a real estate agent and met Fuhrman in 1985. She stated that he told her that "when he sees a 'nigger' driving with a white woman, he would pull them over. . . . [H]e went on to say that he would like nothing more than to see all 'niggers' gathered together and killed. He said something about burning or bombing them." Bell related her conversations in a letter to the defense counsel prior to the trial (the prosecution was aware of it as well).[51]

In this clip, the beginning of Fuhrman's direct examination is shown where Fuhrman discusses that he is nervous about testifying and the amount of his preparation. The second part of the clip shows where he discusses the alleged statements he made to real estate agent Bell. The discussion of Bell occurs very early in the direct examination, just after Fuhrman discusses his nervousness and an incident in 1985 when he responded to O. J.'s house and found Nicole crying outside next to a Mercedes that had a shattered windshield that O. J. had broken with a bat.

Study Questions

1. Does Clark address effectively the potential cross-examination of Fuhrman regarding his trial preparation and alleged statements to Bell?
2. Is Clark successful at getting the details from Fuhrman that she needs?
3. Does Fuhrman appear sincere?
4. Can you identify where Clark asks a leading question?

Clip 2 (Darden): Shipp Discusses Friendship with O. J. and O. J.'s Dream of Killing Nicole (13.5 min.)[52]

Background: Ron Shipp was a Los Angeles Police Department officer from 1974 to 1989. He had met O. J. earlier through Shipp's brother,

---

51. Furhman's statements are contained in the letter shown on the video clip.
52. *People v. Simpson* No. BA097211, 1995 WL 37667 at *18–19 (Cal. Super. Ct. Feb. 1, 1995) (Direct of Ron Shipp) and *People v. Simpson*

who had played football against O. J. in high school. While an officer, he formed a close friendship with O. J. He visited his home sometimes as often as twice a week from 1978 to 1982, when he patrolled West Los Angeles, where O. J.'s home was located. When he was transferred to patrol a different section of Los Angeles in 1982, he saw O. J. less but still maintained the friendship with him. He also became a friend of Nicole's. For example, she asked him for help after she was beaten by O. J. on January 1, 1989. At her request, Shipp spoke to O. J. about the profile of a batterer to see if he would admit to having a problem. O. J. denied that he was a batterer and instead asked Shipp to "take care" of the potential charges. Shipp attempted to do so by talking to the detective handling the case.

Shipp was also with O. J. Simpson on the night of June 13, the evening after the murders, when O. J. had returned from Chicago. At his home that night, O. J. told Shipp that the police had told him that they had found a bloody glove and cap. He asked Shipp how long it would take for DNA to come back. He then revealed that he had had dreams of killing Nicole.

Shipp did not tell the police about this statement at the time because he felt a loyalty to O. J. and did not want to get involved. While not volunteering this information to police and others during the investigation, he did relate the story to Sheila Weller, who wrote a book about the murders that came out before the trial. For the book, Shipp's name was changed to Leo to keep Shipp's identity a secret. Shipp stated that he made the statements to the author because Nicole's cousin asked him to take part in the interview because a portion of the proceeds were going to O. J. and Nicole's children (Sidney and Justin). He also said that he felt burdened by what he knew and felt relieved to tell the author.

Study Questions

1. Are Darden's pacing of questions and eye contact effective?
2. How would you improve the way Darden asks questions about Shipp's friendship with O. J.?

No. BA097211, 1995 WL 37668 at *4–5, 7–10 (Cal. Super. Ct. Feb. 1, 1995) (direct examination of Ron Shipp).

3. Where does Darden use looping questions, and is the use effective?
4. Can you identify where Darden asks overly broad questions?
5. Is Darden successful in eliciting from the witness O. J.'s confession about dreaming of killing Nicole?
6. Does Darden address the weakness in his witness' statement effectively?
7. Does Darden end the examination memorably?
8. Would you have called Shipp as a witness? Why or why not?

Clip 3 (Shapiro): Dr. Huizenga Discusses His Qualifications and Physical Exam of O. J. (8 min.)[53]

Background: At the request of Simpson's attorney, Robert Shapiro, Dr. Robert Huizenga (pronounced *High-zenga*) conducted a physical examination of O. J. just after the murders. Shapiro knew Huizenga well from social gatherings and was a patient of one of Huizenga's partners. Huizenga had even seen Shapiro as a patient from time to time. Here, Dr. Huizenga testifies about his educational background and O. J.'s physical condition shortly after the murders. He states that O. J. was so feeble that he walked like Tarzan's grandfather.

Study Questions

1. What are the different background questions you should ask of an expert as compared to a typical witness?
2. What should you do if a witness is nervous on the stand?
3. Is it permissible for an expert to testify from notes that have not been admitted into evidence?
4. Does Shapiro handle the objection to "foundation" correctly when he asks the doctor about what caused the cuts?
5. Is the witness' narrative answer permissible? Is it effective?

---

53. *People v. Simpson* No. BA097211, 1995 WL 437455 at *6, 7, 10, 20–21, 23 (Cal. Super. Ct. July 14, 1995) (direct examination of Dr. Robert Huizenga).

Clip 4 (Gloves): O. J. Tries on Murder Gloves (4 min.)[54]

Background: This clip shows Darden conducting a demonstration. It also provides context for the following clip. Moreover, both Johnnie Cochran and Marcia Clark will refer to this event in closing arguments.

Study Questions

1. Does O. J. seem to be sincere in trying on the gloves?
2. How would you have handled the demonstration differently?
3. Is it important to maintain your composure in front of the jury? Notice Darden's tone of voice and Clark's facial expressions of frustration and fear.

Clip 5 (Darden): Glove Expert Demonstration (3.5 min.)[55]

Background: A few days earlier in the trial, Darden had asked the court to order O. J. to try on the gloves found at Rockingham and Bundy. In a famous highlight from the trial (see clip 4), O. J. appears to have difficulty trying them on. There are three reasons the gloves did not fit. First, O. J. had latex gloves on when he tried on the crime-scene gloves. Second, he was able to manipulate his fingers and thumb (by sticking thumb out) so that it would seem like the gloves did not fit. Third, the gloves were made to be very tight fitting—almost skin tight. So, to a casual observer who is not familiar with gloves, a normal-fitting pair would seem small. To recover from this disaster, the prosecution recalled Richard Rubin, the prosecution's glove expert, to the stand.

In this clip, Darden asks Rubin if the new gloves in front of him on the witness stand are the same size and style as the gloves found at the murder scene that O. J. had tried on a few days earlier.

---

54. *People v. Simpson* BA097211, 1995 WL 364726 at *38–39 (Cal. Super. Ct. June 15, 1995) (glove demonstration).
55. *People v. Simpson* No. BA097211, 1995 WL 374309 at *13, 14, and 24 (Cal. Super. Ct. June 21, 1995) (direct examination of Richard Rubin).

Study Questions

1. Is the demonstration successful?
2. If you were Darden, what—if anything—would you have done differently?

Chapter Five

─────⦿─────

CROSS-EXAMINATION

More cross-examinations are suicidal than homicidal.
        —*Emory R. Buckner*[1]

5.1 THREE MYTHS ABOUT CROSS-EXAMINATION

There are three myths about cross-examination that must be dispelled from the outset. First is the myth created by the old *Perry Mason* television show and continued by Hollywood that causes young lawyers to feel needlessly petrified of cross-examination. The lawyers' fear comes from the mistaken belief that an attorney is supposed to achieve success on cross-examination like that moment in *A Few Good Men.* In that movie, Tom Cruise plays an inexperienced military defense attorney, Lt. Daniel Kaffee, who is cross-examining Colonel Jessup, played by Jack Nicholson. The climax of the movie is the cross-examination

──────────

1. *Some Comments on the "Uses and Abuses" of Cross-Examination,* in Francis L. Wellman, *The Art of Cross-Examination* at 204 (Macmillan 1936).

of Jessup. Kaffee decides to do the unthinkable for a defense attorney in military courts—accuse an officer of lying without any proof to back it up. Despite the lack of proof, Kaffee's instincts tell him that the power of his questions will force Jessup to admit that he gave an unlawful order (a military crime). However, Kaffee knows that if he fails, he will be punished for falsely accusing an officer. In this famous scene, Kaffee builds his cross-examination and hammers the ultimate demand: "I want to know the truth!" Jessup responds, "You can't handle the truth!" and he arrogantly begins to tell Kaffee why he can't handle the truth, at the same time confessing to giving an unlawful order.

The reality is, however, that the confessions we see in the movies and on TV almost never occur in the courtroom. This chapter will teach you how to prove to the jury that the witness is lying, even though you will never get the witness to admit it.

Another myth is that the witness has the power. At first glance, cross-examination *seems* difficult because the attorney does not know what the witness is going to say, so it would appear the witness has all the leverage. However, the reality is that you get to choose which topics to question the witness on and then which questions to ask. You are in control. You can question the witness on topics that give you the leverage, not him. Nonetheless, attorneys are concerned that even if they ask the right questions, the witness will give an answer that is detrimental to the case. But it does not matter what the witness says; it is whether or not the witness will be believed. With an effective cross-examination, the witness will not be believed.

The third myth is advanced by Thomas A. Mauet in *Trial Techniques*. He instructs that you "ask only enough questions on cross-examination to establish the points you intend to make during your closing argument."[2] Under this theory, "you avoid asking the last question that explicitly drives home your point. Instead, your cross will merely suggest the point. During the closing argument you will rhetorically pose that last question and answer it the way you want it answered, when the witness is not around to give you a bad answer."[3]

---

2. Thomas A. Mauet, *Trial Techniques* at 253 (Aspen 6th ed. 2002).
3. Thomas A. Mauet, *Trial Techniques* at 253 (Aspen 6th ed. 2002).

The problem with Mauet's advice is that it assumes that opposing counsel is not smart enough to ask the witness on redirect examination the ultimate question you have failed to ask on cross-examination. Why would any competent opposing counsel remain silent—oblivious to your line of questioning—and not elicit the bad answer you have avoided on cross? Mauet's advice is a recipe for failure as soon as redirect begins. Instead, choose only those topics on which you are sure to win even after redirect is completed. Do not be subtle. Make your points powerfully and clearly.

> The most important principle of cross-examination is this: it does not matter what the witness says, only whether the witness will be believed.

5.2 THE BASICS OF CLIPS

Every witness can be cross-examined on one of the following areas: (1) *c*redibility, (2) *l*ack of knowledge, (3) *i*mplausible statements, (4) *p*rior inconsistent statements, or (5) to *s*upport your case. You can achieve at least one of these five goals with any witness you cross-examine and be successful.

1. Credibility

Often witnesses have some sort of credibility problem. Have they exaggerated on the stand? How reliable is their memory of the event in question? A credibility issue for many witnesses is one of bias. The witnesses are either for one side or the other. A typical example is a family member of a plaintiff or defendant. Even if these witnesses present devastating testimony, the impact of that testimony can be diminished simply by establishing the close relationship of the witness to the party.

Example 1: Cross-Examination for Bias by Prosecutor in Armed Robbery Trial

Background: The mother of the young defendant has just provided an alibi for the defendant: she was with him watching television at the time of the armed robbery.

Q. You care about your son, don't you?
A. Yes.

> When preparing to cross-examine any witness, there is an acronym that will take away your anxiety and ensure success. Remember CLIPS. Use your questions to attack the witness' *c*redibility, *l*ack of knowledge, *i*mplausible statements, *p*rior inconsistent statements, or to *s*upport your case.

Q. In fact, it goes without saying that you love him very much?
A. Yes.
Q. And for your whole life, you have done just about anything to help him?
A. Yes.

In such an obvious situation of bias, it would be overkill to ask many more questions because the jury might feel you are being unduly harsh on the mother, who has been put in a terrible situation by her son. Do not try to get the witness to confess by asking, "You are lying at trial to protect your son, aren't you?" It is not necessary.

Example 2: Cross-Examination for Bias
(Stephen Jones) from *U.S. v. McVeigh*

Defense counsel Stephen Jones cross-examines government witness Lori Fortier about her agreement to testify for the government in exchange for immunity.

> Q. *Now, under the terms of the immunity grant that you have received from the court, you are required to come in and testify; is that correct?*
> A. *Yes.*
> Q. *And you have provided testimony against Mr. McVeigh.*
> A. *Yes.*
> Q. *And presumably your husband may do the same thing.*
> A. *Yes.*
> Q. *You have avoided all federal charges which could have been brought against you; is that correct?*
> A. *Yes. I have immunity.*[4]

By emphasizing that the witness was given a grant of immunity by the government in exchange for her testimony, the defense tries to

---

4. *United States v. McVeigh* No. 96-CR-68, 1997 WL 209726 at *16–17 (D. Colo. Apr. 30, 1997) (cross-examination of Lori Fortier).

show that the witness is not telling the truth but instead telling the jury only what the prosecutor wants her to say—that McVeigh was the mastermind of the bombing.

Another area of credibility during cross-examination is a witness' prior convictions.[5] A prior conviction can show the jury that a witness is not to be trusted. (e.g., "You were convicted of armed robbery in 2007, weren't you?"). The manner in which a witness can be questioned about a prior conviction varies across the country. The wise practice is to ask the court at the pretrial conference for a ruling regarding the extent the witness can be cross-examined about the conviction.

2. Lack of Knowledge

Lack of knowledge provides a wonderful opportunity in cross-examination. Many witnesses may appear to offer important testimony on direct examination, but on cross-examination, a lack of knowledge can undermine it all.

Example 1: Defense Attorney Cross-Examining
Former Supervisor for Lack of Knowledge
in Employment Discrimination Trial

Q. You testified on direct that you were familiar with the plaintiff's work and believed that she was fired [by the defendant] because of her disability and not because of her bad performance. Is that right?
A. Yes.
Q. The plaintiff was fired in 2006, right?
A. Yes.
Q. You were her supervisor from 1995 to 2000, correct?
A. Yes.

---

5. Fed. R. of Evid. 609, which governs the use of prior convictions, is somewhat complicated, but, in short, a witness may be impeached with any felony conviction or any type of conviction (whether a felony or not) that involves proof of dishonesty or a false statement. In general, the conviction cannot be used for impeachment if more than ten years have elapsed from the date of the witness' release from confinement or the date of conviction if the witness did not go to jail.

Q. So, the last time you reviewed her work was in 2000?

A. Yes.

Q. That was six years before she was fired?

A. True.

Q. So, it is fair to say, that you have no idea how she was performing at work in 2006 when he was fired?

A. Well, yes, that's true.

Example 2: Lack of Knowledge of Character Witness

By using a character witness, a criminal defendant may offer evidence to the jury that he is a person of such fine character that he could not have committed the offense charged.[6] Often the character witness tells the jury that the defendant is an upstanding citizen who has a reputation throughout the community for honesty or peacefulness. However, such testimony provides a wonderful opportunity for the prosecution to cross-examine the witness for lack of knowledge and to argue his theory of the case to the jury.[7]

In this example, a defense witness, the pastor at the defendant's church, testified on direct that the defendant was known as a peaceful person.

Q. Reverend, the defendant was one of hundreds of people in your church?

A. Yes.

Q. You saw him at church functions?

A. Yes.

Q. But you rarely saw him outside of church-related activities?

A. Well, yes, that's true.

Q. Let me turn your attention to the night of December 13 of last year. You weren't at the corner of Commerce and Main at 11:15 at night, were you?

A. No.

Q. In fact, you weren't there when Julia Smith was held up at gunpoint?

A. No, I wasn't.

---

6. Fed. R. Evid. 404(a)(1).
7. Fed. R. Evid. 405(a).

Q. You have no way of knowing whether or not the defendant got out of a black Ford Explorer, approached Julia from behind, stuck a gun in her back, and demanded all her money?

A. No.

Q. You also don't know whether or not the defendant took her purse and ran back to the getaway car and sped off down Commerce Street?

A. No.

Q. In fact, you have no idea about what the defendant was doing on the night of the armed robbery because you never saw him that night, did you?

A. No, I don't know what he did that night.

Q. If it was proven beyond a doubt that the defendant was guilty of armed robbery, that would change your opinion of him, wouldn't it?

A. Well, I can't believe he would do that, but I guess it would.

3. Implausible Statements

Often a witness will make a statement that, based on common sense, provokes disbelief. The technique for cross-examining a witness in this situation by using logical reasoning will be explored in depth later in this chapter, in section 5.6. For now, suffice it to say that any witness can be effectively challenged regarding this type of statement.

4. Prior Inconsistent Statements

Many times witnesses will make statements prior to trial that are inconsistent with what they testify to at trial. The following is a simple example that shows the effect of cross-examining on inconsistent statements.

Example: Cross-Examination on Inconsistent Statements (Stephen Jones) from *U.S. v. McVeigh*

Jones: Ms. Fortier, would you agree with me that you either made false statements to agents of the Federal Bureau of Investigation; your parents, your mother and father; and your mother- and father-in-law and your best friends in

> *late April and May of 1995, or you're making false state-*
> *ments to this jury of strangers yesterday?*
> *Hartzler: I object, Your Honor.*
> *The court: Sustained. . . . You'll have to deal with specific*
> *statements, not generalities like that.*[8]

Although the objection was sustained because the question was compound and not specific enough, the defense attorney had the right idea. At trial, Jones did not cure the objection but moved on to other questions.[9] The correct way to employ Jones' strategy follows.

Q. You are testifying that my client bombed the federal building? [**The attorney's tone is disbelieving.**]

A. Yes.

Q. In fact, the truth is that my client was not involved in the bombing.

A. No. [**It doesn't matter what the witness says, only whether or not she is believed.**]

Q. Do you recall talking about my client's involvement to your parents, friends, and family immediately after his arrest?

A. Yes.

Q. Now, Ms. Fortier, you are close to your parents?

A. Yes.

Q. You love them?

A. Yes.

Q. You are also very close to your in-laws?

A. Yes.

Q. You also have a lot of close friends.

A. Yes.

Q. Let me direct your attention to the few days after my client was arrested. Isn't it a fact that you told your parents that McVeigh did not participate in the bombing?

A. Yes.

Q. Not only did you tell your parents but you also told your in-laws that my client was not involved in any way with the bombing?

---

8. *United States v. McVeigh* No. 96-CR-68, 1997 WL 209383 at *1 (D. Colo. Apr. 30, 1997) (cross-examination of Lori Fortier).

9. An attorney "cures" an objection by rephrasing the question that resolves the concerns of the objection.

A. Yes.

Q. You also told several friends that you knew that McVeigh was innocent?

A. Yes.

Q. In fact, you told the people closest to you, the ones you care about the most, that McVeigh was innocent?

A. Yes.

5. Support Your Case

Although cross-examination is usually thought of as a process of bringing out the weaknesses of a witness, it is also an opportunity to bring out information that will support your case.

Example: Cross-Examining to Support Your Case

In this example, a witness for the plaintiff in a car-wreck case testified on direct that she saw the defendant run the red light and hit the plaintiff's car. See how the defense attorney can cross-examine on the area of limited damages to support his case.

Q. After the accident, you went over to the two cars in the accident?

A. Yes.

Q. You checked to see if everyone was OK?

A. Yes.

Q. There were no cuts on the plaintiff's face, were there?

A. No.

Q. No bruises?

A. No.

Q. No scratches of any kind?

A. No.

Q. You saw the plaintiff get out of her car and inspect her car?

A. Yes.

Q. The plaintiff did not limp?

A. No.

Q. Did not hold her back?

A. No.

Q. Let me turn your attention to the two cars involved in the accident. The only damage was to the plaintiff's rear bumper?

A. Yes.

Q. There was a scratch about 6 inches long?

A. Yes.
Q. And a very small crease in the bumper about 6 inches long?
A. Yes.
Q. No other damage of any kind?
A. No.

5.3 CREATING AN OUTLINE

Having looked at the five main areas where a witness can be cross-examined, let's see how to prepare a cross-examination.

1. Determine Weaknesses

As shown in the previous section, most witnesses have a weakness, or at least they can provide testimony that will support part of your case. Prior to trial, decide where to attack each witness. Remember CLIPS: Does the witness have credibility problems? Is he lacking in knowledge? Is the expected testimony implausible? Has the witness made prior inconsistent statements? Can the witness support part of your case? Think through each of these questions.

A first step in answering these questions is to summarize all the prior oral and written statements of the witness. Many lawyers make the mistake of summarizing everything. Instead, you only need to look for the major points. In a 100-page deposition, it would be reasonable for you to have a 4-page summary that cites to the page numbers of the essence of the witness' testimony. Once you have summarized the statements, organize them by topic on your computer. By doing this, you can determine which category of CLIPS the witness falls into. In addition to looking at written statements, another way to determine a witness' weakness is by interviewing people who know him. They may provide invaluable insights for cross-examination topics.

2. Make Only Three Major Points

Just like your opening statement and direct examination, decide on the themes you want the jury to understand after you have completed your cross-examination. After you decide what the possible themes of cross-examination are, limit your examination to no more than three important points. Not only do you tax the jury's attention span by having more than three themes but each additional theme necessarily takes away the emphasis and importance of the others. Once you pick a theme, each question under that theme must directly relate to it, or you should not ask it.

3. Begin Powerfully and End Memorably

Whatever your order of topics is, start and end with the most important questions. Cross-examination is no time to forget the power of primacy and recency on the jury. Once you have written an outline, divide the outline so that each major point is on a separate sheet of paper. By doing this, you will achieve flexibility in the order you conduct cross-examination, depending on what happens during direct examination.

For example, during direct examination, if the testimony provides fruitful material for cross-examination on a topic you have already prepared, write the key words of the testimony on that topic page of your cross-examination outline. If the testimony involves a new line of inquiry for cross-examination, write it down on a separate sheet of paper. As the direct examination concludes, put your topic sheets in the order you want to proceed, given how the direct examination has developed. The key to cross-examination is to be flexible. If the direct examination ends with testimony that is helpful to you, use it to support your case immediately on cross-examination.

It is absolutely paramount to end your cross-examination on a confrontation you know that you can win. Don't ruin a successful cross-examination by letting the witness leave the jury with the impression that he won the last battle.

Example: Starting Powerfully—Cross-Examination
(Stephen Jones) from *U.S. v. McVeigh*

This example was used earlier in this chapter to explain prior inconsistent statements but is used again here because it is also a good example of trying to start powerfully. Although an objection is sustained because the attorney, Stephen Jones, asks a vague and compound question, his idea is right.

The court: The jury will recall that we heard testimony—direct testimony from witness Lori Fortier, and now we're ready for cross-examination.

Jones: Ms. Fortier, would you agree with me that you either made false statements to agents of the Federal Bureau of Investigation . . . or you're making false statements to this jury of strangers yesterday?

Hartzler: I object, Your Honor.

The court: Sustained.[10]

Example: Ending Memorably—Cross-Examination (Stephen Jones) from *U.S. v. McVeigh*

Here, Jones ends his cross-examination by showing the jury that not only has Fortier received immunity from the federal government for her testimony but that no state charges have been filed nor has her husband been charged as a participant.

Q. *Well, in any event, no charges have been filed against you by Arizona or Oklahoma, have they?*

A. *No.*

Q. *Or anywhere else.*

A. *No.*

Q. *And your husband has not been charged as a participant in this crime; is that correct?*

A. *That's correct.*

Q. *And his sentencing [is still pending]?*

A. *Yes.*

Q. *And you have avoided any jail sentence.*

A. *Yes.*

Q. *You have avoided any forfeiture of your home or car; is that correct?*

A. *Yes.*

Q. *And when this is over with, you will leave the stand and return home to your children; is that correct?*

A. *Yes.*

Jones: No further questions.[11]

---

10. *United States v. McVeigh* No. 96-CR-68, 1997 WL 209383 at *1 (D. Colo. Apr. 30, 1997) (cross-examination of Lori Fortier).

11. *United States v. McVeigh* No. 96-CR-68, 1997 WL 209726 at *16–17 (D. Colo. Apr. 30, 1997) (cross-examination of Lori Fortier).

4. Writing Outline of Cross-Examination

As a general rule, it is better to start your cross-examination eliciting from witnesses facts that will support your case—if you choose this as one of your topics—before you attack the witness on credibility or some other weakness. By doing this, the witness is more likely to answer those questions freely before you suggest to the jury that the witness is a liar through an attack later on cross. However, the key is to be flexible and to use an order that is easy to understand and memorable for the jury, based on what happens during direct examination.

Next to each topic in your outline, reference the item that you can challenge the witness with if he does not answer the way you want. For example, if you are cross-examining a witness to support a part of your case, note the page and line of the deposition where the witness has said what you need. That way, if the witness does not answer correctly, you will have the page cited and can refer to it quickly. Also, tab the relevant page in the deposition.

Example: Outline

Below is a sample of an outline. In this situation, the defense is cross-examining the plaintiff, who was in a car wreck. The plaintiff is claiming at trial that he has a shooting pain in his back that has been constant since the accident a year ago. He also claims that it is an excruciatingly painful condition.

> **Page 1**
> I. Injuries
>> A. Important to Tell Doctors about Injuries
>>> [This line of questioning uses logical reasoning as the leverage to get the answers you want (see section 5.6).]
>>> —went to doctor to get help
>>> —important to tell doctor about pain
>>> —doctor can't help with pain unless you tell him about it
>>
>> B. Exaggerating Injuries at Trial
>>> —did not go to emergency room on night of accident (deposition p. 9, lines 4–7)
>>> —first time went to doctor was one week after accident (deposition p. 15, lines 10–11)

—never complained to doctor about pain in lower back (medical records exhibit 10, p. 117)

—complained only about pain in upper neck (medical records exhibit 10, p. 117)

—went to doctor again two months after accident (medical records exhibit 10, p. 210)

—told doctor "95 percent better" (medical records exhibit 10, p. 212)

—on second visit, did not complain of lower back pain (medical records exhibit 10, p. 212)

—never missed a day of work after accident (deposition p. 20, lines 3–8)

Page 2

II. Very Little Damage to Car

—only damage to plaintiff's car was small dent in rear bumper (exhibit 21: photo of rear bumper)

—no damage to any other part of plaintiff's car (exhibits 22–25: photos of plaintiff's entire car)

—cost of repairs was $200 (exhibit 17: receipt from service center)

—absolutely no damage to defendant's car (exhibits 26–29: photos of defendant's entire car)

5.4 HOW TO ASK QUESTIONS

1. Use Leading Questions

A leading question suggests the answer. The majority—but by no means all—of your questions in cross-examination should be leading. The reason to use leading questions is that you are in a battle and want to force the witness to answer the precise question you are asking. Leading him to answer only "yes" or "no" achieves this result. There are two techniques to master: structure of the question and tone of voice. The structure of the question should be simple. A good rule of thumb is to have only one new fact per question. That way, it is clear to the witness and jury which fact you are asserting as true. Although this sounds simple, it is often difficult because in normal conversation, we rarely speak in sentences that contain only one fact. Second, your tone of voice must be authoritative so that the jurors will understand exactly what the answer should be.

One of the most common mistakes on cross-examination is to ask vague, argumentative, or compound questions. By using only one new fact per question, you will have concise sentences that will force your witness to give you the answer you want.

Example: Asking Concise Questions (Daniel Petrocelli) from *Goldman v. Simpson*[12]

Below is a short exchange by Daniel Petrocelli, the attorney for Fred Goldman, during his questioning of O. J. Simpson. Petrocelli is asking Simpson about a violent confrontation on New Year's Day in 1989 that resulted in Nicole Brown having a bruised and beaten face. See how you would improve the examination.

There is a trick to ensure a successful cross-examination. It is the three Cs. Your cross-examination will be successful if your questioning is clear, concise, and confident. Clear means having obvious themes. Concise means using one fact per question and building questions using logical reasoning (discussed later in this chapter, in section 5.6). Confident means speaking in a tone of voice that conveys the answer you expect—an answer that is supported by the facts in the case and the jury's common sense. Thus, it does not matter what the witness answers.

> Q. Let's talk about 1989, OK?
> That was an angry, intense, physical confrontation, true?
> A. Correct.
> Q. You're what, at the time, six-two, 215 pounds?
> A. Yes.
> Q. Nicole, five-eight, 135 pounds?
> A. Yes.[13]

Each question would have been better if it had only contained one fact. Why? Although Simpson did not deny any of Petrocelli's statements, if he had, it would have been unclear what fact he was denying since there is more than one fact in each question. More important, if

---

12. Simpson was sued for wrongful death in civil court after his acquittal in the criminal trial.
13. *Goldman v. Simpson* No. SC036340, 1996 WL 674551 at *6 (Cal. Super. Ct. Nov. 22, 1996) (direct examination of adverse witness O. J. Simpson).

Petrocelli had put only one fact in each question, the theme of physical domination would have been before the jury for a longer period of time. The following would have been a better way to ask the questions.

Q. Let's talk about 1989, OK? It was a physical confrontation?
A. Yes.
Q. It was an angry confrontation?
A. Yes.
Q. It was intense?
A. Yes.
Q. Now, let me ask you some questions about your size. You are 6 feet 2 inches tall?
A. Yes.
Q. You weigh 215 pounds?
A. Yes.
Q. Now, in contrast, Nicole is 5 feet 8 inches?
A. Yes.
Q. She is 135 pounds?
A. Yes.
Q. So, at the time of this confrontation, you weighed about 80 more pounds than she did?
A. Yes.
Q. And you were half a foot taller?
A. Yes.

Another tool in asking leading questions is to use certain phrases to signal to the witness and the jury that you want a certain answer, such as yes or no. Some of these phrases are in boldface in the following example where the attorney wants a yes answer.

Example: Using Leading Questions to Get Witness to Say Yes.
Q. The robbery happened on January 12, **didn't it?**
A. Yes.
Q. You were near the city park, **right?**
A. Yes.
Q. You were walking, **weren't you?**
A. Yes.
Q. The robber approached you from behind?
A. Yes.

Notice how the words in boldface train the witness to answer yes. After a few questions, there is no need to add these words. Instead, simply ask the question authoritatively, and the witness will realize that the jury is expecting him to answer yes.

Of course, using a leading question doesn't mean that the witness has to answer yes. A leading question simply "leads" the witness to the answer you want. Sometimes having the witness say no is also effective. This is particularly true when you are trying to establish the witness' lack of knowledge. Notice in the following example that the question is in the form of the negative and that phrases at the end of the first few questions train the witness to say no. Then, near the end of the questioning, there is no longer the need for such training.

Whether you are leading the witness to answer yes or leading the witness to answer no, the power you have to make him answer the way you want is based on all the facts of the case. The facts of the case include physical evidence, the witness' prior statements, and the testimony that has come out at trial. With this information, you can lead the witness to provide the answers you want. If the witness fails to answer correctly, you can impeach him (discussed later in this chapter, in section 5.5), or if he gives an unreasonable answer (see section 5.6), the jury won't believe it, so the incorrect answer doesn't matter.

Example: Using Leading Questions to Get Witness to Say No

Q. You weren't at the intersection of Main and Commerce, were you?

A. No.

Q. You did not see what happened there on the night of January 12, **did you?**

A. No.

Q. You did not see a robbery that night, **right?**

A. No.

Q. You don't know if there were one or two robbers?

A. No.

2. Mix in Open-Ended Questions

Open-ended questions—the opposite of leading questions—are questions that you would normally ask on direct examination. They begin with words such as who, what, when, where, why, or how. However, on cross-examination these questions can be freely used when you know what the witness must answer based on a prior statement she has made or the evidence in the case. Such questions provide variety and show the jury that you are not being unduly unfair to the witness by always making her answer yes or no to leading questions. For instance, assume the witness gave a prior statement that she was 20 feet from the intersection when she saw the wreck. For variety, instead of asking the leading question, "You were 20 feet away from the intersection when you saw the accident, weren't you?" You could ask the open-ended question, "How far away from the intersection were you?" For either question, the witness will suffer the penalty of impeachment if she doesn't answer it correctly.

3. Usually Avoid Asking Questions Where Answer Is Unknown

If you don't know what the witness must answer, asking an open-ended question can prove dangerous. A variation of the following well-known example has been taught in law school for years.

> Q. You admit that your head was turned when the large brawl took place?
> A. Yes.
> Q. Then, how can you claim my client bit a part of Mr. Smith's nose off since you didn't see the fight take place?
> A. I saw your client spit it out of his mouth after the brawl.

This example has been used to promote the prohibition that you should *never* ask a question you don't know the answer to. On the contrary, it is perfectly acceptable, and even advisable, to ask a witness an open-ended question when you do not know how the witness will answer—*but* only when the answer simply does not matter. Obviously, in the above example, the answer is detrimental.

So, the rule for most situations, then, is that you should never ask a question unless you know the answer the witness must give or the answer does not matter. The exception to this rule will be discussed after the following example.

Example of Open-Ended Questions Where Answer
Does Not Matter (Daniel Petrocelli) from *Goldman v. Simpson*

Just prior to the example, Petrocelli is asking Simpson about his beatings of Nicole over the years. The one physical altercation O. J. refers to below concerns New Year's Day 1989 when Nicole called 911 after O. J. struck her several times. For context, the passage begins with his answer.

> A. *There was one very physical altercation, and there were other times when they were not so physical.*
> Q. *What do you mean by "not so physical," Mr. Simpson?*
> A. *Well, Nicole hit me a few times, and I didn't consider that too physical.*[14]

Petrocelli asks an open-ended question because there is not an answer that can hurt him. The answer O. J. gives undercuts his prior claim that Nicole could be very physical. It hurts his credibility and would not have been elicited if an open-ended question had not been asked.

There is an important exception to this rule that is often overlooked in textbooks. Mauet declares, "Play it safe. Many witnesses will seize every opportunity to hurt you. Cross-examination is not a discovery deposition. . . . Accordingly, your cross-examination should tread on safe ground."[15] In some criminal trials, however, many defense attorneys would never win if they always treaded on safe ground. Defense attorneys are sometimes forced to ask leading questions where the answer is not absolutely certain because of their inability (through lack of cooperation by the witnesses) to interview police officers and other government witnesses prior to trial. Necessity dictates taking calculated risks. These questions are critical for developing information with which to cross-examine other witnesses or to use later in the cross-examination of the same witness.

---

14. *Goldman v. Simpson* No. SC036340, 1996 WL 674551 at *5 (Cal. Super. Ct. Nov. 22, 1996) (direct examination of adverse witness O. J. Simpson).
15. Thomas A. Mauet, *Trial Techniques* at 252 (Aspen 6th ed. 2002).

4. Make Your Point Clear

As mentioned at the beginning of the chapter, the third myth of cross is Mauet's guidance to be subtle. Let's look at his instruction in more detail. He proclaims:

> The traditional approach to cross-examinations was to make all your points during the cross-examination itself. The modern approach has an entirely different emphasis and level of subtlety. You ask only enough questions on cross-examination to establish the points you intend to make during your closing argument. This means that you will avoid asking the last question that explicitly drives home your point. Instead, your cross will merely suggest the point. During the closing argument you will rhetorically pose that last question and answer it the way you want it answered, when the witness is not around to give you a bad answer.[16]

Mauet provides the following illustration. Here, the attorney wants to prove that the witness did not see the accident until after the impact and thus does not know who caused it.

> Q. You weren't expecting a collision at the intersection, were you?
> A. No.
> Q. The traffic was normal?
> A. Yes.
> Q. As you approached the corner you were talking with your passenger, isn't that right?
> A. Yes.
> Q. The first unusual thing you heard was the sound of the crash, wasn't it?
> A. Yes.
> Q. And that's when you noticed that a crash had just occurred, isn't that true?
> A. Yes.[17]

---

16. Thomas A. Mauet, *Trial Techniques* at 253 (Aspen 6th ed. 2002).
17. Thomas A. Mauet, *Trial Techniques* at 253 (Aspen 6th ed. 2002).

Mauet then instructs, "Don't ask the last obvious question: 'So you didn't really see the cars before the crash occurred, did you?' The witness will always give you a bad answer. Instead, save it for your closing argument."[18] Mauet further teaches, "The problem is always recognizing what that last question you shouldn't ask is, before you inadvertently ask it. Perhaps the best safeguard against doing this is to ask yourself: What's the final point about this witness that I'll want to make during closing arguments? When you decide on the point, make sure you don't ask it as a question during the cross-examination."[19]

His idea to "play it safe" is misguided. By instructing attorneys not to make a clear point but to save it for closing, Mauet creates the wrong mind-set for an attorney. From the first words of the opening statement through the last words of the closing argument, the attorney should be aggressively convincing the jury of his client's position. Mauet's example is not a sound one and proves the point that hypotheticals are often not the best teaching tools. In a real trial, you would gain nothing by your failure to ask the ultimate question. Why not? On redirect examination, the question would get asked. Here's how it would play out.

Example: Redirect Examination That Asks Ultimate Question

Q. On cross-examination, do you recall testifying that the first unusual thing you heard was the sound of the crash and it was at that moment that you noticed a crash had just occurred?

A. Yes.

Q. Did you see any of the cars before the crash occurred?

A. Yes.

Q. How could you if you were talking to your passenger as you approached the intersection?

A. I was not looking at my friend while I was talking to her. I always keep my eyes on the road.

Q. How do you know who caused the accident if the first unusual thing you heard was the sound of the crash?

A. Well, as I was driving and talking to my friend, I saw the light turn red so I slowed down. The car in front of me

---

18. Thomas A. Mauet, *Trial Techniques* at 254 (Aspen 6th ed. 2002).
19. Thomas A. Mauet, *Trial Techniques* at 254 (Aspen 6th ed. 2002).

> It is naive to think that if you don't ask the ultimate question on cross-examination, opposing counsel will fail to do so on redirect examination and allow you to argue the point in your closing. Although you should not ever expect the witness to admit he is a liar, your cross should make powerful points that are clear, not subtle, as Mauet suggests.

ran the red light. I then looked up at the light again to make sure I had seen it turn red, which it had. I did not notice there was a crash until I heard the sound of the car in front of me hitting the car coming from the right that had the green light.

Here, there could be a variety of answers to the last question. However, any good opposing attorney is going to ask the ultimate question on redirect examination. Given the witness' answer here, this line of cross-examination should not have been chosen. Remember, you have the power to choose the topics with which to confront the witness. Obviously, choose only the confrontations you can win. You will know which ones you can win by assessing where the witness is weak (remember CLIPS: *c*redibility, *l*ack of knowledge, *i*mplausible statements, *p*rior inconsistencies, or to *s*upport your case).

The lesson, then, is that—like in every trial skill—your credibility with the jury is at stake. Don't pursue a line of questioning unless you know, at the end, the witness will have to give you the answer you want or that his answer cannot hurt you because it won't be believed.

5.5 IMPEACHMENT WITH PRIOR INCONSISTENT STATEMENTS OR OMISSIONS

Impeachment means to challenge the validity of a witness' testimony or credibility. One way to challenge a witness' testimony on direct is through the use of prior statements or omissions that are inconsistent with trial testimony. In general, a prior inconsistent statement is a witness' oral or written statement given prior to trial that is inconsistent with the witness' testimony at trial. An inconsistent omission is one that occurs when the witness was given an opportunity prior to trial to explain a certain matter in a statement and omitted the explanation but at trial is now explaining the omitted matter.

I. Three Steps for Success

In either case, the following three steps should be taken. First, accuse the witness of making a false statement at trial. Next, build up the prior statement. Build up means to show the jury the trustworthiness of the prior statement with which you intend to impeach the witness. Finally, confront the witness with the prior inconsistent statement or omission.

> Remember the ABCs of impeachment with prior inconsistent statements: *a*ccuse the witness of making a false statement at trial, *b*uild up the trustworthiness of the prior inconsistent statement, and *c*onfront the witness with the prior inconsistency.

Example: Impeaching with Prior Inconsistent Statement

In the following example, assume that the witness testifies at trial that the traffic light was red at the time of the accident, but at her deposition she testified that the light was green. You believe the truth is that the light was green.

> *Step 1: Accuse*
> Q. Your testimony in court here today is that the traffic light was red? [**Your tone should be one of disbelief.**]
> A. Yes.
> Q. Isn't it a fact that the light was green? [**This is the ultimate question. Your tone should be authoritative. You want to make it clear to the jury what you believe the truth is.**]
> A. No. [**You don't care that she says no because you will prove she is lying.**]

This should take no more than two or three questions. The simple goal is to make it clear to the jury that there is an important inconsistency and that you believe the prior statement is the truthful one. The way to achieve step 1 is to ask simple questions and use your tone of voice to indicate to the jury which of the two statements should be believed. Obviously, you cannot say, "You're lying in court, aren't you?" That question would be objectionable as being too argumentative. Also, such a question mistakenly presumes that the witness will admit she is lying in court (see discussion on the three myths of cross-examination discussed at the beginning of this chapter). You are trying to prove the witness is lying, not trying to get her to admit that she is.

Step 2: Build Up

Q. Do you recall giving a deposition in this case?

A. Yes.

Q. The deposition took place at your attorney's office?

A. Yes.

Q. She was present when I asked you questions?

A. Yes.

Q. You were under oath?

A. Yes.

Q. You swore to tell the truth, and nothing but the truth?

A. Yes.

Q. In fact, it was the same oath that you took today?

A. Yes.

This step is essential. Obviously, the courtroom is a formal and important setting. Build up the prior statement to show the jury that the witness knew—or should have known—the importance of the circumstances under which the prior statement was made. Showing that the witness had an attorney present gives the reliability of the prior statement added substance.

Step 3: Confront

Q. Your Honor, may I approach the witness?

The court: Yes.

Q. This is your deposition isn't it? [**Show witness the deposition.**]

A. Yes.

Q. You signed it at the end?

A. Yes.

Q. And you were given an opportunity to review it for any mistakes before you signed it?

A. Yes.

Q. Let me direct your attention to page 30, line 4. [**Point to the relevant lines on the page.**] Isn't it a fact that you were asked the following question and gave the following answer: "Question: What was the color of the traffic light? Answer: Green."

A. Yes.

Q. Did I read that correctly? [**Your tone should be very authoritative.**]

A. Yes.

Notice by asking the last question, the attorney is able to make the witness admit for a second time that she has given a prior inconsistent statement. When confronting the witness with the deposition, it is also an opportunity to continue to build up the reliability of the statement by showing the jury that the witness had the opportunity to review the deposition to correct it for any mistakes. Finally, never let the witness read aloud the prior inconsistent statement during the "confrontation." It is essential that you maintain control of the questioning and use the appropriate tone you want the jury to hear. When a witness is given the opportunity to read her prior statement, she often will speak softly or try and explain away her answer.

The second type of impeachment involves a prior inconsistent omission (omission impeachment). Omission impeachment is used at trial when a witness embellishes testimony that is materially different from a prior statement when it would have been reasonable for the witness to state that fact (the trial embellishment) in the prior statement. This technique is exactly the same as above: accuse, build up, and confront.

One of the most common and damaging mistakes made during impeachment is to ask the witness to contrast—or explain—why there are two inconsistent statements. For example, never ask the witness, "How can you say today the light was red when you said in your deposition that the light was green?"[20] Attorneys do this under the mistaken belief that the witness will somehow admit that they are lying in the courtroom, and the prior statement is true. This never happens. Worse, by asking the question you give control of the flow of information back to the witness, and it takes away from the drama of the impeachment. Although opposing counsel will try and fix the problem on redirect examination, by then it will be too late.

Example: Car-Wreck Trial (Cross-Examination of Plaintiff)
Step 1: Accuse
Q. Your testimony in court here today is that you had a very sharp pain in your back in the twenty-four hours

---

20. This does not mean that you shy away from asking the ultimate question. You have already done that when you ask the witness in step 1, "Isn't it a fact the light was green?"

immediately after the accident? [**Your tone should be one of disbelief.**]

A. Yes.

Q. You said it was so bad that you could barely walk and could not sleep for several days? [**Your tone is still one of disbelief.**]

A. Yes.

Q. In fact, isn't it true that you had absolutely no pain in your back after the accident? [**Here is the ultimate question. Your tone should be authoritative.**]

A. No, that is not true.

Step 2: Build Up

Q. Do you recall giving a deposition in this case?

A. Yes.

Q. The deposition took place at your attorney's office?

A. Yes.

Q. She was present when I asked you questions?

A. Yes.

Q. You were under oath?

A. Yes.

Q. You swore to tell the truth, and nothing but the truth?

A. Yes.

Q. In fact, it was the same oath as if you were in a courtroom?

A. Yes.

Step 3: Confront

Q. Your Honor, may I approach the witness?

The court: Yes.

Q. This is your deposition, isn't it? [**Show the witness the deposition.**]

A. Yes.

Q. You signed it at the end?

A. Yes.

Q. And you were given an opportunity to review it for any mistakes before you signed it?

A. Yes.

Q. Let me direct your attention to page 30, line 4. [**Point to the relevant lines on the page.**] Isn't it a fact that you were asked the following question and gave the following answer: "Question: Describe any and all injuries and pain you experienced in the twenty-four hours immediately after the accident. Answer: I had a bruise on my left forearm and a few scratches on my right hand."

A. Yes.

Q. Did I read that correctly? [Your tone should be very authoritative.]

A. Yes.

[These are additional questions for impeachment by omission.]

Q. Nowhere in this answer did you say that you had pain in your back, did you?

A. No.

Q. Nowhere in the answer did you say that your back pain was so bad that you had difficulty walking?

A. No.

Q. Or that it was so bad that you could not sleep for several days?

A. No.

Q. In fact, nowhere in your entire deposition did you ever say that the accident had caused you back pain? [Your tone has conviction.]

A. No.

> In either type of impeachment, your tone of voice is of paramount importance. From your tone, the jury should never be confused about which statement you believe to be true.

2. Proving up Impeachment

There may be instances where the witness denies making the prior inconsistent statement. This almost never happens when a witness is confronted with a deposition or a signed written statement but is more likely to occur with an oral statement since the witness can more easily deny making it.

Example: Witness Denial of Prior Oral Statement

Q. *Isn't it a fact that you told Officer Smith that the light was green?*

A. *No.*

If this happens, you are allowed to "prove up" the impeachment. In this case, all you have to do is call Officer Smith to the stand to ask him about the statement to prove that the witness is lying. If you were the plaintiff cross-examining a defense witness, you would call Officer

Smith as a rebuttal witness. If you were the defendant cross-examining a plaintiff's witness, you would call Officer Smith in your case in chief.

5.6 LOGICAL REASONING AND PROGRESSION OF QUESTIONS

1. Building a Series of Successful Questions

There are often times when you do not have the tools of a prior inconsistent statement or omission to impeach a witness. One trick in such a situation is to ask a series of questions that requires the witness to answer in your favor or risk being disbelieved by the jury. It can also be used to get the witness to support your case. In criminal trials, where there are few written statements to impeach witnesses with if they answer incorrectly, it is a tactic that defense and prosecuting attorneys live by.

This method is achieved by asking a series of questions, each of which builds on the preceding one. Think of it as building a staircase, each step (or question) leading to a final question or destination.

Example: Using Logical Reasoning in Cross-Examination

Assume that there was a murder committed on the night of January 12 at 11:00 p.m. No suspects are arrested that night, but the police determine several months later that fingerprints found at the scene match the defendant's. The homicide detectives interview the defendant in December, and the defendant claims that he could not have committed the murder because he was with his girlfriend at his apartment watching TV. He gave the detectives a detailed account of his activities that were consistent with his trial testimony. For example, at trial, he explained on direct examination that he picked his girlfriend up at her house at 8:00 p.m. on January 12, and he took her to his apartment at 8:45 p.m. Then, he cooked pasta for dinner around 9:00 p.m. Later, they went down the street to get a beer at Nick's Bar at 10:00 p.m. At 10:30 p.m., they returned to his apartment and watched *Seinfeld*. At 11:45 p.m., they fell asleep together on the couch.

At first glance, it appears that the defendant has an airtight alibi. He is able to account for his activities on the night of the murder, and everything that he has said can be corroborated by his girlfriend. Let's see how the use of questions built carefully on logical reasoning can prove that the defendant is lying.

> Q. Mr. Stanley, you claim that you were at your apartment, with your girlfriend, watching *Seinfeld* at the time of the murder, correct?
>
> A. Yes.
>
> Q. January 12 was an ordinary night for you, wasn't it?
>
> A. Yes.
>
> Q. There was nothing special about it, was there?
>
> A. True.
>
> Q. In fact, there was nothing unusual about it for you or your girlfriend?
>
> A. Yeah.
>
> Q. You will agree, won't you, that in general, the more time passes from an event, the harder it is to remember what happened?
>
> A. Not always.
>
> Q. For example, it is easier to remember what you did yesterday than it is to remember what you did last week?
>
> A. Well, I guess.
>
> Q. You will certainly agree it is easier to remember what you did yesterday than a month ago?
>
> A. Well, I guess that is true, but I remember what I did on January 12.
>
> Q. My question is, it is easier to remember what you did yesterday than a month ago?
>
> A. OK, I agree.
>
> Q. However, you have given a very detailed account of all your actions on the night of January 12 starting at 8:00 p.m?
>
> A. Yeah, I remember because my girlfriend was with me.
>
> Q. Now, it is true that the first time you heard anything about this murder was when the homicide detectives interviewed you in December, correct?
>
> A. Yes.
>
> Q. You told them that you knew nothing about the murder, such as who was killed or when it happened, didn't you?
>
> A. Yes.
>
> Q. The interview was eleven months after the murder, wasn't it?
>
> A. Yes.
>
> Q. That was the first time that anyone had asked you what you had done back in January, right?

A. Right.

Q. And when asked by the detectives and again here in court about what you were doing on January 12, you didn't say, "I don't remember," but you gave a very detailed account instead?

A. Yeah.

Q. You told the jury what you were doing starting at 8:00 p.m. Right?

A. Yes.

Q. Now, let me turn your attention to what were you doing an hour earlier, at 7:00 p.m?

A. Well, I am not sure.

Q. At 6:00 p.m.?

A. I don't remember.

Q. What did you eat for lunch that day?

A. I don't know.

Q. How about the day before January 12, what did you eat for dinner?

A. I am not sure.

Q. Were you with your girlfriend on January 11?

A. I think so.

Q. All right, what time did you pick her up?

A. I don't remember.

Q. The fact is you weren't with your girlfriend at your apartment on the night of January 12, but instead you killed Mr. Gumble in his car, where your fingerprints were found.

A. No, no, I swear I was at my apartment. [**It does not matter what he says; his answer won't be believed.**]

Notice how each question builds on another in a logical progression to the ultimate question. The way to achieve success is to make sure that each question goes only one step further than the proceeding one. The reason the witness is forced to say yes is based on the leverage of the collective wisdom of the jury. Jurors bring a lifetime of experiences into the courtroom. Moreover, they are constantly processing the information presented at trial. These two facts give you the power to cross-examine a witness through logical reasoning.

If you have the power of logical reasoning behind you, you can ask any question that requires an answer that is believable. *Believable* means that your question and the answer it compels are supported by logical reasoning. Therefore, after you ask your question, the jury will silently answer it for the witness and simultaneously expect the proper answer from the witness. If the witness does not answer as the jurors expect and think he should, then the witness will be seen as lying. So, you win either way. The witness either gives the answer that logical reasoning requires—and you win—or the witness gives an unbelievable answer and is seen by the jury as a liar.

On the other hand, do not ask a question that is not supported by logical reasoning and the evidence in the case. If you do, the jury will not silently answer your question as soon as you ask it and will instead believe whatever the witness says. Your integrity before the jury will suffer, and the witness will have won the confrontation.

Suppose instead of building a logical progression of questions, you asked the following questions instead.

Example: Questions Not Built on Logical Reasoning

The key to the above example is the fact that when the detectives interviewed the defendant eleven months after the murder, the defendant told them that he did not know about the murder or when it occurred. This is the linchpin of the cross-examination. If the defendant had told the detectives something different, you would have needed to find a different line of attack. The following shows what can happen if the defendant had already been interviewed by the police prior to meeting with the detectives in December.

> Q. Now, Mr. Stanley, there is **no way** you know what you were doing the night of January 12, **do you?**
> A. Yes, I remember very well that I spent the evening with my girlfriend at my apartment.
> Q. After all of this time, how can you remember that?
> A. On January 13, the cops came to my house and asked me where I was the night before. I remember telling them I was with my girlfriend. . . . It is a day I will never forget. I have never been accused of a crime in my life.

2. Using Evidence and Visual Aids

Cross-examination is no time to forget the power of visual aids. Sometimes a witness' statement at trial can be impeached with physical evidence such as photographs, street diagrams, and company manuals.

For example, a witness' statement can certainly become implausible when compared with the physical evidence in the case. If the witness' testimony does not make sense in light of photographs taken, show the photographs to the witness and jury during your cross-examination. (See video "Cross Clip 3" at the end of this chapter.) Moreover, don't be afraid to use an easel. You can have the witness draw a diagram that will reveal to the jury how implausible the testimony is. Or, if the witness makes some incredible statements, write them on an easel so the jury both sees and hears the words.

5.7 CONTROL OF THE HOSTILE WITNESS

1. Repeat the Question When Witness Does Not Answer

Many attorneys are petrified of cross-examination because they fear that the witness won't answer the question they ask and will instead say something that hurts the case. However, one of the best gifts you can be given during cross-examination is a witness who won't answer your questions. In fact, that should be your hope as you begin each cross-examination. Why? Since you are asking simple questions to prove a particular point, when a witness does not answer the question but argues, is evasive, or tries to sabotage you by giving the jury testimony damaging to your case, you have proven an even more important point: the witness is so biased he cannot be believed. The reason is that jurors expect witnesses to answer the questions that they have been asked. Since your questions will be simple, there is absolutely no reason a witness should not answer them. When he doesn't, you win twice. First, you get to prove that he is not a neutral fact giver but, rather, he is biased for the opposing side; and second, eventually, you will get him to answer your question.

Before moving on to examples from the Simpson civil trial, let's look at how this situation could unfold in the following example.

Example: Witness Who Argues

Here, a police officer is being cross-examined by defense counsel about his police report. In his report, he left blank the boxes used to describe the defendant's clothing.

[Ultimate question]: So, based on your police report, there is no way to know what the defendant was wearing when you arrested him?

A. The defendant was wearing a red jacket and brown pants.

Q. **My question is [said with emphasis],** based on your police report, there is no way to know what the defendant was wearing when you arrested him?

A. My memory is clear. The defendant was wearing a red jacket and brown pants.

Q. My question is, **based on your police report [said with emphasis],** there is no way to know what the defendant was wearing when you arrested him?

A. It does not matter what my police report said; I know that he was wearing a red jacket and brown pants.
[Repeat the question slower this time for emphasis.]

Q. You will agree, officer, based on your police report, there is no way to know what the defendant was wearing when you arrested him?

The court: Officer, answer the question.

A. Yes.

Each time the witness refuses to answer the question, you win by damaging his credibility even more. After repeating the question a few times, the court will jump in and direct the witness to answer. Don't ask the judge for help. It shows your weakness in fearing the witness' answer. In addition, you get the added benefit of having the jury see the judge's frustration with the witness and validating their feelings of annoyance with the witness. Once a witness refuses to answer a question, it really does not matter whether you ever get to the answer (although you will) because the witness has shown the jury that he is untrustworthy and biased.

In any event, some young attorneys feel that they will sound like a broken record if they have to continually repeat the question. However, you can vary your tone of voice and the pace of the question to keep it interesting. By the third or fourth time, ask the question with great deliberation. Either the witness will realize how foolish he looks by not answering the question or the judge will intervene and direct the witness to answer the question.[21]

---

21. In the very rare circumstance where the witness does not answer the question and the judge does not intervene, ask the judge to direct the witness to answer the question.

2. Don't Argue with the Witness

Cross-examination by its nature is combative. Consequently, it is very easy to fall into the trap of arguing with a witness. Juries don't like this. The attorney's goal should be to stay confident and calm, never argumentative. When an attorney lets his emotions take over, the jury no longer sees him as a trustworthy advocate supported by facts. To avoid this problem, take a moment during cross-examination to ask your cocounsel or assistant how your cross is going. Not being in the heat of the battle, he can often tell you whether you should move on to another topic or continue with the line of questions you are pursuing.

In the following three exchanges, Fred Goldman's attorney, Daniel Petrocelli, questions O. J. Simpson about his conversation with police during the low-speed chase in the Bronco prior to Simpson's arrest. In the first example, notice how Petrocelli correctly ignores Simpson's arguing and wins the battle by ignoring his responses.

A. Witness—Not Answering—Makes Request of Direct Examiner

Example: (Daniel Petrocelli) from *Goldman v. Simpson*

Q. And do you recall Detective Lange saying to you, "And nobody's going to get hurt." And you replied, "I'm the only one that deserves it." Do you recall saying that, sir?

A. Not at all.

Q. You deny saying that?

A. I don't recall saying that at all.

Q. If it's on a tape, you wouldn't dispute it, would you?

A. Let me hear the tape. [Simpson argues with Petrocelli. Petrocelli ignores the request because he knows Simpson is trying to divert the jury's attention and interrupt the flow of his examination. Moreover, the tape will be played for the jury in due course, and its contents will be clear. For now, Petrocelli is showing the jury that Simpson can't answer a simple question.]

Q. And you recall telling Mr. Lange near the end, "You've been a good guy, man, you really have. I know you're just doing your job, like you told me. You're a good guy. You did your job well."

Baker: I object to the relevance of this.

Q. Petrocelli: Now, do you recall saying that?

The court: Overruled.

> A. *I don't recall saying it, but I think that's the way I was*
> *feeling toward the police at the time, yes.*[22]

Nothing strikes fear in an inexperienced attorney more than the moment when the witness argues and makes a request of him. One mistake many attorneys make is to snap back, "I am the one who gets to ask the questions. So, please answer." Jurors expect lawyers to be confrontational but not argumentative. In the above example, Petrocelli simply ignores the inappropriate request and continues with his cross. Another way to handle Simpson's response would have been simply to repeat the question, "If it's on a tape, you wouldn't dispute it, would you?" This question would be repeated until Simpson answered the question or the judge interrupted and directed Simpson to answer it.

B. Ask the Judge to Strike the Answer

Another tactic often used when the witness is argumentative is to ask the judge to strike the answer. However, by asking the court to do this, the attorney signals to the jury that he is afraid of the answer. "Moving to strike" is built on the faulty premise that what a witness says can be detrimental to your case. It is only detrimental if it is believed. By showing concern about the answer (i.e., moving to strike it), the attorney gives that answer needless credibility. Instead, simply repeat the question until the witness answers. In this example, Petrocelli makes the mistake of showing his frustration—and giving the answer credibility—by moving to strike and by saying "please."

Example: The Mistake of Asking
the Judge to Strike the Answer
(Daniel Petrocelli) from *Goldman v. Simpson*

> Q. *You never accused Detective Lange of being framed by*
> *the police department, true?*
> A. *I had no idea who Detective Lange was, and I didn't*
> *know what had taken place at all.*

---

22.   *Goldman v. Simpson* No. SC036340, 1996 WL 679699 at *36 (Cal. Super. Ct. Nov. 25, 1996) (direct examination of adverse witness O. J. Simpson).

Q. You never accused whoever you spoke to on the phone of framing you?

A. All I—

Q. True or untrue? [Showing impatience]

A. All I can do is say—and I told him time and time again, I didn't do this.

Q. Move to strike as nonresponsive.

The court: Stricken as nonresponsive.

Q. (By Petrocelli) Please. [Showing impatience]
And the question—you never accused the person on the telephone from the police department when you were talking of planting evidence against you, correct?

A. Correct.[23]

C. Instruct the Witness to Answer Yes or No

It is a sign of weakness when an attorney instructs a witness to "answer yes or no." It shows that the attorney is afraid of the answer or has lost control of the examination. Another common mistake made by attorneys is to interrupt the witness because the attorney is afraid of his answer. You should not care. Remember, it is not what the witness says but whether what he says is believable.

Example: Instructing Witness (Daniel Petrocelli)
from *Goldman v. Simpson*

Q. And remember, you're saying the following:
"Just tell them all I'm sorry. You can tell them later on today and tomorrow that I was sorry and that I'm sorry that I did this to the police department." Do you remember saying that?

A. And I also remember telling them—

Q. Yes or no? [Petrocelli interrupts Simpson's answer.]

A. —I didn't do it.

Q. Do you remember saying that?

A. No, I don't remember that, no. But I probably did.

---

23. *Goldman v. Simpson* No. SC036340, 1996 WL 679699 at *37 (Cal. Super. Ct. Nov. 25, 1996) (direct examination of adverse witness O. J. Simpson).

Q. *Excuse me. Just answer the questions; we'll get through this.* [Petrocelli is clearly growing impatient.]

A. *Oh. Yes.*[24]

Petrocelli gets the answer he wants but not before showing some exasperation. A cleaner way to handle Simpson's nonresponsiveness would have been to repeat the question calmly but forcefully until Simpson answered or the judge intervened spontaneously to direct Simpson to answer the question.

5.8 EXPERT WITNESS

As with any other witness, go through your CLIPS analysis to determine the expert's weaknesses. Credibility rarely fails to be a productive line of attack. Questioning the opposing expert about his education, experience, and the number of times he has testified for plaintiffs or defendants should be fruitful. Since your expert is being paid, just like the other side's, there is no point in cross-examining the expert on the issue that he "is being paid for his testimony."

Example: Cross-Examination Regarding Bias of Plaintiff's Expert Doctor

Q. Doctor, you were hired by the plaintiff in this case?

A. Yes.

Q. How many times have you testified in court?

A. Fifteen times.

Q. Of those fifteen times, how many have been for a plaintiff?

A. Fourteen times.

Q. So, out of all the times you have ever testified in court, only once have you testified for the defense?

A. Yes.

Q. In truth, when you have testified in court, almost 95 percent of the time it has been for a plaintiff?

A. Yes.

---

24. *Goldman v. Simpson* No. SC036340, 1996 WL 679699 at *35–36 (Cal. Super. Ct. Nov. 25, 1996) (direct examination of adverse witness O. J. Simpson).

This cross-examination clearly establishes that the witness must have some bias—although he will never admit it on the stand—since he testifies so often for a plaintiff. Given that this is often a good line of cross-examination, make sure your expert has a history of testifying for both sides or is very well qualified but has rarely testified in court.

Although experts can be very intimidating, the key to cross-examination is to attack their assumptions. By virtue of being an expert—and not an eyewitness—the expert has necessarily made assumptions. Experts have a marked tendency to slant their argument to the side that hired them and to discount the possibility of alternative assumptions that might help the other side. Show the jury that the expert is unwilling to consider reasonable alternatives. Would the expert's opinion change if he had different assumptions? The expert won't admit he used the wrong assumptions, but by showing his unwillingness to consider reasonable assumptions that are different, the jury will see his bias.

Finally, be particularly careful that you know the answer to the questions you ask. The expert has a tremendous amount of knowledge that you don't have. An excellent way to be prepared is to discuss the questions you intend to ask with your own expert to make sure the answer you get won't hurt you. More important, use your expert as a resource to develop questions and themes to cross-examine the opposing expert.

Example: Cross-Examination of Plaintiff's Economist

In this example, the plaintiff has called an economist to calculate his damages. Like all experts, he has necessarily made assumptions.

> Q. You have made certain assumptions at arriving at the estimate of the damages, haven't you?
> A. Yes.
> Q. You have made assumptions about the plaintiff's life expectancy?
> A. Yes.
> Q. You assume in your calculations that the plaintiff will live nine years longer than the average male?
> A. He's in good health.
> Q. My question is, you assume in your calculations that plaintiff will live nine years longer than the average male?

A. Yes.

Q. If you based your assumptions on average life expectancy, you would have arrived at a much lower damages figure?

A. I feel it was reasonable based on his health to use the assumption I did.

Q. My question is, if you based your assumptions on average life expectancy, you would have arrived at a much lower damages figure?

A. Yes.

Q. You also assume that plaintiff would continue to work ten years longer than the average male?

A. Yes.

Q. You also make some assumptions about the economy?

A. Yes.

Q. For example, the inflation rate you assume is higher. . . .

Here, the expert has overreached on his assumptions for life expectancy and expected time of retirement. Those assumptions reveal his bias and undercut his credibility. Necessarily, he has also made assumptions about the inflation rate that will affect his calculation of damages.

The Seven Don'ts of Cross-Examination

1. Don't impeach the witness with minor inconsistencies.
2. Don't argue with the witness.
3. Don't try to get the witness to admit he is wrong.
4. After successfully impeaching the witness, don't ask the witness to reconcile the contradiction.
5. Don't ask complicated questions.
6. Don't play it safe in the hope of tying inferences together in closing.
7. Don't ask a question you don't know the answer to unless whatever the witness says can't hurt you or it won't be believed.

5.9 ANALYSIS OF CROSS-EXAMINATION FROM *GOLDMAN V. SIMPSON*

In a civil case, the plaintiff may call the defendant as an adverse witness in his case in chief. An adverse witness is one who is expected to give testimony that is prejudicial to the party questioning him. In doing so, the plaintiff's attorney is allowed to cross-examine the witness instead of being bound by the rules of direct examination.[25] In the *Simpson* civil trial, the attorney for plaintiff Fred Goldman, Daniel Petrocelli, called Simpson as an adverse witness. Excerpts of his cross-examination follow.

1. Beginning Powerfully

The following are the first questions Petrocelli asked Simpson. See if you can determine what Petrocelli's theme is for these questions.

> Q. *Mr. Simpson, you first met Nicole when she was eighteen years old; is that true?*
> A. *That's correct.*
> Q. *She was a waitress, just having graduated from high school?*
> A. *A waitress, but I think she graduated when she was sixteen.*
> Q. *And you were a football player in the NFL at the time?*
> A. *That's correct.*
> Q. *Almost thirty years old, right?*
> A. *Twenty-nine.*
> Q. *And a month away from thirty, right?* [Petrocelli does not give control to the witness but makes the witness give him the answer he needs.]
> A. *Yes.*
> Q. *And you were married at the time to your then wife?*
> A. *Yes.*
> Q. *And [you had] two children?*
> A. *Yes.*
> Q. *And living together, right?*

---

25. Fed. R. Evid. 611(c) provides: "When a party calls a hostile witness, an adverse party, or a witness identified with an adverse party, interrogation may be by leading questions." After this is done, opposing counsel can conduct an examination consistent with the rules of direct examination or wait and call the witness in his case in chief. If you are in the position of being opposing counsel, the better practice is not to wait and instead conduct the examination so that the witness is not subject to a second cross-examination if you were to recall the witness.

A. *Yes.*

Q. *And when you met Nicole, you struck up, immediately, a romantic relationship with her, right?*

A. *Immediately, yes.*

Q. *And then in a short time, you got her a place to live, and the two of you began your relationship together, right?*

A. *Yes. I helped her get a place to live, yes.*[26]

Petrocelli asks declaratory questions that demand the answer yes from the witness. Notice how almost every question has one simple fact in it. By using simple questions, Petrocelli does not allow the witness any wiggle room in his answers. The witness can't pretend to be confused by the simple questions and must give the answer yes. Also, notice the theme of domination that Petrocelli is starting with: Simpson dominated this relationship because of his age and celebrity status compared with Nicole, who was a young waitress just out of high school when she met Simpson.

2. Impeachment with Prior Inconsistent Oral Statement

After beginning his cross-examination with the theme of Simpson's domination, Petrocelli forces Simpson to admit that it was a problem relationship. Petrocelli knows he will win this confrontation because if Simpson does not admit that there were problems, Petrocelli can call as witnesses the detectives who interviewed Simpson after Nicole's murder to contradict Simpson's denial.

Q. *And you were together, then, with Nicole about seventeen years; is that right?*

A. *Most of seventeen years, yes.*

Q. *And during that period of time, Mr. Simpson, there were some good times and bad times, right?*

A. *Mostly good, yes.*

Q. *And there were bad times, right?*

---

26. *Goldman v. Simpson* No. SC036340, 1996 WL 674551 at *3 (Cal. Super. Ct. Nov. 22, 1996) (direct examination of adverse witness O. J. Simpson).

A. A *few, yes.*

Q. *More than a few, right?*

A. *Well, like any long relationship, there were a few bad times, yes.*

Q. *We're only talking about your relationship, sir, not other relationships. OK?* [Petrocelli is unnecessarily argumentative with this question. He could have simply repeated his previous question to force Simpson to answer.]

A. *Yes.*

Q. *And this was a passionate relationship at times, correct?*

Baker: *Objection; relevance.*

The court: *Overruled.*

A. *Yes.*

Q. Petrocelli: *And it was a problem relationship for you throughout much of the time, true?*

A. *Not true.* [With this denial, Petrocelli is ready to begin his impeachment.]

Q. *Did you not tell the Los Angeles police detectives who interviewed you on June 13, 1994, hours after Nicole's death, that you had always had problems with your relationship with Nicole; it was a problem relationship?*

A. *Yes. We had problems in our relationship, but I don't think it was mostly a problem.* [O. J. does not admit that he "always" had problems.]

Q. *Did you not say that to the police detectives on June 13, 1994? Yes or no?*

A. *Yes.*

Q. *You said that, right?*

A. *Yes.*

Q. *And when you said "I have **always** had problems with her, you know, I, I, um, that—that's our relationship, has been a problem relationship," that was true, correct?*

Baker: *I'm going to object. I'm going to object to reading that transcript because that transcript is inaccurate. If he wants to play the tape, he can play the tape for the jury.*

Petrocelli: *Object to the speaking objections.*

The court: *Overruled.*

Petrocelli: *May I have the question read back? I'm going to repeat it.*

The court: *Leave out—you know, I don't think it's necessary to put in all the "ums" and things.*

Petrocelli: *I just wanted to be accurate, Your Honor, that's all. Mr. Baker, it's page 19.*

Baker: *The transcript is inaccurate.*

> Q. *Petrocelli: Did you not say to Detectives Lange and Van-*
> *natter, on June 13, 1994, concerning your relationship*
> *with Nicole, "I have **always** had problems with her, you*
> *know—that's our relationship, has been a problem rela-*
> *tionship." Did you say that?*
> A. *Yes.*[27]

Petrocelli's persistence pays off. He does not accept Simpson's waf-
fling in his earlier answer when he said, "I don't think it was mostly a
problem." Petrocelli does not stop until Simpson admits he previously
said "always."

3. Impeachment with Deposition Transcripts

In addition to oral statements, another device with which to impeach a
witness is his deposition transcript.

> Q. *Let's talk about 1989, OK? That was an angry, intense,*
> *physical confrontation, true?*
> A. *Correct.*
> Q. *You're what, at the time, six-two, 215 pounds?*
> A. *Yes.*
> Q. *Nicole, five-eight, 135 pounds?*
> A. *Yes.*
> Q. *And you hit her that day, didn't you, sir?*
> A. *No.*
> Q. *Did your hand make contact with her face at all to cause*
> *injuries on her face? Yes or no?*
> A. *I don't know.*
> Q. *Didn't you testify—you remember testifying in this depo-*
> *sition, sir?*
> A. *Yes.*
> Q. *Remember I took your deposition over a number of days*
> *and Mr. Kelly, Mr. Brewer also asked you questions?*
> A. *Yes.*
> Q. *Let me read from that deposition. By the way, you un-*
> *derstand and you understood then, you were under oath*

---

27. *Goldman v. Simpson* No. SC036340, 1996 WL 674551 at *3–4 (Cal.
Super. Ct. Nov. 22, 1996) (direct examination of adverse witness O. J.
Simpson) (emphasis added).

and subject to the same penalty of perjury, just as you are
today?

A. *Yes.*

Petrocelli: Line—page 1,032, Mr. Baker, line 21...
    [Petrocelli reading:]

"Q. You were in such a rage that you don't remember what
    you did; is that right?

A. *I remember exactly what I did."*[28]

Petrocelli successfully impeaches O. J.'s statement at trial that he didn't know whether or not he had hit Nicole with his statement in the deposition that "I remember exactly what I did."

4. Impeachment with Exhibits

Petrocelli displays photos of Nicole's battered and bruised face for the jury and questions Simpson about them.

> *Petrocelli: Let's put some photos up. And I apologize to the*
>   *jury for having to show those photos. Exhibit 3. [The*
>   *plaintiffs' exhibit 3 is displayed on a TV screen.]*
>
> Q. *You've seen those photos before, Mr. Simpson?*
>
> A. *Yes.*
>
> Q. *OK. Tell us how she got the welt over the right eye.*
>
> A. *I don't know specifically how.*
>
> Q. *You did hit her there?*
>
> A. *No.*
>
> Q. *And it's your testimony, before this jury, that you never*
>   *touched her face with your hand, true?*
>
> A. *I don't know, as I told you in the deposition, in wrestling*
>   *her, maybe my hand hit—hit or was on her face. I cer-*
>   *tainly didn't punch her or slap her.*
>
> Q. *You say your hand was on her face. Did you strike her at*
>   *any time?*
>
> A. *As I told you, I had her in a head lock at one point, in*
>   *trying to get her out of the door, so I would assume that*
>   *my hand was somewhere around her—her face.*

---

28. *Goldman v. Simpson* No. SC036340, 1996 WL 674551 at *6–7 (Cal. Super. Ct. Nov. 22, 1996) (direct examination of adverse witness O. J. Simpson).

Q. When you say "head lock," you said in the deposition that you had her head in kind of a head lock to get her out of the room, true?

A. At one point, yes.

Q. Are you saying that that's when that injury to her eye occurred?

A. I don't know when it occurred. But I'm assuming it occurred during the altercation or when she fell outside and—

Q. I would ask—

A. —I was a cause of all of that.

Q. I would ask that you not assume anything. Either tell us what happened or—

Baker: I would ask Mr. Petrocelli not to give my client legal advice.

The court: Overruled.

Q. Petrocelli: I just want to know what your recollection, sir, is; that's all. Just tell us what you remember.

A. I don't—I don't remember specifically when any single mark or injury came on her face, any of them. But I'm assuming they all happened during this altercation.

Q. I would ask that you not assume anything. Just tell us what you—

Baker: Again I ask that Mr. Petrocelli—

The court: Overruled. He may frame the question as he wishes.

Q. Petrocelli: Are you saying now that it's possible that you might have struck her with your hand, delivered a below to her right eye to cause that mark? Yes or no?

A. No.

Q. It's not possible?

A. I did not punch her or slap her. That didn't happen.

Q. Did you strike her with your hand?

A. No.[29]

Petrocelli knows that Simpson is not going to admit on the stand that he beat Nicole. However, that does not stop him from asking this ultimate question, "Did you strike her with your hand?" Remember, it

---

29. *Goldman v. Simpson* No. SC036340, 1996 WL 674551 at *7–8 (Cal. Super. Ct. Nov. 22, 1996) (direct examination of adverse witness O. J. Simpson).

does not matter what Simpson answers; it is whether his answer is believable. With the jury seeing a photo of Nicole's battered and bruised face, Simpson loses credibility every time he denies that he hit Nicole and claims the injuries came from having her in a headlock or when she fell outside the bedroom.

5. Using Open-Ended Questions

Petrocelli asks several open-ended (nonleading) questions in this exchange. The contrast to leading questions makes the examination more interesting for the jury and emphasizes the answer. Remember the rule that you should not ask a question you don't know the answer to unless the answer cannot hurt you or, if it is different than you expect, it won't be believed.

Below, every time Simpson answers "Never" to a nonleading question, Petrocelli is scoring points with the jury because the answer is so preposterous.

> Q. *Well, there was more than one physical altercation, true?*
> A. *I think you'd have to define that. There was one very physical altercation, and there were other times when they were not so physical.*
> Q. *What do you mean by "not so physical," Mr. Simpson?* [nonleading]
> A. *Well, Nicole hit me a few times, and I didn't consider that too physical.*
> Q. *So the ones that were not so physical are the times when you say Nicole hit you, true?*
> A. *Yes. And one time I grabbed her at a door and pushed her outside the door. That—if you call that physical, that's physical, yes.*
> Q. *And how many times did Nicole hit you, as you say?* [nonleading]
> A. *Numerous times.*
> Q. *OK. And how many times, Mr. Simpson, in the course of these physical alterations, did you hit Nicole?* [A series of nonleading questions follows.]
> A. *Never.*
> Q. *How many times did you strike Nicole?*
> A. *Never.*
> Q. *How many times did you slap Nicole?*

A. Never.

Q. How many times did you kick her?

A. Never.

Q. How many times did you beat her, sir?

A. Never.

Q. And if Nicole said you hit her, she would be lying; is that true?

Baker: I object, Your Honor.

The court: Sustained. . . . [Petrocelli's question is argumentative.]

Q. Petrocelli: And you are aware that Nicole has written down in writings that you hit her, true? [Not only is Simpson's version that he was the victim of Nicole's beating incredible but Petrocelli then impeaches Simpson's version with Nicole's writings.]

A. Yes.

Q. And you are aware that her writings describe numerous incidents when you hit her, true?

Baker: I object to this again.

The court: Overruled.

Baker: I think we need to approach.

The court: No. Overruled.

Petrocelli: Please answer the question.

A. Yes.

Q. Petrocelli: And your view is all that is false, true?

A. True, yes.[30]

6. Keeping Eye Contact with Witness

These questions followed the two above examples. Simpson has denied at every opportunity that he ever struck Nicole and caused the bruises on her face. However, watch for the moment when Petrocelli notices that Simpson makes a gesture that becomes an admission of what happened.

> *Q. And you said Nicole is one of the most physically conditioned women you've ever known, right?*

---

30. *Goldman v. Simpson* No. SC036340, 1996 WL 674551 at *5–6 (Cal. Super. Ct. Nov. 22, 1996) (direct examination of adverse witness O. J. Simpson) (emphasis added).

A.   Yes.

Q.   You said, at least that night, she was quite a match for you, right?

A.   It's tough—it was tough to get her out of the room, yes.

Q.   So what you did is, you started to sort of try to, from behind her, put your arms around her and get her out of the room, right?

A.   I don't know if that's necessarily true.

Q.   At some point, you think, in the process of trying to get her out the fifteen feet or so to the door so you could close your door, you got her in a head lock; is that right?

A.   I don't think that's necessarily true.

Q.   Is that a fair description?

A.   No.

Q.   Well, tell us, then.

A.   She jumped on me, on the bed, and with her knees and arms—and then I kind of grabbed her, and we kind of fell over on the floor. And then I was trying to get her— to get her out of the door, and she was grabbing things and hitting. And eventually, I got her out of the door.

Q.   OK. And when you said you grabbed her, you put your right hand into a fist—

A.   Yes.

Q.   —just now. [Petrocelli notices Simpson has made a fist on the stand.] Is that what you did that night when you grabbed her?

A.   Quite possibly when I grabbed her arm, quite possibly I did.

Q.   When you did—now, you just put both hands in a fist. [Petrocelli notices that Simpson has put both hands in a fist.] When you did it that night, did you punch her in the face with your hands?

A.   No. No.[31]

Petrocelli gives us the perfect example why it is important to maintain eye contact with the witness. By doing so, he notices that Simpson makes fists with his hands as he is describing the fight with Nicole. Petrocelli's eyes are not buried in his notes looking ahead to the next question.

---

31.   *Goldman v. Simpson* No. SC036340, 1996 WL 674551 at *9 (Cal. Super. Ct. Nov. 22, 1996) (direct examination of adverse witness O. J. Simpson).

Instead, he is able to see a key moment in the cross-examination. After vehemently denying that he ever struck Nicole that night, Simpson has made two fists during his retelling of the incident and revealed what really happened despite his verbal answers of "No. No."

7. Getting Improbable Answers

If a witness gives answers that don't hold up to common sense, then victory has been achieved. During the cross-examination below, Petrocelli confronted Simpson with a photo of Nicole that showed a red imprint of a hand on her neck. Petrocelli, although not getting the witness to admit yes, achieves the same result by Simpson's improbable answer. It is even better for Petrocelli that Simpson finally admits to touching her throat but not leaving marks.

> Q. Did you put your fingers and hands on her throat and leave marks on her throat, sir?
> A. I don't recall doing that at all, no.
> Q. You are aware she had marks on her throat, are you not?
> A. I'm aware that someone said she did, yes.
> Q. You believe that's false?
> A. I never saw them. And the next day, she showed me all her bruises. . . .
> Q. It's your testimony that you never touched her throat, right?
> A. I don't know. When you say "touched her throat," I was wrestling her; I could have touched her throat, yes.[32]

8. Arguing Case through Witness and Ending Memorably

A cross-examination *must* end memorably. The questioning just prior to this next excerpt concerned the infamous police chase in the white Bronco prior to Simpson's arrest when the police talked to Simpson on a cell phone while he was in the car. Simpson had written a suicide note prior to the police chase.

---

32. *Goldman v. Simpson* No. SC036340, 1996 WL 674551 at *9 (Cal. Super. Ct. Nov. 22, 1996) (direct examination of adverse witness O. J. Simpson).

Here, Petrocelli knows that Simpson is not going to answer yes, but Petrocelli wants to give the jury a concise summary of what happened. In addition, Petrocelli wants the jury to see Simpson being asked the ultimate questions of liability and to judge his credibility as he answers them.

> Q. Please. And the question—you never accused the person on the telephone from the police department when you were talking of planting evidence against you, correct?
>
> A. Correct.
>
> Q. Or framing you for a murder that you did not commit? Correct?
>
> A. That's correct.
>
> Q. And the reason you didn't do so, Mr. Simpson, is because you knew you committed those murders, correct?
>
> A. That's incorrect.
>
> Q. And that is why you were going to kill yourself, because you knew you were going to spend the rest of your life in jail, correct?
>
> A. That's incorrect.
>
> Q. And you knew that you dropped the blood at Bundy, correct?
>
> A. That's incorrect.
>
> Q. And knew, sir, that you went there that night and you confronted Nicole and you killed her—
>
> Baker: Your Honor, I'm going to object.
>
> Q. Petrocelli: —correct?
>
> Baker: This has been asked and a speech is already—
>
> Q. Petrocelli: Correct?
>
> Baker: It's already been asked and answered.
>
> The court: Overruled. You may answer.
>
> A. No, Mr. Petrocelli. That's totally, absolutely incorrect.
>
> Q. And Ronald Goldman came upon you when you were there with Nicole, and you did not expect him that night, correct?
>
> Baker: I'm going to object.
>
> A. I don't know Ron Goldman.
>
> The court: Overruled.
>
> Q. And Ronald Goldman got into a fight with you as he tried to stop you, and you cut him and you slashed him until he died, collapsed in your arms. True or untrue?
>
> A. Untrue.

> Q. And you left him there to die, Mr. Simpson, with his eyes
> open, looking right at you. True or untrue?
> A. That's untrue.
> Petrocelli: I have no further questions.[33]

Petrocelli's questions are all the more devastating because Simpson's attorney is trying vehemently to object. Baker's efforts to protect Simpson from the ultimate questions show that he is afraid of the way Simpson will look before the jury in denying the questions.

5.10 STUDY QUESTIONS FOR CROSS-EXAMINATION VIDEO CLIPS FROM *PEOPLE V. SIMPSON* (DISC 2)

Clip 1 (Bailey): Fuhrman Denies Racial Slurs (4 min.)[34]

Background: Kathleen Bell, a real estate agent who Mark Fuhrman had met in 1985, had sent a letter to both the prosecution and defense stating that Fuhrman had used racial slurs in her presence regarding African Americans. Prior to the clip, F. Lee Bailey had inquired how the prosecution had prepared Fuhrman for cross-examination regarding this issue. Fuhrman stated that he had met with three of the prosecutors who had asked him a total of ten questions about the issue. In this clip, when Bailey begins by asking about "questions put to you by counsel," it is those meetings to which Bailey is referring.

Study Questions

1. Would it be clear to the jury from Bailey's tone of voice what he believes regarding Fuhrman's testimony about trial preparation?
2. Are the majority of Bailey's questions leading?
3. Which questions are argumentative?

---

33. *Goldman v. Simpson* No. SC036340, 1996 WL 679699 at *37 (Cal. Super. Ct. Nov. 25, 1996) (direct examination of adverse witness O. J. Simpson).
34. *People v. Simpson* No. BA097211, 1995 WL 109035 at *22–23 (Cal. Super. Ct. Mar. 15, 1995) (cross-examination of Mark Fuhrman).

4. Does Bailey effectively paint Fuhrman into a corner regarding his prior use of the *N* word?

Clip 2 (Douglas): Shipp Maintains He Is O. J.'s Friend and Does Not Reveal Dream to Investigators (4.5 min.)[35]

Background: Here, defense attorney Carl Douglas attacks Shipp's claim that he was a good friend of O. J.'s and that O. J. actually confessed to Shipp that he had dreamed of killing Nicole.[36]

Study Questions

1. Compare Douglas' style of cross-examination to Bailey's. Which do you think is more effective?
2. Is Douglas effective in casting doubt on Shipp's claim of friendship with O. J.?
3. Does Douglas make effective use of leading questions?
4. Does he vary his voice?
5. Does the witness seem well prepared for Douglas' questions?

Clip 3 (Kelberg): Dr. Huizenga's Lack of Expertise, Failure to Document Finding, Opinion about Injury, and Favoritism toward O. J. (9 min.)[37]

Background: At the request of one of Simpson's attorneys, Robert Shapiro, Dr. Robert Huizenga (pronounced *High-zenga*) conducted a

---

35. *People v. Simpson* No. BA097211, 1995 WL 37668 at *11–12, 16–17, 23–24 (Cal. Super. Ct. Feb. 1, 1995) (cross-examination of Ron Shipp).
36. Joe Brown, who is referred to in one of the questions in the clip, is Douglas' investigator who spoke with Shipp. For a detailed summary of Shipp's testimony on direct relevant to this clip, see the background section of clip 2 and the clip itself at the end of chapter 4. In that clip, Darden asks Shipp about the moment when O. J. confesses to Shipp that he has had dreams of killing Nicole.
37. *People v. Simpson* No. BA097211, 1995 WL 437455 at *19–20, 22–23, 25 (Cal. Super. Ct. July 14, 1995) (cross-examination of Dr.

physical examination of O. J. just after the murders. On direct, Dr. Huizenga testified about his educational background and O. J.'s physical condition. He also stated that O. J. was so feeble that he walked like Tarzan's grandfather. Here, he is questioned about his conclusions regarding O. J.'s frail condition and the cut that O. J. had on his hand.

Note that in the middle of the clip, prosecutor Brian Kelberg has Huizenga take part in a demonstration consistent with the prosecution's theory of the case: O. J. grabbed Goldman from behind, grasped him around his stomach with his left hand, and cut his throat with the knife in his right hand. With this theory, Goldman struggled and removed the left glove—which was found on the scene—from O. J.'s hand, exposing it to scratches and cuts from a knife.

Study Questions

1. Compare attorney Kelberg's tone of voice to Bailey's and Douglas.' Which style do you like better?
2. Does Kelberg make good eye contact with the witness?
3. Is he successful in challenging the doctor's opinion that O. J. walked like Tarzan's grandfather?
4. Notice how you can incorporate demonstrations into a cross-examination. Is Kelberg successful?
5. Is Kelberg's use of "motion to strike an answer" effective?
6. Can you identify the topic that is not in Kelberg's outline but that he addresses given the witness' answer? Is it effective?

Clip 4 (Scheck): Fung Fails to Tell Grand Jury That Assistant Collected Blood Samples (6 min.)[38]

Background: Dennis Fung was a criminalist for the Los Angeles Police Department who collected evidence at the crime scene (Bundy) and O. J.'s house (Rockingham). He was assisted by Andrea Mazzola, who

---

Huizenga) and *People v. Simpson* No. BA097211, 1995 WL 447590 at *10–11 (Cal. Super. Ct. July 17, 1995) (cross-examination of Dr. Huizenga).
38. *People v. Simpson* No. BA097211, 1995 WL 144998 at *27–29 (Cal. Super. Ct. Apr. 4, 1995) (cross-examination of Dennis Fung).

had processed less than five crime scenes in her career. Throughout the cross-examination, Fung was attacked for either making inconsistent statements prior to trial or conducting sloppy police work in the collection of evidence. Hank Goldberg conducted the direct examination, and Barry Scheck handled the cross-examination.

Through these questions, Scheck is setting up Fung for inconsistent statements he made to the grand jury where Scheck contends Fung tried to make it sound like he—with all of his experience—had collected the blood evidence instead of his very junior assistant. The word *swatched* used in this clip refers to the process of collecting blood from a crime scene. It is a collection method in which distilled water is added to a cloth swatch, and the swatch is then placed on a bloodstain so the stain is transferred to the cloth swatch.

Study Questions:

1. Is Scheck's tone of voice effective?
2. Is it clear from the questioning which of the inconsistent statements that the witness made are believed to be true by Scheck?
3. Does Scheck argue with the witness unsuccessfully?
4. How did you react when Scheck looks at the jury as he is making some of his points?

Clip 5 (Scheck): Fung Claims in Error That He Carried O. J.'s Blood Sample (4 min.)[39]

Background: As part of the investigation, O. J. gave a blood sample to the police. Detective Philip Vannatter took the sample to Fung, who was in O. J.'s house conducting an investigation. In this clip, Fung is

---

39. *People v. Simpson* No. BA097211, 1995 WL 215716 at *4 (Cal. Super. Ct. Apr. 12, 1995) (cross-examination of Dennis Fung); *People v. Simpson* No. BA097211, 1995 WL 221962 at *7, 11 (Cal. Super. Ct. Apr. 13, 1995) (cross-examination of Dennis Fung); and *People v. Simpson* No. BA097211, 1995 WL 170091 at *14, 23–24, 26, 35–38 (Cal. Super. Ct. Apr. 11, 1995) (cross-examination of Dennis Fung).

questioned regarding how he carried O. J.'s blood sample from the house to the evidence truck.[40]

Study Questions

1. How well does Scheck get Fung to commit with certainty how Fung carried the vial of blood to the evidence truck?
2. If you were the prosecution, how would you have prepared Fung for this line of cross-examination?
3. Is it effective when Scheck looks directly at the jury?
4. How successful is the impeachment?

Clip 6 (Scheck): Argumentative Questions, Cross to Support Case, and Ending Day Strong (7.5 min.)[41]

Background: In the first part of the clip ("Argumentative Questions"), Scheck is trying to argue to the jury that there was blood planted in O. J.'s Bronco while it was in police custody. He suggests that stain number 305 was present on August 26, 1994 (i.e., planted), but not on June 14, 1994, when stains were "swatched." Scheck also asks Fung why there is no time written down in the evidence report for the collection of the socks from O. J.'s bedroom. Goldberg objects when Scheck asks, "That's something you're just speculating about because you think it sounds good?"

For the second part of the clip ("Cross to Support Case"), it is important to know that there was evidence that there was an area at the Bundy crime scene where dirt had been disturbed as a result of Goldman's struggle with the murderer. Scheck refers to this as the "caged-in area" because the theory was that Goldman had been trapped by the assailant and could not escape. Scheck argues that if O. J. were the murderer, there should be more dirt inside his house.

---

40. Why Vannatter took the blood sample to Fung at O. J.'s house instead of to the LAPD's Scientific Investigative Division (SID) property control room is a question that was never fully resolved at trial.

41. *People v. Simpson* No. BA097211, 1995 WL 170091 at *14, 23–24, 26, 35–38 (Cal. Super. Ct. Apr. 11, 1995) (cross-examination of Dennis Fung).

For the third part of the clip ("Ending Day Strong"), you should be aware that blood was found on the rear gate of Nicole's home. DNA testing showed that the odds of it being someone's blood other than O. J.'s was 1 in 57 billion. What Scheck found suspicious about this blood was that although it was not found until July 3, almost three weeks after the murder, it was almost in pristine condition as compared to blood that had been collected right after the murders and had degraded.[42] This fact fit the defense's theory that after O. J. had given his blood sample to the police, someone had used part of that sample to plant O. J.'s blood. In this video clip, Scheck confronts Fung with a photograph that shows a bloodstain collected on June 13, item number 115. On July 3, Fung collected a blood sample that was item numbers 116 and 117. Neither of those bloodstains appear on the photograph from June 13.

Study Questions

Argumentative Questions
1. Do you agree with the court's rulings on the objections?
2. Would you have made the objections?

Cross to Support Case
1. Does Scheck effectively use the witness' answers to support his theory of the case?
2. Are Scheck's gestures effective or distracting?

Ending Day Strong
1. How persuasive is Scheck's confrontation with Fung?
2. Does Scheck's tone of voice convey his belief to the jury?
3. If you were Scheck, would you have asked any more questions after Judge Ito says, "The lawyers for my 4:30 calendar are here"?
4. Do you think the photographs are powerful impeachment?
5. Is there any explanation why the June 13 photograph does not show the bloodstains recovered on July 3?

---

42. Jeffrey Toobin, *The Run of His Life: The People v. O. J. Simpson* at 340 (Touchstone 1997).

Chapter Six

━━━━◆◆◆◆━━━━

CLOSING ARGUMENT

I have heard an experienced counselor say that he never
feared the effect upon a jury of a lawyer who does not believe
in his heart that his client ought to have a verdict. If he does
not believe it, his unbelief will appear to the jury, despite all
his protestations, and will become their unbelief.[1]

—*Ralph Waldo Emerson*

6.1 THE OVERRATED IMPORTANCE
OF CLOSING ARGUMENT

One of the greatest mistakes a lawyer can make is to save his best argument for the closing argument. It is too late then because the jurors
have almost always already made up their minds. Remember, at least
80 percent of jurors come to a decision "during or immediately after
the opening statements."[2]

---

1. Ralph Waldo Emerson, *Spiritual Laws,* Essays; First Series, 1841, in
    Complete Works of Ralph Waldo Emerson 2:131, 156–157 (Houghton
    Mifflin 1903).
2. James F. McKenzie, *Eloquence in Opening Statement,* Trial Dipl.J. at
    32 (Spring 1987); Donald E. Vinson, *Jury Psychology and Antitrust*

Yet it is understandable why so many attorneys do wait until closings to make their best arguments.

First, opening statements are harder to deliver because it takes a certain amount of courage to predict what the evidence will show; a closing simply has to summarize what has already taken place. Second, some lawyers feel that if they put their best argument in their openings, jurors will lose interest in the trial. These lawyers often like to save some surprise facts for the trial and then use them in their closing. Unfortunately for these lawyers, jurors will go ahead and reach conclusions about who should win after opening statements without the benefit of those facts.

Third, some lawyers feel that if they put their best arguments in their openings, it will tip off the other side to their strategy, and thus they will lose the element of surprise at trial. The problem with this thinking is that the trial begins with the opening statement, not with the first witness. Given that jurors are quickly making up their minds during opening statements, this is not the time to be holding back your strong arguments. Certainly, your opening statement need not give away every surprise you might have at trial. Nonetheless, it should contain your best pieces of evidence and your best arguments.

Even though the importance of closings is overrated, it is paramount that you make your closing as good as it can possibly be. Even if the jurors have already made up their minds, you don't want to give them a reason to change their minds with a subpar performance. Instead, provide jurors with the evidence and arguments to make their deliberations easy. Finally, the importance of opening statements notwithstanding, closings become very important in a close trial. It is then that a trial can be won or lost with closing arguments.

6.2 THE BASICS

1. Openings versus Closings

There are three essential differences between openings and closings. First, while attorneys are not allowed to discuss jury instructions at

---

Trial Strategy, 55 Antitrust L.J. at 591 (1986) (based on 14,000 actual or surrogate jurors, "80 to 90 percent of all jurors come to a decision during or immediately after the opening statements").

length in opening statements, it is imperative that attorneys discuss the important instructions in detail with the jurors in closing. Instructions are often very long and complicated. However, the one or two key instructions need to be summarized by you so the jury can comprehend them (e.g., what constitutes "negligence" in a car wreck).

Second, if you are the plaintiff or prosecutor, you get an opportunity to give a rebuttal to the defendant's closing.[3] This is a significant advantage, which will be discussed later.

Third, it is necessary to explain to the jury which exhibits and trial testimony are important. For example, a typical trial will have many items in evidence, but often the jury only needs to focus on a few of them.

> ### Example: Discussing Important Exhibits
> ### in a Medical Malpractice Case
>
> Ladies and gentlemen, although you will have three volumes of medical records back in the jury room, there really are only two pages you need to look at. On page 60, volume 3, dated February 1 [**show the record on a projection screen for the jury**], a doctor gave my client medication that caused a very severe allergic reaction. However, no changes were made in the hospital computer records or on my client's medical chart to indicate this serious allergic reaction. Instead, the chart indicates "NKDA," which means "no known drug allergies."
>
> On page 90, volume 3, dated February 14 [**show the record on a projection screen**], the record shows that my client was given the very same medication that had caused a serious reaction just two weeks before. This time, the reaction caused my client's death. Was this negligence? Of course it was. There can be no doubt.

2. Damages

In cases involving personal injury, employment discrimination, and others where some damages are intangible (such as pain and suffering

---

3. The plaintiff's or prosecution's first part of the argument is sometimes called opening argument or summation, while the second part is always called rebuttal argument.

or mental anguish damages), the big issue a plaintiff's attorney must re-solve is whether to ask a jury for a specific dollar amount for his client if it is allowed by the court.[4] Great trial lawyers can get into a heated debate about this issue.

Some attorneys feel that it is best not to ask the jury for a specific amount (see Daniel Petrocelli's argument at "Discuss Damages and End Memorably" later in this chapter). The rationale for this view-point is that an attorney may underestimate the value of the case com-pared to what the jury may be thinking. For example, an attorney might ask for $1 million for pain and suffering when the jury would have returned a verdict for $5 million if the attorney had not set the ceiling on damages.

Other attorneys feel that it is a better strategy to ask the jurors for a specific amount.[5] The reason is that they are looking to you—as the authority on the case—to guide them to a proper verdict. The amount you ask for will be determined by how the evidence has come in at trial, the results of your focus group conducted prior to trial, and what verdicts have been returned on similar cases in your jurisdiction.

Below is an example of each type of argument. However you de-cide to argue damages, it is vital that your evidence at trial provides the support you need.[6]

---

4. Compare *Waldorf v. Shula,* 896 F.2d 723, 724 (3d Cir. 1990) ("[P]laintiff's counsel may [not] request a specific dollar amount for pain and suffering in his closing remarks") with *Lightfoot v. Union Carbide,* 110 F.3d 898, 912 (2d Cir. 1997) ("It is best left to the dis-cretion of the trial judge, who may either prohibit counsel from men-tioning specific figures or impose reasonable limitations, including cautionary jury instructions").
5. This has become the more prevalent view in recent years.
6. In cases where punitive damages are allowed, these are usually dis-cussed in separate arguments after the jury has returned a verdict for the plaintiff. If you are the plaintiff, argue that the only way the defen-dant will be deterred in the future is by hurting it (e.g., a corporation) where it counts, in its pocketbook. If you are on the defense, show re-morse and tell the jury that your client accepts the verdict and under-stands clearly the message the jury is sending.

Example: Not Asking for a Specific Amount

Ladies and gentlemen, having discussed the past and future medical expenses for my client, let me turn to the issue of pain and suffering. I am only going to talk about damages that are supported by the overwhelming evidence in this case. Not only did my client have three back surgeries because of the truck driver's reckless actions, he will never be the same. I am not going to pretend that I can tell you how much his pain and suffering is worth. And here is why. A Van Gogh painting sold ten years ago for $135 million. Now, if it were severely damaged, how much would it cost to replace it today?

John [client] is not a painting; he is much more. He is a unique human being. His joy in being able to play catch with his son was not for sale. It has been taken forever. It was robbed from him by the defendant. A rich man would pay anything he could to live a life free of pain, to go one hour without hurting, to be able to do the things that John can't. . . . No lawyer should tell you what John's pain and suffering is worth. Whatever amount you decide, err on the side of mercy because John will never be able to come back here again.

Example: Asking for a Specific Amount

Ladies and gentlemen, having discussed the past and future medical expenses for my client, let me turn to the issue of pain and suffering. I am only going to talk about damages that are supported by the overwhelming evidence in this case. Not only did my client have three back surgeries because of the truck driver's reckless actions, he will never be the same. The evidence is overwhelming that he should be compensated.

A Van Gogh painting sold ten years ago for $135 million. Now, if it were severely damaged, how much would it cost to replace it today? John [client] is not a painting; he is much more. He is a unique human being. His joy in being able to play catch with his son was not for sale. It has been taken forever. It was robbed from him by the defendant. A rich man would pay anything he could to live a life free of pain, to go one hour without hurting, to be able to do the things that John can't. . . . $5 million is the minimum amount of compensation for his pain and suffering. Now, some of you are probably thinking of a much higher amount. Whatever you

do, err on the side of mercy, because John will never be able
to come back here again.

The other question is to what extent a defendant should discuss
damages. This depends on how close the case is. If you are the defense
counsel and feel that you have the upper hand by a large margin, a discussion of damages can certainly be seen as a sign of weakness. If your
case has turned into a disaster, a credible discussion needs to take place
so the jury does not perceive your denial as a reason to award higher
damages than it would have otherwise. If it is a close case, an argument
such as the one below is a good example showing how to deal with the
plaintiff's argument.

Example: Defendant's Discussion of Damages

[Plaintiff's counsel] has mentioned damages in this case, and I
want to discuss them briefly before getting to what this case
is all about. There is no credible explanation for the figure he
has come up with. Let me tell you why. . . . But ladies and
gentlemen, there is absolutely no reason you will need to discuss it. The defendant is not at fault in any way in this case.
There are three reasons why. . . .

3. Prohibitions

Although the scope of this chapter is not intended to cover every prohibition in closing argument, the most common mistakes are discussed
below.[7]

A. Misstating Evidence or Instructions

It goes without saying that attorneys are not allowed to misstate the evidence or the law. First, to do so would undermine your relationship with
the jury. For example, if you recount testimony that is different from
what actually took place, the jurors will lose their trust in you. Second, if
you misstate a jury instruction, it is likely the judge will admonish you in

---

7. For an extremely detailed discussion of prohibitions see Jacob Stein,
   Closing Arguments: The Art and Law, chapter 1, "The Law of Closing
   Argument" (West 2d ed. 2005).

front of the jury—another serious blow to your credibility. Furthermore, such mistakes can lead to reversal of the verdict on appeal.

B. Vouching for Credibility of Witness or Evidence

Attorneys are prohibited from injecting their personal opinions.[8] One way to avoid improperly asserting your opinion is to avoid the use of "I think" or "I believe." As with opening statements, simply make your assertions in the third person instead.

Example: Improper Vouching

1. I believe my client is innocent of murder.
2. I think the prosecution has not proven its case. . . .
3. As a prosecutor, I would not have brought this case if I for one minute thought the defendant was innocent.
4. I have represented a lot of people in my career, but you won't find a more truthful person than my client.

Example: Proper Argument

1. Mr. Jones [client] is innocent.
2. The prosecution has not proven its case.
3. There can be no doubt that the defendant is guilty. We have proven the following. . . .
4. There are at least three reasons you should believe my client's testimony. First, do you remember his demeanor? He answered with sincerity every possible question that was put to him.

C. Appealing to Jurors' Sympathies or Biases

This prohibition is consistent with the standard instruction given to jurors that admonishes them to decide the case on the facts and not be

---

8. See Rule 3.4(e), *Model Rules of Professional Conduct* (2006). The rule states: "A lawyer shall not in trial allude to any matter that the lawyer does not reasonably believe is relevant or that will not be supported by admissible evidence, assert personal knowledge of facts in issue except when testifying as a witness, or state a personal opinion as to the justness of a cause, the credibility of a witness, the culpability of a civil litigant or the guilt or innocence of an accused."

influenced by sympathy for one party or the other. An attempt by an attorney to inflame the jury's sympathies or biases is improper. Of course, almost all important decisions in life are based on a degree of emotion, and a jury verdict is no different. As with the above examples for improper vouching, courts are often concerned with the way in which an argument is phrased as opposed to the message that is conveyed.

> The making of a golden-rule argument (i.e., do unto others as you would have them do unto you) is prohibited in most jurisdictions. That is, you cannot inflame the jurors' sympathy and passion by asking them to put themselves in the shoes of your client and punish the other side as if the wrong at trial had happened to them.

"Imagine" and "Put yourself in my client's position" will almost always draw a successful objection.

Example: Improperly Appealing to Jurors' Sympathies
1. Imagine how my client must have felt when she was hit by the plaintiff's car.
2. Put yourself in the shoes of my client. What would you have done if someone charged at you with a knife? Of course, you would have . . .

Example: Appropriate Argument
1. My client's life was changed forever when she was hit by the plaintiff's car.
2. A person has an absolute right to use self-defense. When John charged my client with a knife, Bob had every right to fight back.

D. Mentioning Insurance
Most states do not allow the mention of insurance at trial. For example, in a car-wreck case, the jurors are unaware that the defendant driver's insurance company is providing counsel and will pay the judgment (pursuant to the terms of the insurance agreement). Since jurors are instructed by courts that they are impartial judges of the facts, it is improper to suggest to the jury that they should find for the plaintiff because the defendant driver is protected by insurance.

E. Missing Witness Argument

The missing witness argument is a very tempting argument to make but can only be done under particular circumstances. The problem for the attorney making the argument is that it is often difficult to satisfy all three requirements. An attorney may argue that the jury can draw a negative inference from the opposing side's failure to call a witness if the witness (1) is in peculiar control of the other side, (2) was available for trial, and (3) the testimony would not have been cumulative. Before making such an argument, you need to get a ruling from the court permitting you to make the argument.

Example: Proper Missing Witness Argument

Plaintiff's counsel: The defendant claims that he fired the plaintiff because she did not perform well at her job. Why is it that the defendant never called her supervisor, Mr. Jones, as a witness at trial? It is because the defendant was afraid of what Mr. Jones would say, namely, that my client was not fired for good cause but rather because she was a woman.

F. Commenting on Criminal Defendant's Failure to Testify

There is no quicker way to have a mistrial declared than for a prosecutor to comment in any way on a defendant's decision not to testify or to put on evidence. However, if the defendant *does* testify or put on witnesses, a prosecutor may fairly ask the jury to judge the credibility of the defense evidence.

G. Commenting on Punishment

In jurisdictions where the judge imposes sentencing, it is improper for either side to comment to the jury on the punishment a defendant might receive if convicted.[9]

---

9. However, where the prosecution has put on a cooperating witness who is testifying because of a plea agreement, defense counsel will attack the witness' testimony as being bought by the plea agreement in closing argument. The consequence is that the jury will know the potential amount of time the witness could have received if convicted (instead of pleading guilty) and, by inference, the amount of prison time the defendant is facing if convicted.

6.3 EIGHT STEPS TO A SUCCESSFUL CLOSING ARGUMENT

1. During Trial, Make a List of Important Testimony

At the beginning of the trial, your table should be clear except for your trial notebook, exhibit notebook, notepad, and computer. During the trial, have a document open in your computer titled "Closing Argument Notes," which lists every witness you expect to be called at trial. As the trial proceeds, type the *important* testimony, verbatim, by the witness' name in this document. If you have an assistant or cocounsel, he will be a tremendous asset in this process. If you are by yourself, type the phrases you remember during breaks in the trial. Important testimony means *important*. In an hour of testimony, you might need to input only a few statements into your computer.

It is extremely critical that you do not start preparing for the next day of trial until you have input the important testimony of the day. There is no way on the following day, much less the night before you give your closing, to remember exactly what was said on the witness stand. Remember that the jurors, given their numbers, have a better chance of remembering what was said than you do, so to maintain your credibility during closing argument, you need to recite the testimony exactly right.

Example: Testimony That Should Be Remembered for Closing (witness Cynthia Lou Klaver) from *U.S. v. McVeigh*

At trial, the prosecution's first witness, Cynthia Lou Klaver, describes the destruction she saw in relation to a photograph of the bombed area.

> Q. *What are we looking at on the ground there?*
> A. *There was twisted—twisted metal everywhere, glass all over, debris. It looked like a war zone to me when I stepped out. The ground was littered, covered.*[10]

---

10. *United States v. McVeigh* No. 96-CR-68, 1997 WL 200045 at *8 (D. Colo. Apr. 25, 1997) (direct examination of Cynthia Lou Klaver).

The witness' words "It looked like a war zone to me when I stepped out" should be written down as she is testifying so that you may use the sentence in closing. For example, if you were giving the closing for the prosecution, you might say, "Ladies and gentlemen of the jury, our first witness, Cynthia Lou Klaver, described the destruction in unforgettable words: 'It looked like a war zone.' She explained that there was—and I quote—'twisted metal everywhere, glass all over.'"

> The most dramatic way to summarize important testimony is to scan selected pages of the transcript into your computer and then display the relevant text on a projection screen for the jury to read along with you. A quicker but slightly less professional way to accomplish the same goal is to copy the selected transcript pages, highlight the quoted text, and put the page on an ELMO brand projector so the jury can see it while you read from the page.[11]

Example: Using Transcripts in Closing Argument

Ideally, you should ask for daily trial transcripts of important witnesses so that you may use them in your closing. Although it is expensive, and court reporters are sometimes reluctant to do this because of the time involved in their preparation, there is nothing more credible and powerful in your closing.

> Remember Ms. White's eyewitness account of the car wreck. She testified, and I am quoting directly from the trial transcript, "The defendant was talking on her cell phone as she drove through the intersection while the light was red." On cross-examination by Ms. Robson [defense counsel], she was asked, "Question: Is it possible that the defendant drove through the intersection while the light was yellow? Answer: No way."

It is obviously more effective to quote verbatim from the trial transcript when you recount a witness' testimony to the jury. However, even if you can't get a trial transcript, reading directly from your notes is an effective way to communicate the important testimony to the jury.

---

11. An ELMO visual presenter projects documents and other tangible items from a flatbed screen to a projection screen that can be seen by the jury.

2. Use the Opening Outline as a Starting Point

Unlike an opening statement, where there is time to write out every word of the first draft, typically there is no such luxury when preparing a closing. Nonetheless, closings are easier because you can use the ideas from your opening, and you have had the entire trial to think about what important evidence you are going to discuss.

Since the promises you made in your opening should have been fulfilled by the evidence at trial, use the outline of your opening statement as your starting point for your closing argument. Throughout the trial, tweak the outline as necessary for closing. The only major difference will be the addition of a discussion of jury instructions and possibly damages.

Closing Argument Outline Form

I.   Begin powerfully with a memorable theme.
     —Incorporate themes from the opening and create new ones.
II. Discuss the important details of the story.
     —Give an overview of strong facts.
     —Present significant evidence that supports strong facts.
     —Use visual aids.
III. Address candidly—but don't dwell on—weaknesses in the case and turn them into strengths.
IV. Briefly discuss important jury instructions.
     —Set forth elements of claim/defense.
     —Address burden of proof.
V.   Discuss damages (civil trial only).
VI. End memorably.

---

3. Incorporate Opening Themes and Create New Ones

There is great opportunity in your closing to be creative and memorable. By listening to the other side's evidence, you will surely be able to add to your opening. This will keep your closing interesting. The jury remembers your opening, so you just can't repeat it. You need to build on it to make your closing memorable. Perhaps the opposing witnesses exaggerated, forgot important facts, or their demeanor was not credible. It may well be that opposing counsel made promises in her opening that were not kept during the trial.

Example: "Broken Promise" Theme

Assume defense counsel stated in her opening that she would bring to court an eyewitness to declare that the plaintiff was negligent in an auto accident—but she never put the witness on the stand. You could state in your closing:

> At the beginning of this trial, I promised that this would be a case about the defendant's reckless behavior. Having heard all the evidence, it is clear that not only is this a case of reckless actions but also a case of promises not being kept. Remember, in Ms. Black's opening statement, she promised to bring you a witness who would testify that my client was negligent. That never happened. There is an old saying, "Fool me once, shame on you; fool me twice, shame on me." Ms. Black's broken promise is all you need to know, but there is more.

4. Tell a Story: Begin Powerfully, Address Weaknesses, and End Memorably

Another advantage a closing argument has over an opening statement is more freedom to use analogies and related stories. The whole world of literature is at your disposal to create an interesting closing. Is there a selection from *Aesop's Fables* that is particularly helpful in explaining your case? Is there something in history that provides a useful analogy? Johnnie Cochran, in his closing argument for *People v. Simpson,* used—with varying degrees of success—analogies from Hitler, the Bible, and the French Revolution to motivate the jury to vote for an acquittal. The important point is to use these tools if they are persuasive and invulnerable to attack by the other side.

Also, just like an opening statement, it is vital that you begin powerfully, candidly discuss the weaknesses in your case, and finish with your best argument. The following examples highlight the importance of these techniques.

Example: Beginning Powerfully—
Prosecution Closing Argument (Larry Mackey)
from *U.S. v. McVeigh*

The court: Mr. Mackey, you're going to present the govern-
ment's case.

Mackey: I am, Your Honor. May it please the court.

The court: Yes.

Mackey: Mr. Jones, Counsel, Mr. Hartzler, my colleagues,
ladies and gentlemen of the jury, good morning.

> *The events that were set in motion two years ago are*
> *drawing to a close. On April 19, 1995, a crime of ghastly*
> *proportions was committed. On that day a truck packed*
> *with explosives parked in downtown Oklahoma City.*
> *Only a wall of windows separated the unsuspecting chil-*
> *dren and women and men inside that building from the*
> *truck and the explosives that sat outside. The truck*
> *bomb exploded, the building gave way, and suddenly*
> *many lives were ended, and many, many more were*
> *changed forever.*
>
> *America stood in shock. Who could do such a thing?*
> *Who could do such a thing? It's a question that began to*
> *ripple across this country coast to coast. And finally it's*
> *come to rest right here in this courtroom. It's fallen to*
> *you as members of this jury to answer that question.*
>
> *Based on the evidence, based on what you've heard,*
> *the answer is clear. Tim McVeigh did it. Tim McVeigh*
> *and Terry Nichols in concert with each other planned*
> *and executed the violent attack on the Murrah Building*
> *and are responsible for the murders of those persons who*
> *died.*[12]

The prosecutor does not waste time getting to his point. He cap-
tures the jurors' attention immediately, just like in the opening statement. As with any good storytelling, whether the first paragraph of a
book, the opening scene in a movie, or the first words in a speech, the
beginning is the one moment when the entire audience is paying attention. It is critical that its attention be captured and the moment not be
wasted. The prosecutor does not waste time thanking the jurors for

---

12. *United States v. McVeigh* No. 96-CR-68, 1997 WL 280943 at *1–2 (D.
Colo. May 29, 1997) (closing argument of Larry Mackey).

their several weeks of service. The jury is ready to begin deliberations, and the prosecutor sets out immediately to give the important reasons for returning a verdict for the government.

After this powerful beginning, the prosecutor gave the jury a brief summary of the remainder of his closing and then resumed quickly with the momentum of his beginning.

Example: Prosecution Closing Continued

When Mr. Hartzler [cocounsel] first spoke to you in the opening and told you what the government intended to do, to fairly present the evidence against Mr. McVeigh, he told you that the evidence would make your job easier, that it would amount to overwhelming evidence of guilt, that it would build brick by brick, witness by witness, a wall, a wall that added up to the guilt of Tim McVeigh. After a month of trial and hammered away at by a very experienced, very skilled team of defense lawyers and experts, that wall still stands, stands tall and strong, and it adds up to the guilt of Tim McVeigh.

When you retire to the jury room, evaluate what promises were made by Joe Hartzler against the evidence and see if we haven't kept our word. We promised and we've proven, in more ways than one, a number of important factual propositions.

Number one, Timothy McVeigh, motivated by hatred of the government, in a rage over the events at Waco, deliberately and with premeditation planned the bombing of the Murrah Building.

Number two, that he educated himself on how to build bombs.

Number three, that he enlisted at least one coconspirator and attempted to recruit yet another, Michael Fortier, to help him.[13]

Also, compare the beginning of this closing to the weak one given by Marcia Clark in the Simpson criminal trial (discussed in section 6.5).

---

13. *United States v. McVeigh* No. 96-CR-68, 1997 WL 280943 at *2 (D. Colo. May 29, 1997) (closing argument of Larry Mackey).

Not only must your closing begin strongly but you also need to discuss candidly the weaknesses in your case.

Example: Addressing Weaknesses—
Defense Closing Argument (Stephen Jones)
from *U.S. v. McVeigh*

Jones: Now, let us not be mistaken. Tim McVeigh was convicted in the court of public opinion not only before the first witness had testified, [but] before the first piece of evidence had been introduced, even before his lawyer was appointed or his preliminary hearing or his indictment. He was convicted because the nature of the crime, as severe as it was and the attention focused on it followed by the dramatic arrest and walkout in Noble County Courthouse, convinced people that the right man had been arrested. But it was not permitted to rest there. For weeks and months and now years later, it continues to be recycled.

I told you in the opening that this evidence in many respects would not be what you expected; things that you might have thought would be presented would not; and there would be things presented that you had never heard of. And I think I was right in that assessment. You may also recall that during the voir dire, Mr. Ryan and Ms. Wilkinson and Mr. Mackey asked you from time to time would you have the fortitude, the courage, the strength to sign a death penalty warrant—or verdict, rather, if it became appropriate and necessary; and each of you said you could and would.

But the question is, now that the evidence is in and knowing what the court of public opinion is, can you vote a verdict of not guilty if, after hearing all the evidence and the argument and the instructions, that is your opinion? If you believe collectively or individually that Mr. McVeigh is not guilty, can you say that? Because if you cannot, then the justice system as we know it in this country has been corrupted far more than any trial that happened in Los Angeles, California.

If we let sympathy overcome reason, then sympathy becomes to this case what race was to another case. When we had the opening statements, I took six minutes and read to you the names of all of the victims who were the subject of this indictment. I did that because all of us understand the victims' plight. They are not the property of any side to this lawsuit. Their collective loss belongs to the country as well as to themselves. There is nothing inconsistent with being Tim McVeigh's counsel and arguing and advocating his position and not having personally and privately and emotionally sympathy and understanding for these individuals. And they are not litigants or parties to this case. Their interest is served by knowing that there is a fair trial so that they have confidence in the verdict. But that requires zealous advocacy, a testing of the evidence, cross-examination, and fierce and sometimes heated argument and discussion about what these facts mean. Because heat generates light, and it is with the light that we will know what the verdict should be.[14]

Jones does not shy away from the greatest hurdles in his case: sympathy for the innocent victims and the public's desire for revenge. He realizes that the trial has not occurred in a vacuum, but he correctly places it in the proper context of the emotions of the nation and of the importance of the trial to the history of criminal justice. While many people may disagree with the propriety of Jones' decision to read the names of the victims in his opening statement (in effect, "How dare he read their names when he represents the murderer?"), he explains that he did it to show that there is nothing inconsistent with grieving for the victims and finding McVeigh innocent. Whether or not you agree if it was effective to read all the names in his opening statement, the point is that Jones gains credibility by confronting the weaknesses of his case—sympathy and revenge—rather than avoiding them.

Finally, just like in an opening statement, you need to end memorably.

Example: Memorable Ending—
Prosecution Closing Argument
(Larry Mackey) from *U.S. v. McVeigh*

That [Ryder] truck crawled to a stop in front of the Murrah Building on that morning, right in front of children and women and men; and then Tim McVeigh ran away.

The law enforcement officers that died that morning were not "treasonous" officials, as Tim McVeigh had declared; "cowardice bastards," as he had described to you.

---

14. *United States v. McVeigh* No. 96-CR-68, 1997 WL 282227 at *3 (D. Colo. May 29, 1997) (closing argument of Stephen Jones).

The credit union employees who disappeared that morning were not tyrants whose blood had to be spilled in order to preserve liberty.

And certainly the nineteen children who died that morning were not storm troopers that Tim McVeigh had said must die, innocent storm troopers who must die because of their association with an evil empire.

In fact, the people who Tim McVeigh murdered on April 19, 1995, weren't one thing. They were bosses and secretaries, they were executives and others. They were blacks, they were whites, they were mothers, they were daughters, they were fathers and sons. They were a community. So who are the real patriots and who is the traitor? You met some of the victims and survivors in this case. Think about that. Compare in your mind the dignity that they exhibited, the characteristics and qualities of good people, and contrast that for a moment with what you've come to know about Tim McVeigh, a man who was intent to kill anyone and everyone and then run away.

In his opening statement, Joe Hartzler talked to you about grievances, and he described one grievance that was going on and being settled in a Democratic fashion by [Cynthia] Lou Klaver that morning, a dispute over water, in democratic fashion, due process at work.

And the other means of resolving grievances that he told you about [were] the means that Tim McVeigh employed on April 19, 1995: terror, violence, and murder.

When Tim McVeigh blew up that truck bomb and brought down the Murrah Building, he did more than simply create the emotional wreckage that you exhibited—or that we saw during the course of this trial. He did more than kill innocent men, women, and children. What he did was he created a new grievance. A new grievance. A grievance against the victims and against the United States of America.

And for myself and each member of this prosecution team, it has been our pleasure to represent those victims and the United States in settling that grievance. We have done so in a way that Tim McVeigh would not choose. We have done so through the due process system; but the process is over now. The process is over. Tim McVeigh has received his due process, and it is now time to render judgment. And your job as jurors, your privilege, your duty, as well as your job, is to do justice. And on behalf of the United States, I ask that *you return a verdict of guilty as charged against Timothy McVeigh.*

Thank you.[15]

Like any great attorney, Mackey ties the themes in his closing into the themes of the opening: cowardice, resolving grievances violently, and innocent children. By doing so, his closing has coherence and is memorable. Finally, he ends his summation[16] forcefully. After discussing the ruthlessness of the bombing and the character of the victims' families who have testified calmly in court—when their range of emotions must have been truly unbearable—Mackey saves his best imagery for last: "[I]t has been our pleasure to represent those victims and the United States in settling that grievance. We have done so in a way that Tim McVeigh would not choose. We have done so through the due process system." What a powerful idea to convey to the jury— that McVeigh would not approve of the trial because it has involved due process; "but the process is over now." And by conveying that idea to the jury, doesn't it make it easier for the jury to return a guilty verdict knowing that McVeigh was given the due process that he denied the innocent victims?

5. Practice Memorizing Ideas, Not Words

6. Use Visual Aids

7. Know Your Ending Cold

8. Create a One-Page Topic Outline

To deliver a closing successfully, follow the last few steps from the "Checklist for the Preparation of an Opening Statement" section in chapter 3. As shown above, those steps are: practice memorizing ideas, not words; use visual aids; know your ending cold; and create a final one-page topic outline.

---

15. *United States v. McVeigh* No. 96-CR-68, 1997 WL 280943 at *51–52 (D. Colo. May 29, 1997) (closing argument of Larry Mackey).

16. After this argument, Jones gave his closing argument for the defendant followed by the prosecution's rebuttal argument.

> # Checklist for Preparation
> ## of a Closing Argument
>
> 1. During trial, make a list of important testimony.
> 2. Use the opening outline as a starting point.
> 3. Incorporate opening themes and create new ones.
> 4. Tell a story: begin powerfully, address weaknesses, and end memorably.
> 5. Practice memorizing ideas, not words.
> 6. Use visual aids.
> 7. Know your ending cold.
> 8. Create a final one-page topic outline.

6.4 THE THREE DON'TS OF CLOSING ARGUMENT

1. Don't Talk Too Much

Keep in mind that the jury is anxious to begin its deliberations. The eagerness a jury had for opening statements has been replaced by an urgency to start deliberating and tune out what lawyers are saying. For the entire trial, jury members have had no control over scheduling, order of witnesses, length of witnesses, or viewing of exhibits. The end is in sight for them, and they are ready to assert their control and reach a decision. Therefore, keep it short and simple.

2. Don't Get Defensive

Whether it is a civil or criminal case, the plaintiff's attorney or prosecutor gets to say the last word by way of rebuttal argument. The argument is a powerful tool because the defense is not allowed to respond to it.

Nonetheless, many good defense attorneys will undermine the rebuttal by telling the jury that opposing counsel needs to answer certain questions in it. The defense attorney—knowing that the other side won't have any good answers—achieves two goals: If the opposing attorney should answer the questions, then his rebuttal can become sidetracked and defensive. If the attorney does not answer the questions, then the jury may interpret that as a sign of weakness.

The following examples show how a defense attorney can success-fully put opposing counsel on the defensive. Effective rebuttals to these arguments are found in the next section.

Example: Putting Prosecutor on Defensive
(Johnnie Cochran) from *People v. Simpson*[17]

Cochran: As such it is Miss Clark's duty to answer for you as best she can any legitimate questions arising from the evidence which we believe casts doubt upon Mr. Simpson's guilt. . . . I do think, after careful deliberation, that it might be fair to suggest fifteen questions, just fifteen ques-tions that literally hang in the air in this courtroom at this moment. . . .

When I'm concluded, for Miss Clark's convenience, should she decide to deal with these very troublesome ques-tions, I'm going to leave her a written list of these questions here when I conclude.

Let me go over these fifteen questions with you just briefly.

1. Why, there on the monitor, did the blood show up on the sock almost two months after a careful search for evi-dence? . . . Do you think that is a fair question in this case? Let's see if she can answer that question.

[Cochran goes through the remaining fourteen questions.]

I'm going to leave those [fifteen] questions for Miss Clark, and we'll see what she chooses to do with and about them. That will be her choice. But I think you have a right to demand answers if you are going to do your job in this case. It seems to me you will need to have answers to those questions.[18]

Analysis: Cochran does a superb job of challenging the prosecution to answer his questions and declares that if it doesn't, the jury should be even more suspicious of the government's case. Notice how Cochran not only discusses the fifteen most important questions but leaves them on a sheet of paper for the prosecution to "see what she chooses to do

---

17. A more detailed excerpt is provided in section 6.5, "Rebuttal Argument."
18. *People v. Simpson* No. BA097211, 1995 WL 697930 at *46–48 (Cal. Super. Ct. Sept. 28, 1995) (closing argument of Johnnie Cochran).

with and about them. That will be her choice."[19] If you were presented with this challenge, what would you do? The answer is discussed in the next section.

Another technique is to engage the jury by asking them to supply the answers to any arguments that are made by the plaintiff/prosecution in the rebuttal argument.

Example: Car-Wreck Case

> Ladies and gentlemen, this is my last chance to talk to you. Ms. Smith [plaintiff's attorney] gets another opportunity because she has to meet a high burden of proof in this case. Given her burden, she may well try and make arguments that I have not had a chance to respond to. However, if she does, ask yourselves, how would I respond to the argument if I were given the chance? Don't let her have the last word. You can supply the responses to any arguments she makes.

If you were giving the rebuttal argument, what would you say in response to this argument? The answer is provided in section 6.5.

3. Don't Misstate the Evidence or Jury Instructions

Throughout the trial, the jury has been judging your integrity by your actions and those of your witnesses. In closing argument, however, the spotlight is solely on you, and it is paramount that you not lose your good standing with the jury. The quickest way to do that is to misstate the evidence. The last thing you want to have happen in deliberations is for a juror to point out that you exaggerated what a witness said or got it wrong altogether.

To avoid this problem, go over the key testimony of the trial each day with your cocounsel and see if there is agreement as to what was said. If you are trying the case by yourself, check your notes from the trial. Better yet, read important testimony in your closing argument directly from the trial transcripts, as seen in the example below.

---

19. *People v. Simpson* No. BA097211, 1995 WL 697930 at *48 (Cal. Super. Ct. Sept. 28, 1995) (closing argument of Johnnie Cochran).

Example: Avoiding the Misstatement of Evidence (Johnnie Cochran) from *People v. Simpson*

Cochran: *I will recall the evidence and speak about the evidence. Should I misstate that evidence, please don't hold that against Mr. Simpson. I will never intentionally do that. In fact, I think you'll find that during my presentation, unlike my learned colleagues on the other side, I'm going to read you testimony of what the witnesses actually said [from transcripts] so there will be no misunderstanding about what was said about certain key things.*[20]

Whatever you do, don't misstate the jury instructions. Judges view instructions very personally (since they read them to the jury) and will not hesitate to admonish you in front of the jury if you misspeak or mischaracterize an instruction. Moreover, appellate courts take instructions very seriously, and many a case has been reversed because a lawyer mischaracterized an instruction for the jury.

6.5 REBUTTAL ARGUMENT

A major difference between openings and closings is the rebuttal argument. Since the plaintiff (or prosecutor) has the burden of proof, she is allowed a chance to rebut the defendant's closing argument. Generally, courts allow the attorney for the plaintiff to decide how much of her allotted time for closing to spend on closing argument and then rebuttal.

The rebuttal requires both the plaintiff and defense to employ strategies that are not needed in openings. The only rule regarding the rebuttal argument is that—by definition—the plaintiff can only talk about subjects that were addressed by the defense in its closing. Consistent with the teachings of this book on other topics, you should begin powerfully and end memorably. If the defense raises an important weakness in your case that you have not already addressed, do so now.

Be aware that the rebuttal is an extremely powerful tool for the plaintiff and should not be squandered. It should contain your most persuasive and powerful argument to which the defense will have no

---

20. *People v. Simpson* No. BA097211, 1995 WL 686429 at *7 (Cal. Super. Ct. Sept. 27, 1995) (closing argument of Johnnie Cochran).

chance to respond. Likewise, the defense should anticipate the plaintiff's rebuttal so that it will not be blindsided by a winning point.

Example: Anticipating Rebuttal
(Johnnie Cochran) from *People v. Simpson*

A shorter excerpt of the argument below was analyzed in the preceding section to show how defense attorneys can put opposing counsel on the defensive in rebuttal. Here, Cochran's argument is set forth in greater detail to show the importance of doing this and how one could rebut it. As you read it, ask yourself how you would respond in rebuttal.

> *Cochran: Now, as it comes time for me to conclude my remarks, I may never have an opportunity again to speak to you, certainly not in this setting, maybe when the case is over. As you have been told many, many times, these are very heavy burdens placed upon the people, and for good reason, to prove this case beyond a reasonable doubt.*
>
> *As such it is Miss Clark's duty to answer for you as best she can any legitimate questions arising from the evidence which we believe casts doubt upon Mr. Simpson's guilt.*
>
> *There may be one thousand such questions in a case like this that could be put to her, but we intend no such exercise. I do think, after careful deliberation, that it might be fair to suggest fifteen questions, just fifteen questions that literally hang in the air in this courtroom at this moment.*
>
> *And as the time approaches for you to decide this case, for us to hand the baton to you.*
>
> *I offer these questions now as a most important challenge to the prosecution, the prosecution that claims that it has met its burden in this case.*
>
> *If that burden has in fact been met, you will be given logical, sensible, credible, satisfying answers to each of these fifteen questions. If the questions are overwhelming and unanswerable, they will be ignored or you will be told that the prosecution has no obligation to answer questions.*
>
> *If you are given anything less than a complete, sensible, and satisfactory response, satisfying you beyond a reasonable doubt to these fifteen questions, you will quickly realize that the case really is transparent and you will think about the scenario that I just went through for you and that—the term smoke and mirrors that you heard about doesn't apply to the defense.*

We proved real hard things for you, things that you can see, things you could take back in that jury room.

And accordingly, you would have to find Mr. Simpson not guilty.

When I'm concluded, for Miss Clark's convenience, should she decide to deal with these very troublesome questions, I'm going to leave her a written list of these questions here when I conclude.

Let me go over these fifteen questions with you just briefly.

1. Why, there on the monitor, did the blood show up on the sock almost two months after a careful search for evidence?

And why, as demonstrated by Dr. Lee and Professor MacDonell, was the blood applied [on the sock] when there was no foot in it?

Do you think that is a fair question in this case? Let's see if she can answer that question.

Question number 2. Why was Mark Fuhrman, a detective who had been pushed off the case, a person who went by himself to the Bronco [and] over the fence to interrogate Kato to discover the glove and the thump, thump, thump area?

Number 3. Why was the glove still moist when Fuhrman found it if Mr. Simpson had dropped it seven hours earlier? As Agent Bodziak told you, as Herb MacDonell has told you, blood dries very rapidly.

4. If Mark Fuhrman, who speaks so openly about his intense genocidal racism to a relative stranger such as Kathleen Bell, how many of his coworkers, the other detectives in this case, were also aware that he lied when he denied using the N word yet failed to come forward? . . .

And finally 15. Given Professor MacDonell's testimony that the gloves would not have shrunk no matter how much blood was smeared on them, and given that they never shrank from June 21, 1994, until now, despite having been repeatedly frozen and thawed, how come the gloves just don't fit?

I'm going to leave those questions for Miss Clark, and we'll see what she chooses to do with and about them. That will be her choice. But I think you have a right to demand answers if you are going to do your job in this case. It seems to me you will need to have answers to those questions. Now,

*there are many, many, many more, but as with everything in
this case, there comes a time when you can only do so much.*

*We took fifteen as representatives, but I can tell you we
had more than fifty questions, but fifteen will be enough,
don't you think? I think so.*[21]

In rebuttal, do not get off track from the powerful ideas you have
prepared. Rather, briefly address the questions in a positive manner.
For example, you could say the following:

> Mr. Cochran asks fifteen questions in his closing. Every ques-
> tion, not just the fifteen that Mr. Cochran lists, but **every**
> question about Mr. Simpson's guilt has been answered and
> proven in this case. Let me discuss the two most important
> questions he raised.

In the preceding section, there was an example of a defense attorney who asked the jurors to pretend the defense attorney could respond to the plaintiff's rebuttal argument and provide the answers that
they thought the defense attorney would provide. Here is one way to
respond to that argument.

Rebuttal Argument in Car-Wreck Case

Even if Ms. White [the defense counsel] had the chance to
speak after me and had all day, there is nothing she could say
that would answer the question, "If the defense's claim is true
that the plaintiff is faking his injuries, why would my client
have back surgery if his back wasn't hurt in the accident?"

Finally, the following are Clark's concluding remarks in her rebuttal argument. See if you can identify the good and bad arguments that
are made.

Example: (Marcia Clark) Rebuttal
Argument from *People v. Simpson*

*Clark: I'd like to conclude my remarks to you today, ladies
and gentlemen. . . .*

---

21. *People v. Simpson* No. BA097211, 1995 WL 697930 at *46–48 (Cal.
Super. Ct. Sept. 28, 1995) (closing argument of Johnnie Cochran).

I want to remind you—because we've come full circle. I've been with you such a long time. It's been so long since we actually had a chance to both talk, and I look forward to the time that we can again.

I wanted to remind you back to the time of jury selection when we first asked questions of you as a group in order to select twelve of you to sit as jurors. . . . [A]nd we talked about what we wanted, what we would ask of you. And if you remember, we expected you to use your common sense, to be open-minded, to be reasonable and to be fair, and to have the moral courage to be just.

And if you'll think back to this time of jury selection when all of you were first together, you will remember that we talked about the United States Supreme Court building in Washington, D.C. It's been so long, I wonder if you remember that, the highest court in the land.

And we asked if you knew what was inscribed on the facade of the Supreme Court building up above the steps, up above the pillars. If you think back, we told you what was written above those marble pillars, "Equal justice under the law." We talked about what that meant, "Equal justice under the law."

You may recall, that means the law is to be applied equally to all persons in this country regardless of whether one is rich or poor or race or creed or color, famous or otherwise. Not even the president of the United States is above the law. You all agreed with that.

We asked you if you had courage to be just to a person. Each of you, each of you said yes, some individually, some responded as a group. . . .

I think that with all you've already gone through, you've shown yourselves to be people of remarkable integrity, strength, courage, and patience, people who will face the hard questions. And this is one of them.

I think it's been hard for all of us to be here and listen to all of the evidence in this case, evidence that proves Mr. Simpson is guilty, because none of us wanted to believe it. We all wanted to believe that our image of him was right. And we all know that we never knew him exactly, but we kind of felt like we did, and it's really kind of hard to have to believe that the man we saw in the movies and commercials could do this. But he did.

And the fact that he did doesn't mean that he wasn't a great football player. It doesn't mean he never did a good thing in his life. Nothing takes that away. That's still here. It will always be here. But so will the fact that he committed these murders.

And even though it's a hard thing, still it cannot mean, it cannot mean that you let a guilty person go free, that someone who commits murder is not held accountable for it. He had strength and he had weaknesses, and it's his weakness that brought us here today, and it's his weakness that's why we're here and Ron and Nicole are not.

And defense would say no motive, no motive. It's one of the oldest motives ever known, ladies and gentlemen: anger, fear of abandonment, jealousy, loss of control of Nicole and of himself.

Usually I feel like I'm the only one left to speak for the victims. But in this case, Ron and Nicole are speaking to you. They're speaking to you, and they're telling you who murdered them.

Nicole started before she even died. Remember back in 1989, she cried to Detective Edwards, "He's going to kill me. He's going to kill me." The children were there.

[In] 1990, she made a safe-deposit box, put photographs of her beaten face and her haunted look in a safe-deposit box along with a will. She was only thirty years old. How many thirty-year-olds you know do that, a will, a safe-deposit box? It's like writing "In the event of my death . . ." She knew. "He's going to kill me."

[In] 1993, the 911 tape, the children were there. He was screaming. She was crying, and she was frightened.

I think the thing that perhaps was so chilling about her voice is that sound of resignation. There was a resignation to it, inevitability. She knew she was going to die.

And Ron, he speaks to you in struggling so valiantly. He forced his murderer to leave the evidence behind that you might not ordinarily have found.

And they both are telling you who did it with their hair, their clothes, their bodies, their blood. They tell you he did it. He did it. Mr. Simpson, Orenthal Simpson, he did it.

They told you in the only way they can. Will you hear them, or will you ignore their plea for justice, or as Nicole said to Detective Edwards, "You never do anything about him." Will you?

I want to play something for you, ladies and gentlemen, that puts it altogether. Let me explain what this is. . . .

This is a compilation of the 1989 tape, 911 call, the 1993 911 call, photographs from the 1989 beating, and the photographs from her safe-deposit box and the photographs from Rockingham and Bundy.

Cochran: I object to that without further explanation, Your Honor.

The court: Overruled.

[Tape played while photos shown on projection screen to jury]

Clark: I don't have to say anything else.

Ladies and gentlemen, on behalf of the people of the state of California, because we have proven beyond a reasonable doubt, far beyond a reasonable doubt that the defendant committed these murders, we ask you to find the defendant guilty of murder in the first degree of Ronald Goldman and Nicole Brown.

Thank you very much.

The court: All right. Thank you, Counsel.[22]

These remarks show Clark at her worst and best. She is at her worst when she preaches to the jury and reminds them of the promises and expectations made in voir dire and that "we expected you to use your common sense, to be open-minded, to be reasonable and to be fair, and to have the moral courage to be just." No one appreciates condescending remarks like these.

Clark also shows too much deference to O. J. when she states, "I think it's been hard for all of us to be here and listen to all of the evidence in this case . . . because none of us wanted to believe it. . . . And the fact that he did doesn't mean that he wasn't a great football player. It doesn't mean he never did a good thing in his life. Nothing takes that away. That's still here. It will always be here. But so will the fact that he committed these murders."

Clark is at her best, however, as she concludes her remarks. What better way to end her rebuttal than to display a compilation of photos and audio that shows O. J.'s prior beating of Nicole and evidence from the crime scene linking him to the murders?

---

22. *People v. Simpson* No. BA097211, 1995 WL 704343 at *35–37 (Cal. Super. Ct. Sept. 29, 1995) (rebuttal argument of Marcia Clark).

6.6 ANALYSIS OF CLOSING ARGUMENTS IN *PEOPLE V. SIMPSON* AND *GOLDMAN V. SIMPSON*

Now that you know how to prepare a closing argument, let's examine excerpts from the civil and criminal trials of O. J. Simpson.[23] Below are examples, both good and bad, of the way experienced attorneys presented closings in these two trials. The excerpts below provide specific examples of each section in the closing argument outline form.

1. Begin Powerfully with a Memorable Theme

Compare these two examples and see which one is more persuasive.

Example 1: Prosecution (Marcia Clark)
from *People v. Simpson*[24]

Clark: Thank you very much. Good morning, ladies and gentlemen.

Jury: Good morning.

Clark: Finally. I feel like it is has been forever since I talked to you. It kind of has.

It is very weird being in the courtroom sitting next to you every day not getting a chance to talk to you. It is very unnatural. I have to tell you as long as I've been doing this, as many years as I've been doing this, at this moment in the trial I always feel the same. I feel like I want to sit down with you and say, "And what do you want to talk about?"

The court: Excuse me, Miss Clark.

Juror 165 needs a pen.

(Brief pause)

---

23. Shortly after the acquittal, the families of Ron and Nicole filed a wrongful death lawsuit against O. J. Simpson. One significant difference from the criminal trial was that the judge did not allow the defense to argue that the police investigation was motivated by racial prejudice. The jury returned a judgment of $8.5 million for compensatory damages for Ron Goldman's family (Nicole's family did not request compensatory damages so that her children would not have to testify against him) and $25 million for punitive damages to be split evenly between the Goldman and Brown families.

24. See also disc 2, Closing Argument: Clark clip 1.

The court: Miss Clark.

Clark: Thank you.

I want to sit down and talk to you and tell you, "What do you want to know? What do you want to talk about?" because that way I don't have to talk about stuff you don't want to hear, stuff that you don't want explained, stuff that you are not interested in, and I can't, and I always have a sense of frustration.

So I'm sorry if I say things that you don't need to hear or I explain things that are already clear to you. Please bear with me because I am not a mind reader and I don't know. [Clark then thanks the jurors for their service.][25]

Example: Plaintiff (Daniel Petrocelli) from *Goldman v. Simpson*

Petrocelli: [Petrocelli thanks the jurors for their service.][26] *We are here to determine responsibility for the deaths of Ronald Goldman and Nicole Brown Simpson. Two vital people who had most of their lives ahead of them.*

Here they are in life. [Indicating to ELMO]

By now, today, Ron Goldman would have been twenty-nine years old, and I think he would have had that restaurant that he wanted to open shaped in the design of an ankh, the Egyptian symbol for eternal life, which Ron always wore around his neck and even had tattooed on his shoulder.

You want to put the other picture up? [Indicating to ELMO]

Nicole Brown Simpson would have been thirty-seven years old.

Not on a day unlike today, I think she would have, like she did every day, gotten up and taken care of her children, feed them, take them to school, karate lessons, dance lessons, bring them home, feed them dinner, play with them, put them to bed.

Ron Goldman will never get to open his restaurant, ladies and gentlemen. And Nicole Brown Simpson will never

---

25. *People v. Simpson* No. BA097211, 1995 WL 672670 at *16 (Cal. Super. Ct. Sept. 26, 1995) (closing argument of Marcia Clark)

26. Given the extraordinary length of the civil and criminal trials, each side thanked the jury for its service and patience. In a normal trial, this is not necessary.

see her children grow up. Because on a Sunday evening in 1994, these two vital people, their lives came to a sudden end in a few moments of uncontrollable rage.

Here they are in death. [Indicating to ELMO]

I apologize for the photograph.

Nicole, as you can imagine, was helpless at the hands of this enraged man, and she died within moments of the gaping cut to her throat. Ron Goldman, instead of running from danger, tried to help a friend, but he too was defenseless against this powerful man with a six-inch knife stabbing over and over and over again until Ron collapsed to the ground and died with his eyes still open.

Now, had Ron lived, ladies and gentlemen, he'd have been on this witness stand, and he would have relived what happened that night, and he would have told us what he saw.

Baker: I object. This is improper evidence.

Petrocelli: Your Honor—

The court: Overruled. It's argument.

Petrocelli: But that is why Ron Goldman was killed. So he could not tell you what he saw that evening. But even though Ron's and Nicole's voices will not be heard in this courtroom, they will not be on that stand, their last struggling moments to stay alive, ladies and gentlemen, provided us the key evidence necessary to identify their killer.

They managed to get a glove pulled off, a hat to drop off, they managed to dig nails into the left hand of this man, cause other injuries to his hand, forcing him to drop his blood next to their bodies as he tried to get away.

And by their blood, they forced him to step, step, step as he walked to the back, leaving shoe prints that are just like fingerprints in this case that tell us who did this, who did this unspeakable tragedy.

So these crucial pieces of evidence after all are the voices of Ron and Nicole speaking to us from their graves, telling us, telling all of you, that there is a killer in this courtroom. [Indicating to Simpson][27]

It is clear that Petrocelli's beginning is infinitely better than Clark's. He immediately reminds the jury what the case is about—the murder of

---

27. *Goldman v. Simpson* No. SC036340, 1997 WL 20765 at *8–9 (Cal. Super. Ct. Jan. 21, 1997) (closing argument of Daniel Petrocelli).

two innocent people. He does this by the choice of his words and photos of Ron and Nicole. On the other hand, Clark starts off with an apology! She says that it feels like "forever" since opening statements. Who is responsible for the slowness of the trial? While the judge and defense can contribute to its length, it is the prosecution's responsibility to put on an efficient trial since it has the burden of proof and is responsible for presenting evidence in an efficient manner. For Clark to concede that it has been forever before she even gets to the substance of her closing is an error. The jury, sequestered as it was, will certainly hold someone accountable for the eight months of freedom that have been taken away. A simple apology at the beginning of the closing won't help.

If the delay is the result of needless questioning by the defense counsel, all the better for the prosecution, since the jury's wrath will be taken out on the defendant. Clark, however, apparently feared that the jury would be angry with the prosecution for the length of the trial. It is too late to change that perception in the closing.

Even worse, Clark apologizes in advance for her closing because she realizes that she may talk about things "you don't need to hear," but the jury will have to bear with her because "I am not a mind reader." Who wants to listen to any speaker who apologizes in advance that her speech will be boring? Finally, Clark concludes her introduction by saying to the jury that she doesn't know what topics it wants to hear her discuss in her closing. That statement, "I don't know," is the ultimate sign of weakness. Why, after eight months of trial in the highest profile case ever, would the lead prosecutor confess to the jury that she does not know what the jury wants to hear in her closing argument? There may be few prohibitions in closing, but here is one: a lawyer should never confess "I don't know" unless it is followed immediately by the statement "but it does not matter."

2. Discuss the Important Details of the Story

Example: Prosecution (Marcia Clark) from *People v. Simpson*
Clark: Now, I would like to start with the evidence in this case with the timing, OK? I think that is the easiest place to start, the timing on June the 12th.

Let's begin with a very brief review of the movements of Ron and Nicole, and we are going to start with the recital in the late afternoon. I'm sure you recall that recital for Sydney at Paul Revere High School.[28]

Example: Plaintiff (Daniel Petrocelli)
from *Goldman v. Simpson*

Petrocelli: Now, I'd like to begin by looking at the most incriminating of the evidence that we have presented to you. And that's the evidence that was found at 875 South Bundy, which is of course where Nicole lived, where the murders occurred, as we know.

To summarize, ladies and gentlemen, at Bundy we have a substantial amount of blood evidence, DNA evidence matching Mr. Simpson's DNA. We have his shoe prints, those unique shoe prints, one of a kind, size 12 Bruno Magli shoes, leading away from the bodies to the back. These are the shoes that Mr. Simpson owned, wore, and lied to you about, as you saw from the photos and his testimony. We also have a single Aris leather light brown glove, extra large, found at the scene between the bodies, and of course Mr. Simpson owned such a glove, as you saw from the photos.

We have hair and fiber evidence at Bundy. We have head hairs of Mr. Simpson in a hat just like hats that he owned. We have blue-black—dark blue-black cotton fibers found on Mr. Goldman's shirt that matched fibers found on Mr. Simpson's socks in his bedroom and on the glove that he dropped at his home in Rockingham, the same blue-black cotton fiber matching, meaning that he was the common source, the messenger between all three of these places.

We also had this rare unique carpet fiber that was found at Bundy, and it was—and it matched the carpet fiber in Mr. Simpson's Bronco. You have blood; you have shoes; you have hair and fiber; you have everything that you need.

Now, I'm going to put up a board in a second and go over this evidence in a little more detail.[29]

Clark starts the summary of her evidence chronologically. Petrocelli is much more effective in starting not chronologically but with the most powerful evidence.

---

28.   *People v. Simpson* No. BA097211, 1995 WL 672670 at *22 (Cal. Super. Ct. Sept. 26, 1995) (closing argument of Marcia Clark).

29.   *Goldman v. Simpson* No. SC036340, 1997 WL 20765 at *13–14 (Cal. Super. Ct. Jan. 21, 1997) (closing argument of Daniel Petrocelli).

3. Address Candidly—but Don't Dwell on— Weaknesses in the Case and Turn Them into Strengths.[30]

Example: Prosecution (Marcia Clark) from *People v. Simpson*

Clark: Let me come back to Mark Fuhrman for a minute. Just so it is clear. Did he lie when he testified here in this courtroom saying that he did not use racial epithets in the last ten years?

Yes.

Is he a racist?

Yes.

Is he the worst LAPD has to offer?

Yes.

Do we wish that this person was never hired by LAPD?

Yes.

Should LAPD have ever hired him?

No.

Should such a person be a police officer?

No.

In fact, do we wish there were no such person on the planet?

Yes.

But the fact that Mark Fuhrman is a racist and lied about it on the witness stand does not mean that we haven't proven the defendant guilty beyond a reasonable doubt.

And it would be a tragedy if with such overwhelming evidence, ladies and gentlemen, as we have presented to you, you found the defendant not guilty in spite of all that, because of the racist attitudes of one police officer.[31]

**Example: Plaintiff (Daniel Petrocelli)
from *Goldman v. Simpson***

Petrocelli: The bottom line here, ladies and gentlemen, is that they would like you to believe that that handsome man with the charming smile, the expensive suit, who's lived the life of fame, celebrity and fortune, and who claims to be dedicated to his family, flawless in character, incapable of telling a lie,

---

30.   See also disc 2, Closing Argument: Clark clip 2.
31.   *People v. Simpson* No. BA097211, 1995 WL 672670 at *19 (Cal. Super. Ct. Sept. 26, 1995) (closing argument of Marcia Clark).

that that man could not possibly be responsible for the deaths of Nicole Brown Simpson and Ronald Goldman.

But it is that very same sense of superiority, ladies and gentlemen, that Mr. Simpson has attained that explains why he has absolutely no sense of responsibility for his actions or his obligation to tell the truth or for anything else. . . . What kind of man, ladies and gentlemen, confronted with this bruised and battered picture of Nicole, says, I take full responsibility for causing all those injuries, but I didn't hit her, I didn't strike her, I didn't slap her, I didn't do anything wrong, I was just defending myself, I was just trying to get her out of my bedroom? . . . What kind of man would try to ruin the lives of innocent people just doing their jobs, accusing them of fabricating evidence, planting evidence, committing perjury, just to protect himself? . . . Well, let me tell you what kind of man says those things, ladies and gentlemen.

Doesn't take a rocket scientist to figure it out.

You can take that down, Steve. [Indicating to ELMO]

A guilty man. A guilty man. A man with no remorse. A man with no conscience.

This man is so obsessed with trying to salvage his image and protect himself that he'll come into this courtroom, knowing the whole world is watching, and he will smear the name and reputation of the mother of his children while she rests in her grave.

This is a man, ladies and gentlemen, who I submit to you has lied and lied and lied to you about every important fact in this case.

Every one.[32]

Both attorneys confront the weaknesses in their case head-on. By way of background, in the criminal trial, Detective Fuhrman had testified that he had never used the N word. After he testified, tape recordings were discovered where Fuhrman was heard to repeatedly use the N word. Clark addresses this issue head-on for the jury. In the civil trial, the judge did not consider Fuhrman's prior use of the N word as relevant evidence, and testimony regarding it was not allowed.

---

32.   *Goldman v. Simpson* No. SC036340, 1997 WL 20765 at *11–12 (Cal. Super. Ct. Jan. 21, 1997) (closing argument of Daniel Petrocelli).

Perhaps Clark goes a little too far in dwelling on the weakness (i.e., "In fact, do we wish there were no such person on the planet? Yes"), thereby turning it into an insurmountable obstacle. However, it was an issue that needed to be confronted directly, and she succeeds.

Although the plaintiff in the civil trial did not have Fuhrman's racist statements to deal with, there were still weaknesses to confront. It was not lost on Petrocelli that during the defendant's opening statement, Simpson's attorney had discussed Simpson's NFL Hall of Fame speech and called Simpson "O. J." and "the Juice" when asking him questions at trial.[33] Clearly, Simpson's defense was going to try to get mileage out of the public's infatuation with celebrities. Petrocelli turns the shield of fame into a sword against O. J. It is a perfect example of turning a weakness into a strength.

4. Briefly Discuss Important Jury Instructions

Prosecution (Marcia Clark) from *People v. Simpson*

Clark: Thank you, Your Honor.

Reasonable doubt.

OK. This is an instruction that we will talk to you about, they are going to talk to you about. This is a real important instruction. It is at the real heart of a case, every case, every criminal case. Because it is the burden of proof that the people have. We don't guess anybody guilty. We prove it beyond a reasonable doubt, which is what we've done in this case. Now, to tell you about reasonable doubt, it is kind of a funny definition because it talks to you about reasonable doubt in very negative terms.

It says: "[T]hat state of the evidence which, after the entire comparison, you cannot say that you have an abiding conviction." It is very weirdly worded, and it is going to take you a while to go through this, so I'm going to go through it pieces at a time to try and give you a little hand here.

First of all, let me point out the first paragraph talks about the fact that it is our burden of proof. I think that one is fine. That is pretty easy.

Now, it talks about how reasonable doubt is defined. This is real important.

---

33. *Goldman v. Simpson* No. SC036340, 1997 WL 20765 at *12 (Cal. Super. Ct. Jan. 21, 1997) (closing argument of Daniel Petrocelli) .

"[I]t is not a mere possible doubt," OK, "because everything relating to human affairs is open to some possible or
imaginary doubt." That is very important. It is a doubt
founded in reason. I'm going to amplify more on that with
examples when we talk about the actual evidence in this case,
but bear that in mind, a possible doubt.

I have a possible doubt that the sun will come up tomorrow. Do I have a reasonable doubt about it? No. I have no
doubt founded in reason that that is going to happen, just for
a very basic example, so think about that, too. We are not
talking about what possible doubt is. It is reasonable doubt.

Now, the other part of it: "[I]t is that state of the case
which after the entire comparison, the entire comparison and
consideration of all of the evidence." Now, what that means,
ladies and gentlemen, is you consider the defense case and
you consider the prosecution case. You consider all of it.

You will probably hear from the defense, multiple times,
"We don't have to prove anything." That is right. They don't.

In every criminal case when the people complete their
presentation, the defense can say no witnesses, we rest, because they can sit and make the state prove its case without
ever calling a witness. That's right. That's correct.

But when they do, when they do, then you must consider
the quality and the nature of the evidence that they have presented. That goes into the mix. That is part of your consideration.

What kind of evidence did they present to demonstrate
something to you? To prove something to you?

If they try to prove something to you, their witnesses,
their evidence gets evaluated by the same rules ours do. The
same jury instruction applies. . . .

But at the conclusion of all of our arguments, when you
open up the windows and let the cool air blow out the smoke
screen that has been created by the defense with the cool
wind of reason, you will see that the defendant has been
proven guilty easily beyond a reasonable doubt. Or to put it
another way: the evidence has conclusively proven that when
Detective Mark Fuhrman said he did not use racial epithets in
the last ten years, he lied, but it is also conclusively proven
that the defendant is guilty beyond a reasonable doubt.[34]

---

34. *People v. Simpson* No. BA097211, 1995 WL 672670 at *19–22 (Cal.
Super. Ct. Sept. 26, 1995) (closing argument of Marcia Clark).

Example: Plaintiff (Daniel Petrocelli)
from *Goldman v. Simpson*

Petrocelli: We did not merely prove that he did these things by a preponderance of the evidence, which, as you will hear later on as the judge will instruct you, is the burden of proof that we have to meet in this case.

We didn't prove it merely by clear and convincing evidence, which is yet another burden of proof.

We didn't prove it merely by proof beyond a reasonable doubt, which is the standard of proof that applies in criminal cases.

We proved it to a certainty. We proved it beyond any doubt.[35]

Which is a more persuasive argument? Notice how Petrocelli, although he only has to prove his case by 51 percent (preponderance of the evidence), argues that he not only has met the highest legal standard possible (beyond a reasonable doubt) but that he has proven his case beyond any doubt. How reassuring, if you were a juror on the case, to hear that your job is easy because the lawyer has proven his case beyond any doubt.

Contrast Petrocelli's concise argument with Clark's tortured one. Her refrain that she only has to prove her case beyond a reasonable doubt but not beyond *any* doubt—not to mention how long it took her to explain the instruction—reveals that she was concerned that jurors might find doubt of some kind in the case. See how much stronger Clark's argument would have been if she had argued like Petrocelli did instead:

> Ladies and gentlemen, the government has the burden of proof in this case. It is burden we embrace. As the judge will instruct you, all we had to do was present evidence of Mr. Simpson's guilt beyond a reasonable doubt. However, we have done more than that, much more. We have proven beyond any doubt whatsoever. Let me tell you why.

---

35. *Goldman v. Simpson* No. SC036340, 1997 WL 20765 at *9–10 (Cal. Super. Ct. Jan. 21, 1997) (closing argument of Daniel Petrocelli).

5. End Memorably (Criminal Trial)

Example: Prosecution (Christopher Darden)
from *People v. Simpson*[36]

The defense got lost in minutia in their attempt to confuse you and to raise a reasonable doubt.

Well, let me explain justice to you this way, and then I will sit down and I will be quiet.

The people put on their case, the defense put on their case, and I assert that the defense case is a bunch of smoke and mirrors, all about distracting you from the real evidence in this case.

So imagine the smoke and imagine a burning house. Imagine that you are standing in front of a burning house, and from inside that burning house you can hear the wail of a baby, a baby's cry, a baby in fear, a baby about to lose its life. And you can hear that baby screaming. You can hear that wail.

Now, that baby, that baby is justice. This is baby justice. Usually justice is a strong woman, but in this case justice is just a baby. And you hear that baby, and you hear that wail, and you see the smoke, you see the defense.

There is all this smoke in front of you and you feel a sense—you have a sense of justice and you have a sense of what the law requires and you have a strong commitment to justice and to the law and you want to do the right thing while justice is about to perish, justice is about to be lost, baby justice is about to be lost.

And so you start to wade through that smoke trying to get to that baby. You have got to save that baby, you have to save baby justice, and you happen to run into smoke, find your way through the smoke, and if you happen to run into a couple of defense attorneys along the way, just ask them to politely step aside and let you find your way through the smoke, because the smoke isn't over, OK? The smoke is [going] to get heavier because they are about to talk to you.

Let's use your common sense. Wade through the evidence. Get down to the bottom line.

And please do the right thing.

---

36.   See also disc 2, Closing Argument: Darden clip 1.

It has been an honor to appear before you, and we will
wait for your verdict.
The court: Thank you, Mr. Darden.[37]

6. Discuss Damages and End Memorably (Civil Trial)

Example: Plaintiff (Daniel Petrocelli)
from *Goldman v. Simpson*

Petrocelli: We now come to the final remarks I'm going to
make to you today. And for me, this is the most difficult area.

We're going to talk very, very briefly about my client,
Fred Goldman, my client's loss, the loss of his son. And you
will be called upon, if you agree Mr. Simpson is liable for the
death of Ronald Goldman—there will be no question that he
is—you will be asked to compensate Mr. Goldman for his
loss.

And I don't need to tell you that there is no amount of
money that could ever compensate Fred Goldman for the loss
of his son. We cannot put a value on human life. You do not
put a price on human life, when there is a loss of life.

There can never be true justice for Fred Goldman. There
can never be true justice for anyone. True justice would be to
see Ron Goldman walk through those doors right now, or
Nicole Brown Simpson, playing with her children. That's true
justice. That will never happen. They're gone forever.

There's nothing I can do; there's nothing you can do;
there's nothing this good judge can do; and there's nothing
that man can do [pointing to Simpson] to bring these people
back.

All you have in your power to do is to bring about some
small measure of justice by recognizing the incalculable loss
my client has suffered, and to require the man who is re-
sponsible for this to pay for this, to pay for the loss he
caused this man.

I would like to talk to you—say a few words about that
loss. I think we would agree, whatever your ethnic, racial,
cultural background is, there isn't any loss greater than a par-
ent losing a child. That loss is no less if a child grows into a
young man. . . .

---

37. *People v. Simpson* No. BA097211, 1995 WL 686428 at *28–29 (Cal.
Super. Ct. Sept. 27, 1995) (closing argument of Christopher Darden).

He will never see the beaming look of satisfaction on Ron's face as Ron might have ushered him through his restaurant. He will never sit down with Ron at a Fourth of July barbecue or Passover Seder, or a birthday party. He will never share the joy of running off to the hospital to see his grandchild, perhaps his first grandchild, a baby that Ron wanted to name Dakota, if you remember.

He will never see again the smile on his son's face. . . . [Indicating to Goldman] Fred has lost all of that and infinitely more forever, and his life will never be the same. His life will never be the same.

I can't, you can't, give him back his son. All you can do is make Mr. Simpson pay for what he did.

Baker: I'm going to object, Your Honor. That's not the law in this state.

Petrocelli: You can make—

The court: Overruled.

Petrocelli: You can make Mr. Simpson compensate my client, that man, that grieving man, for what he has suffered: the loss of companionship, support, love, and affection that he enjoyed with his son; gone forever, ladies and gentlemen.

And I am not going to tell you, or even suggest to you how much you should award him.

I'm just going to leave it up to your good judgment.

I'd like to play for you one more time, one of Fred Goldman's last treasures that he has, he will always have to remember his son by.

Can you play it, Steve?

[Videotape is played.]

Petrocelli: There was a sixteenth-century poet, named Guillaume Du Bartas, who best expressed a relationship between a father and son in a few simple words. Let me read them to you.

"My lovely living boy,
My hope, my happiness,
My love, my life, my joy."
Fred Goldman's lovely living boy is no more.

The court: Ten-minute recess, ladies and gentlemen.[38]

---

38.   *Goldman v. Simpson* No. SC036340, 1997 WL 23183 at *12–13 (Cal. Super. Ct. Jan. 22, 1997) (closing argument of Daniel Petrocelli).

Darden's analogy misses the mark. The worst error is that he makes the jurors believe that they have a very difficult job ahead of them in reaching a just verdict. That is just what the defense wants the jurors to believe. Darden is asking the jurors to risk life and limb to wade through the dense smoke of a fire and find the truth by rescuing baby justice inside a burning house. By using this analogy, Darden concedes how good a job the defense has done.

Compare how Darden ends his closing argument with Petrocelli's ending in the civil case. Petrocelli makes the job of the jurors as easy as possible. He tells them that no amount of money can replace Ron Goldman's life, his smile, or his dream of opening a restaurant. But, they are reminded, they can "bring about some small measure of justice by recognizing the incalculable loss my client has suffered, and to require the man who is responsible for this to pay for this, to pay for the loss he caused this man."

Finally, he ends with a visual image and some powerful words: he plays Ron Goldman's bat mitzvah video and freezes it on the last frame, which shows Ron and his father celebrating together.[39] He then shares three simple lines from a poem about a father's love for his son. Unlike Darden, who puts baby justice inside a burning house, Petrocelli puts justice right in front of the jury: make Simpson pay for destroying the innocent life of Ron Goldman.

7. Rebuttal Argument

Example: Prosecution (Christopher Darden) Rebuttal Argument from *People v. Simpson*[40]

Darden: Well, we have come full circle again it seems. Here you are and here I am.

And as Judge Ito just indicated, this is my last opportunity to speak with you, that is, until after you render your verdict.

If at that time you are kind enough to spare a few moments and allow me to thank you personally at that time, not only for your verdict, but for your service as well.

---

39. Daniel Petrocelli with Peter Knobler, *Triumph of Justice: The Final Judgment on the Simpson Saga* at 613 (Crown Publishers 1998).

40. Darden and Clark split the rebuttal argument. Darden delivered the first half, and Clark presented the second half.

You've got a tough job, a very tough job. I don't envy you in that regard.

But let me tell you something. I have had a tough job, too. The law is a tough thing to enforce in this town. Not everybody, not everybody wants to live up to the law or follow the law. Not everybody thinks that the law applies to them.

I have been a prosecutor for almost fifteen years, and if there is one rule that I have lived by, if there is one rule that means a lot to me, it is this one:

No one is above the law; not the police, not the rich, no one.

And I hope you agree with that. I hope you agree with that rule. I hope you consider that—that motto.

O. J. Simpson isn't above the law.[41]

Example: Plaintiff Rebuttal Argument (Daniel Petrocelli) from *Goldman v. Simpson*

Petrocelli: We're getting there. I'm going to speak to you for a bit. Then I'm going to have my partner, Mr. Lambert, respond to some of the points Mr. Blasier [defense counsel] made. Then I'm going to come back and wrap it up, and I'll be the last lawyer you'll hear from. And then the good judge will instruct you. Then you'll retire for your deliberations. But hang on, we're getting there.

I'd like you to think about this question: What does a man do when his blood is found dripped all over the murder scene? When his hat is found next to the victims' bodies?

When his glove is found there? When his hair is found there? When his clothing fibers are found there? When carpet fibers from his car are found there? When shoe prints in one of the victim's blood are found there; his shoe prints? When his blood is found in his car?

When his blood is found dripped all over his driveway? When his blood is found dripped inside of his house? When his blood is found on his socks? When one of the victim's blood is [also] found on his socks? When the other glove is found on his property; and when that glove has on it his

---

41. *People v. Simpson* No. BA097211, 1995 WL 704342 at *3 (Cal. Super. Ct. Sept. 29, 1995) (rebuttal argument of Christopher Darden).

blood, the blood of each of the victims, the hair from each of the victims, clothing fibers, carpet fibers?

When he has no alibi? When he was involved in a deeply conflicted relationship with one of the murdered victims? When he is seen in photos wearing the possible murder clothes?

When he is seen in photos wearing the possible murder gloves? When he is seen in photos wearing the murder shoes that he lied and lied about?

And when he has injuries all over his left hand? Now, what does he do? What does this guy do; especially if this man has money and resources? What does he do? He hires an army of lawyers, experts, investigators, consultants, you name it; he hires them all, and they sit down, and they figure out what to say about all of this evidence. . . . And what you have heard in this courtroom, ladies and gentlemen, from the defense over the last four months, and from these lawyers over the last two days, is what a guilty man has to say in response to all of this evidence.

It was all planted. It's all contaminated. All of the photos are fake. All the law-enforcement people are corrupt or incompetent. Every witness who gets on that stand and testifies against me is lying or mistaken. There's a conspiracy the likes of which has never before been witnessed, all to get me.

That's what a guilty man does. And what's the reason? Why? Why would there be this conspiracy? Why would people do such a thing?

Why would they all gang up and conspire to frame an innocent man; particularly a celebrity who's got a lot of money and who's going to draw massive attention, maybe the highest profile case ever?

And people, innocent people who are doing their jobs, criminalists, lab technicians, patrol officers, rookies, seasoned detectives, FBI agents, coroner, assistant coroner; all these people have to be in on this to one extent or another, either they're in on it by planting and fabricating and making up evidence, or they got on that witness stand and lied.

That's what you have to believe, ladies and gentlemen. That's what they're trying to sell you. You know there's an old expression: "Necessity is the mother of invention." I'm sure you've all heard that. What does that mean?

That means when it's necessary, you'd better come up with something. And that's what you have heard: inventions.

Inventions. They have invented argument. They have invented defenses that have no basis in reality. They have no facts to support them. They have no evidence. They're made up.

What you just heard Mr. Baker [defense counsel] describe for you was that police officers planted evidence and gloves, and this and that. And we're going to get into that in detail because, boy, we couldn't wait to hear him try to explain this so we could get the opportunity to let you know, once and for all, that this whole thing that we've heard about from the moment Mr. Baker started asking you questions in jury selection, from the moment he made his opening statement, and all the questions he asked charged with all this inflammatory language about planting and conspiracy and all this stuff.

We couldn't wait for the day, finally, when we got a chance to hear him lay it out. Ladies and gentlemen, it's a fraud. It's a fraud on you. It's a big lie. It never happened. It's what—it never happened.

It's what guilty men do. They've been doing it for hundreds of years. They've refined it to a new art form because they've got the money. They got big-shot experts, fancy lawyers come in here, figure out all the little discrepancies in the documents. Oh, they didn't pick up this, they didn't pick up that. Let's say this, let's say that. Making it up as they go along.[42]

Why would Darden—in the first couple of sentences—admit to the jurors that he thinks their job is tough? Not just a tough job but in his words, "a very tough job." There is no good answer. Then, in a failed effort to get sympathy from the jury, he says how tough *his* job has been.

Unlike Darden, Petrocelli gets right to the heart of the case. He reassures the jury that he will address the defense counsel's argument, but he will do it in due course. By starting his rebuttal with a series of questions, Petrocelli focuses the jury on the motives behind Simpson's defense and severely undercuts the defense theory of a conspiracy.

---

42. *Goldman v. Simpson* No. SC036340, 1997 WL 29312 at *2–3 (Cal. Super. Ct. Jan. 27, 1997) (rebuttal argument of Daniel Petrocelli).

6.7 STUDY QUESTIONS FOR CLOSING ARGUMENT VIDEO CLIPS FROM *PEOPLE V. SIMPSON* (DISC 2)

As you look at all the attorneys, compare the different styles of Clark, Darden, Cochran, and Scheck. Whose style do you like the best? What is the best quality of each attorney? What is the worst?

1. Clark Closing Argument

Clark clip 1: Beginning of Clark's Closing Argument (4 min.) [43]

Background: Clark begins her closing argument. This clip is discussed in detail in the preceding section of this chapter regarding Clark's failure to begin her closing strongly. Therefore, no study questions are presented.

Clark clip 2: Clark Addresses Weaknesses in Prosecution's Case (4 min.) [44]

Background: Clark addresses Fuhrman's racism and lying on the witness stand. She emphasizes the jury instruction requiring jurors not to be motivated by sympathy.

Study Questions

1. Does Clark effectively address the weaknesses in her case?
2. Do you agree with the amount of time Clark spends discussing Fuhrman's racism? Why or why not?

---

43. *People v. Simpson* No. BA097211, 1995 WL 672670 at *16–17 (Cal. Super. Ct. Sept. 26, 1995) (closing argument of Marcia Clark).
44. *People v. Simpson* No. BA097211, 1995 WL 672670 at *18–19 (Cal. Super. Ct. Sept. 26, 1995) (closing argument of Marcia Clark).

Clark clip 3: Clark Explains Glove Demonstration (3 min.) [45]

Background: Clark reasons why the gloves found at the murder scene did not fit Simpson when he tried them on at trial.

Study Questions

1. Does Clark offer a credible explanation for the gloves not fitting?
2. Is the analogy that Clark uses regarding a child trying on shoes persuasive?
3. Does Clark maintain good eye contact with the jury?

Clark clip 4: Clark Concludes Closing (4 min.) [46]

Background: Clark concludes her closing by discussing the important pieces of physical evidence while having an exhibit that shows Simpson's face being filled in like pieces of a puzzle.

Study Questions

1. Is the exhibit of the puzzle persuasive? Why or why not?
2. Compare Clark's cadence and eye contact to those in the preceding clip. In which are they more effective, and why?

2. Darden Closing Argument

Darden clip 1: Darden Concludes Closing (2 min.) [47]

Background: Darden concludes his closing by comparing justice to a baby who needs rescuing from a burning house. In addition to the

---

45. *People v. Simpson* No. BA097211, 1995 WL 672671 at *38–39 (Cal. Super. Ct. Sept. 26, 1995) (closing argument of Marcia Clark).
46. *People v. Simpson* No. BA097211, 1995 WL 672671 at *60 (Cal. Super. Ct. Sept. 26, 1995) (closing argument of Marcia Clark).
47. *People v. Simpson* No. BA097211, 1995 WL 686428 at *8–29 (Cal. Super. Ct. Sept. 27, 1995) (closing argument of Christopher Darden).

study questions, this passage is discussed in detail in the previous section of this chapter.

Study Questions

1. Does Darden make good eye contact with the jury?
2. Does Darden appear confident?

3. Cochran Closing Argument

Cochran clip 1: Cochran Argues Lack of Blood, Puts on Knit Cap, and Discusses Glove Demonstration (4 min.)

Part 1: Cochran Argues Lack of Blood (1 min.)[48]

Background: Cochran argues that there should be more blood at Simpson's house if he had committed murders and returned home as the prosecution claimed.

Part 2: Cochran Puts on Knit Cap (1 min.)[49]

Background: Cochran mocks Clark's argument that the knit cap found at the murder scene was worn by Simpson. He puts on a knit cap to show that it does not disguise him, nor would it have disguised Simpson had he worn it.

Part 3: Cochran Discusses Glove Demonstration (3 min.)[50]

Background: Cochran reviews the glove demonstration.

Study Questions

1. Is Cochran's point about the lack of blood compelling?
2. Does he make a strong argument when he puts on the knit cap for a demonstration?

---

48. *People v. Simpson* No. BA097211, 1995 WL 686429 at *25 (Cal. Super. Ct. Sept. 27, 1995) (closing argument of Johnnie Cochran).
49. *People v. Simpson* No. BA097211, 1995 WL 686429 at *26 (Cal. Super. Ct. Sept. 27, 1995) (closing argument of Johnnie Cochran).
50. *People v. Simpson* No. BA097211, 1995 WL 686429 at *30 (Cal. Super. Ct. Sept. 27, 1995) (closing argument of Johnnie Cochran).

3. Does Cochran make good eye contact when discussing the glove demonstration?

Cochran clip 2: Cochran Considers the Twins of Deception (2.5 min.)[51]

Background: Cochran first discusses Detective Philip Vannatter. Vannatter was the lead detective who arrived at O. J.'s house around 5:30 a.m. to notify him of Nicole's death and that his children had been taken to the police station. Vannatter and other detectives saw blood on O. J.'s Bronco parked at the house and entered the property fearing that O. J. or another victim was inside in need of help. He takes Vannatter to task for testifying that O. J. was "no more a suspect" than O. J.'s attorney, Robert Shapiro. Cochran says that statement was "preposterous." Cochran cites the book of Luke in the Bible to show that if the people lie in small things, they can't be trusted in bigger things.

Study Questions

1. Is there conviction in Cochran's tone of voice?
2. Is Cochran's analogy to the Bible compelling?
3. Is the persuasive aid of Fuhrman's lies effective?

Cochran clip 3: Cochran Discusses Racism (4 min.)[52]

Background: Cochran compares Fuhrman to Hitler and tells the jurors that the reason for their being selected is to say "no more" to racism in the Los Angeles Police Department (LAPD).

Study Questions

1. Do you think Cochran's argument is improper?
2. How would you object to his argument?

---

51. *People v. Simpson* No. BA097211, 1995 WL 697928 at *5 (Cal. Super. Ct. Sept. 27, 1995) (closing argument of Johnnie Cochran).
52. *People v. Simpson* No. BA097211, 1995 WL 697928 at *12–13 (Cal. Super. Ct. Sept. 27, 1995) (closing argument of Johnnie Cochran).

3. Even if you could object, would you?

4. Scheck Closing Argument

Scheck clip 1: Scheck Asserts Opinion about Innocence (3 min.) [53]

Background: This is the beginning of Barry Scheck's closing argument.

Study Questions

1. Is Judge Ito correct in sustaining objections to Scheck's use of the phrases "I think" and "We believe"?
2. How does Scheck respond to the objections after the sidebar at the bench?
3. How persuasive is Scheck's aid of the black hole?

Scheck clip 2: Scheck Summarizes Problems with Scientific Evidence (3 min.) [54]

Background: Just prior to this clip, Scheck summarized the unacceptable levels of risk of cross-contamination that took place at the LAPD lab. For example, one contention the defense had was that the DNA tests could not be trusted because blood from the crime scene had been improperly stored and mixed together and that the blood had been mixed with the sample of blood O. J. gave after his arrest. When the clip begins, Scheck addresses the worst mistake: the spillage of blood that occurs when LAPD criminalist Collin Yamauchi is handling the sample of blood that was taken from O. J. while he is analyzing swatches (or samples) of blood from the crime scene.

---

53. *People v. Simpson* No. BA097211, 1995 WL 697929 at *5–6 (Cal. Super. Ct. Sept. 28, 1995) (closing argument of Barry Scheck).
54. *People v. Simpson* No. BA097211, 1995 WL 697930 at *8–9 (Cal. Super. Ct. Sept. 28, 1995) (closing argument of Barry Scheck).

Study Questions

1. How would you evaluate Scheck's recitation of Yamauchi's testimony?
2. How would you rate Scheck's eye contact with the jury?
3. Does Scheck overwhelm the jury with details?
4. What is Scheck's theme?
5. How would you improve Scheck's argument?

Scheck clip 3: Scheck Talks about Contamination at Crime Scene and Cover-Up (4 min.) [55]

Background: In this clip, Scheck summarizes testimony that showed that the crime scene was contaminated because the glove and an envelope found near the bodies had been moved. Ron Goldman's body had also been moved. In the last part of the clip, he criticizes Dennis Fung for misleading testimony in the grand jury and preliminary hearing where he said "I collected" evidence when in fact a trainee, Andrea Mazzola, had done a majority of the collection. Michele Kestler, who is mentioned in this clip, was the assistant director of the LAPD crime lab.

Study Questions

1. What is Scheck's theme in this clip?
2. Is his theme powerful?

Scheck clip 4: Scheck Concludes Closing Argument (1 min.) [56]

Background: Scheck concludes his closing remarks by reminding the jurors of the sloppy police work and its ramifications for the rights of

---

55. *People v. Simpson* No. BA097211, 1995 WL 697930 at *31–32 (Cal. Super. Ct. Sept. 28, 1995) (closing argument of Barry Scheck).
56. *People v. Simpson* No. BA097211, 1995 WL 697930 at *33 (Cal. Super. Ct. Sept. 28, 1995) (closing argument of Barry Scheck).

citizens set forth in the Constitution. In the clip there is a reference to EDTA. EDTA is a preservative that was used in the tube that contained O. J.'s blood sample. An expert testified at trial that EDTA was found on the gate at Nicole's home with the implication that the blood had been planted there.

Study Questions

1. Compare Scheck's conclusion to Darden's above. Which do you think is more forceful?
2. Compare not only what Scheck and Darden say but how they say it. Which do you think is more forceful?

5. Darden Rebuttal Argument

Darden clip 1: Darden Cites Constitution (4 min.)[57]

Background: In response to Scheck's argument that the sloppy way in which the police investigated the case proves the "Constitution means nothing" (Scheck, clip 4, "Scheck Concludes Closing Argument"), Darden responds by talking about what the Constitution means to the victims and that the victims had a right to the pursuit of happiness and that O. J. did not have the right to kill them.

Study Questions

1. How do you evaluate the effectiveness of Darden's response?
2. Is Darden too emotional?
3. Is any part of Darden's argument improper?
4. Does Darden patronize the jury?
5. How could Darden improve his delivery?

---

57. *People v. Simpson* No. BA097211, 1995 WL 704342 at *5–6 (Cal. Super. Ct. Sept. 29, 1995) (rebuttal argument of Christopher Darden).

6. Clark Rebuttal Argument

Clark clip 1: Clark Summarizes Uncontradicted Evidence (6 min.)[58]

Background: Clark summarizes the uncontradicted evidence of the prosecution. The clip begins by discussing Allan Parks, the limo driver, who was waiting at O. J.'s home to take him to the airport. He had repeatedly rung the intercom, but there had been no answer until he saw a man resembling O. J. enter the home at 10:54 p.m.

Study Questions

1. Does Clark make a good argument about O. J.'s alibi?
2. If you were Judge Ito, would you rule that Clark's argument about the defense's failure to produce the gloves is improper?
3. What are the good and bad qualities about the persuasive aid Clark uses?

---

58. *People v. Simpson* No. BA097211, 1995 WL 704343 at *33–34 (Cal. Super. Ct. Sept. 29, 1995) (rebuttal argument of Marcia Clark).

Chapter Seven

———⧉———

EXHIBITS AND OBJECTIONS

I would sooner trust the smallest slip of paper for truth than the strongest and most retentive memory ever bestowed on mortal man.

—Joseph Henry Lumpkin, American jurist[1]

vidence can be divided into two categories: (1) exhibits and (2) testimony that comes from witnesses at trial. Exhibits are nothing more than tangible items shown to the jury during trial. Some exhibits are admitted into evidence and seen by the jury during deliberations. Others are simply shown to the jury during the trial but cannot be viewed by the jury during deliberations. This chapter focuses primarily on the techniques needed to introduce a wide variety of exhibits into evidence and common objections to exhibits. The last section of the chapter addresses basic evidentiary objections to testimony and lawyers' questions during trial.

---

1.   *Miller v. Cotten*, 5 Ga. 341, 349 (1848).

7.1 THREE TYPES OF EXHIBITS

Exhibits can be divided into three categories: (1) real, (2) illustrative, and (3) persuasive aids. Real exhibits come from the actual event in question. For example, real exhibits in an armed-robbery case could be the victim's stolen purse, the handgun found in the defendant's pocket, and the brown jacket the defendant was wearing. In a car-wreck case, the real exhibits would be the medical records of the plaintiff at the emergency room and the repair bills for the plaintiff's car. Real exhibits go to the jury room for deliberations.[2]

The second category is illustrative (sometimes called demonstrative) exhibits. Illustrative exhibits are tangible items created after the event in question and used at trial to explain relevant facts for the jury. For example, in the armed-robbery example above, an illustrative exhibit would be a diagram of the intersection that was created a week before the trial in order for the victim to explain better—or illustrate—what she saw. In the car-wreck example, a photo taken a month after the accident showing different parts of the intersection to aid the witnesses in explaining their testimony would be an illustrative exhibit.

A judge has broad discretion in deciding to what extent illustrative exhibits are admitted into evidence. For example, with the armed-robbery case, the diagram of the intersection can (1) go to the jury room like any real exhibit or (2) be shown to the jury only during the trial (i.e., admitted into evidence for illustrative purposes only). Generally, you would prefer your illustrative exhibit to go to the jury room. However, either outcome above is beneficial because your exhibit is going to have its most significant impact when your witness talks about it during trial.

Persuasive aids comprise the third category of exhibits. Persuasive aids are not admitted into evidence but may be shown to the jury during trial. Examples are timelines used by attorneys in opening statements, enlargements of the text of important jury instructions and trial

---

2. However, be aware that a few judges, in exercising their discretion, won't allow admitted evidence to go to the jury room unless the jury has seen it during the trial.

testimony used in closing arguments, and PowerPoint presentations used by attorneys in openings and closings.

7.2 MAJORITY OF EXHIBITS EASILY ADMITTED

There is a misconception that a lawyer has to run through a maze of technicalities before getting evidence admitted. Most exhibits are easily admitted into evidence. Since most state evidentiary rules are modeled after the Federal Rules of Evidence, those rules are discussed in this chapter. Federal Rule of Evidence 402 plainly states that exhibits containing relevant evidence are generally admissible.[3] So, at trial, the presumption is that relevant exhibits are admissible unless there is a good objection for keeping them out.

Another reason exhibits are easy to admit is that attorneys and judges know that if objections are made, the offering attorney can then either ask the right questions or she can call another witness to cure the objection. Finally, judges—particularly in federal court—encourage the parties to agree on the admission of as many exhibits as possible prior to trial so that court time is not taken up by attorneys' laying technical foundations for exhibits that are ultimately admissible. In state courts, where the pace of litigation can be more frantic, you will need to be persistent prior to trial in getting opposing counsel to agree to the admissibility of exhibits for mutual benefit, saving everyone time.

Despite the ease of admitting exhibits, you need to know the basics of admissibility. Rule 401 defines relevant evidence as "evidence having any tendency to make the existence of any fact that is of consequence to the determination of the action more probable or less probable than it would be without the evidence."[4] However, just because an exhibit is helpful to prove your case does not mean it is admissible. It still must contain evidence that is more probative than prejudicial. Rule 403 declares, "Although relevant, evidence may be excluded if its probative value is substantially outweighed by the danger of unfair

---

3. Fed. R. Evid. 402.
4. Fed. R. Evid. 401.

prejudice, confusion of the issues, or misleading the jury, or by considerations of undue delay, waste of time, or needless presentation of cumulative evidence."[5]

Once these two requirements have been met—that the exhibit is relevant and more probative than prejudicial—you must establish that the item is what your witness claims it to be.[6] This process is known as laying the foundation.

7.3 LAYING THE FOUNDATION

Rule 902 sets forth ten categories of exhibits, such as newspapers and certified copies of public records, that are self-authenticating. If the exhibit is self-authenticating, nothing more needs to be done at trial other than offering its admission into evidence.[7] For those exhibits that are not self-authenticating, Rule 901(b) provides illustrations of a nonexclusive list of ten types of exhibits and how they can be authenticated. In short, the witness simply needs to testify from personal knowledge that the exhibit is what it is claimed to be.

7.4. THE SIX STEPS FOR GETTING EXHIBITS ADMITTED

The six steps for getting exhibits admitted into evidence follow.

Step 1. *Mark the exhibit with an identification sticker.* Prior to trial, your exhibits should be premarked with an exhibit sticker. Bring extra stickers to trial because something unforeseen always comes up, and you will invariably need to mark an item with an exhibit sticker.

Step 2. *Show opposing counsel the exhibit (preferably before trial).* Opposing counsel needs to have the opportunity to view any exhibit you discuss with a witness. If the other side does not have a copy prior to trial, show opposing counsel your exhibit before asking questions of the witness. Contrary to one trial textbook, there is no need to say,

---

5.   Fed. R. Evid. 403.
6.   Fed. R. Evid. 901.
7.   As noted, the exhibit can be admitted into evidence if it is relevant and more probative than prejudicial.

"For the record. I am showing [opposing counsel] Plaintiff's exhibit #1."[8] This is a cumbersome step that achieves nothing in the way of making the trial or appellate record clear. Just show the exhibit to opposing counsel.

Step 3. *Show the witness the exhibit.* For example, "Ms. Witness, can you turn to exhibit 5 in the notebook on the witness stand." Having the exhibits in a notebook at the witness stand avoids the necessity of your having to walk to the witness stand and hand the witness an exhibit every time you want to discuss a new exhibit.[9] If you need to discuss several items that are not in the witness notebook on the stand because they won't fit in it (e.g., a stolen purse, an article of clothing, and so forth), show them all at once to opposing counsel and take them up to the witness stand before the testimony begins, thereby avoiding the interruption of approaching the witness each time you discuss a different piece of evidence.

Step 4. *Lay the foundation for admission of the exhibit.* Authenticate the exhibit to show that it is what it purports to be. Be careful that your questions do not elicit substantive answers about the exhibit before it is admitted into evidence. It is your responsibility to ensure that evidence is not seen or heard by the jury before it is properly admitted, so you will need to guide the witness in this area especially with regard to the contents of documents.

Example: Laying the Foundation in a Civil Case.

The following is an example showing how to lay the foundation for a letter without revealing its contents prior to its admission. The letter was written by the witness offering to sell her computer to John Smith in Chicago.

> Q. Do you recognize exhibit 4?
> A. Yes.
> Q. Without going into the details of the document, can you tell me what it is?

---

8. Thomas A. Mauet, *Trial Techniques* at 170 (Aspen 6th ed. 2002). Mauet states that the "common practice is to state what you are doing so that the trial record is clear."
9. Many courts require attorneys to ask the judge for permission before approaching the witness stand.

A. Yes. It is a letter I wrote about my computer.

Q. What is the date on the letter?

A. August 6, 2006.

Q. Who wrote the letter?

A. I did.

Q. Who did you write it to?

A. John Smith in Chicago.

Q. Your Honor, I move exhibit 4 into evidence.

The court: Any objections?

Opposing counsel: No, Your Honor.

The court: Exhibit 4 is admitted.

[Show the letter on a projection screen and have the witness explain it.]

Example: Laying the Foundation in a Criminal Case

Assume your witness is a crime-scene officer who took photos of the murder victim. The particular photo you are introducing shows a lot of blood coming from the victim's head but is probative of the force that was used when she was bludgeoned with a club by the murderer.

Q. Without holding up the photo marked as exhibit 5, can you tell me if you recognize it?

A. Yes.

Q. Again, without describing the details of the photo, how can you recognize it?

A. I recognize it because I took this photo when I arrived at the crime scene on the night of July 1. You can see where . . . [Officer then begins to hold up the picture.]

Q. Don't show the picture yet! [The witness complies.] Thank you. Is it a fair and accurate depiction of the victim's body as you found it?

A. Yes.

Q. Your Honor, I move exhibit 5 into evidence.

The court: Any objections?

Opposing counsel: Yes, it is inflammatory.

The court: Let me see the picture. [The court looks at it.] Overruled. Exhibit 5 is admitted.

[Now, have the witness show the photograph and describe it.]

Step 5. *Move the exhibit into evidence.* Typically, one says, "Your Honor, [plaintiff/government/defendant/we] [offer(s) or move(s)] exhibit 5 into evidence." The court will ask if there are any objections, rule on them, and say "Sustained" or "Overruled." If the objection is sustained, the attorney offering the exhibit will be given an opportunity to ask more questions in light of the objection—unless there is no way to cure it (as would be the case with an inflammatory photograph). If the objection is overruled, the court will say, "Exhibit 5 is admitted."

Generally, if the exhibit is illustrative, the court will either admit it or—after hearing opposing counsel's objection—inform you that it is only being admitted for illustrative purposes (and therefore can't go back to the jury room). Don't be surprised if the court asks you whether you are admitting it for "illustrative [or demonstrative] purposes only." If you need it to go back to the jury room, say no. However, the judge's inquiry is a good signal of his likely ruling that you will only be able to show it to the jury during the trial.[10]

If you aren't trying to get the illustrative exhibit back into the jury room but only need it admitted so the jury can see it at that moment (and realize the judge is not going to let it go back to the jury room anyway), simply ask the witness when you are laying the foundation if the exhibit will assist the witness in explaining his testimony.

Some exhibits are admitted "conditionally." That is, there may be exhibits that require several witnesses to lay the foundation for their admission. To allow the first witness to discuss the substance of the exhibit even though it has not been admitted, courts may allow you to offer an exhibit into evidence (often referred to as "conditional admission") subject to other witnesses completing the foundation for its actual admission. This allows the first witness to show the exhibit to the jury and discuss it even though all the technical requirements for laying the foundation have not been accomplished. Courts will allow conditional admission only where it can be clearly shown that the exhibit will be admitted through other witnesses.

---

10. Occasionally, illustrative exhibits can go back to the jury room with a limiting instruction that tells the jury that it is not real evidence (e.g., a stocking hat that is similar to the one worn by the defendant in the armed robbery).

> Many attorneys are so caught up in the technical aspects of having evidence admitted that they fail to get a persuasive impact from the exhibit once it is admitted. If the exhibit is important, the jury needs to see it immediately upon its admission into evidence.

If additional testimony turns out to be insufficient for the exhibit's admission, however, opposing counsel should ask the court to instruct the jury to disregard what they have seen and heard about the exhibit. If the exhibit and the testimony have been highly prejudicial, opposing counsel should ask for a mistrial.

Be aware that when several witnesses are needed for authentication, you may forget to move the exhibit into evidence while the final witness is on the stand. This is not a fatal error. You can move any exhibit into evidence at any time before you rest your case. Be aware that the court reporter and judge will likely keep track of which exhibits have been admitted. Before resting your case, review your list of exhibits to see which ones have been admitted and which ones you question. Then check your list against the court reporter's. If there is a discrepancy, ask the court about the exhibit's status if it is important (you don't want to try the court's patience with too many questions, since it is your job to know the status of an exhibit).

Then, when the court asks if you are ready to rest, you can say, "At this time, the plaintiff would offer into evidence exhibits 17–20, and after their admission, the plaintiff rests."

Step 6. *Display the exhibit for the jury and have the witness discuss it after its admission.* Now that the item is in evidence, show the exhibit to the jury and continue your examination of the witness. If it is a document or photograph, you should have scanned it into your computer so you can now display it for the jury on a large screen in the courtroom. Step 6 is an ideal situation for enlarging portions of an admitted document or photograph so the jury can see the exact part of the exhibit about which the witness is testifying.

Thomas A. Mauet states that you should ask the court's permission to "publish the exhibit" to the jury.[11] The reason you ask permission is because you are approaching the jury box and handing the exhibit to

---

11.   Thomas A. Mauet, *Trial Techniques* at 173 (Aspen 6th ed. 2002).

the jury as opposed to just having the witness show it to them. However, it is an antiquated technique. In modern trials, you should have all your exhibits scanned into your computer to be shown on a projection screen in court once they are admitted. At the least, your exhibits should be enlarged on foam board so that the jurors can see them as the witness testifies.[12] Since you are not approaching the jury box to hand the jurors the exhibit, there is no need to ask the court for permission to publish it. The only time you would need to ask for permission to publish an exhibit is if it were something that the jury could not see or understand without holding it.

Checklist for Offering Exhibit into Evidence

1. Mark the exhibit with an identification sticker.
2. Show opposing counsel the exhibit (preferably before trial).
3. Show the witness the exhibit. (Most courts will allow you to have a copy of the exhibits in a notebook at the witness stand. If not, ask the court for "permission to approach" and show the witness the exhibit.)
4. Lay the foundation for admission of the exhibit.
5. Move the exhibit into evidence. (State "I offer/move exhibit number ___ into evidence.")
6. Display the exhibit for the jury and have the witness discuss it after its admission.

7.5 THE RIGHT WITNESS

The key to getting exhibits admitted into evidence is having the right witness on the stand. During discovery, decide who this will be. You may need more than one witness. It is best to be overinclusive on your

---

12. There may still be an occasional exhibit item that needs to be passed out to the jury, but this should be done rarely. Realize that any time you pass an exhibit around to the jurors, each juror will want to study it. Then everyone waits for the exhibit to get passed to all the jurors. This should be avoided at all costs. You could have a copy of the exhibit for each juror, but then the jury will be studying the exhibit while the momentum of your direct examination is completely lost.

trial witness list so that you can call the necessary one, should opposing counsel raise an objection.[13] If the witness is out of the subpoena range of the court, take the witness' deposition.[14]

The witness must have personal knowledge of the exhibit, since you have to establish that the exhibit is what your witness claims it to be.[15] Also, keep in mind that even though an exhibit is admitted, the key is the weight that the jury gives to it—the degree to which the jury believes it to be the truth.

For example, a victim of an armed robbery may be able to identify an exhibit as a gun that looks "similar" to the one that was pointed at her on the night of the holdup. However, the officer who recovered it from the defendant's pocket and who scratched his initials on the gun is a better witness to establish that the gun is the one used in the robbery. For the best emotional impact on the jury, have both witnesses testify about the exhibit.

7.6 BENCH MEMOS

While federal courts insist on pretrial conferences to sort out significant evidentiary battles before trial, many state courts do not have this luxury of time. Therefore, state court judges often have to make key rulings without the benefit of thorough research. If you anticipate that there is going to be a significant challenge to a key exhibit or if you have a significant challenge to your opponent's exhibits, prepare a bench memo prior to trial. The memo is simply a summary of the relevant case law

---

13. Prior to trial, you will file with the court a document that lists your expected trial witnesses.
14. Always ask yourself, "How will I get this witness to court if he does not cooperate?" In federal court, a witness cannot be compelled to attend if the witness is "at a greater distance than 100 miles from the trial or hearing," according to Fed. R. Civ. P. 32(3)(B). If the witness lives more than 100 miles away and will not voluntarily appear for trial, you will need to use the deposition at trial.
15. Fed. R. Evid. 901(a) states that "the requirement of authentication or identification as a condition precedent to admissibility is satisfied by evidence sufficient to support a finding that the matter in question is what its proponent claims." Fed. R. Evid. 901(b) illustrates that the rule can be satisfied by a witness' "testimony that a matter is what it is claimed to be."

supporting your position. Attach the most important case referred to in the memo and have the holding of the case tabbed and highlighted.

For example, assume you are the plaintiff, and you are trying to introduce a 911 call of an unknown witness who exclaims that she saw the defendant run a red light and hit the plaintiff. Although you are confident that you can authenticate the audiotape containing the 911 call through the record custodian at police headquarters, there is still the issue of whether the statement itself is admissible because it might not fall under an exception to the hearsay rule. Anticipate the day of trial the exhibit will be offered into evidence and hand the court a bench memo at the start of that day so the judge can read it during a break. If you choose carefully your evidentiary battles with opposing counsel and don't overwhelm the judge with research every time you anticipate an objection or make one, you will be able to educate him and gain an advantage over opposing counsel.

7.7 EXAMPLES OF ADMITTING REAL AND ILLUSTRATIVE EXHIBITS

Remember, there is a presumption that relevant exhibits are admissible.[16] The following are examples showing how to admit commonly used exhibits. They assume that steps 1 and 2 above (marking the exhibit and showing it to opposing counsel) have been done.

To illustrate the requirements of offering particular exhibits into evidence, the examples show the minimum questions needed. However, once these requirements have been learned, add the appropriate questions that will lend even more credibility to the exhibit so that the jury will be persuaded of its reliability.

1. Document (Purchase Agreement to Buy a Car in a Suit by Buyer to Recover Deposit Because Car Was Not Delivered)

> *Witness: Plaintiff (Buyer)*
> Q. Please turn to exhibit 9 in the notebook at the witness stand. Do you recognize that document?

---

16.   Fed. R. Evid. 402.

A. Yes.

Q. What is it?

A. It is a copy of the purchase agreement for an SUV.

Q. How do you recognize it?

A. At the bottom of the second page is my signature and the date I signed it. I also recognize the basic terms of the agreement, which I remember reading before I signed it.

Q. Is there another signature on the purchase agreement?

A. Yes, there is the signature of the salesman I dealt with. He signed it just after I did.

Q. Your Honor, I offer exhibit 9 into evidence.

The court: If there are no objections, it will be admitted.

Opposing counsel: No objection.

The court: Exhibit 9 is admitted.

Here, the witness is able to authenticate the purchase agreement by having personal knowledge of its terms and recognizing her signature on it. Federal Rule of Evidence 901(b)(2) allows for authentication through the "nonexpert opinion as to the genuineness of handwriting," and 901(b)(4) states that authentication can be established by testimony about "appearance, contents, substance, internal patterns, or other distinctive characteristics." Finally, in addition to getting the exhibit admitted, you could gain more impact by asking the following:

Q. Why do you remember the signing of this purchase agreement?

A. I was so excited because I had been searching for this car all over town and was promised that if they could not get the SUV for me that I would get my deposit back.

2. Photograph of a Crime Scene from *U.S. v. McVeigh*

Witness: Cynthia Lou Klaver (She Worked in the Water Resources Building Next to the Murrah Building)

Q. *Would you turn to exhibit number 958?*

A. *OK.*

Q. *Could you identify that for the jury, please?*

A. It's an aerial photo of downtown Oklahoma City, color Xerox copy.

Q. Is it a true and accurate photograph of an aerial view of Oklahoma City?

A. It looks to be a true and accurate photograph.

Prosecutor: Your Honor, the government would offer exhibit 958.

The court: Any objection?

Defense counsel: No, Your Honor.

The court: Received.[17]

Photographs are among the easiest exhibits to get admitted. As the prosecutor did, simply ask, "Is exhibit __ a fair and accurate picture of [whatever is depicted in the picture at the relevant time]?"

3. Photograph or Videotape Taken after Event (e.g., Auto Accident)

Witness: Hired Investigator for the Plaintiff

Q. Investigator Lightbourn, let me direct your attention to exhibit number 3. Without showing it to the jury, could you identify it, please?

A. It is a photo [or video] of the intersection of Newark and Wisconsin Avenue, where the accident occurred.

Q. When was it taken?

A. I took it about a month after the accident.

Q. Is it a fair and accurate photograph [or video] of that intersection as it was at the time of the accident?

A. Yes, the time of the day is the same. Nothing has changed except there are obviously different cars there.

Q. Your Honor, I offer exhibit 3 into evidence.

Some lawyers ask two additional foundational questions: (1) "Are you familiar with the intersection?" and (2) "How are you familiar with it?" However, photographs are so commonly accepted by courts that you don't even need to ask these questions, since it is assumed that

---

17. *United States v. McVeigh* No. 96-CR-68, 1997 WL 200045 at *3 (D. Colo. Apr. 25, 1997) (direct examination of Cynthia Lou Klaver).

the witness is familiar with the place in question; otherwise, the witness would not be able to identify the photograph.

To get the exhibit admitted, you do not even need to have the person who took the photograph testify. See the following:

> *Witness: A Pedestrian Who Has Testified That She Saw the Accident*
> Q. Would you look at exhibit 3? Is it a fair and accurate photograph of that intersection on that day?
> A. Yes. The lighting is the same, but the cars are different.
> Q. Your Honor, I offer exhibit 3 into evidence.

4. Diagram from *U.S. v. McVeigh*

Witness: Cynthia Lou Klaver (She Worked in the Water Resources Building Next to the Murrah Building)

> Q. Would you look at exhibit 940 . . . in front of you there? Could you identify that for the jury?
> A. Exhibit 940 is a copy or a diagram of the buildings downtown around the Murrah Building and the Water Board.
> Q. Does it accurately depict the downtown area?
> A. Yes, it does.
> Q. And the location of the buildings relative to one another?
> A. Yes, it does.
> The court: Are you going to offer this 940?
> Prosecutor: I'm sorry. Yes, I would offer government's exhibit 940.
> Defense counsel: No objection.
> The court: All right, 940 is received.[18]

Leading questions are generally permissible in laying the foundation for an exhibit so that a witness does not talk about the substance of the exhibit before it is admitted. It also allows attorneys to quickly lay the foundation.

Here, the court admitted this illustrative exhibit. A majority of courts will allow evidence like this to go to the jury room. Others will admit it only for illustrative purposes during the witness' testimony. Whatever

---

18. *United States v. McVeigh* No. 96-CR-68, 1997 WL 200045 at *3 (D. Colo. Apr. 25, 1997) (direct examination of Cynthia Lou Klaver).

the case may be, some courts expect the attorney to ask an additional question of the witness: "Will this diagram assist you in explaining your testimony to the jury?" While there is no harm in asking this question, there is no need to ask this question unless there is an objection.

Ideally, you will find out from other attorneys how your judge is likely to rule on illustrative exhibits. If the court only admits for illustrative purposes, you will still get all the impact you need from your witness during trial.

5. Witness' Drawing

In most cases, it is best to have a layperson describe events from an illustrative exhibit created prior to trial by a professional. For example, in the *Fordyce v. Harris and Felson* case file, discussed in chapter 2, you would need to have the witnesses explain what happened in the bar by using a diagram of it (see, e.g., figure 7.1).[19] This can be done by creating the exhibit prior to trial and then having the witness state that the exhibit is a fair and accurate diagram of Gus' Bar & Grill.

There are times, however, when you won't have this luxury. If that is the case, use the questions in the following example.

> *Witness: Eva Long (adapted from the* Fordyce v. Harris and Felson *Case File)*[20]
>
> Q. Ms. Long, you have testified that Mr. Felson threatened Mr. Fordyce with a broken beer bottle. With the court's permission, I am going to ask you to come down from the witness stand and approach the easel.
>
> A. OK. [The witness goes to the easel, which is in front of the jury.]
>
> Q. Would you draw a basic diagram of the area where you were sitting and where defendants Felson and Harris were sitting?
>
> [The witness draws a diagram.]
>
> Q. Your Honor, I move exhibit 2 into evidence.

---

19. *Fordyce v. Harris and Felson*, by Abraham P. Ordover (NITA 1992).
20. *Fordyce v. Harris and Felson*, by Abraham P. Ordover (NITA 1992).

Gus' Bar & Grill

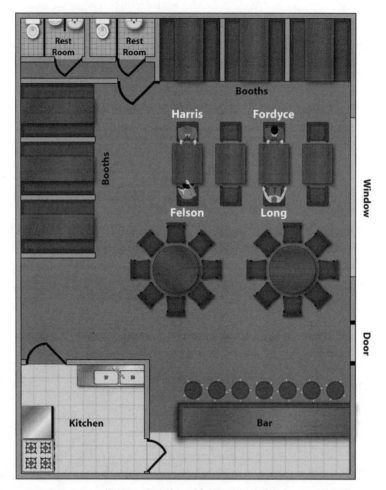

Figure 7.1. Diagram of Scene. (Produced by DecisionQuest)

> The court: There being no objections, the exhibit will be admitted.

Like the diagram in the *McVeigh* example, this diagram is admissible as an exhibit under Rule 901(a) because it is what the witness claims it to be. Notice that the jury sees the exhibit before it is admitted. The reason is that there is a presumption that drawings will be admitted. A strategic question is whether you *want* the exhibit to go to the jury room. Since the drawings are generally somewhat crude, you might not want the jury poring over their details during deliberations but, rather, you would prefer to get the impact just when the witness makes her drawings. If so, have the witness draw the diagram and then do not offer it into evidence.

Warning! It is not a good idea to have a witness practice freehand drawing in trial without having practiced before trial. There is nothing worse than getting locked into a bad illustration at trial.

6. Demonstration

An in-court demonstration by the witness is not an exhibit but, instead, is the testimony of the witness. Since it is such an effective visual aid, however, it will be discussed here.

> *Witness: Eva Long (adapted from the* Fordyce v. Harris and Felson *Case File)*[21]
> Q. Ms. Long, you have testified that in the bar, Mr. Felson threatened Mr. Fordyce with a broken beer bottle. Your Honor, may the witness step down from the witness stand and come before the jury box for a demonstration?
> The court: Yes.
> Q. Ms. Long, please come over to the front of the jury box.
> [The witness complies.]
> Q. Could you position me where Mr. Fordyce was and demonstrate what you saw Mr. Felson do to Mr. Fordyce?
> [The witness demonstrates.]

Since this is only testimony, there is no need to offer anything into evidence. If, however, the witness demonstrates something important, you will need to preserve the action for the possibility of appeal after trial. Because the court reporter does not transcribe demonstrations into the trial record, you can say the following: "Your Honor, may the record reflect that Ms. Long raised her right hand as she approached. . . ." Use this technique sparingly since it can interrupt the flow of the demonstration; note that jurors will become skeptical if you don't relate precisely what happened, so take care when stating what the record should reflect.

---

21. *Fordyce v. Harris and Felson,* by Abraham P. Ordover (NITA 1992).

7. Recorded Recollection

Sometimes you need your witness to testify to specifics that are impossible to remember. In such a situation, Federal Rule of Evidence 803(5) provides a solution. The rule states that a record containing information that a witness once knew but is not able to remember and that was made by the witness at a time when the information was fresh in the witness' mind may be read into evidence but not go to the jury room.

In the following example, the victim had her high-definition television and her digital camcorder stolen from her house. She does not remember the serial numbers of the items but had written them down on a sheet of paper when she bought them.

> *Witness: Victim of Burglary*
> Q. Ms. Cavendish, can you remember the serial numbers of your TV and digital camcorder that were stolen from your house?
> A. No.
> Q. If you saw them again, would they refresh your memory as to what they were?
> A. No. I never had them memorized because the numbers were too long.
> Q. Did you ever make a record of them?
> A. Yes. When I bought them, I wrote the serial numbers down on a piece of paper and put it in my safe-deposit box.
> Q. Do you recognize exhibit 13?
> A. Yes.
> Q. What is it?
> A. It is the sheet of paper that I just told you about.
> Q. Your Honor, I move that the witness be allowed to read exhibit 13 into evidence.

The first few questions are asked to signal the judge that you are offering the exhibit as a past recollection recorded and not to refresh the witness' recollection. If the witness could see the numbers and then remember them (e.g., a driver's license number), the exhibit would not be introduced into evidence after being shown to the witness but, instead, would be shown to refresh her recollection. In this case, where the numbers are too long to remember, the exhibit is admitted as evidence of what the serial numbers were, but it is not permitted in the jury room because of Rule 803(5)'s restrictions.

8. Audio Recording

Witness: Undercover Police Officer (Officer Had Testified That He Had Several Conversations with the Defendant, One of Which He Recorded)

Q. Officer, can you identify exhibit 9?
A. Yes, it is a tape recording I made.
Q. Have you listened to it?
A. Yes, all of it.
Q. Without telling us the conversation on it, can you tell us whose voices are on it?
A. My voice and the defendant's.
Q. When was the tape made?
A. On the night of March 15.
Q. Is it a fair and accurate recording of the conversation that took place?
A. Yes, but some of the words are hard to understand the first time you listen to the tape.
Q. Your Honor, I move exhibit 9 into evidence.

Although the same question can be used for an audiotape as for a photograph, there is an additional evidentiary hurdle with an audiotape—hearsay. Here, the statement is not hearsay because it is an admission by a "party-opponent."[22]

9. Transcript of Audiotape

Witness: Same Undercover Officer as in Preceding Example

Q. Officer, you mentioned that some of the words on exhibit 9 were difficult to understand? [**See example above.**]

---

22. Fed. R. Evid. 801(d)(2) declares in part that a statement is not hearsay if the statement is "offered against a party and is the party's own statement." So, the defendant's statements on the tape are admissible. Be aware that there are a host of constitutional issues regarding proper police procedures to ensure that a defendant's statements were not coerced. Those issues are raised prior to trial through a motion to suppress statements filed by defense counsel.

A. Yes.
Q. Let me direct your attention to exhibit 10. Can you tell me what it is?
A. It is a transcript I made of exhibit 9.
Q. When did you make it?
A. Sometime prior to trial, I played the tape several times and created a transcript of the conversation that took place on the tape.
Q. Is your transcript accurate?
A. Yes. Where I could not understand a word, I wrote the word inaudible.
Q. Your Honor, I offer exhibit 10 into evidence.

Whether or not a transcript—being an illustrative exhibit—goes to the jury room depends on the court. Even if the judge only allows its admission for illustrative purposes, you can use it to great advantage during the witness' testimony. There is no point in playing an audio-tape that is difficult to understand without a transcript. Make the jurors' job easy and create a transcript as an exhibit so they can follow along as the tape is being played.

10. Physical Evidence from Crime Scene

Let's assume there was an armed robbery. The defendant was arrested after the crime in a nearby alley. He had with him the victim's purse, a gun used in the robbery, and a stocking used to cover his face. All of these can be authenticated under Rule 901(b). The witness must be the officer who took the evidence from the defendant. Although the evidence has changed hands several times while in police custody, as long as the officer who recovered the evidence can identify it, the evidence will be admitted.

Witness: Officer Johnson (Arresting Officer)
[The attorney offering exhibits shows opposing counsel the three exhibits and takes them to the witness stand as the officer enters the courtroom to take the stand. This is done to save time and keep the testimony flowing so that the attorney does not have to take each exhibit to the witness stand during the testimony.]
Q. Do you recognize the three exhibits in front of you?

A. Yes.

Q. What is exhibit 1?

A. It is the victim's purse, which was recovered from the defendant.

Q. How do you know?

A. When I arrested the defendant, I recovered it from the bag he was carrying, I put a tag on it with my initials, the date, and the defendant's name.

Q. Is that tag on the bag?

A. Yes.

Q. What is exhibit 2?

A. It is the .38-caliber gun I recovered from the defendant's jacket.

Q. How do you know that?

A. When I took the gun out of his jacket, I scratched my initials on the gun and put a property tag on it when I got to the station. I see my initials right here.

Q. Finally, can you identify exhibit 3?

A. Yes, it is the stocking found in the defendant's bag. I kept it as evidence because it matched the clothing description the victim had given. I tagged it with this tag here when I got to the station.

Q. Your Honor, at this time I offer exhibits 1, 2, and 3 into evidence.

The court: They are admitted.

Q. Now, officer, let's go through each exhibit in some detail now that you can show them to the jury.

There is no need to offer each exhibit separately into evidence. Moreover, as the trial progresses, you will get a feel for the degree to which opposing counsel will object to your exhibits. Usually, she won't object because she knows they will ultimately be admitted. Once you know there is little chance of objection, you could offer the above three exhibits with one question:

Q. *Officer, can you identify the three exhibits in front of you and briefly tell us how you can identify them?*

A. *I recovered exhibit 1, the purse, exhibit 2, the gun, and exhibit 3, the stocking, from the defendant on the night of the arrest. They each have a tag with my initials and other information.*

Q. *Your Honor, I move exhibits 1, 2, and 3 into evidence.*

If opposing counsel objects, all you have to do is fill in a few details, which the prior example has. Remember that you are in control. The jury will become impatient if you go through the litany of asking every possible question to get an item admitted. Make the other side object and bear the penalty of exasperated looks from the jury for causing you to go through every detail to lay a foundation after an objection.

11. Chain of Custody Issues
(Seized Drugs in a Criminal Case)

Unlike the above example, where not every officer who handled the crime-scene exhibits is needed to get the exhibits admitted, chain of custody becomes important in admitting exhibits that are not unique. Money and drugs are classic examples. They are not unique in any way, so you must do more to establish that they are what they purport to be—pieces of evidence connected to the defendant. For example, in a crack-cocaine trial where a baggie of crack was found in the defendant's jacket pocket, the following testimony would be needed. Officer 1 would testify that he recovered a baggie (a small plastic sandwich bag) of drugs containing a rocklike substance from the defendant's jacket pocket during a pat-down search. He then gave the baggie to Officer 2. The second officer would testify that he got a baggie of drugs from Officer 1; performed a field test on the substance (to see if it was a narcotic) and put the baggie and drugs in a heat-sealed envelope (like a large Ziploc bag); wrote his initials, the date, the defendant's name, and other identifying information on the envelope; and put the envelope in the property room at the police station. The chemist would testify that she received a heat-sealed envelope that was intact from the property room (or from the police courier) and tested the substance. She determined that it was crack cocaine and noted on the envelope that she had opened and closed it. She then returned it to the property room.

By having all three witnesses testify, the court is assured that the heat-sealed envelope in court is what the witnesses claim it to be, the crack that was recovered from the defendant's pocket.[23] Sometimes

---

23. Fed. R. Evid. 406 states, "Evidence of the habit of a person or of the routine practice of an organization, whether corroborated or not and

several more officers will handle the baggie of drugs at the scene of the crime. In such a situation, not every officer is needed to testify in court for admissibility, but to the extent there is a break in the chain of custody, the defense can use that break to challenge the authenticity of the evidence.

12. Medical Records, X-rays, MRIs, and CAT Scans (Business Records)

In admitting medical records, there is no difference among those that contain the patient's statements, doctor's notes, treatment plans, and so forth and X-rays, MRIs, and CAT scans. They are all medical records and fall under the umbrella of the business records exception to the hearsay rule. See Federal Rule of Evidence 803(6). The patient's statements contained in the records are admissible under Federal Rule of Evidence 803(4) because they are statements made for the purpose of medical diagnosis.

> *Witness: Custodian of Records at a Hospital*
> Q. Can you identify exhibit number 11?
> A. Yes. They are the medical records [or CAT scans] of Sue Smith.
> Q. Were the events, opinions, and diagnoses recorded at or near the time they occurred? [Or were the CAT scans recorded contemporaneously with the procedure?]
> A. Yes.
> Q. Were those records [CAT scans] made in the course of regularly conducted business at the hospital?
> A. Yes.
> Q. Was it the regular practice of the hospital to make these records [or to take CAT scans]?
> A. Yes.
> Q. And you obtained these from the hospital records room?
> A. Yes.

---

regardless of the presence of eyewitnesses, is relevant to prove that the conduct of the person or organization on a particular occasion was in conformity with the habit or routine practice." So, if an officer were missing from this chain of custody, counsel would need to argue that he has established through the other two witnesses a routine sufficient to show authenticity.

The business records exception to the hearsay rule, Federal Rule of Evidence 803(6), is the vehicle for the admission of many documents at a typical civil trial. In the above example, the attorney followed the steps to offer medical records under Rule 803(6). In reality, however, medical records are often admitted by agreement among counsel, or they have already been authenticated through the use of a deposition upon written questions for the custodian of records (Fed. R. Civ. P. 31). A third way to get medical records and other types of business records admitted is through the provisions of Rule 902(11) and (12), allowing one to meet the requirements of Rule 803(6) prior to trial through certification of the records by a qualified person.

Remember that the witness does not have to be a "custodian of records" but simply any qualified person. In the above example, it could be a doctor or nurse who performed or recorded the test instead of the custodian of records.

13. Business Record from *U.S. v. McVeigh*

Since the business record exception is so often used, here is another example of how it is done, in this instance, with an audiotape that is a business record.[24] The exhibit below is an audiotape of the legal proceeding in the Water Resources Building that accidentally recorded the sound of the explosion at the federal building next door.

> Q. *Now, you have looked, have you not, and listen[ed] to government exhibit 942, which is an audiotape?*
> A. *Yes, I have.*
> Q. *Is that the audiotape that your secretary was maintaining for the administrative hearing that started at 9:00 on April 19th?*

---

24. In a civil case, beginning lawyers often mistakenly believe that because a business maintains a document in its file, it is admissible under the business records exception. For example, a company may receive a complaint from several customers about a subject relevant to a lawsuit. That letter—although it is kept in the normal course of a regularly conducted business activity—is not "made" by the business. Therefore, it cannot come in under this exception (but may come in under other exceptions, depending on the circumstances).

A. *Yes, it is.*

Q. *I take it that is the standard procedure as you've described to the jury.*

A. *Yes.*

Q. *And is it the customary and ordinary practice of the board to make a tape recording of all of these hearings?*

A. *Yes, it is.*

Prosecutor: Your Honor, we would offer government's exhibit 942.

Defense counsel: No objection, Your Honor.

The court: 942 is received.

Q. *It's a true and accurate recording of what occurred that day?*

A. *Yes, it is.*[25]

To make the admission of the tape more meaningful to the jury, the prosecutor should have woven his last question about the tape's accuracy into his questions that had laid the foundation.

Checklist for Business Records Exception (Federal Rule of Evidence 803(6))

1. A person with knowledge transmitted the information that makes the record.
2. The record or data was made at or near the time the event occurred.
3. The record was kept in the course of a regularly conducted business activity.
4. It was the regular practice of the business to make the record.

14. Examples of Admissible and Inadmissible Records under Business Records Exception

Since many exhibits are offered as business records, below are some common examples of what is admissible and what is not.[26] Courts

---

25. *United States v. McVeigh* No. 96-CR-68, 1997 WL 200045 at *5–6 (D. Colo. Apr. 25, 1997) (direct examination of Cynthia Lou Klaver).

26. For a detailed discussion of the business record exception, see Michael Graham, *Federal Practice and Procedure,* vol. 30B at 497–653 (West

view the exception broadly and favor admission. For those examples below that are inadmissible, be aware that they may very well be admissible under another rule of evidence, such as an admission of a party-opponent.[27]

A. Admissible Records
1. Employee's official personnel file
2. Medical records
3. Computer printouts of qualifying business records
4. Bank records of a customer's account
5. Business appointment calendars kept by an employee

B. Inadmissible Records
1. Personal notes created by an employee at a business and related to personal matters (not regular practice of the business to make the record or keep it)
2. Documents prepared in anticipation of litigation (lack of routine and motivation for preparation undermine trustworthiness of a business record exception)
3. Reports made by employees that were not part of their official duties (not regular practice of the business to make the record)
4. Accident report made by an employee a week after the incident (record not made at or near time event occurred)
5. Letters of complaint by customers to a business (not made by someone at the business with knowledge)
6. Statements to a police officer at the scene of an accident or crime that are recorded in an officer's notes (the witness does not have a "business" duty to report information to an officer; this fact undermines the reliability of the statement; this is inadmissible hearsay within admissible hearsay—the part the officer has knowledge of).[28]

2006) and Paul Rothstein, *Federal Rules of Evidence* at 526–540 (West 2003).
27. See Fed. R. Evid. 801(d)(2).
28. See Fed. R. Evid. 805. "Hearsay included within hearsay is not excluded under the hearsay rule if each part of the combined statements

Although it is often a good idea to get exhibits admitted with as few questions as possible, when you need to make an important point, you can use the process of laying the foundation to your advantage. For example, with business records, instead of breezing through the first requirement that a person with knowledge transmitted the information, you could have the witness explain who the person "with knowledge" is and why the transmission of the information is important to the business (e.g., the business' success depends on the trustworthiness of the information). For medical records, let the jury know that doctors and staff rely on the records to provide accurate treatment. If the hospital is able to rely on them in the regular course of its business, then the jury should be able to rely on their accuracy in relating what occurred.

15. Computer Issues

A. Computer Records

Just because records have been kept on a computer does not make them difficult to admit into evidence. The business records exception above applies exactly the same way, whether the records have been stored on a computer or not.[29]

B. E-mails

Don't assume that e-mails are a business record. Usually, they are not. While they may be admissible under other evidentiary rules, it is unlikely that inflammatory e-mails were made in the regular course of business or that it was the practice of the business to maintain that record.[30]

---

conforms with an exception to the hearsay rule provided in these rules."

29. See *United States v. Fujii*, 301 F.3d 535, 539 (7th Cir. 2002).

30. See *Monotype Corp. v. International Typeface Corp.*, 43 F.3d 443, 450 (9th Cir. 1994) (an inflammatory e-mail sent by employee to his supervisor about another person was not a regularly conducted business activity as compared to a monthly inventory printout).

Here is an example of how to admit an e-mail that does not qualify as a business record but yet is admissible as an admission by a party opponent under Rule 801(d)(2).

> *Witness: Plaintiff Suing Her Supervisor, Mr. Smith, Who Allegedly Sexually Harassed Her*
> Q. Do you recognize exhibit 13?
> A. Yes.
> Q. What is it?
> A. It is an e-mail from a supervisor at my company.
> Q. How do you recognize it?
> A. I received it on the morning of May 1, and I remember how shocked I was when I received it.
> Q. Your Honor, I move exhibit 13 into evidence.

C. Internet Web Sites

Postings on Web sites are a relatively new evidentiary problem. Don't assume that statements from a party's Web site are those made by the person or business you claim made them. You must authenticate that the statement on the Web site is truly that of the party you are claiming it to be.[31]

D. Computer Illustrations and Animations

Many lawyers overthink the requirements of getting a computer illustration or animation into evidence. Lawyers mistakenly believe that since a computer created it, there must be additional hurdles to overcome. That is not the case.

Suppose the owner of a warehouse was suing the manufacturer of a fire door because the door failed to close and protect the warehouse's inventory when there was a fire in an adjoining space. The defense of the manufacturer of the fire door was that the door worked properly but that there were altered physical conditions at the warehouse that caused the door to malfunction. Doubtlessly, a defense witness—assuming that the witness has knowledge of how the door works—could draw on an easel a door, sensors, and other markings to show how the door should have functioned when there was a fire. To get the diagram

---

31. See, e.g., *United States v. Jackson*, 208 F.3d 633, 638 (7th Cir. 2000) (holding that evidence from the Internet was unauthenticated).

admitted as an illustrative exhibit, all the witness would need to do is testify that the exhibit is what it purports to be. That is, the drawing does "fairly and accurately" depict the fire door and how it works. Obviously, the drawing would not be to scale and would not contain every detail of the door and warehouse. Those failings would only go to how much the jury credited it—the weight of the evidence—not its admissibility. If opposing counsel were to make an objection to its accuracy that is sustained, you could rephrase your question and ask, "Would your drawing help explain your testimony to the jury?"

Likewise, if your exhibit were a computer drawing that had perfectly straight lines for the door and was drawn to scale, the question to the witness would still be the same: "Does the exhibit fairly and accurately depict the fire door and how it works?"

So, if you created a series of slides on the computer that showed the sequence of the sensors being set off by heat and the doors actually closing, the question would still be the same. The only difference is that the more accurate your exhibit is, the more the jury will trust it (see figure 7.2 for an example of a highly detailed drawing of fire doors).[32]

The logic for the admission of computer illustrations applies to computer animations. In this example, an animation might be a more complicated version of the door illustration that would be converted into moving digital images.

In short, if the witness is knowledgeable about the exhibit and if the testimony would come in if there were no exhibit, the exhibit can certainly be admitted as long as it illustrates what the witness is talking about. If the illustration or animation is created by an expert witness, then special issues may arise. That type of exhibit is discussed below under "Scientific Exhibits."

E. PowerPoint Presentations

A PowerPoint presentation is a visual aid that is created on a computer. It is essentially a slide show that can contain documents, explanatory

---

32. This computer "slide show" is on disc 1 under the heading "Exhibits: Slideshow" and labeled "Using Graphics to Demonstrate a Mechanical Concept." The slides for all the exhibits have been converted to a video clip so you can fast-forward, pause, and rewind when necessary. You can also skip to the next slide by using the "seek" button.

Figure 7.2. Detailed Exhibit. (Produced by DecisionQuest)

text, photos, videos, and animations. An example is on disc 1 under "Exhibits: Slideshow" and labeled "Using Builds to Present Complex Information."[33]

A PowerPoint presentation is often used by an expert witness to help explain his testimony. In such situations, it is an illustrative exhibit, and the evidentiary question is whether it should be allowed to go back to the jury room. To the extent the presentation contains the witness' conclusions (e.g., explanatory text below satellite photographs), then it won't be allowed in the jury room and can only be used by the expert to assist his explanation to the jury.

In a complex case, however, there can be great benefit to crafting the exhibit so that the jury can view it on a computer during deliberations instead of just once when the witness testifies. Create two exhibits. One would have the PowerPoint with the expert's explanations

---

33. All the exhibits on disc 1, Exhibits: Slideshow, were produced by DecisionQuest.

that the jury would see during his testimony. The other one would not have those explanations but only items of evidence that you are certain will be admitted (and in fact are admitted at trial) (e.g., satellite photos). You will have a much better chance of getting the latter exhibit into the jury room along with a computer to view it on. That way, jurors will at least see key pieces of evidence organized in a PowerPoint that they can review during deliberations.

> Well in advance of trial, experienced trial lawyers will seek agreement from opposing counsel to the admissibility of computer-generated exhibits. If you wait until trial to see if there is an objection, there will be no time to cure the objection and create an acceptable exhibit. If opposing counsel is not reasonable prior to trial, seek a hearing with the court prior to trial to get a ruling.

16. Scientific Exhibits

Scientific exhibits can include DNA evidence, comparison of fingerprints, blood-splatter analysis, Breathalyzer tests, accident reconstructions, footprint comparisons, voice spectrographic analysis, and much more.[34] Let's look at a computer animation created by an accident reconstructionist. (An example is on disc 1 under "Exhibits: Scruggs Animation."[35]) The example on the disc shows a car failing to brake in time, hitting a child. (Still frames from the animation can be found in figures 7.3 through 7.5.) Since the exhibit purports to be a real-time re-

---

34. For a good introduction to the types of testimony and exhibits allowed under Rule 702, see Paul F. Rothstein, *Federal Rules of Evidence* at 375–423 (West 3d ed. 2003). For a more detailed discussion, see Federal Judicial Center, *Reference Manual on Scientific Evidence* (2d. ed. 2000).

35. This is an animation created by the plaintiff's expert. There are several scenarios portrayed. For convenience of viewing, each scenario is repeated. The first scenario is a real-time sequence that shows what happened when the defendant failed to brake in time. A red light on the dash lights up to indicate when the defendant brakes. The second scenario (feasibility study #1) shows what would have happened if the defendant had applied the brakes when the truck did. The third scenario (feasibility study #2) demonstrates what would have happened if the defendant had applied the breaks at the same distance from the child as the truck did.

Child clears the path of the Truck. Kia is approx. 90' away.

Child at center of road. Kia begins braking, approx. 40' away.

Kia impacting child.

Figure 7.3. Animation Still.   *Figure 7.4. Animation Still.*   *Figure 7.5. Animation Still.*

creation of the accident created by the plaintiff's expert (it shows the accident occurring as the defendant would have seen it), a layperson would not be competent to authenticate its accuracy, and you would need an expert, such as an accident reconstructionist.

Like that of any expert, the reconstructionist's testimony would have to satisfy the requirements established by the Supreme Court in *Daubert v. Merrell Dow Pharmaceuticals, Inc.,* 509 U.S. 579 (1993) and *Kumho Tire Co. v. Carmichael,* 526 U.S. 137, 141 (1999).[36] Under *Daubert,* a trial judge, faced with a proffer of expert testimony that is either scientific, technical, or otherwise specialized, must determine at the outset, pursuant to Federal Rule of Evidence 702, that "(1) the testimony is based upon sufficient facts or data, (2) the testimony is the product of reliable principles and methods, and (3) the witness has applied the principles and methods reliably to the facts of the case." Pertinent considerations in making this determination are (1) whether a theory or technique can be (and has been) tested; (2) whether it has been subjected to peer review and publication; (3) the known or potential

---

36. Unless a *Daubert* challenge is raised by opposing counsel, there is no need to go into all the details to satisfy *Daubert* unless you feel the questions lend credibility to the testimony. Generally, if a *Daubert* challenge is made, a hearing will be held outside of the jury to determine if the witness is qualified. See *Kumho Tire Co. v. Carmichael,* 526 U.S. 137, 141 (1999) (holding that *Daubert* applies to testimony based on scientific knowledge as well as technical and other specialized knowledge. In addition, *Daubert's* list of factors is flexible and "neither necessarily nor exclusively applies to all experts or in every case").

rate of error; (4) the existence and maintenance of standards and controls in the methodology; and (5) whether the theory or technique is
generally accepted.

The accident reconstructionist could meet these requirements. As
part of her testimony, she would testify about the science of determining driver reaction times and braking distances and how she determined the speed of the child running.

17. Self-Authenticating Documents

A. Court Judgment of Witness' Prior
Felony Conviction (Public Record)[37]

When you decide to impeach a witness who has a conviction that
meets the standards of Federal Rule of Evidence 609, your exhibit if he
denies the conviction is the actual judgment that sets forth the prior
conviction. This judgment is a public record that is self-authenticating
under Federal Rule of Evidence 902(4) as long as it is certified as being
so by someone authorized to make the certification. The judgment
along with the attached certification can be admitted into evidence at
trial without having to call any witnesses.

B. Other Public Records from U.S. v. McVeigh

The following are examples showing how easily public records were
admitted into evidence in the *McVeigh* trial.

> Hartzler: Your Honor, we would also move the admission
> under Rule 902 of certain public records that we have
> shown the defense. The first is government exhibit 53,
> which is a certified copy of an application for a Michigan
> license.
> The court: Any objection to 53?
> Jones: No, Your Honor.
> The court: Received.
> Hartzler: The second is 266, which is a certified copy of a
> title history for a J2000 Pontiac.

---

37. Exhibits used for impeachment such as prior convictions or prior inconsistent statements do not fall neatly into categories of real or illustrative exhibits.

Jones: No objection.

The court: 266 received. . . .

*Hartzler: Government exhibit[s] 321, 322, and 323 are certi-
fied copies of information obtained from the South
Dakota Bureau of Motor Vehicles.*

Jones: No objection.

The court: 321, 322, 323 received.[38]

18. Summary Chart from *U.S. v. McVeigh*

Summary charts are routine in complex litigation. They are used to summarize voluminous information for the jury.[39] The following example illustrates their use in aiding the jury to match the counts in the indictment with the relevant evidence.

Witness: Chief Medical Examiner for Oklahoma

*Q. Now, Dr. Jordan, I'm going to—you should have on
your screen here in a moment a list of eight law enforcement officers who comprise eight murder counts in this
case, exhibit 1264. What does this exhibit tell us? Don't
tell us the content, but what is it designed to do?*

*A. The exhibit lists the victims and the method of identifica-
tion.*

Ryan: Your Honor, we would offer exhibit 1264.

Jones: No objection.

The court: Received. 1264 may be shown.

*Ryan: Now, if you would, Dr. Jordan, with respect to these
eight murder counts, would you tell us how these officers
were identified by your office.*

A. Individually?

Q. Yes, sir. Just go down the list.

*A. Cynthia Campbell Brown was identified by fingerprints.
Paul Broxterman by fingerprints.*[40]

---

38. *United States v. McVeigh* No. 96-CR-68, 1997 WL 266800 at *3 (D. Colo. May 21, 1997).

39. See Fed. R. Evid. 1006.

40. *United States v. McVeigh* No. 96-CR-68, 1997 WL 266800 at *34 (D. Colo. May 21, 1997).

Prior to the excerpt shown here, the witness had detailed the process his team had used to identify the bodies. Federal Rule of Evidence 1006 provides for the admission into evidence of a summary of voluminous writings, recordings, or photographs that cannot be conveniently examined in court. All you have to show is that (1) the summary is accurate, (2) the records reviewed would be admissible in evidence if offered, and (3) the records would "not be convenient" for the court to examine.

19. Prior Inconsistent Statement

The extent to which an exhibit containing a prior inconsistent statement is admissible depends on a few factors. If the statement was made under oath and at a previous court hearing or in a deposition, it may be admissible—depending on the jurisdiction and whether or not the witness denies having made it—to prove the truth of the facts asserted in that statement (as an exemption from the hearsay rule).[41] Likewise, if it was not made under oath, extrinsic evidence (such as the document it was written on), may or may not be admissible depending on the court. However, don't get bogged down in these rules. Remember, the persuasive impact of any inconsistent statement occurs the moment that the jury sees the witness confronted with it during trial. That is all you need.

20. Stipulations from *U.S. v. McVeigh*

Stipulations are agreements between parties regarding the admission of evidence. They can be used to agree to the admission of exhibits and testimony to save time for the jury. The following are examples of the use of stipulations:

> *The court: Members of the jury, good morning.*
> *We're going to begin this morning with reading to you some stipulations. Stipulation is a word we use in legal proceedings, a fancy word to mean agreement, when certain things have been agreed between both sides in the case. . . .*

---

41.   See Fed. R. Evid. 801(d)(1)(A) and 613(b).

Remember, the majority of lawyers are not going to object to evidence that they know is admissible despite the failure technically to lay a proper foundation. Why not? Because the objection can be cured by filling in the details after the objection is made. Opposing counsel knows that objections are distracting to the jury, and she realizes that the more she objects, the more likely needless objections to her exhibits will be made. Also, the jury will not look favorably on an attorney who continually objects to the admissibility of evidence that is ultimately admitted after the objections are cured.

So I'm going to read to you what has been stipulated with respect to these witnesses.

And the first of these is with respect to a William Davis. And the parties have agreed that if he were called as a witness in this case, he would testify as follows: "I am married to Patricia Davis, who is the sister of the defendant, Timothy James McVeigh. In early 1993, I owned and operated a business known as Bill Davis Electric, which was then located in my home at 11240 N.W. 27th Court, Plantation, Florida, 33323. . . .

There's also an agreement about certain facts. Now, what the jury does with these stipulations is, first, those that relate to what witnesses would say, you, of course, accept that testimony as you would the testimony of any other witness who does come in and testify here before you.

With respect to this stipulation, these are statements of fact and they are agreed as fact and the jury will accept these as facts without the need for calling any witnesses or introducing any other evidence with respect to these facts.

"The parties stipulate and agree:

"(1) That Special Agent Paul Gregory Broxterman . . . was a federal law enforcement officer with the Office of Inspector General, Housing and Urban Development, and engaged in the performance of his official duty on April 19, 1995. . . .

"(4) That government exhibits 1070, 1074, and 1136 are admissible."

So with that—those particular exhibits are admitted.[42]

---

42. *United States v. McVeigh* No. 96-CR-68, 1997 WL 266800 at *1–3 (D. Colo. May 21, 1997).

7.8 PERSUASIVE AIDS

Persuasive aids are underutilized in almost every trial. No opening statement or closing argument should be given without them. The persuasive aid can be anything that visually tells your story. Almost every opening would benefit from the use of a chart that shows the relationship of the important people in the case and a timeline that shows the chronology of events. Moreover, if you have a key piece of evidence, for impact show it to the jury in your opening statement. Is there a key statement of the opposing party contained in an e-mail? Scan it into your computer and show the key phrase on a projection screen.

Since persuasive aids are not admitted into evidence, there is no need to lay the foundation. The court has broad discretion in determining what is permissible to use in openings and closing arguments. As long as your persuasive aid fairly represents what the evidence will be at trial (or has been), then it is permissible. The reason is that judges will instruct the jury both before opening statements and again at the end of trial that the lawyer's arguments are not evidence. So, if you could say the statement without the exhibit, there is nothing wrong with saying it and using a visual aid to convey your point better.

What your persuasive aids look like is only limited by your imagination and, to some extent, your budget. At a minimum, you could stand before the jury with an easel and write the four facts you will prove in your case. Even better, you could use an ELMO to emphasize important exhibits.[43] The ELMO allows you to zoom in and turn an exhibit over with ease. Or you could put together a PowerPoint presentation that combines exhibits with explanatory text.

7.9 EXAMPLES OF PERSUASIVE AIDS

The saying that "a picture is worth a thousand words" is certainly true in the courtroom. The power of the visual image cannot be

---

43. The ELMO visual presenter allows you to put a document, photo, or tangible object—like a gun—on a flat screen and then project an image of the object onto a large projection screen for viewing.

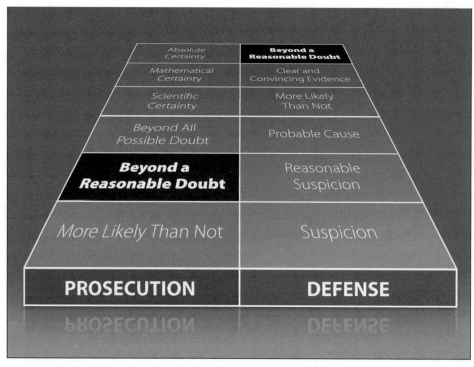

PROSECUTION	DEFENSE
Absolute Certainty	Beyond a Reasonable Doubt
Mathematical Certainty	Clear and Convincing Evidence
Scientific Certainty	More Likely Than Not
Beyond All Possible Doubt	Probable Cause
Beyond a Reasonable Doubt	Reasonable Suspicion
More Likely Than Not	Suspicion

Figure 7.6. Burden of Proof. (Produced by DecisionQuest)

overestimated. Let's look at how the concept of burden of proof in a criminal case might be explained. Figure 7.6 is an exhibit that shows how the burden of proof can be portrayed differently depending on which side is arguing. The left side of the diagram shows how the prosecution might argue it, while the right side shows the defense perspective. Notice how the different columns create starkly different images that are very persuasive, depending on which side you are arguing.[44]

---

44. The right side shows a quantifiable progression of required proof. In contrast, the left side is not as quantifiable, since reasonable people could argue whether scientific certainty is more certain than mathematical certainty and so on. Nonetheless, a prosecutor could argue that all of the categories above "beyond a reasonable doubt" require more proof than that which is needed in a criminal trial.

1. Examples of Still Images

The following are examples of several different types of persuasive aids that were created by DecisionQuest and used in actual cases.[45] In figure 7.7, the graphic was used by the defense in an employment case that dealt with retiree benefits. The plaintiffs were retirees from the late 1980s and early 1990s, a time when health benefits were at elevated levels. The plaintiffs sought to lock in these elevated benefits by having them vest at the time of retirement.

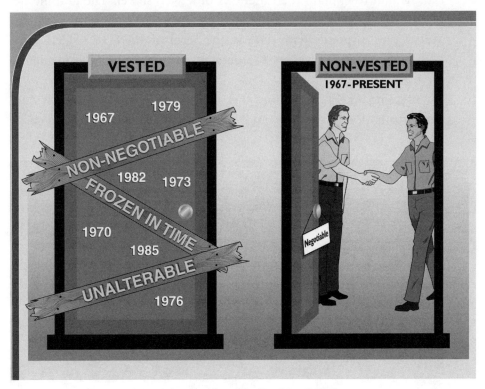

Figure 7.7. To Vest or Not to Vest. (Produced by DecisionQuest)

---

45.   Where noted, the exhibits in this section and on the enclosed DVD have been created by DecisionQuest. For examples of additional exhibits, go to www.decisionquest.com (accessed December 1, 2006). From the home page, go to "Courtroom Graphics," then click on "Featured Graphic," and then click on "Archive."

The graphic visually demonstrates that by vesting at the time of retirement, benefits become "frozen in time" and "nonnegotiable"—to the detriment of hundreds of earlier retirees from the 1960s, 1970s, and 1980s, who had retired with less advantageous health benefits. Rather than leaving the earlier retirees with lackluster health benefits, the defense took an "open door" policy of negotiations that accrued to the benefit of all retirees.

Figure 7.8 is a simple flowchart that was used in a patent case in which the attorney had to educate the jurors (e.g., opening statement) about highly technical Web-based control issues. As part of that tutorial, he had to explain the functions of a Web server. The graphic depicts how the Web browser sends a request to the Web server, and the Web server responds with data in the form of XML or HTML. The Web browser then displays the data in an understandable format to the user.

By using an exhibit such as this, an attorney can more quickly convey information to the jury, and the jury will remember it more easily

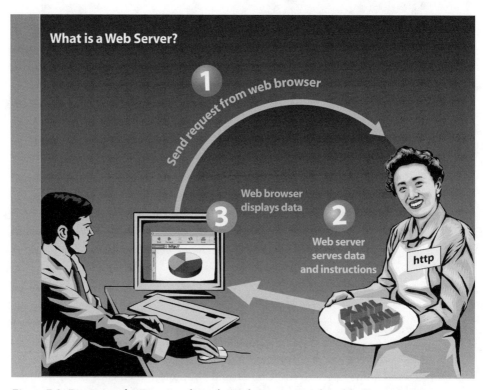

Figure 7.8. Depicting the Functionality of a Web Server. (Produced by DecisionQuest)

because a picture is associated with the information. Notice how the image for the Web server is a waitress "serving" information.

Figure 7.9 shows how space and size can maximize your message. Here, the attorney wanted to convey that exposure to asbestos involves several steps as opposed to a single event. Space is used in the layout to visually convey that "exposure" is several steps removed from simple contact. Additionally, space is used to illustrate the physical pathway to exposure. Size conveys that each step is of equal value. The graphic shows that it is not one step but nine equal and significant ones that result in asbestos exposure.

Figure 7.10 shows how a large number of statistics can be presented in a coherent fashion for the jury.[46] This chart summarized a portion of an expert's testimony in a product liability test. Several bar graphs were used at trial. To make each bar graph more engaging and memorable, visual icons creating simple associations between the numbers and a picture were used with each graph. This made the key message of each graph instantaneous for jurors and also broke up the monotonous nature of numerous bar graphs. From this graph, jurors were left with a clear message that the graph related to seat belts.

A series of still images can also be used. An excellent example is the "Strategic Timeline" exhibit which can be found on disc 1, "Exhibits: Slideshow."[47] It was designed for a case alleging the wrongful death of two chemical plant workers. In the case, the plaintiffs ran out of air and, pursuant to standard protocols, were provided new tanks, which were supposed to be filled with oxygen (the hot swap). However, an independent

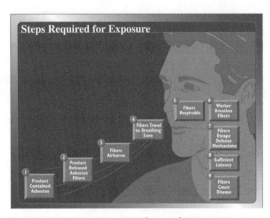

Figure 7.9. Using Space, Color, and Size to Maximize Your Message. (Produced by DecisionQuest)

---

46. An expanded version of this exhibit is on disc 1, "Exhibits: Slideshow" and labeled "Bar Graph."
47. It is the third series of slides on "Slideshow."

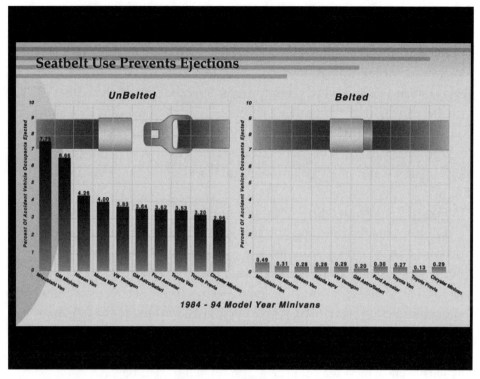

Figure 7.10. Bar Graph. (Produced by DecisionQuest)

vendor had inadvertently filled the oxygen tanks with a dangerous gas, and the men died of asphyxiation within moments of inhaling the dangerous gas. The strategic concept of this timeline was to avoid a finding of negligence on the part of the plant for not responding to the emergency sooner. The exhibit demonstrates that the best-case emergency response time was greater than the time it took the men to die.

The slide show summarizes the testimony of the key experts at trial. From the time of loss of consciousness, death occurred within two minutes, according to expert Allan. Expert Johnson testified that time of death was three minutes from the time of loss of consciousness. Under either scenario, death occurred well before the fastest, best-case emergency response time of five minutes, as testified by expert Griffin. The timeline dramatically demonstrates that there was no way the men could have been saved. This exhibit would be powerful in closing argument.

2. Examples of Animations

Visual aids that have color and movement are very effective.

On disc 1, "Exhibits: Animation Reel," there is a wide variety of computer animations that shows how powerful visual images can be in court.[48] They can be used with witnesses or in openings and closing arguments. It is not necessary to explain each of the many types of animations shown. Suffice it to say that the visual images are unique in their ability to help you argue your case.

7.10 OBJECTIONS TO EXHIBITS AND TESTIMONY

Use objections sparingly. Why make an objection if it can be easily cured by opposing counsel asking the right question or calling another witness? Jurors don't understand objections and will hold accountable the attorney who causes too many interruptions. However, when the testimony or exhibit is critical and you are on solid legal ground, object vigorously.

In most federal courts (as well as in an increasing number of state courts), attorneys are directed by the court to limit their objections to one word (such as "Objection") or to a short phrase ("Objection; hearsay"). The reason is that in the past, "speaking" objections were very common. A speaking objection is one in which an attorney improperly uses an objection as an opportunity to speak to the jury by arguing his case (e.g., "Your Honor, I object; opposing counsel's question assumes a fact not

> Instead of seeing how many objections you can make throughout a trial, see how few you can make. If you make numerous objections, causing interruptions and delays, the jury may very well hold it against you by the time of closing argument. Let the other side make the objections and suffer the anger of the jury. Pick your fights very carefully.

---

48. The animation reel was produced by DecisionQuest.

in evidence. There is absolutely no proof by the plaintiff that the defendant was talking on her cell phone at the time of the car wreck").

1. Common Objections Used at Trial

A. Hearsay

One of the most important objections you can make is "hearsay." Hearsay is an out-of-court statement offered in evidence to prove the truth of the matter asserted in the statement.[49] The objection is important because many exhibits contain statements by other persons who may not testify at trial and be subject to cross-examination. Moreover, opposing counsel will also ask witnesses about oral statements—not in exhibits—made by other people. It is vital to object when this happens unless the statements are admissible hearsay.

For example, assume there is a car-wreck trial and one of the plaintiff's key exhibits is an audiotape of a 911 call made by a witness an hour after the accident. (The witness called when she got home.) The witness declares on the tape that the defendant ran the red light. During the trial, when the plaintiff's attorney tries to get the audiotape admitted through the records custodian at police headquarters, you must make a hearsay objection (i.e., simply say "Objection" or "Objection; hearsay"). Make the opposing counsel call the witness. It may turn out that the witness is unavailable, and, therefore, the devastating statement made on the 911 call will not be heard by the jury.

B. Lack of Foundation

Familiarize yourself with the foundations required for admission of every important exhibit opposing counsel intends to offer. If opposing counsel fails to set forth a requirement, and you believe an objection is worth making (see discussion above), state your specific objection. As mentioned above, many courts prefer attorneys to say "Objection" without giving a reason or with a very short reason. If the judge wants more information, she will ask you. Prudence dictates getting guidance from the court. Below, the reason for the objection is given in case the court wants the reason for the objection.

---

49.   Fed. R. Evid. 801(c).

Example: Lease Agreement

Objection, Your Honor. The witness lacks personal knowledge regarding the contents of the document.

Example: Business Record

Objection, Your Honor. There has not been testimony that this record was made in the ordinary course of business. [It was prepared for use at trial.]

Example: Diagram of Intersection

Objection, Your Honor. The witness lacks familiarity with the intersection in question.

Example: Signature Identification

Objection, Your Honor. There has been no testimony that the witness is familiar with the defendant's signature on the document.

C. Relevancy and Unfair Prejudice

Other important objections should be used when necessary. If opposing counsel is offering an exhibit or testimony that is irrelevant and doesn't hurt you, don't object. Let him confuse the jury to his detriment. However, object if it is irrelevant and hurtful (Rule 402) or relevant and unfairly prejudicial (Rule 403).

2. Objections to Form of Question

There are any number of objections to opposing counsel's questions. One important objection is "leading." Use it during critical parts of the trial where you feel opposing counsel is testifying and truly giving the answers to the witness.

Example: Armed Robbery Trial

In this example, the defense attorney is questioning his client about his alibi during the armed robbery.

> Q. At 9:00 p.m., you went to your girlfriend's apartment after eating dinner at the restaurant, didn't you?
> Prosecutor: Objection; leading the witness.
> The court: Sustained. [**The defense attorney rephrases the question.**]

Q. Where did you go after eating dinner at the restaurant?
A. I went to my girlfriend's apartment at 9:00 p.m.

Although the objection appears fruitless because opposing counsel can rephrase the question, it is important to make it for a couple of reasons. First, it alerts the judge that defense counsel is inappropriately leading during a key part of the testimony. The judge will now be vigilant during defense counsel's remaining questions. The next time you object, opposing counsel is likely to be sternly rebuked by the judge. Second, the objection points out to the jury that defense counsel is suggesting important answers to the defendant.

Other objections to the form of the question include "argumentative," "compound question," "assumes facts not in evidence," "confusing," "ambiguous," "calls for speculation," "calls for a narrative [answer]," and "[question has been] asked and answered."[50] These objections are self-explanatory. There are also objections to a witness' answer such as "nonresponsive" and "narrative." These objections are governed by Rule 611, which states that the court shall "exercise reasonable control over the mode and order of interrogating witnesses . . . so as to (1) make the interrogation and presentation effective for the ascertainment of the truth, (2) avoid needless consumption of time, and (3) protect witnesses from harassment or undue embarrassment."[51]

A well-prepared witness will be able to handle many of opposing counsel's objectionable questions. Often, even if you could win an objection, it is better to remain silent. If opposing counsel is arguing with the witness, don't object; let the jury see that he is being unfair to your witness. If his questions are ambiguous or confusing, trust that the witness (through your preparation) will ask the attorney to rephrase the question. If opposing counsel is unorganized and stumbling, asking the

---

50. The "asked and answered" objection is best used when opposing counsel is conducting direct examination. When opposing counsel is conducting cross-examination, the proper objection for a question that has been repeated and answered is "argumentative" or "badgering the witness."

51. See Fed. R. Evid. 611(a). The remainder of the rule governs the scope of cross-examination and the use of leading questions.

same question in different ways, or asking confusing questions, the jury will become annoyed by him. If opposing counsel is sinking his own ship, don't distract the jury by objecting.

3. The Rule on Excluding Witnesses

Federal Rule of Evidence 615 requires the court—if you request—to exclude witnesses from the courtroom so they cannot hear the trial testimony of each other. Obviously, invoking "the rule," as it is commonly known, is very important. The rule does not apply to parties or expert witnesses or those essential to the presentation of a party's case.

4. Motion in Limine

Another way to prevent unwanted testimony or exhibits from being introduced into evidence is through a motion in limine. It is filed prior to trial and asks the court to prevent the opposing side from introducing irrelevant or unfairly prejudicial evidence at trial. It is a useful tool to educate the judge on the important evidentiary issues at trial.

Typically, the motion requests that opposing counsel be required to approach the bench to seek the court's specific permission before trying to introduce any evidence mentioned in the motion. Be aware that if the court grants your motion, you still must object at trial if opposing counsel violates the order. For example, assume you represent the defendant in a car-wreck case. Assume that you directed the plaintiff's attorney to approach the bench and seek the court's permission before asking any questions related to defendant's involvement in previous car accidents.

Now, suppose that once trial starts, the plaintiff's attorney ignores the court's ruling and asks the defendant if he has been in any other accidents. If you do not object to the question, not only will you fail to get the court's ruling on the improper question, you will fail to preserve the issue for appeal.

Chapter Eight

⸻◦◦◦⸻

CONCLUSION

There is no getting around the fact that there is an art to winning at trial. Webster's dictionary defines art as "the conscious use of skill and creative imagination."[1] The goal of this book has been to teach the necessary skills for trial and to inspire readers' creative imaginations. By using your skills and creative imagination, you will reach the emotions of jurors, and you will win at trial.

To achieve the goal of this book, I have presented the teaching of trial techniques in an innovative way. Too often, practicing lawyers are asked to share their wisdom in trial advocacy classes and wind up telling war stories from their trials in the vain attempt to teach skills. These stories are not effective because they are usually embellished. Even when they stick to the facts, it is hard to re-create the surrounding context of the story so that the lesson can be useful to the students.

If war stories are not used, contrived hypothetical examples are examined from textbooks or created by the instructor. Such examples often make poor teaching tools because the facts of the hypothetical

---

1. *Merriam-Webster's Collegiate Dictionary* at 69 (Merriam-Webster 11th ed. 2003)

are manipulated specifically in order to teach a skill. The manipulation of the facts takes them away from the realities of the courtroom.

That is why every effort has been made in this book to teach trial skills grounded in actual transcripts or videos of real trials. Where hypothetical situations have been used, they have not been artificially contrived but rather have been modeled after common situations that occur in courtrooms across the country.

Three famous trials (*People v. Simpson, Goldman v. Simpson,* and *U.S. v. McVeigh*) provide memorable teaching tools, showing successful trial skills used and mistakes made. In addition, I expect that readers will find such encouragement by looking at these trials, especially the video clips, that they will master trial skills without needing to be involved in hundreds of trials or made a part of the Trial of the Twentieth Century (*People v. Simpson*). One of the lessons of this book that should give beginning lawyers confidence is that some of the most famous lawyers make very basic mistakes that should not ever be made. Likewise, in this book are examples of some of the best trial skills on display (e.g., Joseph Hartzler's opening statement in *U.S. v. McVeigh*), which are worthy of great effort to emulate.

What should you do now, after reading this book, in order to develop your trial skills? While learning the basic and advanced skills taught here is essential, the next step is to develop your own style of trial advocacy. Know your strengths and weaknesses. Do you need to be more passionate, or do you need to be less emotional in order to strike the right chord with the jury? Do you prepare too much and consequently get lost in details at trial, or do you have a tendency to wing it and get surprised by a devastating fact at trial? Do you view a trial from the jury's perspective or your own?

Finally, although the video clips from this book go a long way toward answering the need to see lawyers in action, there is no substitute for watching as many trial lawyers as possible. Learn from their strengths and weaknesses and model your style accordingly. Sitting through a typical trial for one day, you will see how truly boring many of them can be. If you are bored, so is the jury. Watch great lawyers and see how they can make a trial extremely interesting. Watch great lawyers and see how they can take the usual and make it extraordinary.

You will find that they are passionately telling a concise compelling story with lots of visual aids.

No matter where you are in your journey as a trial lawyer, you can think now about new ways to try your next case in your own unique way and win at trial.

Appendix One

⎯⎯⎯⎯⎯◦◦◦◦⎯⎯⎯⎯⎯

BACKGROUND FOR
PEOPLE V. SIMPSON

SUMMARY OF FACTS

Around 10:15 p.m. on the night of June 12, 1994, O. J. Simpson's ex-wife, Nicole Brown, and an acquaintance of hers, Ron Goldman, were stabbed to death outside of Nicole's condominium at 875 South Bundy (often referred to simply as "Bundy" throughout the trial) in Los Angeles, California.[1] The defendant at trial, O. J. Simpson, was a Heisman Trophy winner while at the University of Southern California, a Hall of Fame running back for the Buffalo Bills, and a well-known celebrity who had appeared in such movies as *The Naked Gun.*

When O. J. first met Nicole, he was a famous athlete and thirty years old; she was a waitress and eighteen years old. They married in 1985 (his second marriage) and had two children—a daughter, Sydney, and a son, Justin. On New Year's Day 1989, Nicole called 911 from their home. When Detective John Edwards arrived, he found Nicole, partially clothed, hiding in the bushes. She told the detective that O. J. was "going to kill me." The police took photographs of Nicole's bruised face and neck. O. J. pled "no contest" to

---

1. Background based on trial transcripts, *The O. J. Simpson Murder Trial: A Headline Court Case,* by Michael J. Pellowski (Enslow 2001), and *The Run of His Life: The People v. O. J. Simpson,* by Jeffrey Toobin (Touchstone 1997).

a misdemeanor for this incident and received probation. The couple was divorced in October 1992.

On the evening of the murders, O. J. and Nicole attended the dance recital of their daughter, Sydney, at Paul Revere Junior High School. After the recital, Nicole had dinner with her mother, other members of her family, and friends at the restaurant Mezzaluna, where Ron Goldman worked. Meanwhile, O. J. went back to his house on Rockingham Avenue in Brentwood, California (often referred to as "Rockingham" throughout the trial). Once there, he and Kato Kaelin (who lived in O. J.'s guesthouse) went to McDonald's and returned with their food at approximately 9:35 p.m. Kaelin went to his guesthouse to eat his dinner, and O. J. went inside his house.

At approximately 9:50 p.m., Ron Goldman went to Nicole's condominium to return her mother's eyeglasses, which had been left at the restaurant. Around 10:15 p.m., a neighbor of Nicole's, Pablo Fenjves, heard the "plaintive wail" of a dog. Meanwhile, Allan Park, a limousine driver, arrived at O. J.'s home at 10:25 p.m. to drive O. J. to the airport for a trip to Chicago. Park, who had come early, did not see O. J.'s white Ford Bronco. At 10:40 p.m., he used the intercom to tell O. J. he had arrived, but no one answered. He repeatedly used the intercom for the next ten minutes; there was still no answer.

At approximately 10:55 p.m., Park saw an African American man wearing dark clothing enter O. J.'s house. At this same time, Kaelin came out of his guesthouse—because he had heard a thumping noise on his wall—and approached Park to ask if O. J. had overslept his flight. Park used the intercom again. O. J. answered for the first time around 11:00 p.m. At 11:15 p.m., O. J. came out of the house and was driven to the airport.

Around midnight, Nicole's dog, Kato (named after Kato Kaelin), his paws covered in blood, was found wandering the neighborhood by some of Nicole's neighbors. He led one neighbor, Sukru Boztepe, to the dead bodies of Nicole and Ron. When a policeman, Officer Robert Riske, arrived, he found Nicole's body at the foot of a short set of stairs leading to her front door. Ron's body was nearby, up against a fence. A black hat, a left-hand leather glove, and a white envelope were lying near Ron's body. The bodies appeared to have been stabbed, and there were pools of blood near them.

The police then went to O. J.'s mansion in Brentwood to notify him of the death of his ex-wife. When Detectives Mark Fuhrman and Phillip Vannatter arrived, they found a trail of blood leading from O. J.'s Bronco to the house. Blood (later determined to match O. J.'s) was also found on the door handle of the Bronco. Blood on the center console of the Bronco matched a mixture of O. J.'s and Ron's blood. It was also determined later that there were several more drops in the driver's area of the Bronco that matched O. J.'s and one drop that matched Nicole's. In O. J.'s bedroom, two socks with blood on them were found. One spot matched O. J.'s blood type; another spot matched Nicole's. Near the guesthouse where Kato lived, Detective Fuhrman found a right-hand leather glove, which matched the one at Bundy.

At the scene of the crime, there were bloody footprints leading away from the victims to the alley, with fresh drops of blood to the left of the footprints.

(When O. J. was questioned by police the next day, he had a cut on a finger of his left hand.) The footprints were made by Bruno Magli loafers, size twelve— O. J.'s size. The loafers are very uncommon and expensive. (O. J. was later to incriminate himself at the civil trial when he said in a deposition that he would never be caught wearing an "ugly ass" pair of Bruno Magli shoes. At that trial, he was confronted with a photo showing him wearing those shoes.) A knit cap was also found at the murder scene. Black hairs from the cap matched samples taken from O. J.; a hair found on Goldman's shirt also matched O. J.'s. Carpet fibers found in the cap matched the carpet of O. J.'s Bronco. Blood drops at the scene were consistent with O. J.'s blood but consistent with less than that of 0.5 percent of the world's population.

The left-hand leather glove found at Bundy and the matching right-hand glove found by Detective Fuhrman at O. J.'s home were a rare and distinct style of glove known as Aris Lights. The glove found outside O. J.'s home had hair fibers like those of Nicole and Goldman and fibers like those from Goldman's shirt. The glove also had carpet fibers like those found in O. J.'s Bronco. Additionally, the glove had blood that was consistent with a mixture of blood from Nicole, Goldman, and O. J.

On June 17, 1994, O. J. was charged with two counts of murder, and arrangements were made for his voluntary surrender. O. J. failed to show. Later, he was spotted in the back of a white Ford Bronco (different from O. J.'s) driven by his friend Al Cowlings. The slow-speed "chase" by police lasted for several hours. Around 8:51 p.m., O. J. surrendered. A fake beard and moustache and O. J.'s passport were found in the car. In his pocket, Cowling had $8,750, which O. J. had given him.

The jury that returned the verdict was composed of eight African American women, one African American man, one Hispanic man, and two white women. The foreperson was Amanda Cooley, an African American woman who had attended several years of college. Based on jury questionnaires, (1) nine jurors believed that O. J. was less likely to have killed Nicole because of his success in football, (2) two jurors were college graduates, (3) no juror read the newspaper regularly, (4) five of the jurors or members of their families had experienced a bad encounter with the police, (5) five thought it was acceptable to use force with a member of the family, (6) all were Democrats, (7) two jurors had management experience, (8) nine rented homes, and (9) three owned homes. Each side, prosecution and defense, had been given twenty preemptory strikes; the prosecution did not use all of them.

The not guilty verdict was returned on October 3, 1995. The only testimony reviewed by the jury prior to the verdict was that of the limo driver, Allan Park. The jury deliberated approximately four hours.

MARK FUHRMAN

Detective Fuhrman, one of the first detectives to arrive at Bundy, also accompanied three other detectives to O. J.'s house to notify him of Nicole's death. While there, he found a bloody glove that matched the other glove found at Bundy.

The prosecution knew, prior to his testimony, that Fuhrman would be accused of being a racist. Among other things, they were aware of allegations that in 1984 an eighteen-year-old African American had filed a complaint against Fuhrman, claiming that Fuhrman had put him in a choke hold and declared that he would "kill him" for a jaywalking offense. Moreover, Kathleen Bell, a real estate agent who had met Fuhrman in 1985, had also gone public with statements charging that Fuhrman had said that "when he sees a nigger driving with a white woman he would pull them over," and he wanted "nothing more than to see all 'niggers' gathered together and killed." Fuhrman denied making these statements on direct examination. On cross-examination, he denied having used the N word in the past ten years. During trial, a tape recording surfaced in which Fuhrman was heard using the N word repeatedly, as well as other very offensive language about African Americans. This tape was in the possession of Laura McKinney, a freelance screenwriter who had met many times with Fuhrman as a source for her writing of a fictional account about women in the Los Angeles Police Department (LAPD). Judge Ito restricted the defense's use of this evidence to playing two excerpts from the tape in which Fuhrman used the N word and in allowing McKinney to testify that Fuhrman had said the N word forty-one times.

DNA TESTING

Marcia Clark explained in her opening that there are two kinds of DNA testing: restriction fragment length polymorphism (RFLP) and polymerase chain reaction (PCR). Both tests were used in the crime-scene investigation, and both are tests of exclusion rather than inclusion. That is, the sample from the crime scene is compared to a sample from the defendant to see if the defendant can be excluded as a suspect. RFLP is more precise than PCR. For example, at trial RFLP testing showed that for one of the drops of blood on the path outside of Nicole's home, the odds were 1 in 170 million that it came from someone other than O. J. The blood found on the socks on the floor in O. J.'s bedroom had a 1 in 6.8 billion chance of coming from someone other than Nicole. The blood found on the gate at Nicole's home had a 1 in 57 billion chance of being blood other than O. J.'s. The PCR tests generally came back with odds of 1 in a few thousand.

Note that hair and fiber analysis is not DNA testing but, rather, is comparison under a microscope.

THE DEFENSE STRATEGY

The defense vigorously fought the forensic evidence linking O. J. to the murders. They put on evidence to show that the methods to collect evidence used by LAPD criminologist Dennis Fung and his assistant, Andrea Mazzola, were suspect. It was Mazzola's first case where she was the primary person responsible for gathering blood evidence and only her third occasion to be at a crime scene. The defense made a number of attacks: (1) Detective Vannatter carried a vial of O. J.'s blood in an unsealed envelope for several hours before logging it in the property room; (2) 1.5 cc. of O. J.'s blood were unaccounted for by the police (giving the police the opportunity to frame O. J. with his own blood); (3) vials of blood samples were not accounted for throughout the collection process; (4) police claimed that blood was found on the pair of socks in O. J.'s bedroom, but when the socks were originally discovered, no such finding was documented; (5) the crime scene was contaminated by shoddy police procedures, not the least of which was the covering of the bodies with a blanket from Nicole's home, instead of with a clean sheet, in accordance with police procedures; (6) the coroner dragged Goldman's body over the glove found at the scene; and (7) the blood samples recovered by Fung at the crime scene were stored in plastic bags in a non air-conditioned vehicle for several hours, leading to a lack of quality in the samples.

THE CIVIL TRIAL

Shortly after the acquittal, the families of Ron and Nicole filed a wrongful death lawsuit against O. J. in Santa Monica, California. The judge was Hiroshi Fujisaki. The jury in the civil trial was made up of one juror of mixed African American and Hispanic ancestry, one Asian, one Hispanic, and nine whites. One significant difference from the criminal trial was that the judge did not allow the defense to argue that the police investigation was motivated by racial prejudice.

The jury returned a judgment of $8.5 million for compensatory damages for Ron Goldman's family (Nicole's family did not request compensatory damages so that her children would not have to testify against him) and $25 million for punitive damages to be split evenly between the Goldman and Brown families.

Appendix Two

BACKGROUND FOR
U.S. V. MCVEIGH

On the morning of April 19, 1995, a Ryder truck filled with home-made explosives was parked in front of the Murrah Federal Building. The bomb inside the truck exploded at 9:02 a.m., shattering the building and others nearby. It was the greatest act of domestic terrorism on U.S. soil. The explosion killed 168 people, including 19 children.

By chance, Timothy McVeigh was stopped 78 miles north of Oklahoma City on Interstate 35 for driving his 1977 Mercury Marquis without a license plate. It was seventy-five minutes after the bombing. When Trooper Charlie Hanger approached McVeigh, he noticed a bulge under McVeigh's jacket. He asked McVeigh what it was, and McVeigh volunteered that he was armed. McVeigh was arrested for possession of a concealed weapon. McVeigh was stopped almost exactly where someone would be if he had left the Murrah Building at 9:02 a.m. and driven within the speed limit.

On the front seat of the car was an envelope containing excerpts from McVeigh's favorite book, *The Turner Diaries*. On one of the pages was the sentence, "But the real value of our attacks today . . ." At the bottom of the page McVeigh wrote, "Maybe now there will be liberty." McVeigh was also wearing a T-shirt that had a likeness of Abraham Lincoln. On the back was the expression, "The tree of liberty must be refreshed from time to time with the blood of patriots and tyrants" and on the front side the Latin phrase, "Sic semper tyrannous," which means thus always to tyrants.

The prosecution theory was that McVeigh bombed the federal building to seek revenge against the United States for its "attack" against citizens at the

Branch Davidian compound in Waco, Texas. In fact, McVeigh detonated his bomb on the second anniversary of the raid at Waco.

The eleven-count indictment included charges that McVeigh conspired with Terry Nichols to use a truck bomb to destroy the Murrah Building and that McVeigh murdered eight law-enforcement officers in the performance of their official duties.

The federal trial began on April 24, 1997, in Denver, Colorado, before U.S. District Judge Robert Matsch. It had been moved from Oklahoma City, Oklahoma, to ensure a fair jury. Terry Nichols, McVeigh's army buddy and coconspirator, was tried separately.[1]

Two of the key witnesses for the prosecution were Michael Fortier and his wife, Lori. They were very close friends of McVeigh and lived in Kingman, Arizona. Indeed, McVeigh had been the best man at their wedding. Among other things, Lori Fortier testified at trial that when McVeigh was on one of his many visits to see them, he took some soup cans out of her kitchen cabinet and used them to simulate barrels full of explosive material to show her how he intended to configure the bomb. She also related that she had helped make a fake driver's license for him in the name of Robert Kling, which McVeigh used to rent the Ryder truck used in the bombing. In addition, she testified that McVeigh had told her about bombing the Murrah Building, but she had not taken him seriously. In exchange for her testimony, the government gave her immunity so that she could not be prosecuted.

Michael Fortier further told the jury about McVeigh's actions including a time when they were casing the Murrah Building. At the time, McVeigh told Michael Fortier that it would be an easy target. Fortier further stated that McVeigh had told him that he wanted to take offensive action against the government. When Fortier asked him what he meant by that, McVeigh said that he wanted to bomb a federal building. McVeigh tried to recruit Fortier to join Nichols and him in their plan, but Fortier refused.

Michael Fortier pled guilty to four charges, including conspiracy to transport stolen firearms and making false statements to the FBI about his knowledge of McVeigh and Nichol's plan. In return for his cooperation and testimony at trial, the government agreed to seek a reduction of his prison sentence. After the trial, Michael Fortier was sentenced to twelve years in prison. He was facing a maximum of twenty-three years.

The government also showed that the McVeigh and Nichols' conspiracy included the robbing of a gun dealer to get money to fund the materials needed for their homemade bomb. One of those materials was ammonium nitrate. There was proof that they had bought 4,000 pounds of it in September and October 1994 from a co-op located in McPherson, Kansas. There was also evidence of McVeigh's fingerprint on one of the receipts for 2,000 pounds of ammonium nitrate. McVeigh confided to the Fortiers that he had bought ammonium nitrate for the bomb. The government also proved that McVeigh

---

1. Nichols was found guilty at trial and sentenced to life imprisonment without parole.

bought 160 gallons of nitromethane, another necessary ingredient to build the bomb. Finally, Michael Fortier testified that McVeigh and Nichols showed up in Kingman, Arizona, and took him to a storage shed where they showed him twelve containers of explosives they say they had stolen from a quarry near Nichols' house.

When McVeigh was arrested, the police found explosive residues on his shirt and pants' pockets. McVeigh's sister, Jennifer, also testified about her brother's anger against the government for the raid at Waco and his promises to avenge the deaths of the more than seventy people who died there. In addition, the government put on evidence that showed McVeigh used *The Turner Diaries* as a blueprint for his plan. The fictional book describes how revolutionaries in America can incite a civil war through selected acts of terrorism. One of the acts of terror is the truck bombing of the FBI building in Washington, D.C.

As for the defense, Stephen Jones, counsel for McVeigh, stated that the government spent only two weeks investigating the bombing and then spent the next two years focusing on McVeigh's alleged guilt to the exclusion of other evidence. Jones declared that the government failed to follow evidence that led to John Doe No. 2, a stocky person with olive complexion that was seen getting out of the Ryder truck just moments before it exploded. The defense labeled the Fortiers as morally corrupt drug abusers. It suggested on cross-examination that the Fortiers were lying in order to get a deal from the government for their testimony. The defense also presented evidence of the many statements the Fortiers made to their friends, family, and the press where they declared McVeigh's innocence immediately after the bombing. Jones also presented evidence that there were no eyewitnesses placing McVeigh at the scene of the crime and that McVeigh's fingerprints were not found on the ignition key to the Ryder truck that was found at the crime scene.

On June 2, 1997, after twenty-three hours of deliberations, McVeigh was convicted on all counts. On June 13, 1997, the jury unanimously sentenced McVeigh to death. On June 10, 2001, McVeigh was executed by lethal injection.

Appendix Three

⫷⬥⬥⫸

DVD MENUS

DISC 1[1]

Focus Group:

Juror Profiles (1.5 min.)

Focus Group (37 min.)

> Part One: Liability and Past Medical Expenses (11 min.)
> Part Two: Future Medical Expenses (6 min.)
> Part Three: Loss of Enjoyment of Life Damages (4 min.)
> Part Four: Conclusions (7 min.)
> Part Five: Discussion with Moderator after Verdict (9 min.)
> [Note: To quickly find the start of each part of this clip, click on the "seek" button of your DVD player.]

Voir Dire:

Voir Dire (22 min.)[2]

---

1. The video excerpts of the Simpson trial are intended to supplement the detailed analysis of those trial techniques discussed in the book. In an effort to include as many relevant clips as possible, production considerations necessitated that the video be reproduced at a quality sufficient for teaching purposes but not of broadcast quality.
2. You can go to different parts of this clip by using the "seek" button. The first chapter is at 2 min. 56 sec., which is the beginning of a discussion

Opening Statements:

Darden clip 1: Darden's Opening Remarks (12 min.)
Darden clip 2: Darden Discusses Beating on New Year's Day, 1989 (6 min.)
Darden clip 3: Darden Concludes Opening Statement (3 min.)
Clark clip 1: Clark's Opening Remarks (4 min.)
Clark clip 2: Clark Explains the Scientific Evidence Linking O. J. to the Crime (6 min.)
Cochran clip 1: Cochran's Opening Remarks (8 min.)
Cochran clip 2: Cochran Responds to Darden's Claim That Wife Beating Leads to Murder (3 min.)
Cochran clip 3: Cochran Attacks Forensic Evidence (4 min.)

Jury Verdict:

O. J. Simpson Jury Verdict (October 3, 1995) (8 min.)

Exhibits:

Animation Reel (3.5 min.)
Slideshow (4.5 min.)
Scruggs Animation (2 min.)

DISC 2

Direct Examination:

Clip 1 (Clark): Fuhrman Begins Direct—Acts Nervous and Denies Racism (4.5 min.)
Clip 2 (Darden): Shipp Discusses Friendship with O. J. and O. J.'s Dream of Killing Nicole (13.5 min.)
Clip 3 (Shapiro): Dr. Huizenga Discusses His Qualifications and Physical Exam of O. J. (8 min.)
Clip 4 (Gloves): O. J. Tries on Murder Gloves (4 min.)
Clip 5 (Darden): Glove Expert Demonstration (3.5 min.)

Cross Examination:

Clip 1 (Bailey): Fuhrman Denies Racial Slurs (4 min.)
Clip 2 (Douglas): Shipp Maintains He Is O. J.'s Friend and Does Not Reveal Dream to Investigators (4.5 min.)

---

of the burden of proof. The next chapter is at 9 min. 12 sec., which is a discussion about lawsuits "getting out of hand." The third chapter is at 16 min. 13 sec. and begins with a discussion of Sam's supervision.

Clip 3 (Kelberg): Dr. Huizenga's Lack of Expertise, Failure to Document Finding, Opinion about Injury, and Favoritism Toward O. J. (9 min.)

Clip 4 (Scheck): Fung Fails to Tell Grand Jury That Assistant Collected Blood Samples (6 min.)

Clip 5 (Scheck): Fung Claims in Error That He Carried O. J.'s Blood Sample (4 min.)

Clip 6 (Scheck): Argumentative Questions, Cross to Support Case, and Ending Day Strongly (7.5 min.)

Closing Argument:

Clark clip 1: Beginning of Clark's Closing Argument (4 min.)

Clark clip 2: Clark Addresses Weaknesses in Prosecution's Case (4 min.)

Clark clip 3: Clark Explains Glove Demonstration (3 min.)

Clark clip 4: Clark Concludes Closing (4 min.)

Darden clip 1: Darden Concludes Closing (2 min.)

Cochran clip 1: Cochran Argues Lack of Blood, Puts on Knit Cap, and Reminds Jury of Glove Demonstration (6 min.)

Cochran clip 2: Cochran Considers the Twins of Deception (2.5 min.)

Cochran clip 3: Cochran Discusses Racism (4 min.)

Scheck clip 1: Scheck Asserts Opinion about Innocence (3 min.)

Scheck clip 2: Scheck Summarizes Problems with Scientific Evidence (3 min.)

Scheck clip 3: Scheck Talks about Contamination at Crime Scene and Cover-Up (4 min.)

Scheck clip 4: Scheck Concludes Closing Argument (1 min.)

Rebuttal:

Darden clip 1: Darden Cites Constitution (4 min.)

Clark clip 1: Clark Summarizes Uncontradicted Evidence (6 min.)

Appendix Four

SAMPLE NEWSPAPER AD AND FOCUS GROUP QUESTIONNAIRE

NEWSPAPER AD:

We will be conducting a mock trial in [name of city] on [date and time]. The trial will be interesting and will last approximately four hours. Jurors will be paid $60 for their work and lunch will be provided. If you are interested, please call [name of staff member] at [office phone number].

QUESTIONNAIRE:[1]

The following is a questionnaire that can be used by the plaintiff or defendant in a typical car-wreck case.

---

1.   The questionnaire was created by Bill Bailey and used with his permission.

VERDICT QUESTIONS:

1. VOTE ON LIABILITY

1.1 If you had to vote right now, who would win:

_____ Plaintiff

_____ Defendant

1.2 List the three main reasons you voted the way you did:

(1) _____

_____

_____

(2) _____

_____

_____

(3) _____

_____

_____

1.3 What do you believe is the key issue or major point about who should win?

1.4 After listening to the facts of this case, do you believe everything that the plaintiff, who has brought the lawsuit, is saying or claiming? _____ If not, explain please:

1.5 After listening to the facts of this case, do you believe everything that the defendant who is being sued is saying or claiming? _____ If not, please explain your areas of concern:

1.6 Would you like more information to decide this case? _____ What?

2. VOTE ON AWARDING DAMAGES

*2.1 If you had to vote right now, would you award
damages to the plaintiff?*

_____ Yes

_____ No

*2.2 If yes, how much would you award in the
following categories?*

2.3 Plaintiff for past lost income:

2.4 Plaintiff for future lost income:

*2.5 Plaintiff for past pain, suffering, disability, and loss of
enjoyment of life:*

*2.6 Plaintiff for future pain, suffering, disability, and loss of
enjoyment of life:*

2.7 Plaintiff for medical expenses:

*2.8 If you had to vote right now, would you award damages to the
plaintiff's wife for loss of consortium?*

_____ Yes

_____ No

2.9 If yes, how much would you award to the plaintiff's wife for loss of consortium:

3. GENERAL VIEWS ABOUT CASE

3.1 Is there anything else you think important for the people involved in this case to know about this case and how you feel about it?

CONFIDENTIAL INFORMATION ABOUT YOU:

This information is confidential and is only for use in connection with this jury study. We need to know some background about you in order to evaluate the accuracy of the panel's opinions. DO NOT sign your name to this document as the information is entirely confidential.

1. INFORMATION ABOUT YOU

1.1 Male ____ Female ____ Age ____ yrs.

Place of birth: _____

1.2 How long have you lived at the place where you live now?

1.3 Do you rent? ____ Or own? ____

1.4 How long have you lived in this country? _____ State? _____

1.5 Are you:

Married _____

Divorced _____

Separated _____

Widowed _____

Single _____

1.6 Do you have any children? Yes ____ No ____
If so, please list their sex, ages, and occupation:

1.7 Who is your present employer? _____

How long have you been employed there? _____

What is your job title and what do you do? _____

Job before that? _____

1.8 If you are retired, unemployed, and/or disabled, what kind of
work did you do in the past? _____

1.9 How far did you go in school? _____

Degrees _____

Technical or other training _____

1.10 Is your spouse employed? ____ Where? _____

Job _____ How long? _____

1.11 Your spouse's formal education _____

Degrees _____

1.12 Children? _____ Ages _____

Are they employed? _____
Their work:

1.13 Do you drive a car? Yes ____ No ____
1.14 What organizations are you active in?

What do you do for these organizations?

1.15 What magazines do you regularly read?

2. EXPERIENCES WITH LEGAL SYSTEM

2.1 Are you or any close friend or family related to any person connected with the courts or justice system? Yes ____ No ____

If so, please explain:

2.2 Have you served as a juror before? Yes ____ No ____
If yes, did you serve on: Criminal case ____
Civil damage case ____

When? _____

Where? _____

2.3 Have you ever sued or made a claim for injuries?

Yes ____ No ____

Why? _____

_____

When? _____

What was the outcome? _____

2.4 Have you ever sued or made a claim other than for injuries?

Yes ____ No ____ Why? _____

When? _____

What was the outcome?

2.5 Has anyone sued you? Yes ____ No ____

Why?

What was the outcome?

2.6 Have you ever been a witness in a lawsuit? Yes ___ No ___

Was it Criminal? ___ Civil? _____ When? _____
Why?

3. DISABILITIES

3.1 Have you or a family member ever suffered any serious injury or illness?

3.2 Yes ___ No ___

3.3 Please explain:

4. JUROR'S GENERAL ATTITUDE AND OPINIONS

4.1 Ever had a similar experience to facts of this case? ____

If so, please explain:

4.2 Any medical training or experience? ____

What?

4.3 Any insurance claims training or experience? _____

What?

4.4 Any police training or experience? _____

What?

4.5 Any legal training or experience? _____

What?

4.6 Can you think of any reason why you might have strong feelings about a case like this one because of your background? ____ *Why?*

5. JUROR'S ATTITUDES REGARDING THE JUSTICE SYSTEM

5.1 Have you telephoned or written any newspaper or legislature about any tort reform legislation, high verdicts, insurance rates, lawsuits, or changes in civil justice laws? Yes ____ *No* ____

5.2 Why?

5.3 Do you regularly listen to talk radio? If so, who or what station(s)?

5.4 Have you had any bad personal experiences in your business or family life that you felt was due to lawsuits and high jury verdicts? Yes ____ *No* ____ *Please explain:*

5.5 Do you have any strong feelings about jury verdicts in cases like this one or the amount of jury verdicts for any reason at all? Yes ____ *No* ____ *Please explain:*

6. CONCLUSION

6.1 Is there anything else we should know about in evaluating your answers to the questions about this case that might affect your thinking in a case of this nature?

Appendix Five

FEDERAL RULES

OF EVIDENCE

as amended to
December 1, 2006

ARTICLE I. GENERAL PROVISIONS

Rule 101. Scope

These rules govern proceedings in the courts of the United States and before the United States bankruptcy judges and United States magistrate judges, to the extent and with the exceptions stated in rule 1101.

Rule 102. Purpose and Construction

These rules shall be construed to secure fairness in administration, elimination of unjustifiable expense and delay, and promotion of growth and development of the law of evidence to the end that the truth may be ascertained and proceedings justly determined.

Rule 103. Rulings on Evidence

(a) **Effect of erroneous ruling.**—Error may not be predicated upon a ruling which admits or excludes evidence unless a substantial right of the party is affected, and

(1) **Objection.**—In case the ruling is one admitting evidence, a timely objection or motion to strike appears of record, stating the specific ground of objection, if the specific ground was not apparent from the context; or

(2) **Offer of proof.**—In case the ruling is one excluding evidence, the substance of the evidence was made known to the court by offer or was apparent from the context within which questions were asked.

Once the court makes a definitive ruling on the record admitting or excluding evidence, either at or before trial, a party need not renew an objection or offer of proof to preserve a claim of error for appeal.

(b) **Record of offer and ruling.**—The court may add any other or further statement which shows the character of the evidence, the form in which it was offered, the objection made, and the ruling thereon. It may direct the making of an offer in question and answer form.

(c) **Hearing of jury.**—In jury cases, proceedings shall be conducted, to the extent practicable, so as to prevent inadmissible evidence from being suggested to the jury by any means, such as making statements or offers of proof or asking questions in the hearing of the jury.

(d) **Plain error.**—Nothing in this rule precludes taking notice of plain errors affecting substantial rights although they were not brought to the attention of the court.

Rule 104. Preliminary Questions

(a) **Questions of admissibility generally.**—Preliminary questions concerning the qualification of a person to be a witness, the existence of a privilege, or the admissibility of evidence shall be determined by the court, subject to the provisions of subdivision (b). In making its determination it is not bound by the rules of evidence except those with respect to privileges.

(b) **Relevancy conditioned on fact.**—When the relevancy of evidence depends upon the fulfillment of a condition of fact, the court shall admit it upon, or subject to, the introduction of evidence sufficient to support a finding of the fulfillment of the condition.

(c) **Hearing of jury.**—Hearings on the admissibility of confessions shall in all cases be conducted out of the hearing of the jury. Hearings on other preliminary matters shall be so conducted when the interests of justice require, or when an accused is a witness and so requests.

(d) **Testimony by accused.**—The accused does not, by testifying upon a preliminary matter, become subject to cross-examination as to other issues in the case.

(e) **Weight and credibility.**—This rule does not limit the right of a party to introduce before the jury evidence relevant to weight or credibility.

Rule 105. Limited Admissibility

When evidence which is admissible as to one party or for one purpose but not admissible as to another party or for another purpose is admitted, the court, upon request, shall restrict the evidence to its proper scope and instruct the jury accordingly.

Rule 106. Remainder of or Related Writings or Recorded Statements

When a writing or recorded statement or part thereof is introduced by a party, an adverse party may require the introduction at that time of any other part or any other writing or recorded statement which ought in fairness to be considered contemporaneously with it.

ARTICLE II. JUDICIAL NOTICE

Rule 201. Judicial Notice of Adjudicative Facts

(a) **Scope of rule.**—This rule governs only judicial notice of adjudicative facts.

(b) **Kinds of facts.**—A judicially noticed fact must be one not subject to reasonable dispute in that it is either (1) generally known within the territorial jurisdiction of the trial court or (2) capable of accurate and ready determination by resort to sources whose accuracy cannot reasonably be questioned.

(c) **When discretionary.**—A court may take judicial notice, whether requested or not.

(d) **When mandatory.**—A court shall take judicial notice if requested by a party and supplied with the necessary information.

(e) **Opportunity to be heard.**—A party is entitled upon timely request to an opportunity to be heard as to the propriety of taking judicial notice and the tenor of the matter noticed. In the absence of prior notification, the request may be made after judicial notice has been taken.

(f) **Time of taking notice.**—Judicial notice may be taken at any stage of the proceeding.

(g) **Instructing jury.**—In a civil action or proceeding, the court shall instruct the jury to accept as conclusive any fact judicially noticed. In a criminal case, the court shall instruct the jury that it may, but is not required to, accept as conclusive any fact judicially noticed.

ARTICLE III. PRESUMPTIONS IN CIVIL ACTIONS AND PROCEEDINGS

Rule 301. Presumptions in General in Civil Actions and Proceedings

In all civil actions and proceedings not otherwise provided for by Act of Congress or by these rules, a presumption imposes on the party against whom it is directed the burden of going forward with evidence to rebut or meet the presumption, but does not shift to such party the burden of proof in the sense of the risk of non-persuasion, which remains throughout the trial upon the party on whom it was originally cast.

Rule 302. Applicability of State Law in Civil Actions and Proceedings

In civil actions and proceedings, the effect of a presumption respecting a fact which is an element of a claim or defense as to which State law supplies the rule of decision is determined in accordance with State law.

ARTICLE IV. RELEVANCY AND ITS LIMITS

Rule 401. Definition of "Relevant Evidence"

"Relevant evidence" means evidence having any tendency to make the existence of any fact that is of consequence to the determination of the action more probable or less probable than it would be without the evidence.

Rule 402. Relevant Evidence Generally Admissible; Irrelevant Evidence Inadmissible

All relevant evidence is admissible, except as otherwise provided by the Constitution of the United States, by Act of Congress, by these rules, or by other rules prescribed by the Supreme Court pursuant to statutory authority. Evidence which is not relevant is not admissible.

Rule 403. Exclusion of Relevant Evidence on Grounds of Prejudice, Confusion, or Waste of Time

Although relevant, evidence may be excluded if its probative value is substantially outweighed by the danger of unfair prejudice, confusion of the issues, or misleading the jury, or by considerations of undue delay, waste of time, or needless presentation of cumulative evidence.

Rule 404. Character Evidence Not Admissible to Prove Conduct; Exceptions; Other Crimes

(a) Character evidence generally.—Evidence of a person's character or a trait of character is not admissible for the purpose of proving action in conformity therewith on a particular occasion, except:

(1) Character of accused.—In a criminal case, evidence of a pertinent trait of character offered by an accused, or by the prosecution to rebut the same, or if evidence of a trait of character of the alleged victim of the crime is offered by an accused and admitted under Rule 404(a)(2), evidence of the same trait of character of the accused offered by the prosecution;

(2) Character of alleged victim.—In a criminal case, and subject to the limitations imposed by Rule 412, evidence of a pertinent trait of character of the alleged victim of the crime offered by an accused, or by the prosecution to rebut the same, or evidence of a character trait of peacefulness of the alleged victim offered by the prosecution in a

homicide case to rebut evidence that the alleged victim was the first aggressor;

(3) **Character of witness.**—Evidence of the character of a witness, as provided in rules 607, 608, and 609.

(b) **Other crimes, wrongs, or acts.**—Evidence of other crimes, wrongs, or acts is not admissible to prove the character of a person in order to show action in conformity therewith. It may, however, be admissible for other purposes, such as proof of motive, opportunity, intent, preparation, plan, knowledge, identity, or absence of mistake or accident, provided that upon request by the accused, the prosecution in a criminal case shall provide reasonable notice in advance of trial, or during trial if the court excuses pretrial notice on good cause shown, of the general nature of any such evidence it intends to introduce at trial.

Rule 405. Methods of Proving Character

(a) **Reputation or opinion.**—In all cases in which evidence of character or a trait of character of a person is admissible, proof may be made by testimony as to reputation or by testimony in the form of an opinion. On cross-examination, inquiry is allowable into relevant specific instances of conduct.

(b) **Specific instances of conduct.**—In cases in which character or a trait of character of a person is an essential element of a charge, claim, or defense, proof may also be made of specific instances of that person's conduct.

Rule 406. Habit; Routine Practice

Evidence of the habit of a person or of the routine practice of an organization, whether corroborated or not and regardless of the presence of eyewitnesses, is relevant to prove that the conduct of the person or organization on a particular occasion was in conformity with the habit or routine practice.

Rule 407. Subsequent Remedial Measures

When, after an injury or harm allegedly caused by an event, measures are taken that, if taken previously, would have made the injury or harm less likely to occur, evidence of the subsequent measures is not admissible to prove negligence, culpable conduct, a defect in a product, a defect in a product's design, or a need for a warning or instruction. This rule does not require the exclusion of evidence of subsequent measures when offered for another purpose, such as proving ownership, control, or feasibility of precautionary measures, if controverted, or impeachment.

Rule 408. Compromise and Offers to Compromise

(a) **Prohibited uses.**—Evidence of the following is not admission on behalf of any party, when offered to prove liability for, invalidity of, or amount of a claim that was disputed as to validity or amount, or to impeach through a prior inconsistent statement or contradiction:

(1) furnishing or offering or promising to furnish or accepting or offering or promising to accept a valuable consideration in compromising or attempting to compromise the claim; and

(2) conduct or statements made in compromise negotiations regarding the claim, except when offered in a criminal case and the negotiations related to a claim by a public office or agency in the exercise of regulatory, investigative, or enforcement authority.

(b) **Permitted uses.** This rule does not require exclusion if the evidence is offered for purposes not prohibited by subdivision (a). Examples of permissible purposes include proving a witness's bias or prejudice; negating a contention of undue delay; and proving an effort to obstruct a criminal investigation or prosecution.

Rule 409. Payment of Medical and Similar Expenses

Evidence of furnishing or offering or promising to pay medical, hospital, or similar expenses occasioned by an injury is not admissible to prove liability for the injury.

Rule 410. Inadmissibility of Pleas, Plea Discussions, and Related Statements

Except as otherwise provided in this rule, evidence of the following is not, in any civil or criminal proceeding, admissible against the defendant who made the plea or was a participant in the plea discussions:

(1) a plea of guilty which was later withdrawn;

(2) a plea of nolo contendere;

(3) any statement made in the course of any proceedings under Rule 11 of the Federal Rules of Criminal Procedure or comparable state procedure regarding either of the foregoing pleas; or

(4) any statement made in the course of plea discussions with an attorney for the prosecuting authority which do not result in a plea of guilty or which result in a plea of guilty later withdrawn.

However, such a statement is admissible (i) in any proceeding wherein another statement made in the course of the same plea or plea discussions has been introduced and the statement ought in fairness be considered contemporaneously with it, or (ii) in a criminal proceeding for perjury or false statement if the statement was made by the defendant under oath, on the record and in the presence of counsel.

Rule 411. Liability Insurance

Evidence that a person was or was not insured against liability is not admissible upon the issue whether the person acted negligently or otherwise wrongfully. This rule does not require the exclusion of evidence of insurance against liability when offered for another purpose, such as proof of agency, ownership, or control, or bias or prejudice of a witness.

Rule 412. Sex Offense Cases; Relevance of Alleged Victim's Past Sexual Behavior or Alleged Sexual Predisposition

(a) **Evidence Generally Inadmissible.**—The following evidence is not admissible in any civil or criminal proceeding involving alleged sexual misconduct except as provided in subdivisions (b) and (c):

> (1) Evidence offered to prove that any alleged victim engaged in other sexual behavior.
>
> (2) Evidence offered to prove any alleged victim's sexual predisposition.

(b) **Exceptions.**

> (1) In a criminal case, the following evidence is admissible, if otherwise admissible under these rules:
>
> > (A) evidence of specific instances of sexual behavior by the alleged victim offered to prove that a person other than the accused was the source of semen, injury or other physical evidence;
> >
> > (B) evidence of specific instances of sexual behavior by the alleged victim with respect to the person accused of the sexual misconduct offered by the accused to prove consent or by the prosecution; and
> >
> > (C) evidence the exclusion of which would violate the constitutional rights of the defendant.
>
> (2) In a civil case, evidence offered to prove the sexual behavior or sexual predisposition of any alleged victim is admissible if it is otherwise admissible under these rules and its probative value substantially outweighs the danger of harm to any victim and of unfair prejudice to any party. Evidence of an alleged victim's reputation is admissible only if it has been placed in controversy by the alleged victim.

(c) **Procedure to Determine Admissibility.**

> (1) A party intending to offer evidence under subdivision (b) must—
>
> > (A) file a written motion at least 14 days before trial specifically describing the evidence and stating the purpose for which it is offered unless the court, for good cause requires a different time for filing or permits filing during trial; and
> >
> > (B) serve the motion on all parties and notify the alleged victim or, when appropriate, the alleged victim's guardian or representative.
>
> (2) Before admitting evidence under this rule the court must conduct a hearing in camera and afford the victim and parties a right to attend and be heard. The motion, related papers, and the record of the hearing must be sealed and remain under seal unless the court orders otherwise.

Rule 413. Evidence of Similar Crimes in Sexual Assault Cases

(a) In a criminal case in which the defendant is accused of an offense of sexual assault, evidence of the defendant's commission of another offense or offenses of sexual assault is admissible, and may be considered for its bearing on any matter to which it is relevant.

(b) In a case in which the Government intends to offer evidence under this rule, the attorney for the Government shall disclose the evidence to the defendant, including statements of witnesses or a summary of the substance of any testimony that is expected to be offered, at least fifteen days before the scheduled date of trial or at such later time as the court may allow for good cause.

(c) This rule shall not be construed to limit the admission or consideration of evidence under any other rule.

(d) For purposes of this rule and Rule 415, "offense of sexual assault" means a crime under Federal law or the law of a State (as defined in section 513 of title 18, United States Code) that involved—

> (1) any conduct proscribed by chapter 109A of title 18, United States Code;
>
> (2) contact, without consent, between any part of the defendant's body or an object and the genitals or anus of another person;
>
> (3) contact, without consent, between the genitals or anus of the defendant and any part of another person's body;
>
> (4) deriving sexual pleasure or gratification from the infliction of death, bodily injury, or physical pain on another person; or
>
> (5) an attempt or conspiracy to engage in conduct described in paragraphs (1)–(4).

Rule 414. Evidence of Similar Crimes in Child Molestation Cases

(a) In a criminal case in which the defendant is accused of an offense of child molestation, evidence of the defendant's commission of another offense or offenses of child molestation is admissible, and may be considered for its bearing on any matter to which it is relevant.

(b) In a case in which the Government intends to offer evidence under this rule, the attorney for the Government shall disclose the evidence to the defendant, including statements of witnesses or a summary of the substance of any testimony that is expected to be offered, at least fifteen days before the scheduled date of trial or at such later time as the court may allow for good cause.

(c) This rule shall not be construed to limit the admission or consideration of evidence under any other rule.

(d) For purposes of this rule and Rule 415, "child" means a person below the age of fourteen, and "offense of child molestation" means a crime under Federal law or the law of a State (as defined in section 513 of title 18, United States Code) that involved—

> (1) any conduct proscribed by chapter 109A of title 18, United States Code, that was committed in relation to a child;
>
> (2) any conduct proscribed by chapter 110 of title 18, United States Code;
>
> (3) contact between any part of the defendant's body or an object and the genitals or anus of a child;
>
> (4) contact between the genitals or anus of the defendant and any part of the body of a child;

(5) deriving sexual pleasure or gratification from the infliction of death, bodily injury, or physical pain on a child; or

(6) an attempt or conspiracy to engage in conduct described in paragraphs (1)–(5).

Rule 415. Evidence of Similar Acts in Civil Cases Concerning Sexual Assault or Child Molestation

(a) In a civil case in which a claim for damages or other relief is predicated on a party's alleged commission of conduct constituting an offense of sexual assault or child molestation, evidence of that party's commission of another offense or offenses of sexual assault or child molestation is admissible and may be considered as provided in Rule 413 and Rule 414 of these rules.

(b) A party who intends to offer evidence under this Rule shall disclose the evidence to the party against whom it will be offered, including statements of witnesses or a summary of the substance of any testimony that is expected to be offered, at least fifteen days before the scheduled date of trial or at such later time as the court may allow for good cause.

(c) This rule shall not be construed to limit the admission or consideration of evidence under any other rule.

ARTICLE V. PRIVILEGES

Rule 501. General Rule

Except as otherwise required by the Constitution of the United States or provided by Act of Congress or in rules prescribed by the Supreme Court pursuant to statutory authority, the privilege of a witness, person, government, State, or political subdivision thereof shall be governed by the principles of the common law as they may be interpreted by the courts of the United States in the light of reason and experience. However, in civil actions and proceedings, with respect to an element of a claim or defense as to which State law supplies the rule of decision, the privilege of a witness, person, government, State, or political subdivision thereof shall be determined in accordance with State law.

ARTICLE VI. WITNESSES

Rule 601. General Rule of Competency

Every person is competent to be a witness except as otherwise provided in these rules. However, in civil actions and proceedings, with respect to an element of a claim or defense as to which State law supplies the rule of decision, the competency of a witness shall be determined in accordance with State law.

Rule 602. Lack of Personal Knowledge

A witness may not testify to a matter unless evidence is introduced sufficient to support a finding that the witness has personal knowledge of the matter.

Evidence to prove personal knowledge may, but need not, consist of the witness' own testimony. This rule is subject to the provisions of rule 703, relating to opinion testimony by expert witnesses.

Rule 603. Oath or Affirmation

Before testifying, every witness shall be required to declare that the witness will testify truthfully, by oath or affirmation administered in a form calculated to awaken the witness' conscience and impress the witness' mind with the duty to do so.

Rule 604. Interpreters

An interpreter is subject to the provisions of these rules relating to qualification as an expert and the administration of an oath or affirmation to make a true translation.

Rule 605. Competency of Judge as Witness

The judge presiding at the trial may not testify in that trial as a witness. No objection need be made in order to preserve the point.

Rule 606. Competency of Juror as Witness

(a) **At the trial.**—A member of the jury may not testify as a witness before that jury in the trial of the case in which the juror is sitting. If the juror is called so to testify, the opposing party shall be afforded an opportunity to object out of the presence of the jury.

(b) **Inquiry into validity of verdict or indictment.**—Upon an inquiry into the validity of a verdict or indictment, a juror may not testify as to any matter or statement occurring during the course of the jury's deliberations or to the effect of anything upon that or any other juror's mind or emotions as influencing the juror to assent to or dissent from the verdict or indictment or concerning the juror's mental processes in connection therewith. But a juror may testify about (1) whether extraneous prejudicial information was improperly brought to the jury's attention, (2) whether any outside influence was improperly brought to bear upon any juror, or (3) whether there was a mistake in entering the verdict onto the verdict form. A juror's affidavit or evidence of any statement by the juror may not be received on a matter about which the juror would be precluded from testifying.

Rule 607. Who May Impeach

The credibility of a witness may be attacked by any party, including the party calling the witness.

Rule 608. Evidence of Character and Conduct of Witness

(a) **Opinion and reputation evidence of character.**—The credibility of a witness may be attacked or supported by evidence in the form of opinion or reputation, but subject to these limitations: (1) the evidence may refer only to character for truthfulness or untruthfulness, and (2) evidence of truthful character is admissible only after the character of the witness for truthfulness has been attacked by opinion or reputation evidence or otherwise.

(b) **Specific instances of conduct.**—Specific instances of the conduct of a witness, for the purpose of attacking or supporting the witness' character for truthfulness, other than conviction of crime as provided in rule 609, may not be proved by extrinsic evidence. They may, however, in the discretion of the court, if probative of truthfulness or untruthfulness, be inquired into on cross-examination of the witness (1) concerning the witness' character for truthfulness or untruthfulness, or (2) concerning the character for truthfulness or untruthfulness of another witness as to which character the witness being cross-examined has testified.

The giving of testimony, whether by an accused or by any other witness, does not operate as a waiver of the accused's or the witness' privilege against self-incrimination when examined with respect to matters that relate only to character for truthfulness.

Rule 609. Impeachment by Evidence of Conviction of Crime

(a) **General rule.**—For the purpose of attacking the character for truthfulness of a witness,

> (1) evidence that a witness other than an accused has been convicted of a crime shall be admitted, subject to Rule 403, if the crime was punishable by death or imprisonment in excess of one year under the law under which the witness was convicted, and evidence that an accused has been convicted of such a crime shall be admitted if the court determines that the probative value of admitting this evidence outweighs its prejudicial effect to the accused; and
>
> (2) evidence that any witness has been convicted of a crime shall be admitted regardless of the punishment, if it readily can be determined that establishing the elements of the crime required proof or admission of an act of dishonesty or false statement by the witness.

(b) **Time limit.**—Evidence of a conviction under this rule is not admissible if a period of more than ten years has elapsed since the date of the conviction or of the release of the witness from the confinement imposed for that conviction, whichever is the later date, unless the court determines, in the interests of justice, that the probative value of the conviction supported by specific facts and circumstances substantially outweighs its prejudicial effect. However, evidence of a conviction more than 10 years old as calculated herein, is not admissible unless the proponent gives to the adverse party sufficient advance written notice of intent to use such evidence to provide the adverse party with a fair opportunity to contest the use of such evidence.

(c) **Effect of pardon, annulment, or certificate of rehabilitation.**—Evidence of a conviction is not admissible under this rule if (1) the conviction has been the subject of a pardon, annulment, certificate of rehabilitation, or other equivalent procedure based on a finding of the rehabilitation of the person convicted, and that person has not been convicted of a subsequent crime which was punishable by death or imprisonment in excess of one year, or (2) the conviction has been the subject of a pardon, annulment, or other equivalent procedure based on a finding of innocence.

(d) **Juvenile adjudications.**—Evidence of juvenile adjudications is generally not admissible under this rule. The court may, however, in a criminal case allow evidence of a juvenile adjudication of a witness other than the accused if conviction of the offense would be admissible to attack the credibility of an adult and the court is satisfied that admission in evidence is necessary for a fair determination of the issue of guilt or innocence.

(e) **Pendency of appeal.**—The pendency of an appeal therefrom does not render evidence of a conviction inadmissible. Evidence of the pendency of an appeal is admissible.

Rule 610. Religious Beliefs or Opinions

Evidence of the beliefs or opinions of a witness on matters of religion is not admissible for the purpose of showing that by reason of their nature the witness' credibility is impaired or enhanced.

Rule 611. Mode and Order of Interrogation and Presentation

(a) **Control by court.**—The court shall exercise reasonable control over the mode and order of interrogating witnesses and presenting evidence so as to (1) make the interrogation and presentation effective for the ascertainment of the truth, (2) avoid needless consumption of time, and (3) protect witnesses from harassment or undue embarrassment.

(b) **Scope of cross-examination.**—Cross-examination should be limited to the subject matter of the direct examination and matters affecting the credibility of the witness. The court may, in the exercise of discretion, permit inquiry into additional matters as if on direct examination.

(c) **Leading questions.**—Leading questions should not be used on the direct examination of a witness except as may be necessary to develop the witness' testimony. Ordinarily leading questions should be permitted on cross-examination. When a party calls a hostile witness, an adverse party, or a witness identified with an adverse party, interrogation may be by leading questions.

Rule 612. Writing Used to Refresh Memory

Except as otherwise provided in criminal proceedings by section 3500 of title 18, United States Code, if a witness uses a writing to refresh memory for the purpose of testifying, either—

(1) while testifying, or

(2) before testifying, if the court in its discretion determines it is necessary in the interests of justice, an adverse party is entitled to have the writing pro-

duced at the hearing, to inspect it, to cross-examine the witness thereon, and to introduce in evidence those portions which relate to the testimony of the witness. If it is claimed that the writing contains matters not related to the subject matter of the testimony the court shall examine the writing in camera, excise any portions not so related, and order delivery of the remainder to the party entitled thereto. Any portion withheld over objections shall be preserved and made available to the appellate court in the event of an appeal. If a writing is not produced or delivered pursuant to order under this rule, the court shall make any order justice requires, except that in criminal cases when the prosecution elects not to comply, the order shall be one striking the testimony or, if the court in its discretion determines that the interests of justice so require, declaring a mistrial.

Rule 613. Prior Statements of Witnesses

(a) **Examining witness concerning prior statement.**—In examining a witness concerning a prior statement made by the witness, whether written or not, the statement need not be shown nor its contents disclosed to the witness at that time, but on request the same shall be shown or disclosed to opposing counsel.

(b) **Extrinsic evidence of prior inconsistent statement of witness.**—Extrinsic evidence of a prior inconsistent statement by a witness is not admissible unless the witness is afforded an opportunity to explain or deny the same and the opposite party is afforded an opportunity to interrogate the witness thereon, or the interests of justice otherwise require. This provision does not apply to admissions of a party-opponent as defined in rule 801(d)(2).

Rule 614. Calling and Interrogation of Witnesses by Court

(a) **Calling by court.**—The court may, on its own motion or at the suggestion of a party, call witnesses, and all parties are entitled to cross-examine witnesses thus called.

(b) **Interrogation by court.**—The court may interrogate witnesses, whether called by itself or by a party.

(c) **Objections.**—Objections to the calling of witnesses by the court or to interrogation by it may be made at the time or at the next available opportunity when the jury is not present.

Rule 615. Exclusion of Witnesses

At the request of a party the court shall order witnesses excluded so that they cannot hear the testimony of other witnesses, and it may make the order of its own motion. This rule does not authorize exclusion of (1) a party who is a natural person, or (2) an officer or employee of a party which is not a natural person designated as its representative by its attorney, or (3) a person whose presence is shown by a party to be essential to the presentation of the party's cause, or (4) a person authorized by statute to be present.

ARTICLE VII. OPINIONS AND EXPERT TESTIMONY

Rule 701. Opinion Testimony by Lay Witnesses

If the witness is not testifying as an expert, the witness' testimony in the form of opinions or inferences is limited to those opinions or inferences which are (a) rationally based on the perception of the witness, and (b) helpful to a clear understanding of the witness' testimony or the determination of a fact in issue, and (c) not based on scientific, technical, or other specialized knowledge within the scope of Rule 702.

Rule 702. Testimony by Experts

If scientific, technical, or other specialized knowledge will assist the trier of fact to understand the evidence or to determine a fact in issue, a witness qualified as an expert by knowledge, skill, experience, training, or education, may testify thereto in the form of an opinion or otherwise, if (1) the testimony is based upon sufficient facts or data, (2) the testimony is the product of reliable principles and methods, and (3) the witness has applied the principles and methods reliably to the facts of the case.

Rule 703. Bases of Opinion Testimony by Experts

The facts or data in the particular case upon which an expert bases an opinion or inference may be those perceived by or made known to the expert at or before the hearing. If of a type reasonably relied upon by experts in the particular field in forming opinions or inferences upon the subject, the facts or data need not be admissible in evidence in order for the opinion or inference to be admitted. Facts or data that are otherwise inadmissible shall not be disclosed to the jury by the proponent of the opinion or inference unless the court determines that their probative value in assisting the jury to evaluate the expert's opinion substantially outweighs their prejudicial effect.

Rule 704. Opinion on Ultimate Issue

(a) Except as provided in subdivision (b), testimony in the form of an opinion or inference otherwise admissible is not objectionable because it embraces an ultimate issue to be decided by the trier of fact.

(b) No expert witness testifying with respect to the mental state or condition of a defendant in a criminal case may state an opinion or inference as to whether the defendant did or did not have the mental state or condition constituting an element of the crime charged or of a defense thereto. Such ultimate issues are matters for the trier of fact alone.

Rule 705. Disclosure of Facts or Data Underlying Expert Opinion

The expert may testify in terms of opinion or inference and give reasons therefor without first testifying to the underlying facts or data, unless the court requires otherwise. The expert may in any event be required to disclose the underlying facts or data on cross-examination.

Rule 706. Court Appointed Experts

(a) Appointment.—The court may on its own motion or on the motion of any party enter an order to show cause why expert witnesses should not be appointed, and may request the parties to submit nominations. The court may appoint any expert witnesses agreed upon by the parties, and may appoint expert witnesses of its own selection. An expert witness shall not be appointed by the court unless the witness consents to act. A witness so appointed shall be informed of the witness' duties by the court in writing, a copy of which shall be filed with the clerk, or at a conference in which the parties shall have opportunity to participate. A witness so appointed shall advise the parties of the witness' findings, if any; the witness' deposition may be taken by any party; and the witness may be called to testify by the court or any party. The witness shall be subject to cross-examination by each party, including a party calling the witness.

(b) Compensation.—Expert witnesses so appointed are entitled to reasonable compensation in whatever sum the court may allow. The compensation thus fixed is payable from funds which may be provided by law in criminal cases and civil actions and proceedings involving just compensation under the fifth amendment. In other civil actions and proceedings the compensation shall be paid by the parties in such proportion and at such time as the court directs, and thereafter charged in like manner as other costs.

(c) Disclosure of appointment.—In the exercise of its discretion, the court may authorize disclosure to the jury of the fact that the court appointed the expert witness.

(d) Parties' experts of own selection.—Nothing in this rule limits the parties in calling expert witnesses of their own selection.

ARTICLE VIII. HEARSAY

Rule 801. Definitions

The following definitions apply under this article:

(a) Statement.—A "statement" is (1) an oral or written assertion or (2) nonverbal conduct of a person, if it is intended by the person as an assertion.

(b) Declarant.—A "declarant" is a person who makes a statement.

(c) Hearsay.—"Hearsay" is a statement, other than one made by the declarant while testifying at the trial or hearing, offered in evidence to prove the truth of the matter asserted.

(d) Statements which are not hearsay.—A statement is not hearsay if—

(1) Prior statement by witness.—The declarant testifies at the trial or hearing and is subject to cross-examination concerning the statement, and the statement is (A) inconsistent with the declarant's testimony, and was given under oath subject to the penalty of perjury at a trial, hearing, or other proceeding, or in a deposition, or (B) consistent

with the declarant's testimony and is offered to rebut an express or implied charge against the declarant of recent fabrication or improper influence or motive, or (C) one of identification of a person made after perceiving the person; or

(2) **Admission by party-opponent.**—The statement is offered against a party and is (A) the party's own statement, in either an individual or a representative capacity or (B) a statement of which the party has manifested an adoption or belief in its truth, or (C) a statement by a person authorized by the party to make a statement concerning the subject, or (D) a statement by the party's agent or servant concerning a matter within the scope of the agency or employment, made during the existence of the relationship, or (E) a statement by a coconspirator of a party during the course and in furtherance of the conspiracy. The contents of the statement shall be considered but are not alone sufficient to establish the declarant's authority under subdivision (C), the agency or employment relationship and scope thereof under subdivision (D), or the existence of the conspiracy and the participation therein of the declarant and the party against whom the statement is offered under subdivision (E).

Rule 802. Hearsay Rule

Hearsay is not admissible except as provided by these rules or by other rules prescribed by the Supreme Court pursuant to statutory authority or by Act of Congress.

Rule 803. Hearsay Exceptions; Availability of Declarant Immaterial

The following are not excluded by the hearsay rule, even though the declarant is available as a witness:

(1) **Present sense impression.**—A statement describing or explaining an event or condition made while the declarant was perceiving the event or condition, or immediately thereafter.

(2) **Excited utterance.**—A statement relating to a startling event or condition made while the declarant was under the stress of excitement caused by the event or condition.

(3) **Then existing mental, emotional, or physical condition.**—A statement of the declarant's then existing state of mind, emotion, sensation, or physical condition (such as intent, plan, motive, design, mental feeling, pain, and bodily health), but not including a statement of memory or belief to prove the fact remembered or believed unless it relates to the execution, revocation, identification, or terms of declarant's will.

(4) **Statements for purposes of medical diagnosis or treatment.**—Statements made for purposes of medical diagnosis or treatment and describing medical history, or past or present symptoms, pain, or sensations, or the inception or general character of the cause or ex-

ternal source thereof insofar as reasonably pertinent to diagnosis or treatment.

(5) **Recorded recollection.**—A memorandum or record concerning a matter about which a witness once had knowledge but now has insufficient recollection to enable the witness to testify fully and accurately, shown to have been made or adopted by the witness when the matter was fresh in the witness' memory and to reflect that knowledge correctly. If admitted, the memorandum or record may be read into evidence but may not itself be received as an exhibit unless offered by an adverse party.

(6) **Records of regularly conducted activity.**—A memorandum, report, record, or data compilation, in any form, of acts, events, conditions, opinions, or diagnoses, made at or near the time by, or from information transmitted by, a person with knowledge, if kept in the course of a regularly conducted business activity, and if it was the regular practice of that business activity to make the memorandum, report, record or data compilation, all as shown by the testimony of the custodian or other qualified witness, or by certification that complies with Rule 902(11), Rule 902(12), or a statute permitting certification, unless the source of information or the method or circumstances of preparation indicate lack of trustworthiness. The term "business" as used in this paragraph includes business, institution, association, profession, occupation, and calling of every kind, whether or not conducted for profit.

(7) **Absence of entry in records kept in accordance with the provisions of paragraph (6).**—Evidence that a matter is not included in the memoranda reports, records, or data compilations, in any form, kept in accordance with the provisions of paragraph (6), to prove the nonoccurrence or nonexistence of the matter, if the matter was of a kind of which a memorandum, report, record, or data compilation was regularly made and preserved, unless the sources of information or other circumstances indicate lack of trustworthiness.

(8) **Public records and reports.**—Records, reports, statements, or data compilations, in any form, of public offices or agencies, setting forth (A) the activities of the office or agency, or (B) matters observed pursuant to duty imposed by law as to which matters there was a duty to report, excluding, however, in criminal cases matters observed by police officers and other law enforcement personnel, or (C) in civil actions and proceedings and against the Government in criminal cases, factual findings resulting from an investigation made pursuant to authority granted by law, unless the sources of information or other circumstances indicate lack of trustworthiness.

(9) **Records of vital statistics.**—Records or data compilations, in any form, of births, fetal deaths, deaths, or marriages, if the report thereof was made to a public office pursuant to requirements of law.

(10) **Absence of public record or entry.**—To prove the absence of a record, report, statement, or data compilation, in any form, or the

nonoccurrence or nonexistence of a matter of which a record, report, statement, or data compilation, in any form, was regularly made and preserved by a public office or agency, evidence in the form of a certification in accordance with rule 902, or testimony, that diligent search failed to disclose the record, report, statement, or data compilation, or entry.

(11) **Records of religious organizations.**—Statements of births, marriages, divorces, deaths, legitimacy, ancestry, relationship by blood or marriage, or other similar facts of personal or family history, contained in a regularly kept record of a religious organization.

(12) **Marriage, baptismal, and similar certificates.**—Statements of fact contained in a certificate that the maker performed a marriage or other ceremony or administered a sacrament, made by a clergyman, public official, or other person authorized by the rules or practices of a religious organization or by law to perform the act certified, and purporting to have been issued at the time of the act or within a reasonable time thereafter.

(13) **Family records.**—Statements of fact concerning personal or family history contained in family Bibles, genealogies, charts, engravings on rings, inscriptions on family portraits, engravings on urns, crypts, or tombstones, or the like.

(14) **Records of documents affecting an interest in property.**—The record of a document purporting to establish or affect an interest in property, as proof of the content of the original recorded document and its execution and delivery by each person by whom it purports to have been executed, if the record is a record of a public office and an applicable statute authorizes the recording of documents of that kind in that office.

(15) **Statements in documents affecting an interest in property.**—A statement contained in a document purporting to establish or affect an interest in property if the matter stated was relevant to the purpose of the document, unless dealings with the property since the document was made have been inconsistent with the truth of the statement or the purport of the document.

(16) **Statements in ancient documents.**—Statements in a document in existence twenty years or more the authenticity of which is established.

(17) **Market reports, commercial publications.**—Market quotations, tabulations, lists, directories, or other published compilations, generally used and relied upon by the public or by persons in particular occupations.

(18) **Learned treatises.**—To the extent called to the attention of an expert witness upon cross-examination or relied upon by the expert witness in direct examination, statements contained in published treatises, periodicals, or pamphlets on a subject of history, medicine, or other science or art, established as a reliable authority by the testimony or admission of the witness or by other expert testimony or by judicial notice. If admitted, the statements may be read into evidence but may not be received as exhibits.

(19) Reputation concerning personal or family history.—Reputation among members of a person's family by blood, adoption, or marriage, or among a person's associates, or in the community, concerning a person's birth, adoption, marriage, divorce, death, legitimacy, relationship by blood, adoption, or marriage, ancestry, or other similar fact of personal or family history.

(20) Reputation concerning boundaries or general history.—Reputation in a community, arising before the controversy, as to boundaries of or customs affecting lands in the community, and reputation as to events of general history important to the community or State or nation in which located.

(21) Reputation as to character.—Reputation of a person's character among associates or in the community.

(22) Judgment of previous conviction.—Evidence of a final judgment, entered after a trial or upon a plea of guilty (but not upon a plea of nolo contendere), adjudging a person guilty of a crime punishable by death or imprisonment in excess of one year, to prove any fact essential to sustain the judgment, but not including, when offered by the Government in a criminal prosecution for purposes other than impeachment, judgments against persons other than the accused. The pendency of an appeal may be shown but does not affect admissibility.

(23) Judgment as to personal, family, or general history, or boundaries.—Judgments as proof of matters of personal, family or general history, or boundaries, essential to the judgment, if the same would be provable by evidence of reputation.

Rule 804. Hearsay Exceptions; Declarant Unavailable

(a) **Definition of unavailability.**—"Unavailability as a witness" includes situations in which the declarant—

(1) is exempted by ruling of the court on the ground of privilege from testifying concerning the subject matter of the declarant's statement; or

(2) persists in refusing to testify concerning the subject matter of the declarant's statement despite an order of the court to do so; or

(3) testifies to a lack of memory of the subject matter of the declarant's statement; or

(4) is unable to be present or to testify at the hearing because of death or then existing physical or mental illness or infirmity; or

(5) is absent from the hearing and the proponent of a statement has been unable to procure the declarant's attendance (or in the case of a hearsay exception under subdivision (b)(2), (3), or (4), the declarant's attendance or testimony) by process or other reasonable means.

A declarant is not unavailable as a witness if exemption, refusal, claim of lack of memory, inability, or absence is due to the procurement or wrongdoing of the proponent of a statement for the purpose of preventing the witness from attending or testifying.

(b) Hearsay exceptions.—The following are not excluded by the hearsay rule if the declarant is unavailable as a witness:

(1) **Former testimony.**—Testimony given as a witness at another hearing of the same or a different proceeding, or in a deposition taken in compliance with law in the course of the same or another proceeding, if the party against whom the testimony is now offered, or, in a civil action or proceeding, a predecessor in interest, had an opportunity and similar motive to develop the testimony by direct, cross, or redirect examination.

(2) **Statement under belief of impending death.**—In a prosecution for homicide or in a civil action or proceeding, a statement made by a declarant while believing that the declarant's death was imminent, concerning the cause or circumstances of what the declarant believed to be impending death.

(3) **Statement against interest.**—A statement which was at the time of its making so far contrary to the declarant's pecuniary or proprietary interest, or so far tended to subject the declarant to civil or criminal liability, or to render invalid a claim by the declarant against another, that a reasonable person in the declarant's position would not have made the statement unless believing it to be true. A statement tending to expose the declarant to criminal liability and offered to exculpate the accused is not admissible unless corroborating circumstances clearly indicate the trustworthiness of the statement.

(4) **Statement of personal or family history.**—(A) A statement concerning the declarant's own birth, adoption, marriage, divorce, legitimacy, relationship by blood, adoption, or marriage, ancestry, or other similar fact of personal or family history, even though declarant had no means of acquiring personal knowledge of the matter stated; or (B) a statement concerning the foregoing matters, and death also, of another person, if the declarant was related to the other by blood, adoption, or marriage or was so intimately associated with the other's family as to be likely to have accurate information concerning the matter declared.

(5) **[Other exceptions.]** [Transferred to Rule 807]

(6) **Forfeiture by wrongdoing.**—A statement offered against a party that has engaged or acquiesced in wrongdoing that was intended to, and did, procure the unavailability of the declarant as a witness.

Rule 805. Hearsay Within Hearsay

Hearsay included within hearsay is not excluded under the hearsay rule if each part of the combined statements conforms with an exception to the hearsay rule provided in these rules.

Rule 806. Attacking and Supporting Credibility of Declarant

When a hearsay statement, or a statement defined in Rule 801(d)(2)(C), (D), or (E), has been admitted in evidence, the credibility of the declarant may be attacked, and if attacked may be supported, by any evidence which would be admissible for those purposes if declarant had testified as a witness. Evidence of a statement or conduct by the declarant at any time, inconsistent with the declarant's hearsay statement, is not subject to any requirement that the declarant may have been afforded an opportunity to deny or explain. If the party against whom a hearsay statement has been admitted calls the declarant as a witness, the party is entitled to examine the declarant on the statement as if under cross-examination.

Rule 807. Residual Exception

A statement not specifically covered by Rule 803 or 804 but having equivalent circumstantial guarantees of trustworthiness, is not excluded by the hearsay rule, if the court determines that (A) the statement is offered as evidence of a material fact; (B) the statement is more probative on the point for which it is offered than any other evidence which the proponent can procure through reasonable efforts; and (C) the general purposes of these rules and the interests of justice will best be served by admission of the statement into evidence. However, a statement may not be admitted under this exception unless the proponent of it makes known to the adverse party sufficiently in advance of the trial or hearing to provide the adverse party with a fair opportunity to prepare to meet it, the proponent's intention to offer the statement and the particulars of it, including the name and address of the declarant.

ARTICLE IX. AUTHENTICATION AND IDENTIFICATION

Rule 901. Requirement of Authentication or Identification

(a) **General provision.**—The requirement of authentication or identification as a condition precedent to admissibility is satisfied by evidence sufficient to support a finding that the matter in question is what its proponent claims.

(b) **Illustrations.**—By way of illustration only, and not by way of limitation, the following are examples of authentication or identification conforming with the requirements of this rule:

(1) **Testimony of witness with knowledge.**—Testimony that a matter is what it is claimed to be.

(2) **Nonexpert opinion on handwriting.**—Nonexpert opinion as to the genuineness of handwriting, based upon familiarity not acquired for purposes of the litigation.

(3) **Comparison by trier or expert witness.**—Comparison by the trier of fact or by expert witnesses with specimens which have been authenticated.

(4) **Distinctive characteristics and the like.**—Appearance, contents, substance, internal patterns, or other distinctive characteristics, taken in conjunction with circumstances.

(5) **Voice identification.**—Identification of a voice, whether heard firsthand or through mechanical or electronic transmission or recording,

by opinion based upon hearing the voice at any time under circumstances connecting it with the alleged speaker.

(6) **Telephone conversations.**—Telephone conversations, by evidence that a call was made to the number assigned at the time by the telephone company to a particular person or business, if (A) in the case of a person, circumstances, including self-identification, show the person answering to be the one called, or (B) in the case of a business, the call was made to a place of business and the conversation related to business reasonably transacted over the telephone.

(7) **Public records or reports.**—Evidence that a writing authorized by law to be recorded or filed and in fact recorded or filed in a public office, or a purported public record, report, statement, or data compilation, in any form, is from the public office where items of this nature are kept.

(8) **Ancient documents or data compilation.**—Evidence that a document or data compilation, in any form, (A) is in such condition as to create no suspicion concerning its authenticity, (B) was in a place where it, if authentic, would likely be, and (C) has been in existence 20 years or more at the time it is offered.

(9) **Process or system.**—Evidence describing a process or system used to produce a result and showing that the process or system produces an accurate result.

(10) **Methods provided by statute or rule.**—Any method of authentication or identification provided by Act of Congress or by other rules prescribed by the Supreme Court pursuant to statutory authority.

Rule 902. Self-Authentication

Extrinsic evidence of authenticity as a condition precedent to admissibility is not required with respect to the following:

(1) **Domestic public documents under seal.**—A document bearing a seal purporting to be that of the United States, or of any State, district, Commonwealth, territory, or insular possession thereof, or the Panama Canal Zone, or the Trust Territory of the Pacific Islands, or of a political subdivision, department, officer, or agency thereof, and a signature purporting to be an attestation or execution.

(2) **Domestic public documents not under seal.**—A document purporting to bear the signature in the official capacity of an officer or employee of any entity included in paragraph (1) hereof, having no seal, if a public officer having a seal and having official duties in the district or political subdivision of the officer or employee certifies under seal that the signer has the official capacity and that the signature is genuine.

(3) **Foreign public documents.**—A document purporting to be executed or attested in an official capacity by a person authorized by the laws of a foreign country to make the execution or attestation, and accompanied by a final certification as to the genuineness of the signature and official position (A) of the executing or attesting person, or (B) of

any foreign official whose certificate of genuineness of signature and official position relates to the execution or attestation or is in a chain of certificates of genuineness of signature and official position relating to the execution or attestation. A final certification may be made by a secretary of an embassy or legation, consul general, consul, vice consul, or consular agent of the United States, or a diplomatic or consular official of the foreign country assigned or accredited to the United States. If reasonable opportunity has been given to all parties to investigate the authenticity and accuracy of official documents, the court may, for good cause shown, order that they be treated as presumptively authentic without final certification or permit them to be evidenced by an attested summary with or without final certification.

(4) **Certified copies of public records.**—A copy of an official record or report or entry therein, or of a document authorized by law to be recorded or filed and actually recorded or filed in a public office, including data compilations in any form, certified as correct by the custodian or other person authorized to make the certification, by certificate complying with paragraph (1), (2), or (3) of this rule or complying with any Act of Congress or rule prescribed by the Supreme Court pursuant to statutory authority.

(5) **Official publications.**—Books, pamphlets, or other publications purporting to be issued by public authority.

(6) **Newspapers and periodicals.**—Printed materials purporting to be newspapers or periodicals.

(7) **Trade inscriptions and the like.**—Inscriptions, signs, tags, or labels purporting to have been affixed in the course of business and indicating ownership, control, or origin.

(8) **Acknowledged documents.**—Documents accompanied by a certificate of acknowledgment executed in the manner provided by law by a notary public or other officer authorized by law to take acknowledgments.

(9) **Commercial paper and related documents.**—Commercial paper, signatures thereon, and documents relating thereto to the extent provided by general commercial law.

(10) **Presumptions under Acts of Congress.**—Any signature, document, or other matter declared by Act of Congress to be presumptively or prima facie genuine or authentic.

(11) **Certified domestic records of regularly conducted activity.**— The original or a duplicate of a domestic record of regularly conducted activity that would be admissible under Rule 803(6) if accompanied by a written declaration of its custodian or other qualified person, in a manner complying with any Act of Congress or rule prescribed by the Supreme Court pursuant to statutory authority, certifying that the record—

> (A) was made at or near the time of the occurrence of the matters set forth by, or from information transmitted by, a person with knowledge of those matters;

(B) was kept in the course of the regularly conducted activity; and

(C) was made by the regularly conducted activity as a regular practice. A party intending to offer a record into evidence under this paragraph must provide written notice of that intention to all adverse parties, and must make the record and declaration available for inspection sufficiently in advance of their offer into evidence to provide an adverse party with a fair opportunity to challenge them.

(12) **Certified foreign records of regularly conducted activity.**—In a civil case, the original or a duplicate of a foreign record of regularly conducted activity that would be admissible under Rule 803(6) if accompanied by a written declaration by its custodian or other qualified person certifying that the record—

(A) was made at or near the time of the occurrence of the matters set forth by, or from information transmitted by, a person with knowledge of those matters;

(B) was kept in the course of the regularly conducted activity; and

(C) was made by the regularly conducted activity as a regular practice. The declaration must be signed in a manner that, if falsely made, would subject the maker to criminal penalty under the laws of the country where the declaration is signed. A party intending to offer a record into evidence under this paragraph must provide written notice of that intention to all adverse parties, and must make the record and declaration available for inspection sufficiently in advance of their offer into evidence to provide an adverse party with a fair opportunity to challenge them.

Rule 903. Subscribing Witness' Testimony Unnecessary

The testimony of a subscribing witness is not necessary to authenticate a writing unless required by the laws of the jurisdiction whose laws govern the validity of the writing.

ARTICLE X. CONTENTS OF WRITINGS, RECORDINGS, AND PHOTOGRAPHS

Rule 1001. Definitions

For purposes of this article the following definitions are applicable:

(1) **Writings and recordings.**—"Writings" and "recordings" consist of letters, words, or numbers, or their equivalent, set down by handwriting, typewriting, printing, photostating, photographing, magnetic impulse, mechanical or electronic recording, or other form of data compilation.

(2) **Photographs.**—"Photographs" include still photographs, X-ray films, video tapes, and motion pictures.

(3) **Original.**—An "original" of a writing or recording is the writing or recording itself or any counterpart intended to have the same effect by a person executing or issuing it. An "original" of a photograph includes the negative or any print therefrom. If data are stored in a computer or similar device, any printout or other output readable by sight, shown to reflect the data accurately, is an "original."

(4) **Duplicate.**—A "duplicate" is a counterpart produced by the same impression as the original, or from the same matrix, or by means of photography, including enlargements and miniatures, or by mechanical or electronic re-recording, or by chemical reproduction, or by other equivalent techniques which accurately reproduces the original.

Rule 1002. Requirement of Original

To prove the content of a writing, recording, or photograph, the original writing, recording, or photograph is required, except as otherwise provided in these rules or by Act of Congress.

Rule 1003. Admissibility of Duplicates

A duplicate is admissible to the same extent as an original unless (1) a genuine question is raised as to the authenticity of the original or (2) in the circumstances it would be unfair to admit the duplicate in lieu of the original.

Rule 1004. Admissibility of Other Evidence of Contents

The original is not required, and other evidence of the contents of a writing, recording, or photograph is admissible if—

(1) **Originals lost or destroyed.**—All originals are lost or have been destroyed, unless the proponent lost or destroyed them in bad faith; or

(2) **Original not obtainable.**—No original can be obtained by any available judicial process or procedure; or

(3) **Original in possession of opponent.**—At a time when an original was under the control of the party against whom offered, that party was put on notice, by the pleadings or otherwise, that the contents would be a subject of proof at the hearing, and that party does not produce the original at the hearing; or

(4) **Collateral matters.**—The writing, recording, or photograph is not closely related to a controlling issue.

Rule 1005. Public Records

The contents of an official record, or of a document authorized to be recorded or filed and actually recorded or filed, including data compilations in any form, if otherwise admissible, may be proved by copy, certified as correct in accordance with rule 902 or testified to be correct by a witness who has compared it with the original. If a copy which complies with the foregoing cannot be obtained by the exercise of reasonable diligence, then other evidence of the contents may be given.

Rule 1006. Summaries

The contents of voluminous writings, recordings, or photographs which cannot conveniently be examined in court may be presented in the form of a chart, summary, or calculation. The originals, or duplicates, shall be made available for examination or copying, or both, by other parties at reasonable time and place. The court may order that they be produced in court.

Rule 1007. Testimony or Written Admission of Party

Contents of writings, recordings, or photographs may be proved by the testimony or deposition of the party against whom offered or by that party's written admission, without accounting for the nonproduction of the original.

Rule 1008. Functions of Court and Jury

When the admissibility of other evidence of contents of writings, recordings, or photographs under these rules depends upon the fulfillment of a condition of fact, the question whether the condition has been fulfilled is ordinarily for the court to determine in accordance with the provisions of rule 104. However, when an issue is raised (a) whether the asserted writing ever existed, or (b) whether another writing, recording, or photograph produced at the trial is the original, or (c) whether other evidence of contents correctly reflects the contents, the issue is for the trier of fact to determine as in the case of other issues of fact.

ARTICLE XI. MISCELLANEOUS RULES

Rule 1101. Applicability of Rules

(a) **Courts and judges.**—These rules apply to the United States district courts, the District Court of Guam, the District Court of the Virgin Islands, the District Court for the Northern Mariana Islands, the United States courts of appeals, the United States Claims Court, and to United States bankruptcy judges and United States magistrate judges, in the actions, cases, and proceedings and to the extent hereinafter set forth. The terms "judge" and "court" in these rules include United States bankruptcy judges and United States magistrate judges.

(b) **Proceedings generally.**—These rules apply generally to civil actions and proceedings, including admiralty and maritime cases, to criminal cases and proceedings, to contempt proceedings except those in which the court may act summarily, and to proceedings and cases under title 11, United States Code.

(c) **Rule of privilege.**—The rule with respect to privileges applies at all stages of all actions, cases, and proceedings.

(d) Rules inapplicable.—The rules (other than with respect to privileges) do not apply in the following situations:

(1) Preliminary questions of fact.—The determination of questions of fact preliminary to admissibility of evidence when the issue is to be determined by the court under rule 104.

(2) Grand jury.—Proceedings before grand juries.

(3) Miscellaneous proceedings.—Proceedings for extradition or rendition; preliminary examinations in criminal cases; sentencing, or granting or revoking probation; issuance of warrants for arrest, criminal summonses, and search warrants; and proceedings with respect to release on bail or otherwise.

(e) Rules applicable in part.—In the following proceedings these rules apply to the extent that matters of evidence are not provided for in the statutes which govern procedure therein or in other rules prescribed by the Supreme Court pursuant to statutory authority: the trial of misdemeanors and other petty offenses before United States magistrate judges; review of agency actions when the facts are subject to trial de novo under section 706(2)(F) of title 5, United States Code; review of orders of the Secretary of Agriculture under section 2 of the Act entitled "An Act to authorize association of producers of agricultural products" approved February 18, 1922 (7 U.S.C. 292), and under sections 6 and 7(c) of the Perishable Agricultural Commodities Act, 1930 (7 U.S.C. 499f, 499g(c)); naturalization and revocation of naturalization under sections 310–318 of the Immigration and Nationality Act (8 U.S.C. 1421–1429); prize proceedings in admiralty under sections 7651–7681 of title 10, United States Code; review of orders of the Secretary of the Interior under section 2 of the Act entitled "An Act authorizing associations of producers of aquatic products" approved June 25, 1934 (15 U.S.C. 522); review of orders of petroleum control boards under section 5 of the Act entitled "An Act to regulate interstate and foreign commerce in petroleum and its products by prohibiting the shipment in such commerce of petroleum and its products produced in violation of State law, and for other purposes," approved February 22, 1935 (15 U.S.C. 715d); actions for fines, penalties, or forfeitures under part V of title IV of the Tariff Act of 1930 (19 U.S.C. 1581–1624), or under the Anti-Smuggling Act (19 U.S.C. 1701–1711); criminal libel for condemnation, exclusion of imports, or other proceedings under the Federal Food, Drug, and Cosmetic Act (21 U.S.C. 301–392); disputes between seamen under sections 4079, 4080, and 4081 of the Revised Statutes (22 U.S.C. 256–258); habeas corpus under sections 2241–2254 of title 28, United States Code; motions to vacate, set aside or correct sentence under section 2255 of title 28, United States Code; actions for penalties for refusal to transport destitute seamen under section 4578 of the Revised Statutes (46 U.S.C. 679); actions against the United States under the Act entitled "An Act authorizing suits against the United States in admiralty for damage caused by and salvage service rendered to public vessels belonging to the United States, and for other purposes," approved March 3, 1925 (46 U.S.C. 781–790), as implemented by section 7730 of title 10, United States Code.

Rule 1102. Amendments

Amendments to the Federal Rules of Evidence may be made as provided in section 2072 of title 28 of the United States Code.

Rule 1103. Title

These rules may be known and cited as the Federal Rules of Evidence.

INDEX

References are to pages.

Accident reconstructions, 341–343

Acquittal, motion for judgment of, 22

Alternative arguments, 18–19

Animations, 338–339
  accident scene reconstructions, 341–343
  as persuasive aids, 353

Arguing your case, 17–19. *See also* Closing arguments; Opening statements

Attitude of "less is more," 14–15

Audiotapes, 329
  as business records, 334–335
  transcripts of, 329–330

Background questioning, 185–186
  experts, qualifications of, 181–184

Batson challenges, 37

Bench *versus* jury trials, 21

Blood-spatter analysis, 341

Breathalyzer tests, 341

Burden of proof, 18
  opening statements, discussion in, 87, 119–120, 128
  voir dire in civil cases, 49

Business records, 334
  admissibility examples, 335–337
  audiotapes, 334–335
  checklist for, 335

Case-in-chief, 22

CAT scans, 333

Chain of custody issues, 332–333

Challenges for cause, 36
  Batson challenges, 37

Charisma, 19–20

Closing arguments, 22
  beginning powerfully, 269–271, 286–289
  biases of jurors, appealing to, 263–264
  credibility of witness, vouching for, 263
  damages, discussion of, 259–262, 297–299
  defensive behavior, 276–278
  "don'ts" of, 276–279
  ending memorably, 273–275, 296–299
  evidence
    misstating evidence, 262–263, 278–279
    vouching for credibility of evidence, 263
  insurance, mention of, 264
  jury instructions
    important instructions, discussion of, 293–295
    misstating instructions, 262–263, 278–279
  memorizing ideas, not words, 275
  "missing witness" argument, 265
  misstating evidence, 262–263, 278–279
  misstating instructions, 262–263, 278–279
  opening themes, incorporation of, 268–269, 275
  openings *versus* closings, 258–259

outline
  final outline, 275
  form of, 268
overrated importance of, 257–258
preparation checklist, 276
prohibited conduct, 262–265
punishment, commenting on, 265
rebuttal argument, 279–285,
  299–302, 309–310
steps to achieving success,
  266–267
storytelling, 269–271, 289–290
sympathies of jurors, appealing to,
  263–264
talking too much, 276
visual aids, use of, 275
weaknesses of case, discussion of,
  272–273, 291–293
Computer animations/illustrations,
  338–339
accident scene reconstructions,
  341–343
as persuasive aids, 349–353
Computer records, 337
Consultants, use of, 10–12, 38
Convictions
  confronting on direct, 167–169
  records of, 343
Credibility of witnesses
  cross-examination, 203–205
  vouching for credibility in closing
    argument, 263
Cross-examination
  asking questions on
    avoiding where answer is
      unknown, 218–219
    building a series of questions,
      228–231
    leading questions, 214–217
    logical reasoning, use of,
      228–231
    making your point clear,
      220–222
    open-ended questions, 217–218,
      246–247
  beginning powerfully, 211–212,
    240–241

credibility of witness, 203–205
"don'ts" of, 239
ending memorably, 210, 211,
  249–251
evidence, use of, 231–232
expert witnesses, 237–239
eye contact with witness, 247–249
hostile witnesses. *See* Hostile
  witnesses
impeachment on, 207–209. *See
  also* Impeachment of witnesses
implausible statements, 207, 249
knowledge, lack of, 205–207
leading questions, 214–217
logical reasoning, use of, 228–231
myths about, 201–203
open-ended questions, 217–218,
  246–247
outline of, 213–214
prior inconsistent statements,
  207–209
  impeachment of witness,
    222–228, 241–243
supporting your case with,
  209–210
themes, determination of, 210–211
visual aids, use of, 231–232
weaknesses, determination of, 210

Damages
  closing arguments, discussion in,
    259–262, 297–299
  voir dire, 49–51
Demonstrations/demonstrative
  exhibits, 312. *See also* Exhibits
  during direct examination,
    152–155
  in-court, 327
Deposition testimony, use of,
  163–164
Deposition transcripts, impeachment
  with, 243–244
Diagrams, 324–325
Direct examination, 135–136
  background questioning, 185–186
  experts, qualifications of,
    181–184

beginning powerfully, 136–139
comfort level of witness, 141–143
  letting witnesses approximate,
    186
commands, use of, 149
controlling the witness, 177–178
  with commands, 149
delivery, style of, 159–160
deposition testimony, use of,
    163–164
details
  corroboration of, 187–188
  development of, 188–191
  getting from witness, 164–165
difficult problems on, 164–170
ending memorably, 139, 193–194
expert witnesses, 179–185
eye contact with the witness,
    160–161
frequency technique, 157
goal of, 155–157
impeachment-proofing your
    witness, 144–146
jury comprehension, simplifying
    testimony for, 176
leading questions, 152
  how to ask nonleading
    questions, 146–147
"less" as "more," 139–141
listening to answers, 178–179
"looping" questions, 149–151,
    186–187
mistakes on, 176–179
open-ended questions, 147–148
order of questions, 155
order of witnesses, 136–141
outlines, 161–163
preparation for, 141–146, 161–164
primacy technique, 157–19
prior convictions of witness,
    167–169
recency technique, 157
redirect examination, 171–176
refreshing recollection, 166–167
strategies of, 136–146
techniques of, 146–155
  frequency technique, 157

primacy technique, 157–159
  recency technique, 157
themes
  discussing testimony in context
    of, 143–144
  failure to create, 179
  selection of, 161
transitions, use of, 148–149
videotaped testimony, use of,
    163–164
visual aids, use of, 152–155
weaknesses of witnesses
  addressing, 169–170, 177,
    192–193
word usage, 176
Directed verdict, motion for, 22
DNA evidence, 341
Documents
  business records. *See* Business
    records
  computer records, 337
  as exhibits, 321–322
  medical records, 333
  public records, 343–344
  recorded recollections, 328–329
  self-authenticating documents,
    343–344
Drugs seized in criminal case,
    332–333
DVD menus, 373–375

E-mails, 337–338
Evidence
  closing arguments
    misstating evidence, 262–263,
      278–279
    vouching for credibility of
      evidence, 263
  cross-examination, use during,
    231–232
  documents. *See* Documents
  exhibits. *See* Exhibits
  misstating in closing argument,
    262–263, 278–279
Examination of witnesses
  cross-examination. *See* Cross-
    examination

direct examination. *See* Direct
  examination
order of, 22
redirect examination, 171–176
Exclusion of witnesses, 357
Exhibits, 311
  admissibility, 313–314
    agreement with courtroom
      deputy following trial, 22–23
    business records examples,
      335–337
    checklist, 319
    steps to, 314–319
  audiotapes, 329
    transcripts of, 329–330
  bench memos, 320–321
  business records, 334
    admissible/inadmissible records
      examples, 335–337
    checklist for, 335
    from *McVeigh case,* 334–335
  CAT scans, 333
  chain of custody issues, 332–333
  checklist for offering into evidence,
    319
  computer animations/illustrations,
    338–339
    accident scene reconstructions,
      341–343
    as persuasive aids, 349–353
  computer records, 337
  demonstrations. *See*
    Demonstrations/demonstrative
    exhibits
  diagrams, 324–325
  direct examination, use during,
    152–155
  displaying to jury, 318–319
  documents, 321–322
    self-authenticating documents,
      343–344
  drawing(s) of witnesses, 325–327
  drugs seized in criminal case,
    332–333
  e-mails, 337–338
  evidence
    admissibility, *above*
    moving into, 316–318

expert witnesses, use with,
    184–185
felony convictions, records of, 343
foundation for, 314, 315–316
graphic images, 349–352
illustrative exhibits, 312
impeachment with, 244–246
Internet, 338
marking exhibits, 314
medical records, 333
motions *in limine,* use of, 357
MRIs, 333
objections, 353–354
  foundation, lack of, 354–355
  "hearsay" objection, 354
  "relevancy" objection, 355
  "unfair prejudice" objection,
    355
persuasive aids, 312–313, 347
  animations. Computer
    animations/illustrations, *above*
  examples of, 347–353
  still images, 349–352
photographs
  accident scenes, 323–324
  crime scenes, 322–323
PowerPoint presentations,
    339–341
prior inconsistent statements, 345
public records, 343–344
real evidence from crime scene,
    330–332
real exhibits, 312
recorded recollections, 328–329
scientific exhibits, 341–343
self-authenticating documents,
    343–344
showing exhibits
  to opposing counsel, 314–315
  to witness, 315
stipulations, 345–346
summary charts, 344–345
types of, 312–313
videotapes, 323–324
Web sites, 338
witnesses
  discussing exhibits with, 318
  drawings of, 325–327

recorded recollections,
328–329
the right witness, 319–320
showing exhibits to, 315
x-rays, 333
Expert witnesses
asking expert her opinion, 180–181
cross-examination, 237–239
direct examination, 179–185
exhibits, use of, 184–185
narrative answers, 180
qualifications of, 180
background questions to
establish, 181–184

Federal Rules of Evidence,
387–414
Felony convictions, records of, 343
Fingerprint comparisons, 341
Focus group questionnaire,
377–385
Focus groups, use of, 10–12
video clips *(Scruggs v. Snyder)*,
23–30
Footprint comparisons, 341
Foundation for exhibits, 314,
315–316

Goldman v. Simpson (excerpts and
analysis)
closing arguments, 287–289, 290,
291–293, 295, 297–299,
300–302
cross-examination, 215–216, 219,
235–237, 239–251
hostile witnesses, 235–237
openings, gestures during, 96
Graphic images, 349–352

"Hearsay" objection, 354
Hostile witnesses
arguing with, 234–237
asking judge to strike an answer,
235–236
control of, 232–237
instructing witness to answer "yes"
or "no," 236–237
repeating questions to, 222–223

requests made to examiner,
234–235

Illustrative exhibits, 312
Impeachment of witnesses
on cross-examination, 207–209
with deposition transcripts,
243–244
with exhibits, 244–246
making witness on direct
unimpeachable, 144–146
with prior inconsistent statements
and omissions, 222–228,
241–243
"proving up" impeachment,
227–228
In limine motions, 357
Inconsistent statements. *See* Prior
inconsistent statements
Influencing the outcome of a trial,
2–3
Instructions to jury. *See* Jury
instructions
Insurance, closing argument
comments on, 264
Integrity, 15–17
Internet, 338
Irrelevancy, objection to, 355

Jurors
challenges for cause, 36
Batson challenges, 37
closing arguments to. *See* Closing
arguments
opening statements to. *See*
Opening statements
preemptory strikes, 36–37
presentation of case to, 13–14
seeing your case through jury's
eyes, 9–14
verdict. *See* Verdict of jury
voir dire. See Voir dire
Jury instructions, 22
closing arguments
important instructions,
discussion of, 293–295
misstating instructions, 262–263,
278–279

important instructions, discussion of, 293–295

misstating in closing argument, 262–263, 278–279

preliminary instructions, 22

Jury questionnaires, 38

Jury selection. *See Voir dire*

Jury *versus* bench trials, 21

Leading questions
  during cross-examination, 214–217
  on direct examination, 152
  how to ask nonleading questions, 146–147

Listening to opposing counsel's opening, 103–104

Listening to witness's answers, 178–179

"Looping" questions, 149–151, 186–187

Marking exhibits, 314

McVeigh, U.S. v. (excerpts and analysis)
  audiotapes as business records, 334–335
  background for, 369–371
  closing arguments, 266–267, 270–275
  cross-examination, 204–205, 207–209, 211–212
  direct examination, 137–139, 150, 151, 153, 157–159, 164–165, 169–170, 178–179, 185–194
  expert witness direct examination, 181–185
  opening statements
    defense counsel's opening, 121–129
    prosecution's opening, 87, 101, 106, 110–121
  redirect examination, 172–176
  stipulations, 345–346
  summary charts, use of, 344–345

Medical records, 333

Memory
  recorded recollections, 328–329
  refreshing recollection, 166–167

"Missing witness" argument, 265

Motion for directed verdict, 22

Motion for judgment of acquittal, 22

Motions *in limine,* 357

MRIs, 333

Newspaper ads, 377

Objections, 353–354
  to exhibits, 353–355
  form of question, 355–357
  foundation, lack of, 354–355
  "hearsay" objection, 354
  pretrial conference, use of, 21–22
  "relevancy" objection, 355
  "unfair prejudice" objection, 355

O. J. Simpson cases
  Goldman v. Simpson. See Goldman v. Simpson (excerpts and analysis)
  People v. Simpson. See Simpson, People v. (excerpts and analysis)

Open-ended questions
  on cross-examination, 217–218, 246–247
  on direct examination, 147–148

Opening statements
  argument, rule against, 75–76
  "Bad Facts" preparation list, 78
  beginning powerfully, 82–84, 110–114, 121–124
  breathing "to calm nerves," 99
  burden of proof, discussion of, 87, 119–120, 128
  car-wreck cases, 106–107
  checklists
    delivery of opening, 96
    "don'ts" of openings, 105
    overcoming courtroom fears, 100
    preparation checklist, 93

closings *versus* openings, 258–259

conviction, speaking with, 95

courtroom fears, overcoming, 96–100

courtroom visit beforehand, 99

delivering openings, 93–96

"don'ts" of, 100–106

draft of entire opening, 88

dressing appropriately, 96

elements of claim, discussion of, 87, 119–120, 128

emotion and theme, 67–68
 car wreck cases, 106–107
 creation of theme, 80–82
 drafting your outline, 86
 employment discrimination cases, 107–108
 famous speeches, examples from, 69–74
 medical malpractice cases, 108–110
 reaching the jurors' emotions, 68–69

employment discrimination cases, 107–108

ending memorably, 85–87, 120–121, 128–129

explaining to jurors what an opening is, 102–103

eye contact during, 93–94

fears, overcoming, 96–100

feedback when preparing, 96

gestures, use of, 95–96

where to give, 74

"Good Facts" preparation list, 78

juror's perspective, 77

knowing your ending cold, 91

length of, 74

listening to opposing counsel's opening, 103–104

making jurors' job easy, not more difficult, 100–101

making openings important and interesting, 67–68

medical malpractice cases, 108–110

memorizing ideas, not words, 88–90

mistakes, allowing yourself to make, 97–98

nervous energy, 99–100

outlines
 final outline, 91–92
 first, 86–87
 form of outline, 88

physical distractions, limiting, 94

preparation
 being prepared, 97
 steps to use in preparing openings, 77–93

prohibited conduct, 75–77

realizing the jury wants you to succeed, 98

steps to use in preparing openings, 77–93

storytelling, 82–87, 114–115, 124–125

"talking down" to jurors, 104–105

theme. Emotion and theme, *above*

theory of case, determination of, 78–80

time to give, 74

underrated importance of, 65–67

varying your voice, 94–95

visual aids, use of, 90

visualizing success, 98–99

vocal distractions, limiting, 94

weaknesses, discussion of, 84–85, 116–119, 125–128

word usage, 104–105

Outlines
 closing arguments
  final outline, 275
  form of outline, 268
 cross-examination, 213–214
 direct examination, 161–163
 opening statements
  final outline, 91–92
  first draft of outline, 86–87
  form of outline, 88

People v. Simpson. See Simpson, People v.

Persuasive exhibits, 312–313, 347.
    See also Exhibits
    animations, 353. *See also*
        Animations
    examples of, 347–353
    still images, 349–352
Photographs
    accident scenes, 323–324
    crime scenes, 322–323
Physical evidence from crime scene,
    330–332
PowerPoint presentations, 339–341
Preemptory strikes, 36–37
Prejudice, objection to, 355
Preparation
    closing argument checklist, 276
    of cross-examination theme(s),
        210–211
    for direct examination, 141–146,
        161–164
    importance of, 14
    of opening statements. *See*
        Opening statements
Pretrial conference, 21–22
Prior convictions
    confronting on direct, 167–169
    records of, 343
Prior inconsistent statements
    cross-examining witnesses about,
        207–209
    exhibits, 345
    impeachment with, 222–228,
        241–243
"Proving up" impeachment,
        227–228
Public records, 343–344
Punishment, closing argument
        comments on, 265

Qualities of great trial lawyers, 3–21
Questionnaire, 377–385

Radiographs, 333
Real evidence from crime scene,
    330–332
Real exhibits, 312
Rebuttal closing argument, 279–285,
    299–302, 309–310

Recollection
    recorded recollections, 328–329
    refreshing recollection, 166–167
Redirect examination, 171–176
Refreshing recollection, 166–167
"Relevancy" objection, 355
"Rule of three," 14–15

Scientific exhibits, 341–343
Self-authenticating documents,
    343–344
Sequestration of witnesses, 357
Simpson, People v. (excerpts and
        analysis)
    background for, 363–367
    closing arguments
        defense's closing, 104–105,
            277–278, 279, 280–282,
            305–309
        prosecution's closing, 282–287,
            289–290, 293–297, 299–300,
            303–305, 309–310
        video excerpts, 303–310
    cross-examination video clips,
        251–256
    direct examination
        expert witnesses, 181, 197–199
        video excerpts, 194–199
    expert witness direct examination,
        181, 197–199
    opening statements
        defense's opening, 103, 132–133
        prosecution's opening, 84, 85,
            101, 102, 129–132
        video excerpts, 129–133
Stipulations, 345–346
Storytelling
    beginning powerfully, 4–5
    closing arguments, 269–271,
        289–290
    compelling stories, 4–9
    memorable moments, creation of,
        5–6
    opening statements, 82–87,
        114–115, 124–125
    theme development, 6–9
Style in lawyering
    development of, 3–4

direct examination, delivery of, 159–160
Summary charts, 344–345

Theme(s)
 cross-examination preparation, 210–211
 direct examination. *See* Direct examination
 opening statements. *See* Opening statements and storytelling, 6–9
Theory of case
 determining a winning theory, 9–14
 opening statements, preparation of, 78–80
Timothy McVeigh case. *See* McVeigh, U.S. v. (excerpts and analysis)
Trial consultants, 10–12, 38
Trial notebook, 23–26
Trial process, 21–23

"Unfair prejudice" objection, 355
U.S. v. McVeigh. *See* McVeigh, U.S. v.

Verdict of jury, 23
 researching verdicts, 13
Videotapes
 exhibits, 323–324
 testimony, use of, 163–164
Visual aids. *See also* Exhibits
 closing argument, use in, 275
 cross-examination, use during, 231–232
 direct examination, use on, 152–155
 opening statements, use in, 90
Voice spectrographic analysis, 341
Voir dire, 22, 31–32
 burden of proof, 49
 challenges for cause, 36
  Batson challenges, 37
 in civil trials, 47–48
  burden of proof, 49
  damages, 49–51

defendant's *voir dire*, 53–57, 60–62
 plaintiff's *voir dire*, 48–53, 57–60
 consultants, use of, 38
 in criminal trials, 38–39
  defense's *voir dire*, 43–47
  prosecution's *voir dire*, 40–43
  summary of facts, 39–40
 damages, 49–51
 federal court *voir dire*, 34–36
 jury questionnaires, 38
 preemptory strikes, 36–37
 prohibited conduct, 37–38
 prosecution's *voir dire*, 40–43
 strategies for, 32–34
 video clips *(Scruggs v. Snyder)*, 62–63

Web sites, evidence of, 338
Witnesses
 credibility
  cross-examination, 203–205
  vouching for credibility in closing argument, 263
 examination
  cross-examination. *See* Cross-examination
  direct examination. *See* Direct examination
  order of, 22
  redirect examination, 171–176
 exclusion of, 357
 exhibits
  discussing exhibit with witness, 318
  drawing(s) of witnesses, 325–327
  recorded recollections, 328–329
  the right witness, 319–320
  showing exhibit to witness, 315
 expert witnesses. *See* Expert witnesses
 eye contact
  during cross-examination, 247–249
  during direct examination, 160–161
  during opening statement, 93–94

hostile witnesses. *See* Hostile
    witnesses
impeachment
    with deposition transcripts,
      243–244
    with exhibits, 244–246
    making witness on direct
      unimpeachable, 144–146
    with prior inconsistent
      statements and omissions,
      222–228, 241–243
    "proving up" impeachment,
      227–228
implausible statements, 207, 249
inconsistent statements. Prior
    inconsistent statements, *below*

knowledge, lack of, 205–207
listing important testimony during
    trial, 266–267
"missing witness" argument,
    265
motions *in limine*, use of, 357
objections to testimony. *See*
    Objections
prior inconsistent statements
    cross-examination, 207–209
    exhibits, 345
    impeachment with, 222–228,
      241–243
redirect examination, 171–176

X-rays, 333

ABOUT THE AUTHOR[1]

S hane Read is a graduate of Yale University and the University of Texas School of Law. He began his legal career in 1989 at Akin Gump in Dallas, Texas, before joining the U.S. Attorney's Office in Washington, D.C., from 1992 to 1998. Since 1998, he has worked at the U.S. Attorney's Office in Dallas. He has been lead counsel on countless civil and criminal trials over the past eighteen years. In addition, he has served as lead counsel for numerous oral arguments before appellate courts.

He has also held a wide variety of teaching positions during his career. He is currently an adjunct professor at Southern Methodist University Dedman School of Law. Here he has taught Trial Advocacy, coached mock trial teams, and currently is teaching a unique seminar on trial strategies. He has also taught both new and experienced lawyers at NITA's seminars on trial skills and at the Department of Justice's National Advocacy Center. For more information about the author or this book, go to www.shaneread.com.

---

1. The views expressed in this book are solely those of the author and do not necessarily reflect the views of the Department of Justice.